A·N·N·U·A·L E·D·I·T·I·O·N·S

Arrendale Library Piedmont College

Educational Psychology

Fifteenth Edition

00/01

D0140666

EDITORS

Kathleen M. Cauley
Virginia Commonwealth University

Kathleen M. Cauley received her Ph.D. in educational studies/human development from the University of Delaware in 1985. Her research interests center on applying cognitive developmental research to school learning. Currently, she is studying children's mathematical understanding.

Fredric Linder
Virginia Commonwealth University

Fredric Linder received an A.B. in American civilization from the University of Miami, Florida, an M.A. in psychology from the New School for Social Research, and a Ph.D. in educational psychology from the State University of New York at Buffalo. His research focuses on the values and cognitive learning styles of students.

James H. McMillan
Virginia Commonwealth University

James H. McMillan received his bachelor's degree from Albion College in 1970, an M.A. from Michigan State University in 1972, and a Ph.D. from Northwestern University in 1976. He has reviewed and written extensively in educational psychology.

Dushkin/McGraw-Hill
Sluice Dock, Guilford, Connecticut 06437

Visit us on the Internet
http://www.dushkin.com/annualeditions/

Discarded by
Arrendale Library
Piedmont College

Credits

1. Perspectives on Teaching
Unit photo—© 2000 by Cleo Freelance Photography, Inc.
2. Development
Unit photo—United Nations photo by John Isaac.
3. Exceptional and Culturally Diverse Children
Unit photo—© 2000 by Cleo Freelance Photography, Inc.
4. Learning and Instruction
Unit photo—© 2000 by Cleo Freelance Photography, Inc.
5. Motivation and Classroom Management
Unit photo—© by Steve Takatsuno.
6. Assessment
Unit photo—© 2000 by Cleo Freelance Photography, Inc.

Copyright

Cataloging in Publication Data
Main entry under title: Annual Editions: Educational Psychology. 2000/2001.
    1. Educational psychology—Periodicals. 2. Teaching—Periodicals. I. Cauley, Kathleen M., *comp.*; Linder, Fredric, *comp.*; McMillan, James H., *comp.* II. Title: Educational psychology.
ISBN 0–07–236547–1   370.15′05   82–640517   ISSN 0731–1141

© 2000 by Dushkin/McGraw-Hill, Guilford, CT 06437, A Division of The McGraw-Hill Companies.

Copyright law prohibits the reproduction, storage, or transmission in any form by any means of any portion of this publication without the express written permission of Dushkin/McGraw-Hill, and of the copyright holder (if different) of the part of the publication to be reproduced. The Guidelines for Classroom Copying endorsed by Congress explicitly state that unauthorized copying may not be used to create, to replace, or to substitute for anthologies, compilations, or collective works.

Annual Editions® is a Registered Trademark of Dushkin/McGraw-Hill, A Division of The McGraw-Hill Companies.

Fifteenth Edition

Cover image © 2000 PhotoDisc, Inc.

Printed in the United States of America   1234567890BAHBAH543210   Printed on Recycled Paper

Members of the Advisory Board are instrumental in the final selection of articles for each edition of ANNUAL EDITIONS. Their review of articles for content, level, currentness, and appropriateness provides critical direction to the editor and staff. We think that you will find their careful consideration well reflected in this volume.

EDITORS

Kathleen M. Cauley
Virginia Commonwealth University

Fredric Linder
Virginia Commonwealth University

James H. McMillan
Virginia Commonwealth University

ADVISORY BOARD

Roberta Ahlquist
San Jose State University

Thomas L. Bennett
Bowling Green State University

Robert G. Brown
Florida Atlantic University

Edward J. Caropreso
Clarion University

Karen G. Duffy
SUNY at Geneseo

Godfrey Franklin
University of West Florida

Albert H. Gardner
University of Maryland College Park

Ines Gomez
San Francisco State University

William L. Goodwin
University of Colorado Denver

William M. Gray
University of Toledo

Cheryl Greenberg
University of North Carolina

Stephanie L. Hinson
West Chester University

Anabel L. Jensen
College of Notre Dame

Elaine C. Koffman
Northeastern Illinois University

Golam Mannan
Indiana University–Purdue University

Laura J. Massey
Montana State University

Martha J. Meyer
Butler University

Kyra J. Osmus
Mercer University

Robert G. Saba
North Georgia College & State University

Donald H. Saklofske
University of Saskatchewan

Fred Schultz
University of Akron

Thomas J. Shuell
SUNY at Buffalo

Sandra M. Stokes
University of Wisconsin Green Bay

Harvey N. Switzky
Northern Illinois University

Lani M. Van Dusen
Utah State University

EDITORIAL STAFF

Ian A. Nielsen, Publisher
Roberta Monaco, Senior Developmental Editor
Dorothy Fink, Associate Developmental Editor
Addie Raucci, Senior Administrative Editor
Cheryl Greenleaf, Permissions Editor
Joseph Offredi, Permissions/Editorial Assistant
Diane Barker, Proofreader
Lisa Holmes-Doebrick, Senior Program Coordinator

PRODUCTION STAFF

Brenda S. Filley, Production Manager
Charles Vitelli, Designer
Lara M. Johnson, Design/ Advertising Coordinator
Laura Levine, Graphics
Mike Campbell, Graphics
Tom Goddard, Graphics
Eldis Lima, Graphics
Juliana Arbo, Typesetting Supervisor
Marie Lazauskas, Typesetter
Kathleen D'Amico, Typesetter
Karen Roberts, Typesetter
Larry Killian, Copier Coordinator

Editors/Advisory Board

Staff

To the Reader

In publishing ANNUAL EDITIONS we recognize the enormous role played by the magazines, newspapers, and journals of the public press in providing current, first-rate educational information in a broad spectrum of interest areas. Many of these articles are appropriate for students, researchers, and professionals seeking accurate, current material to help bridge the gap between principles and theories and the real world. These articles, however, become more useful for study when those of lasting value are carefully collected, organized, indexed, and reproduced in a low-cost format, which provides easy and permanent access when the material is needed. That is the role played by ANNUAL EDITIONS.

New to ANNUAL EDITIONS is the inclusion of related World Wide Web sites. These sites have been selected by our editorial staff to represent some of the best resources found on the World Wide Web today. Through our carefully developed topic guide, we have linked these Web resources to the articles covered in this ANNUAL EDITIONS reader. We think that you will find this volume useful, and we hope that you will take a moment to visit us on the Web at *http://www.dushkin.com* to tell us what you think.

Educational psychology is an interdisciplinary subject that includes human development, learning, intelligence, motivation, assessment, instructional strategies, and classroom management. The articles in this volume give special attention to the application of this knowledge to teaching.

Annual Editions: Educational Psychology 00/01 is divided into six units, and an overview precedes each unit, which explains how the unit articles are related to the broader issues within educational psychology.

The first unit, *Perspectives on Teaching*, presents issues that are central to the teaching role. The articles' authors provide perspectives on being an effective teacher and the issues facing teachers in the twenty-first century.

The second unit, entitled *Development*, is concerned with child and adolescent development. It covers the biological, cognitive, social, and emotional processes of development. The essays in this unit examine the issues of parenting, moral development, the social forces affecting children and adolescents, as well as the personal and social skills needed to cope with school learning and developmental tasks.

The third unit, regarding exceptional and culturally diverse students, focuses on the learning disabled, the gifted, and multicultural education. Diverse students require an individualized approach to education. The articles in this unit review the characteristics of these children and suggest programs and strategies to meet their needs.

In the fourth unit, *Learning and Instruction*, articles about theories of learning and instructional strategies are presented. The different views of learning, such as information processing, behaviorism, and constructivist learning, represent the accumulation of years of research on the way humans change in thinking or behavior due to experience. The principles generated by each approach have important implications for teaching. These implications are addressed in a section on instructional strategies, covering such topics as instructional methods, authentic instruction, and learning styles.

The topic of motivation is perhaps one of the most important aspects of school learning. Effective teachers need to motivate their students both to learn and to behave responsibly. How to manage children and what forms of discipline to use are issues that concern parents as well as teachers and administrators. The articles in the fifth unit, *Motivation and Classroom Management*, present a variety of perspectives on motivating students and discuss approaches to managing student behavior.

The articles in the sixth unit review assessment approaches that can be used to diagnose learning and improve instruction. The focus is on how alternative assessments, such as performance and portfolios, can be integrated with instruction to enhance student learning. Approaches to grading are also reviewed.

A feature that has been added to this edition are selected *World Wide Web* sites, which can be used to further explore the articles' topics. These sites are cross-referenced by number in the *topic guide*.

This fifteenth edition of *Annual Editions: Educational Psychology* has been revised in order to present articles that are current and useful. Your responses to the selection and organization of materials are appreciated. Please complete and return the postage-paid *article rating form* on the last page of the book.

Kathleen M. Cauley
Editor

Fredric Linder
Editor

James H. McMillan
Editor

Contents

UNIT 1

Perspectives on Teaching

Four selections discuss the importance of research and the value of scientific inquiry to the teaching process.

UNIT 2

Development

Six articles examine how social interaction in the classroom influences child and adolescent development.

The concepts in bold italics are developed in the article. For further expansion please refer to the Topic Guide and the Index.

UNIT 3

Exceptional and Culturally Diverse Children

Seven articles look at the problems and positive effects of educational programs for learning disabled, gifted, and culturally diverse children.

The concepts in bold italics are developed in the article. For further expansion please refer to the Topic Guide and the Index.

UNIT 4

Learning and Instruction

Twelve selections explore the important types of student/teacher interaction.

The concepts in bold italics are developed in the article. For further expansion please refer to the Topic Guide and the Index.

C. INSTRUCTIONAL STRATEGIES

UNIT 5

Motivation and Classroom Management

Eight selections discuss
student control and moti-
vation in the classroom.

The concepts in bold italics are developed in the article. For further expansion please refer to the Topic Guide and the Index.

B. CLASSROOM MANAGEMENT AND DISCIPLINE

The concepts in bold italics are developed in the article. For further expansion please refer to the Topic Guide and the Index.

UNIT 6

Assessment

Four articles discuss the implications of educational measurement for the classroom decision-making process and for the teaching profession.

The concepts in bold italics are developed in the article. For further expansion please refer to the Topic Guide and the Index.

This topic guide suggests how the selections and World Wide Web sites found in the next section of this book relate to topics of traditional concern to educational psychology students and professionals. It is useful for locating interrelated articles and Web sites for reading and research. The guide is arranged alphabetically according to topic.

The relevant Web sites, which are numbered and annotated on pages 4 and 5, are easily identified by the Web icon (◎) under the topic articles. By linking the articles and the Web sites by topic, this ANNUAL EDITIONS reader becomes a powerful learning and research tool.

TOPIC AREA	TREATED IN	TOPIC AREA	TREATED IN
Alternative Assessment	39. Practicing What We Preach in Designing Authentic Assessments 40. Lessons Learned about Student Portfolios ◎ **30, 31, 32**	**Cognitive Learning**	18. Brain Basics 19. In Search of . . . Brain-Based Education ◎ **23, 24, 25, 26**
At-Risk Behavior	10. Out of the Mouths of Babes ◎ **16, 28, 29**	**Constructivism**	23. Constructivist Theory in the Classroom 24. Challenges of Sustaining a Constructivist Classroom Culture ◎ **6, 9, 10, 14**
Behaviorism	22. Caution—Praise Can Be Dangerous 30. New Look at School Failure and School Success ◎ **1, 12, 14, 15**	**Differentiated Instruction**	28. Mapping a Route toward Differentiated Instruction ◎ **16, 17, 18, 19, 23, 24, 25, 26**
Brain-Based Education	18. Brain Basics 19. In Search of . . . Brain-Based Education ◎ **2, 3, 8, 9, 10, 24, 25**	**Disabilities**	11. Taking Inclusion into the Future 12. Good Questions to Ask ◎ **16, 21, 29**
Character Education	19. In Search of . . . Brain-Based Education 25. Keeping in Character: A Time-Tested Solution ◎ **2, 3, 8, 9, 10, 12**	**Discipline**	37. Salinas, California: Peace Breaks Out ◎ **27, 28, 29**
Child/ Adolescent Development	5. What Do We Know from Brain Research? 6. Moral Child 7. Reevaluating Significance of Baby's Bond with Mother 8. Helping Children Become More Prosocial ◎ **12, 13, 14, 15**	**Diverse Students**	15. Goals and Track Record of Multicultural Education 16. Multiculturalism at a Crossroads 17. Voices and Voces ◎ **16, 17, 18, 19, 20, 22**
Classroom Management	33. Moving beyond Management As Sheer Compliance 34. Connecting Instruction and Management in a Student-Centered Classroom 35. Teaching Students to Regulate Their Own Behavior 36. How to Defuse Defiance, Threats, Challenges, Confrontations ◎ **27, 28, 29**	**Early Childhood**	5. What Do We Know from Brain Research? 8. Helping Children Become More Prosocial 13. Meeting the Needs of Gifted Learners in the Early Childhood Classroom ◎ **1, 14, 15**
		Educational Issues	3. Schools and Curricula for the 21st Century 4. What Issues Will Confront Public Education in the Years 2000 and 2020? ◎ **10**
Cognitive Development	5. What Do We Know from Brain Research? 6. Moral Child ◎ **14, 15**	**Effective Teaching**	1. Year That I Really Learned How to Teach 2. Reflection Is at the Heart of Practice ◎ **25, 26**

● AE: Educational Psychology

The following World Wide Web sites have been carefully researched and selected to support the articles found in this reader. If you are interested in learning more about specific topics found in this book, these Web sites are a good place to start. The sites are cross-referenced by number and appear in the topic guide on the previous two pages. Also, you can link to these Web sites through our DUSHKIN ONLINE support site at *http://www.dushkin.com/online/*.

The following sites were available at the time of publication. Visit our Web site—we update DUSHKIN ONLINE regularly to reflect any changes.

General Sources

1. American Psychological Association
http://www.apa.org/psychnet/
By exploring the APA's "PsychNET," you will be able to find links to an abundance of articles and other resources that are useful in the field of educational psychology.

2. Educational Resources Information Center
http://www.accesseric.org:81
This invaluable site provides links to all ERIC sites: clearinghouses, support components, and publishers of ERIC materials. Search the ERIC database for what is new.

3. National Education Association
http://www.nea.org
Something—and often quite a lot—about virtually every education-related topic can be accessed at or through this site of the 2.3-million-strong National Education Association.

4. National Parent Information Network/ERIC
http://npin.org
This is a clearinghouse of information on elementary and early childhood education as well as urban education. Browse through its links for information for parents.

5. U.S. Department of Education
http://www.ed.gov/pubs/TeachersGuide/
Government goals, projects, and grants are listed here, plus many links to teacher services and resources.

Perspectives on Teaching

6. The Center for School Reform
http://www.educenter.org
This is the home page of the Center for School Reform, self-described as a "not-for-profit, non-partisan research organization" focusing on K–12 education reform strategies. Click on its links about school privatization.

7. Classroom Connect
http://www.classroom.net
This is a major Web site for K–12 teachers and students, with links to schools, teachers, and resources online. It includes discussion of the use of technology in the classroom.

8. Education World
http://www.education-world.com
Education World provides a database of literally thousands of sites that can be searched by grade level, plus education news, lesson plans, and professional-development resources.

9. EdWeb/Andy Carvin
http://edweb.cnidr.org
The purpose of EdWeb is to explore the worlds of educational reform and information technology. Learn about trends in education policy and information infrastructure development, and examine success stories of computers in the classroom.

10. Goals 2000: A Progress Report
http://www.ed.gov/pubs/goals/progrpt/index.html
Open this site to survey a progress report by the U.S. Department of Education on the Goals 2000 reform initiative. It provides a sense of the goals that educators are reaching for as they look toward the future.

11. Teacher Talk Forum
http://education.indiana.edu/cas/tt/tthmpg.html
Visit this site for access to a variety of articles discussing life in the classroom. Clicking on the various links will lead you to electronic lesson plans, covering a variety of topic areas, from Indiana University's Center for Adolescent Studies.

Development

12. Association for Moral Education
http://www.wittenberg.edu/ame/
AME is dedicated to fostering communication, cooperation, training, curriculum development, and research that links moral theory with educational practices. From here it is possible to connect to several sites on moral development.

13. Child Welfare League of America
http://www.cwla.org
The CWLA is the United States' oldest and largest organization devoted entirely to the well-being of vulnerable children and their families. This site provides links to information about issues related to morality and values in education.

14. Guidelines for Developmentally Appropriate Early Childhood Practice
http://www.newhorizons.org/naeyc.html
Here is a 23-page exerpt from a report, edited by Sue Bredekamp, that covers every aspect of appropriate programs that serve children from birth through age 8, published on the Web by the National Association for the Education of Young Children.

15. The National Academy for Child Development
http://www.nacd.org
This international organization is dedicated to helping children and adults reach their full potential. Its home page presents links to various programs, research, and resources into such topics as ADD/ADHD.

Exceptional and Culturally Diverse Children

16. ERIC Clearinghouse on Disabilities and Gifted Education
http://www.cec.sped.org/gifted/gt-faqs.htm
This page will give you access to information on identifying and teaching gifted children, attention-deficit disorders, and other topics in gifted education.

17. Global SchoolNet Foundation
http://www.gsn.org
Access this site for multicultural education information. The site includes news for teachers, students, and parents, as well as chat rooms, links to educational resources, programs, and contests and competitions.

18. International Project: Multicultural Pavilion
http://curry.edschool.virginia.edu/curry/centers/
multicultural/papers.html
Here is a forum for sharing of stories and resources and for learning from the stories and resources of others, in the form of articles on the Internet that cover every possible racial, gender, and multicultural issue that could arise in the field of multicultural education.

19. Let 1000 Flowers Bloom/Kristen
   Nicholson-Nelson
http://teacher.scholastic.com/professional/
assessment/100flowers.htm
Open this page for Kristen Nicholson-Nelson's discussion of ways in which teachers can help to nurture children's multiple intelligences. She provides a useful bibliography and resources.

20. Multicultural Publishing and Education Catalog
http://www.mpec.org
This is the home page of the MPEC, a networking and support organization for independent publishers, authors, educators, and librarians fostering authentic multicultural books and materials. It has excellent links to a vast array of resources related to multicultural education.

21. National Attention Deficit Disorder Association
http://www.add.org
This site, some of which is under construction, will lead you to information about ADD/ADHD. It has links to self-help and support groups, outlines behaviors and diagnostics, answers FAQs, and suggests books and other resources.

22. National MultiCultural Institute (NMCI)
http://www.nmci.org
NMCI is one of the major organizations in the field of diversity training. At this Web site, NMCI offers conference data, resource materials, diversity training and consulting service information, and links to other related sites.

Learning and Instruction

23. Education Week on the Web
http://www.edweek.org
At this page you can open archives, read special reports, keep up on current events, and access a variety of articles in educational psychology. A great deal of material is helpful in learning and instruction.

24. Online Internet Institute
http://www.oii.org
A collaborative project among Internet-using educators, proponents of systemic reform, content-area experts, and teachers who desire professional growth, this site provides a learning environment for integrating the Internet into educators' individual teaching styles.

25. Teachers Helping Teachers
http://www.pacificnet.net/~mandel/
This site provides basic teaching tips, new teaching-methodology ideas, and forums for teachers to share their experiences. It features educational resources on the Web, with new ones added each week.

26. The Teachers' Network
http://www.teachnet.org
Bulletin boards, classroom projects, online forums, and Web mentors are featured on this site, as well as the book *Teachers' Guide to Cyberspace* and an online, 4-week course on how to use the Internet.

Motivation and Classroom Magement

27. Canada's Schoolnet Staff Room
http://www.schoolnet.ca/home/e/
Here is a resource and link site for anyone involved in education, including special-needs educators, teachers, parents, volunteers, and administrators.

28. Early Intervention Solutions
http://www.earlyintervention.com
EIS presents this site to address concerns about children's stress and reinforcement. It suggests ways to deal with negative behaviors that may result from stress and anxiety among children.

29. National Institute on the Education of At-Risk
   Students
http://www.ed.gov/offices/OERI/At-Risk/
The At-Risk Institute supports a range of research and development activities designed to improve the education of students at risk of educational failure due to limited English proficiency, race, geographic location, or economic disadvantage. Access its work and links at this site.

Assessment

30. Awesome Library for Teachers
http://www.neat-schoolhouse.org/teacher.html
Open this page for links and access to teacher information on everything from assessments to child development topics.

31. Phi Delta Kappa International
http://www.pdkintl.org
This important organization publishes articles about all facets of education. You can check out the online archive of the journal, *Phi Delta Kappan*, which has resources such as articles having to do with assessment.

32. Washington (State) Center for the
   Improvement of Student Learning
http://cisl.ospi.wednet.edu/CISLALT.html
This Washington State CISL site is designed to provide access to information about the state's new academic standards, assessments, and accountability system. Many resources and Web links are included.

We highly recommend that you review our Web site for expanded information and our other product lines. We are continually updating and adding links to our Web site in order to offer you the most usable and useful information that will support and expand the value of your Annual Editions. You can reach us at:
http://www.dushkin.com/annualeditions/.

www.dushkin.com/online/

Unit Selections

Key Points to Consider

❖ Describe several characteristics of effective teachers.

❖ How does reflection improve teaching?

❖ As we move into the twenty-first century, what new demands will be placed on teachers and schools? What demands will fade?

DUSHKIN ONLINE Links

www.dushkin.com/online/

These sites are annotated on pages 4 and 5.

The teaching-learning process in school is enormously complex. Many factors influence pupil learning—such as family background, developmental level, prior knowledge, motivation, and, of course, effective teachers. Educational psychology investigates these factors to better understand and explain student learning. We begin our exploration of the teaching-learning process by considering the characteristics of effective teaching.

In the first article, Ranae Hagan Stetson describes her experiences as a professor who returns to a first grade classroom to try out her ideas about student-centered instruction. Next, Dwight L. Rogers and Leslie Babinski describe one characteristic of effective teaching—reflection. They describe two protocols that teachers can follow to make reflection more useful.

Finally, we look toward the future and the educational issues that may ultimately change the teacher's role. The third article, "Schools and Curricula for the 21st Century: Predictions, Visions, and Anticipations," maintains that educational technology will dominate thinking about education. The authors discuss ways in which technology will change curriculum, teaching strategies, and schools in general. The fourth article, "What Issues Will Confront Public Education in the Years 2000 and 2020? Predictions of Chief State School Officers," suggests dramatic changes in the way children are educated by the year 2020. These authors, too, suggest that technology will not only change what happens in classrooms, but will enable more children to be educated at home or in the workplace. This will raise questions about school governance, professional development for teachers and other school personnel, and adequate preparation of students for the workplace.

Educational psychology is a resource for teachers that emphasizes disciplined inquiry, a systematic and objective analysis of information, and a scientific attitude toward decision making. The field provides information for decisions that are based on quantitative and qualitative studies of learning and teaching rather than on intuition, tradition, authority, or subjective feelings. It is our hope that this aspect of educational psychology is communicated throughout these readings, and that, as a student, you will adopt the analytic, probing attitude that is part of the discipline.

While educational psychologists have helped to establish a knowledge base about teaching and learning, the unpredictable, spontaneous, evolving nature of teaching suggests that the best they will ever do is to provide concepts and skills that teachers can adapt for use in their classrooms. The issues raised in these articles about effective teaching, and the issues facing teachers in the twenty-first century, help us understand the teaching role and its demands. As you read articles in other chapters, consider the demands they place on the teaching role as well.

The Year That I Really Learned How to Teach

Ten years ago, I left my teaching position at the University of Nevada, Las Vegas, and returned to a 1st grade classroom in the Clark County School District. It was time for me to either "walk the talk" about child-centered, integrated-literacy instruction or never again preach to my university students how to do something I had never tried doing myself.

"No big deal," I told myself. "After all, I'm an experienced K–1 classroom teacher, almost finished with my doctorate in education, and armed with a thorough understanding of the research base supporting integrated-literacy instruction."

Reality Bites

As Nevada state law requires, I received a textbook for every child in every subject—306 textbooks in all! Somehow I was supposed to shovel this mountain of information into the minds of my 6-year-olds in the next nine months. How could we possibly get through these books and still study mammals, space, earthquakes, or the dozens of other topics that 1st graders are interested in learning? As I was repeatedly reminded throughout that year, the year-end tests would be on mandated curriculum, not on all that "other stuff"—the topics that interested the children.

The temperature was already close to 100 degrees when the children arrived. Each class had its number and a corresponding line painted on the

playground where teachers were to pick up their students. Decked out in my new red suit and high heels, I welcomed what seemed an endless line of excited and nervous faces. Suddenly, one child leaped out of line, wrapped both of his arms around my thighs, and began sobbing hysterically. After determining that he was neither bleeding nor near death, I asked him what was wrong. My heart broke as he shrieked between sobs that he *could not read.*

I thought of all the textbooks in my classroom and knew that I wouldn't be passing them out after all. Then I did a really stupid thing—

I bent down to look into his eyes and told him not to worry. By the end of the day, I promised, he would be able to read. My distraught student, Trevor, clung to me as I finished mak-

ing my way down the line. I berated myself: How could I have just made that promise to a child about whom I knew absolutely nothing? Frantic, I mentally reviewed my academic plans for the day.

No books changed hands that day as we popped popcorn and used our observations to write a language-experience story. We ate popcorn. We sang popcorn songs. We smelled popcorn before, during, and after popping. We measured equal portions of popcorn to eat. We created popcorn art. By the end of the day, we had read our popcorn story at least 15 times, and Trevor could read it all by himself. Whether or not he memorized the story didn't matter in the least to Trevor—or to me—because now he believed that he could read.

Lessons Learned

The year was both the hardest and the most rewarding that I have ever had professionally. My class did study mammals, space, earthquakes, jungles, marine biology, and dozens of other

> Child-centered instruction does work.
> And best of all, the children are worth the
> effort it takes to make it happen.

topics. I began to understand more about how important the job of a classroom teacher really was. Classroom teachers are sometimes the only buffer between the children and the

From *Educational Leadership*, May 1999, pp. 78-79. © 1999 by the Association for Supervision and Curriculum Development. All rights reserved. Reprinted by permission.

regulations that can hamper the learning process that they are supposed to help. Daily, I agonized whether I was doing the right thing by teaching the topics that the children were interested in studying. I was questioned by some of the more traditional teachers—the 2nd grade teachers in particular wanted to make sure that I covered volume 1 of the textbooks so that the children would be ready for volume 2 in 2nd grade.

I had unbelievable parental support, however. Parents loved the books that their children were creating, the stories that they were writing, and the knowledge of current topics that their children were developing. For example, we studied why the columns on the two-tier freeways in California collapsed in perfect symmetry with one another during a major earthquake. We looked at both sides of the tuna fish boycott that resulted in the dolphin-safe labels on the tuna cans. And when one of my students brought in a piece of the Berlin Wall, we studied that as well.

We never did make it all the way through volume 1 of the handwriting, the spelling, or the language-arts textbooks, but somehow my class's average on the year-end test was in the 90th percentile.

I now teach at a private, urban university in Texas. I am often deluged with the "Yes, buts" from my graduate and undergraduate students questioning the feasibility of implementing child-centered, integrated instructional practices. I happily play the videotapes of my 1st grade classes as I explain how I bucked the system. It can be done, I tell them. You will survive. Child-centered instruction does work. And best of all, the children are worth the effort it takes to make it happen.

Ranae Hagen Stetson is Associate Professor of early childhood education for the School of Education, Texas Christian University, TCU Box 297900, Ft. Worth, TX 76129.

Simon Hole and Grace Hall McEntee

Reflection Is at the Heart of Practice

The ordinary experiences of our teaching days are the essence of our practice. Using a guide to reflect on these experiences—either individually or with colleagues—is an entry to improving our teaching.

The life force of teaching practice is thinking and wondering. We carry home those moments of the day that touch us, and we question decisions made. During these times of reflection, we realize when something needs to change.

A protocol, or guide, enables teachers to refine the process of reflection, alone or with colleagues. The Guided Reflection Protocol is useful for teachers who choose to reflect alone. The Critical Incidents Protocol, which we developed through our work with the Annenberg Institute for School Reform at Brown University, is used for shared reflection. The steps for each protocol are similar; both include writing.

Guided Reflection Protocol

The first step in guided reflection is to collect possible episodes for reflection. In his book *Critical Incidents in Teaching: Developing Professional Judgement* (1993), David Tripp encourages us to think about ordinary events, which often have much to tell us about the underlying trends, motives, and structures of our practice. Simon's story, "The Geese and the

Guided reflection is a way to find the meaning within the mundane.

Blinds," exemplifies this use of an ordinary event.

Step One: What Happened?

Wednesday, September 24, 9:30 a.m. I stand to one side of the classroom, taking the morning attendance. One student glances out the window and sees a dozen Canada geese grazing on the playground. Hopping from his seat, he calls out as he heads to the window for a better view. Within moments, six students cluster around the window. Others start from their seats to join them. I call for attention and ask them to return to their desks. When none of the students respond, I

walk to the window and lower the blinds.

Answering the question What happened? is more difficult than it sounds. We all have a tendency to jump into an interpretive or a judgmental mode, but it is important to begin by simply telling the story. Writing down what happened—without analysis or judgment—aids in creating a brief narrative. Only then are we ready to move to the second step.

Step Two: Why Did It Happen?

Attempting to understand why an event happened the way it did is the

We all have a tendency to jump into an interpretive or a judgmental mode, but it is important to begin by simply telling the story.

From *Educational Leadership*, May 1999, pp. 34-37. © 1999 by the Association for Supervision and Curriculum Development. All rights reserved. Reprinted by permission.

beginning of reflection. We must search the context within which the event occurred for explanations. Simon reflects:

> It's not hard to imagine why the students reacted to the geese as they did. As 9-year-olds, they are incredibly curious about their world. Explaining my reaction is more difficult. Even as I was lowering the blinds, I was kicking myself. Here was a natural opportunity to explore the students' interests. Had I stood at the window with them for five minutes, asking questions to see what they knew about geese, or even just listening to them, I'd been telling a story about seizing the moment or taking advantage of a learning opportunity. I knew that even as I lowered the blinds. So, why?

Searching deeper, we may find that a specific event serves as an example of a more general category of events. We need to consider the underlying structures within the school that may be a part of the event and examine deeply held values. As we search, we often find more questions than answers.

> Two key things stand out concerning that morning. First, the schedule. On Wednesdays, students leave the room at 10:00 a.m. and do not return until 15 minutes before lunch. I would be out of the classroom all afternoon attending a meeting, and so this half hour was all the time I would have with my students.
>
> Second, this is the most challenging class I've had in 22 years of teaching. The first three weeks of school had been a constant struggle as I tried strategy after strategy to hold their attention long enough to have a discussion, give directions, or conduct a lesson. The hectic schedule and the need to prepare the class for a substitute added to the difficulty I've had "controlling" the class, so I closed the blinds.

There's something satisfying about answering the question Why did it happen? Reflection often stops here. If the goal is to become a reflective practitioner, however, we need to look more deeply. The search for meaning is step three.

Step Three: What Might It Mean?

Assigning meaning to the ordinary episodes that make up our days can feel like overkill. Is there really meaning behind all those events? Wouldn't it be more productive to wait for something extraordinary to happen, an event marked with a sign: "Pay attention! Something important is happening." Guided reflection is a way to find the meaning within the mundane. Split-second decision making is a crucial aspect of teaching. Given the daily madness of life in a classroom, considering all the options and consequences is difficult. Often, it is only through reflection that we even recognize that we had a choice, that we could have done something differently.

> Like a football quarterback, I often make bad decisions because of pressure. Unlike a quarterback, I don't have an offensive line to blame for letting the pressure get to me. While it would be nice to believe that I could somehow make the pressure go away, the fact is that it will always be with me. Being a teacher means learning to live within that pressure, learning from the decisions I make and learning to make better decisions.

Our growing awareness of how all events carry some meaning is not a new concept. In *Experience and Education* (1938), John Dewey wrote about experience and its relationship to learning and teaching: "Every experience affects for better or worse the attitudes which help decide the quality of further experiences" (p. 37). He believed that teachers must be aware of the "possibilities inherent in ordinary experience" (p. 89), that the "business of the educator [is] to see in what direction an experience is heading" (p. 38). Rediscovering this concept through the examination of ordinary events creates a fresh awareness of its meaning.

The search for meaning is an integral part of being human. But understanding by itself doesn't create changes in classroom practice. The last phase of guided reflection is more action oriented and involves

holding our practice to the light of those new understandings.

Step Four: What Are the Implications for My Practice?

Simon continues:

> My reaction to the pressure this year has been to resort to methods of control. I seem to be forever pulling down the blinds. I'm thinking about how I might better deal with the pressure.
>
> But there is something else that needs attention. Where is the pressure coming from? I'm sensing from administration and parents that they feel I should be doing things differently. I've gotten subtle and overt messages that I need to pay more attention to "covering" the curriculum, that I should be finding a more equal balance between process and product.
>
> Maybe they're right. What I've been doing hasn't exactly been a spectacular success. But I think that what is causing the lowering of the

---

Guided Reflection Protocol (For Individual Reflection)

1. *Collect stories.* Some educators find that keeping a set of index cards or a steno book close at hand provides a way to jot down stories as they occur. Others prefer to wait until the end of the day and write in a journal.

2. *What happened?* Choose a story that strikes you as particularly interesting. Write it succinctly.

3. *Why did it happen?* Fill in enough of the context to give the story meaning. Answer the question in a way that makes sense to you.

4. *What might it mean?* Recognizing that there is no one answer is an important step. Explore possible meanings rather than determine the meaning.

5. *What are the implications for practice?* Consider how your practice might change given any new understandings that have emerged from the earlier steps.

blinds stems from my not trusting enough in the process. Controlling the class in a fairly traditional sense isn't going to work in the long run. Establishing a process that allows the class to control itself will help keep the blinds up.

Cultivating deep reflection through the use of a guiding protocol is an entry into rethinking and changing practice. Alone, each of us can proceed step-by-step through the examination of a particular event. Through the process, we gain new insights into the implications of ordinary events, as Simon did when he analyzed "The Geese and the Blinds."

Whereas Guided Reflection is for use by individuals, the Critical Incidents Protocol is used with colleagues. The goal is the same: to get to the heart of our practice, the place that pumps the lifeblood into our teaching, where we reflect, gain insight, and change what we do with our students. In addition, the Critical Incidents Protocol encourages the establishment of collegial relationships.

Critical Incidents Protocol

Schools are social places. Although too often educators think and act alone, in most schools colleagues do share daily events. Stories told in teachers' lounges are a potential

Telling stories has the potential for changing individual practice and the culture of our schools.

source of rich insight into issues of teaching and learning and can open doors to professional dialogue.

Telling stories has the potential for changing individual practice and the culture of our schools. The Critical Incidents Protocol allows practitioners to share stories in a way that is useful to their own thinking and to that of the group.

Three to five colleagues meet for the purpose of exploring a "critical incident." For 10 minutes, all write a brief account of an incident. Participants should know that the sharing of their writing will be for the purpose of getting feedback on what happened rather than on the quality of the writing itself.

Next, the group decides which story to use with the protocol. The presenter for the session then reads the story while the group listens carefully to understand the incident and the context. Colleagues ask clarifying questions about what happened or why the incident occurred, then they discuss what the incident might mean in terms of the presenter's practice.

During this time, the presenter listens and takes notes. The presenter then responds, and the participants discuss the implications for their own practice. To conclude, one member leads a conversation about what happened during the session, how well the process worked, and how the group might change the process.

The sharing of individual stories raises issues in the fresh air of collegial support. If open dialogue is not already part of a school's culture, however, colleagues may feel insecure about beginning. To gain confidence, they may choose to run through the protocol first with a story that is not theirs. For this purpose, Grace offers a story about an incident in the writing lab from her practice as a high school English teacher.

Step One: What Happened?

We went into the computer lab to work on essay drafts. TJ, Neptune, Ronny, and Mick sat as a foursome. Their sitting together had not worked last time. On their single printer an obscene message had appeared. All four had denied writing it.

The next day Ronny, Neptune, and Mick had already sat together. Just as TJ was about to take his seat, I asked him if he would mind sitting over at the next bay of computers. He exploded. "You think I'm the cause of the problem, don't you?"

Actually I did think he might be, but I wasn't at all certain. "No," I said, "but I do want you to sit over here for today." He got red in the face, plunked down in the chair near the three other boys, and refused to move.

I motioned for him to come with me. Out in the hall, I said to him quietly, "The bottom line is that all of you need to get your work done." Out of control, body shaking, TJ angrily spewed out, "You always pick on me. Those guys. . . .

Critical Incidents Protocol (For Shared Reflection)

1. *Write stories.* Each group member writes briefly in response to the question: What happened? (10 minutes)

2. *Choose a story.* The group decides which story to use. (5 minutes)

3. *What happened?* The presenter reads the written account of what happened and sets it within the context of professional goals. (10 minutes)

4. *Why did it happen?* Colleagues ask clarifying questions. (5 minutes)

5. *What might it mean?* The group raises questions about the incident in the context of the presenter's work. They discuss it as professional, caring colleagues while the presenter listens. (15 minutes)

6. *What are the implications for practice?* The presenter responds, then the group engages in conversation about the implications for the presenter's practice and for the participants' own practice. A useful question at this stage might be, What new insights occurred? (15 minutes)

7. *Debrief the process.* The group talks about what just happened. How did the process work? (10 minutes)

You. . . ." I could hardly hear his words, so fascinated was I with his intense emotion and his whole-body animation.

Contrary to my ordinary response to students who yell, I felt perfectly calm. I knew I needed to wait. Out of the corner of my eye, I saw two male teachers rise out of their chairs in the hallway about 25 feet away. They obviously thought that I, a woman of small stature, needed protection. But I did not look at them. I looked at TJ and waited.

When he had expended his wrathful energy, I said softly, "You know, TJ, you are a natural-born leader." I waited. Breathed in and out. "You did not choose to be a leader; it was thrust upon you. But there you are. People follow you. So you have a tremendous responsibility, to lead in a positive and productive way. Do you understand what I am saying?"

Like an exhalation after a long in-breath, his body visibly relaxed. He looked down at me and nodded his head. Then he held out his hand to me and said, "I'm sorry."

Back in the room, he picked up his stuff and, without a word, moved to the next bay of computers.

Step Two: Using the Critical Incidents Protocol

At first you'll think that you need more information than this, but we think that you have enough here. One member of the group will take the role of Grace. Your "Grace" can answer clarifying questions about what happened or why it happened in whatever way he or she sees fit. Work through the protocol to figure out what the incident might mean in terms of "Grace's" practice. Finally, discuss what implications the incident in the writing lab might have for her practice and for your own as reflective educators. Then, try an event of your own.

We think that you will find that whether the group uses your story or someone else's, building reflective practice together is a sure way to get to the heart of teaching and learning.

References

Dewey, J. (1938). *Experience and education.* New York: Macmillan.

Tripp, D. (1993). *Critical incidents in teaching: Developing professional judgement.* New York: Routledge.

Simon Hole is a 4th grade teacher at Narragansett Elementary School in Narragansett, Rhode Island. He may be reached at 36 White Oak Dr., Wyoming, RI 02898 (e-mail: ropajavi@aol.com). **Grace Hall McEntee** is cofounder of Educators Writing for Change. She may be reached at Box 301, Prudence Island, RI 02872 (e-mail: Gmcente@aol.com).

Schools and Curricula for the 21st Century: Predictions, Visions, and Anticipations

By Weldon F. Zenger and Sharon K. Zenger

If the research on education for the 21st century were to be summed up in three words, they would be technology, technology, and technology. Almost without exception, information regarding education in the 21st century directly or indirectly involves technology in some way. How might technology affect education and schools in the next century?

Society is becoming more and more involved in thinking about and planning for tomorrow's world. Technology will be a determining factor in how and what the teacher will use for instruction (Berliner, 1992). Classroom management must change so technology can be used. Sandra Welch, Executive Vice President at PBS (Baker, 1993), envisions schoolchildren having a device the size of a tape recorder that serves as a source of knowledge from all over the world. Sharon Bell, director of technology for New Orleans Public Schools (Baker, 1993), sees children with hand-held pads containing one million times more power than any computer today. This power pad would recognize handwriting and voice, and would type, register, respond, and store this information.

Literacy skills needed for the 21st century include accessing, thinking, and communication.

Literacy skills needed for the 21st century include accessing, thinking, and communication (Hill, 1992). According to the U.S. National Commission on Libraries and Information Science, "Our nation's schools

Weldon F. Zenger is professor emeritus of education and President's Distinguished Scholar at Fort Hays State University (1993), Hays, Kans., as well as adjunct professor emeritus of education at Kansas State University, Manhattan, conducting research; Sharon K. Zenger is professor emeritus of education at Tabor College, Hillsboro, Kans. The authors may be reached at 2504 Meadowood Drive, Manhattan, Kans. 66502.

Reprinted with permission from *NASSP Bulletin*, April 1999, pp. 49-59. © 1999 by the National Association of Secondary School Principals. For more information concerning NASSP services and/or programs, please call (703) 860-0200.

must recognize information literacy as an essential skill and strive to develop an information literate society" (1989, p. xiii). For students to be information literate, "they must know how to find, analyze, synthesize, evaluate, and communicate information and ideas" (p. xiii). The Commission maintains that information processing will be a determining factor in an individual's ability to succeed and will be the focus of education in the 21st century.

Future curricula must be developed around major or universal themes such as change and adaptability, global interdependence, cultural diversity, quality of life, increasing technology, self-actualization, lifelong learning, and world economic systems in balance with the national environment (Wilson et al., 1991). State-of-the-art communication systems, technology, and transportation have all fostered the globalization of business (Carlock, 1991). Education must provide students with an international perspective.

crease in lifelong learning will all be a part of this demand for more assistive technology instruction.

By the year 2010, every job will require some skill in information-processing technology (Cetron, 1989). Many public schools will be open 24 hours a day, retraining adults and renting out computer systems after the school day ends. Vocational education will become as crucial as traditional education. School days and years will lengthen. Class sizes will be cut from an average of 17 to 10. Students will be promoted by performance, not on the time spent in class. Teachers will also be recruited from business and industry. Computer-aided learning programs will be replacing books. Schools will work more with business and industry.

The biggest challenge is funding. In places like Independence, Mo.—the first 21st Century School site—parent fees nearly cover operating expenses. Parental involvement in school affairs is undoubtedly going to increase in schools of the future (Murphy, 1991). School

By the year 2010, every job will require some skill in information-processing technology.

Awareness of the global economy and the basics of international business is the first step in preparing students to compete in the business world of the future (McCaslin, 1992). In the future, global education will include the study of the environment, migratory pollution, national security, nuclear war, economics, world population, and food distribution (Smith, 1990). Our youth need to be educated about these concerns. Legislation is already being passed in many states to develop and improve global knowledge in schools. All subjects can, and should, be taught from a global perspective. Many topics will be controversial.

More emphasis must be placed on the education of the poor and minorities. All schools should expect the same high standards. Schools will use more apprenticeships and internships, especially for at-risk students. Increased learner diversity, including the increase in the number of older Americans, will increase the use of instructional assistive technologies (Hofmeister, Menlove, and Thorkildsen, 1992). With the increase in learner diversity and increased availability of videos, open and closed captioning in video courseware may be the most important trend in schools for the 21st century. An increase in the number of hearing impaired students in public and higher education, an increase in learners of English as a second language at all levels, and an in-

councils will consist of parents with varying political, social, cultural, and economic values that will require school leaders to become more politically astute if they are to survive.

Schools and Curricula in the 21st Century

Curriculum planners in the 21st century will have knowledge of real-world requirements and will be able to set guidelines for the skills needed for elementary, middle, and high school students (Cetron, 1985). Instead of talking about which grade they are in, students will talk in terms of outcomes, topics, issues, job experiences, projects, or community applications with which they are working.

As has been noted, technology dominates the ideas and predictions for the 21st century schools. Interwoven with technology are information, communication, and globalism. The parents, home, community, and businesses will play a larger role in schools of the future. Some very thought-provoking, challenging, and perhaps alarming predictions for schools of the next century follow, some of which have already come to fruition.

Lewis (1991) gives us a taste of what we might see in the 21st century schools:

- Computers may be integrated into the desktop of students and teachers.
- Students and teachers will travel from class to class with their own personal computer. In a few years, battery-powered notebook computers that can be plugged into a school's network will be available.
- Video wallpaper where images surround students may be a part of the classroom.

- Outcomes-based learning as opposed to covering the content
- Individualized testing as opposed to norm-referenced testing
- Performance-based assessment as opposed to nonauthentic assessment
- Personal learning plans as opposed to group-based content delivery
- Cooperative learning as opposed to adversarial learning
- Learning centers as opposed to adversarial learning

The parents, home, community, and businesses will play a larger role in schools of the future.

Berliner (1992) has very insightful projections for schools of the future. They include:

- Notebook or backpack computers assigned to all students in the place of textbooks will be possible.
- Textbooks will be on disks with interactive elements and dynamic rather than static graphics, and will allow erasing and rerecording.
- Sophisticated calculators with animated graphics will be used for mathematical work and problem solving.
- Communications from home to school will easily be carried out through local communication networks.
- Teachers will be seen as managers of information and complex environments rather than authoritative sources of information.
- Teachers will become more collegial and informal due to the individual use of technology and will be viewed more as facilitators or coaches, leading to higher levels of productivity for both students and teachers.
- New technology will make more individual and group projects possible, promoting a multidimensional classroom approach.
- Project methods of intrinsic interests to students will be used to teach critical thinking skills.

Reigeluth (1992) offers the emerging features of an information-age educational system compared to the current industrial-aged system:

- Continuous progress as opposed to grade levels

- Teachers as coach or facilitator of learning as opposed to teacher as dispenser of knowledge
- Thinking, problem-solving skills, and meaning-making as opposed to memorization of meaningless facts
- Communication skills as opposed to isolated reading, writing skills
- Advanced technologies as tools as opposed to books as tools (p. 12).

Reigeluth (1992) also offers the following features for an information-age educational system based on changes in the family:

- A "teacher" is responsible for a child for a period of about 4 years.
- That teacher is responsible for educating the whole child.
- Each school has no more than 10 teachers, to create a smaller caring environment (schools-within-schools).
- Each student develops a quarterly contract with the teacher and parents (p. 12).

Reigeluth (1992) also indicated the need for a new paradigm in education based on massive changes in the conditions and educational needs of an emerging information society. Reigeluth and Garfinkle (1992) present a more detailed image of the features that appear to be emerging from those new conditions and educational needs of the information society. They call that image "LearningSphere 2000." The purpose of LearningSphere

2000 is to present one possible image of a different paradigm for education.

Reigeluth and Garfinkle caution that the features in this new paradigm are illustrative rather than prescriptive and are to stimulate thinking rather than to present a solution. Not all aspects of the paradigm should be considered as necessary or even advisable for any given community. Some of the features of the LearningSphere 2000 paradigm are:

- Mastery of tasks before progression
- Tasks completed in a variety of ways within and outside the school
- Teacher as facilitator and instructional manager
- Teacher as guide for a student for 3–5 years
- Clusters of guides (4–10 per cluster) functioning somewhat independent of the school district
- Parents requesting the guides for their student
- Learning centers providing instruction in areas of

need for a new paradigm in education based on massive changes in the information society. As the information age reaches maturity and the bioengineering age develops, he contends that the ability to learn will become the driving force to success. Lines between grades and levels of education will disappear and as the electronic learning environments develop, a whole new array of educational providers will enter the scene.

Bauer (1991) seems to sum it up with some predictions for the curriculum of the 1990s and beyond, including the following elements:

- The microcomputer will be used as a standard tool for learning.
- Software will become easier to learn and all students will know word processing, database, spreadsheet, and desktop publishing software.
- Advanced typewriting will be replaced with advanced word processing applications.

...the emerging new format of education for the 21st century is struggling to be born in 19th-century buildings.

focus whether in a traditional discipline area or a cross-discipline thematic area such as pollution
- Learning contracts developed for each student, each period with input from the guide, parents, and student
- Five levels of development, starting with birth. The earliest level (birth to age 3) will take place at home or in a "home room" daycare situation provided by the school
- Students' progress assessed across the disciplines through real-world projects as well as separately in the academic disciplines
- Technology such as multimedia, hypermedia, electronic networks, and computer-based simulations used at all levels
- Social services provided through the schools, including child care services, health care and family services, as well as parenting education
- Peer tutoring, parents, and senior citizens as well as other volunteers used to reduce the labor costs of education.

Edward Hammond (1997), president of Fort Hays State University and a visionary committed to computerization and information technology, agrees there is a

- Records management will be absorbed into database applications.
- Desktop publishing will move from word processing into document processing.
- Office administration will rely on integrated computer skills.
- Secretaries will be known as support staff, with an increase in administrative duties and salaries.
- The three R's will be replaced with the four C's: comprehension, critical thinking, communication, and coping.
- Blackboards will be obsolete; modular seating, personal computers, and encyclopedias stored on disks will be common.
- Voice activated keyboards will be used.
- There will be a greater emphasis on visual education.
- The new computers will be able to read handwriting with almost human accuracy and convert handwritten notes into typewritten form and store the information in the computer's memory.
- Adaptability will be the survival skill. As job requirements change and electronics affect technological skills, adaptability will be the key to success (p. 21).

Halsted (1992) is concerned that the emerging new format of education for the 21st century is struggling to be born in 19th-century buildings. Drawing from the major concerns of educators and architects who met for the purpose of identifying school designs for the future, Halsted suggests that schools should be hospitable environments and welcoming places for no more than 400–500 students, and where:

- Classrooms will be like studios.
- Each student will have his or her own workstation and research space.
- There will need to be an array of spaces of various sizes, including:

  ✓ Central gathering places for the school community

  ✓ Work spaces for cooperative learning by groups of different sizes

  ✓ Quiet, private areas for one-on-one sessions with a teacher, mentor, or fellow student

  ✓ Nooks where students can think and work independently

  ✓ Offices for teachers where they can work as true professionals, do individual testing and counseling, organize individualized study programs for their students, and do their own research, with telephone and voice mail access to parents and teacher colleagues.

- There will be a need to incorporate the wide range of existing and anticipated educational technology, making it accessible to all.
- There should be a full range of social services in or near the school: preschool education, daycare, parent education, health, mental health, employment, recreational, substance abuse, and family counseling.
- Above all, the new schools should be institutions where all feel welcome and have a sense of belonging in spaces that flow from social and public areas to smaller work areas, to private spaces that encourage contemplation (p. 47).

Infotech-Based Education in the 21st Century

In an article entitled "Cyberspaced out by 2025?" Cornish (1996) gives us one of the most recent and complete anticipations of how technology could shape education in the future. He is careful to point out these are possible future developments and *not* predictions.

- Infotech will allow children to start formal education in their cribs. Interactive instruction can begin in infancy, especially as equipment is adapted to cradle, crib, and playpen. Playing electronic games should stimulate early development of mental faculties. Some youngsters will teach themselves to read before age 3.

- The education experience will be dramatically enhanced by multimedia, computer stimulation, virtual reality, etc. Interactive programs will offer virtual-reality experiences of stirring events.
- There will be a boom in packaged educational products. Highly engaging and effective products should become increasingly available at reasonable cost. Parents and teachers must see that children use these "automated tutors" properly. These products should greatly benefit children taught at home by parents.
- The stupendous increase in knowledge in libraries and databases will pose the question: What do youngsters really need to learn? Youths can study only the tiniest bit of the knowledge base at our disposal. Deciding wisely what they should learn becomes essential for students' long-term success. Society must make hard choices about what children must know and what is merely useful or interesting.
- Teachers will be better able to handle classes of students with widely different abilities and interests. Educational infotech should permit most students to learn mainly on their own. Computerized multimedia courses reduce the need for constant instruction by a human teacher. However, youngsters will still need guidance to stay focused on what they need to learn.
- Handicapped people will be special beneficiaries of infotech-based education. The homebound can take courses from teachers all over the world in any subject. The blind, deaf, and paralyzed will have equipment that largely offsets their handicaps.
- Infotech will enable students to get personal help with homework without parents. Homework hotlines are multiplying. New teleconferencing systems will enable youngsters to work easily with distant teachers. And a student who wants a general review of any standard school topic should be able to summon up a computer tutor for a quick briefing.
- Incredible information resources will be available for students doing papers. One problem is the temptation to copy from electronic source material rather than writing one's own thoughts.
- Global universities will emerge, connecting students, lecturers, and researchers in many nations via computer networks, satellite television, etc. Students may be required to spend little or no time at a university campus.
- Future infotech alone will not ensure good education: Teachers will continue to be needed. The many exciting technologies will not necessarily be used effectively and may even be abused. Most students have difficulty staying on task without a human teacher. So the future teacher's main task may be to provide one-on-one guidance, supervision, and intimate discussion.
- Teachers will resist infotech in education when it threatens jobs or privileges but may accept it when it frees them for more interesting tasks.

- Infotech will allow students to take courses at their own pace and get credit whenever material is mastered. College students in a hurry could whip through a course, while others, with less time, might spend several years. Increased efficiency in pumping information into students' minds through infotech should also permit students to spend more time in other important developmental activities.

- Education may become compulsory for adults as well as children. As more adults waste their lives because they lack skills for good jobs, interpersonal relationships, and global citizenship, society will reassess letting people escape badly needed training simply because they are no longer youngsters (pp. 5–7).

A Word of Caution

All these predictions, projections, visions, and anticipations of education for the 21st century could lead one to believe that technology will solve all the problems of education. Many of the authors cited by these writers warned against doing this. Postman (1994) goes so far as to say technology is part of the problem, not the solution. He contends that the great problems of education are social and moral and have nothing to do with dazzling new technologies. He believes our children, like the rest of us, now suffer from information glut, not information scarcity.

McCluskey (1994) agrees technology will not solve the problems facing education. He does not dispute that technology has an important and vital role in education of the future. In fact, he reminds us that it does, but it may also produce unanticipated and perhaps unpleasant consequences. Further, he contends that if more and more advanced technology is introduced into the educational scheme without a concomitant emphasis on knowledge acquisition, it will allow some students to operate at lower levels of thinking. Students who possess knowledge will tend to use technology as a tool, and those who do not will use it as a crutch.

Sequencing Content into the School Curriculum

In further search of how technology and other predictions for education may affect education in the future, these writers are extending their research with a study of placement, scope, and sequencing content into the infotech school curricula of the 21st century. To do this, in addition to reviewing the literature and curriculum planning books, the following are being contacted: All 50 state chief school officers, national councils and committees of education, major textbook publishers, major universities and educational leaders who can be identified.

The early response from chief school officers has been excellent. Some designs appear to be taking shape, especially at the state level, pertaining to what is guiding and may guide the scope and sequencing of school curricula in the new millennium.

Almost all states responding to a written survey report that curriculum development, especially scope and sequencing of content to specific grade levels, is left up to local school systems. Most of them did indicate, however, that they develop standards, benchmarks, frameworks, goals, or essential learning outcomes to assist and provide guidance for local systems to follow as they develop curricula. Most of these broad standards are not grade-level specific. In developing these state-level standards, the following were listed as sources and guidelines: National and international standards, other state standards, standards from the National Assessment of Educational Progress, New Standards Project, national councils and commissions of education in specific subject areas, existing research, professional judgment, current practice, and teacher expertise. The processes for developing these standards were described by some states responding, in which case many educators from all levels were involved as well as some outside the field of education.

To this point in the current study, the only response indicating that specific criteria have been established to scope and sequence content is by the National Council for the Social Studies. Through a series of task force studies, 24 criteria and six scope and sequence models have been developed that can be used by local school districts to guide scope and sequencing social studies subject content to grade levels. Responses from state chief school officers indicate that placing and sequencing content to grade levels is left to the local districts.

A review of curriculum planning and development books has identified criteria that could be used, but what actually is being used by local districts is not clear. The primary purpose in further researching this area is to identify criteria that have been used to place, scope and sequence subject matter content to specific grade levels in the past, are being used in the present, and project that which will be appropriate for use in the infotech schools of the future. *Any suggestions or ideas for helping to locate this information will be welcomed by these writers.*

Authors' Note: The original idea and much of the impetus for this research was the brainchild of Charles Leftwich, Dean of the College of Education at Fort Hays State University. An earlier version of this article including a section on higher education was published in the "Record," a publication of the Kansas Association for Supervision and Curriculum Development.

References

Baker, D. E. "Technovisions." *America's Agenda* 1(1993): 34–35.

Bauer, D. E. "Predicting the Next Ten Years." *Business Education Forum,* April 1991.

Berliner, D. C. "Redesigning Classroom Activities for the Future." *Educational Technology,* October 1992.

Carlock, L. L. "Internationalizing the Business Education Curriculum." *National Business Education Yearbook* 29(1991): 1–7.

Cetron, M. "Long-Term Trends Affecting Undergraduate Education into the Twenty-First Century." Paper presented at the National Educational Conference, Kansas City, Mo., September 1988.

_____. "Preparing Education for the Year 2000." *The Education Digest,* April 1989.

_____. *Schools of the Future: How American Business and Education Can Cooperate To Save Our Schools.* New York: McGraw-Hill, 1985.

Cornish, E. "Cyberspaced Out by 2025?" *The Education Digest,* April 1996.

Halsted, H. "Designing Facilities for a New Generation of Schools." *Educational Technology,* October 1992.

Hammond, E. Interviewed by authors January 8, 1997, Hays, Kans.

Hill, M. "The New Literacy." *Electronic Learning,* September 1992.

Hofmeister, A. M.; Menlove, M.; and Thorkildsen, R. "Learner Diversity and Instructional Video: Implications for Developers." *Educational Technology,* July 1992.

Lewis, P. H. "The Technology of Tomorrow: Here's a Taste of What You Can Expect in 21st Century Schools." *Principal* 71(1991): 6–7.

McCaslin, J. "Preparing for Success in the World Economy: A Governmental perspective." *The Balance Sheet,* January/February 1992.

McCluskey, L. "Gresham's Law, Technology, and Education." *Phi Delta Kappan.* 7(1994): 550–52.

Murphy, P. J. "Collaborative School Management: Implications for School Leaders," *NASSP Bulletin,* October 1991.

Postman, N. "Technology as Dazzling Distraction." *The Education Digest,*. April 1994.

Reigeluth, C. M. "The Imperative for Systemic Change." *Educational Technology,* November 1992.

Reigeluth, C. M. and Garfinkle, R. J. "envisioning a New System of Education." *Educational Technology,MD* November 1992.

Smith, A. F. "First Steps and Future Trends." *Momentum,*. February 1990.

U.S. National Commission on Libraries and Information Science. *Information Literacy and Education for the 21st Century: Toward an Agenda for Action.* Chicago, ILL.: American Association of School Librarians. ERIC Document No. ED 330 343, 1989.

Wilson, C., and Others. *A Vision of a Preferred Curriculum for the 21st Century: Action Research in School Administration.* Rochester, Mich.: Oakland University, Schools of Education and Human Services. ERIC Document No. 344 275, 1991.

What Issues Will Confront Public Education in the Years 2000 and 2020? Predictions of Chief State School Officers

ALAN D. MORGAN, MYRNA MATRANGA, GARY L. PELTIER, and GEORGE C. HILL

National education goals notwithstanding, public education remains a state-level responsibility by virtue of the Tenth Amendment to the U.S. Constitution. Specifically, state education systems must ensure access to a free public education for every citizen.

To carry out that responsibility, the average state spends over 45 percent of its general fund budget to educate children in our elementary and secondary schools (NEA 1994). Thus, public education commands a greater proportion of state funds than that appropriated for highways, corrections, or even public health services. Although it is true that the percentage assigned for public education from state-level budgets has declined in the past decade, actual total appropriations for public education have steadily increased during the period. Despite that increased expenditure, however, the public perception is that "public schools have frittered away vast sums without much visible improvement in student performance" (Mandel 1995, 64).

From the perspective of professional educators, there are many reasons for the lackluster performance of public education, ranging from low expectations to inadequate financial support. Whatever the reason, however, one

Alan D. Morgan, formerly the New Mexico superintendent of public instruction, is executive vice president for governmental relations, Voyager Expanded Learning, Inc., in Albuquerque, New Mexico. Myrna Matranga is the chair of the Department of Educational Leadership, Gary L. Peltier is a professor of educational leadership, and George C. Hill is an associate professor of educational leadership, all in the College of Education, University of Nevada, Reno.

overlooked strategy to *improve* school performance is to emphasize goal setting and long-range planning, especially by anticipating the future needs of, and demands upon, the public education system. In the face of a current lack of information regarding those future needs and demands, we surveyed the chief state school officer (CSSO) in each state to determine what he or she saw as the critical issues that will confront public education in the future. The chief state school officer—known as commissioner, state superintendent, or director of education—is the person in each state who oversees and administers the state education system and so is in a particularly advantageous position to predict what the education issues of the future will be.

A questionnaire was mailed to all 51 CSSOs. Forty-eight returned the data collection instrument (for a response rate of 94 percent). In the questionnaire, we asked the CSSOs to rank the level of importance of eleven critical issues of public education policy for the years 2000 and 2020; the issues were as follows: utilization of technology in instruction, site-based decision making, equity in funding school operations, equity in funding capital projects, student preparation for the workplace, services for special populations, educator preparation and licensure, preschool and early childhood education, assessment of student progress, safe environment for learning, and adult learning.

Results

The three most frequently chosen public education issues perceived as likely to be very important in the year 2000 (of the eleven given) were (1) student preparation for the workplace (81 percent), (2) utilization of technol-

From *The Clearing House*, July/August 1998, pp. 339–341. Reprinted with permission of the Helen Dwight Reid Educational Foundation. Published by Heldref Publications, 1319 Eighteenth St., NW, Washington, DC 20036-1802. © 1998.

ogy in instruction (79 percent), and (3) providing a safe environment for learning (79 percent). The three issues perceived most often as not likely to be important or not likely to be very important for the year 2000 were (1) equity in funding capital projects, (2) educator preparation and licensure, and (3) services for special populations.

The predictions for the year 2020 were somewhat different. The three most frequently chosen were (1) utilization of technology in instruction (73 percent), (2) student preparation for the workplace (71 percent), and (3) preschool and early childhood education (58 percent). Four of the eleven public education policy issues were rated by 30 percent or more of the respondents as not likely to be important or not likely to be very important in 2020: (1) equity in funding of capital projects, (2) site-based decision making, (3) equity in funding school operations, and (4) educator preparation and licensure.

The questionnaire also invited respondents to make written comments regarding public education policy issues of the future. Among the issues identified in those narrative responses were the following: (1) concern over the potential withdrawal of public support, and funding, of public institutions such as local schools; (2) a vision of schools becoming the primary architects of societal values in ways not thought of in the twentieth century, such as through genetic engineering and the creation of new life forms; (3) the burgeoning of individual and self-paced learning, at home or in the workplace, coupled with currently unknown technologies, thus eliminating the need for school building, school campuses, and traditional school-funding mechanisms; and (4) the possibility that society will put an increased value on education, as seen in the increasing support for lifelong learning and intergenerational partnerships.

Regional differences. The only issue regarding which statistically significant differences existed between the responses from CSSOs of different regions in the country was preschool and early childhood education as seen for the year 2000. Specifically, the CSSOs of the Pacific West perceived the issue of pre-school and early childhood education as being considerably more important than did their counterparts in the other four regions of the country.

Selection differences. Each respondent had been asked to indicate the method by which he or she was selected to the position of chief state school officer. (Responses indicated that 27 percent of the CSSOs were elected by popular vote, 58 percent were appointed to their positions by state boards of education, and 15 percent were appointed by the governors of their states.) Based on the method of selection, the only issue for which a statistically significant difference existed (identified at the .05 level) was "safe environment for learning" in the year 2020. Elected CSSOs viewed a safe environment as being of much greater importance than did the chief state school officers who had been appointed by governors or state boards of education.

Gender differences. This study found a statistically significant difference (at the .01 level) between male respondents and female respondents with regard to the perceived importance of site-based decision making in the year 2000. Female CSSOs were far more certain than their male counterparts that site-based decision making would continue to be an important issue. Several male respondents, on the other hand, shared the perception that, in the future, schooling would not happen in discrete school buildings and on campuses but rather would occur through a more eclectic arrangement, one tailored to the needs of individual students in the workplace, home, and other physical settings—thus obviating the need for school site-based decision making. Both males and females perceived site-based decision making as likely to be less important by the year 2020 than it is now.

Implications

Most respondents availed themselves of the opportunity to add comments to the survey. (A total of eighty-six individual comments were received from the forty-eight respondents.) The comments suggested that a wide variety of public education policy issues await communities and states in the relatively near future:

1. By the year 2000, as much as 75 percent of the present teaching force will still be on the job. Therefore, the greatest pending policy issue requiring attention in and before the year 2000, as noted in the comments, will be continuous professional development of teachers and professional staff to improve student learning.

2. No policy dilemma will exceed that of governance. Respondents observed that by the year 2000 a clear indication must be evident to answer the question of who controls the education of children. With the advent of charter schools, vouchers, and privatization of services, local school boards may be a fading memory in the governance schema of the future.

3. One chief state school officer provided insight, and qualified pessimism, by noting that the age wave and global competitiveness are likely to be the driving forces behind the changes in schools by the year 2000. The baby boomers, now 35 to 50 years of age, will represent 76 million persons ages 40 to 55 by 2000. Equity will be of less concern than it has been, given the heightened emphasis on achievement. Also, the children of 2000 will be considerably more economically and linguistically diverse, and born to less-well-paid parents, than children in the past; families, therefore, will require more day care for the youngest children and more job training and retraining for the adults. Finally, greater achievement will be required to re-establish America's pre-eminence in the global marketplace. It is likely that schools will be the governmental entities with the breadth and depth of experience and the human resources—as well as the public confidence—to meet these changing priorities.

In regard to the year 2020, comments included the following:

> Public schools will not likely exist as known in 1995. School-aged students may participate in a government-sponsored and publicly funded range of experiences. A child's early years may include more structured group processes. As children age, they may more likely be tutored, guided, and instructed through new partnerships representing the home, a work sponsor, and an educational liaison utilizing new technologies and advanced applications of learning theories. America's new demographics warrant a new vision of public education. By the year 2020, almost 50 percent of the population under seventeen years of age will be composed of ethnic minority children. This trend suggests the projected change in composition will result in a substantial increase in the proportion of educationally disadvantaged children, thus requiring an unparalleled commitment to new teaching techniques, new technologies, new efficiencies, and new resources.

The Future

The results of the study led us to speculate about emerging or continuing demands within education. For example, it is possible that, by 2020,

- the use of technology will not be seen to be as critical an issue as it is today because technology will be so pervasive as to be institutionalized;
- equity in funding capital projects will diminish in import because students will be learning at home and in other community environments;
- adult learning will gain increased attention as the population grows older overall and demands life-long opportunities for learning and an extended work life; and
- site-based decision making will be less of an issue in the future because school "sites" as we know them today will no longer exist.

Studies such as this one rely on the knowledge, insight, and "connectedness" of the respondents. The country's chief state school officers have given us a look with a special lens into the future of public education policy issues.

REFERENCES

Mandel, J. M. 1995. Will schools ever get better? *Business Week* 41 (17 April): 64–68.
National Education Association. 1994. *Ranking of the states.* Washington, D.C.: NEA Research Division.

Unit 2

Key Points to Consider

❖ How can parents and teachers provide children and adolescents with experiences that promote their cognitive, moral, social, and emotional development?

❖ What are the needs of youth in early, middle, and late adolescence?

❖ What can at-risk adolescents tell us about their perceptions of caring?

 **Links** | **www.dushkin.com/online/**

These sites are annotated on pages 4 and 5.

The study of human development provides us with knowledge of how children and adolescents mature and learn within the family, community, and school environments. Educational psychology focuses on description and explanation of the developmental processes that make it possible for children to become intelligent and socially competent adults. Psychologists and educators are presently studying the idea that biology as well as the environment influences cognitive, personal, social, and emotional development and involve predictable patterns of behavior.

Jean Piaget's theory regarding the cognitive development of children and adolescents is perhaps the best known and most comprehensive. According to this theory, the perceptions and thoughts that young children have about the world are often quite different when compared to those of adolescents and adults. That is, children may think about moral and social issues in a unique way. Children need to acquire cognitive, moral, and social skills in order to interact effectively with parents, teachers, and peers. If human intelligence encompasses all of the above skills, then Piaget may have been correct in saying that development is the child's intelligent adaptation to the environment.

Today the cognitive, moral, social, and emotional development of children takes place in a rapidly changing society. A child must develop positive conceptions of self within the family as well as at school in order to cope with the changes and become a competent and socially responsible adult. In "What Do We Know From Brain Research?" Pat Wolfe and Ron Brandt discuss the potential that such research has for teaching and learning, while the articles "The Moral Child" and "Helping Children Become More Prosocial: Ideas for Classrooms, Families, Schools, and Communities" discuss the moral and social skills of children. Adolescence brings with it the ability to think abstractly and hypothetically and to see the world from many perspectives. Adolescents strive to achieve a sense of identity by questioning their beliefs and tentatively committing to self-chosen goals. Their ideas about the kinds of adults they want to become and the ideals they want to believe in sometimes lead to conflicts with parents and teachers. Adolescents are also sensitive about espoused adult values versus adult behavior. The articles in this unit discuss the cognitive, social, and emotional changes that confront adolescents and also suggest ways in which the family and school can help meet the needs of adolescents.

Development

What Do We Know from Brain Research?

The recent explosion of neuroscientific research has the exciting potential to increase our understanding of teaching and learning. But it's up to educators to carefully interpret what brain science means for classroom practice.

Pat Wolfe and Ron Brandt

In July 1989, following a congressional resolution, President Bush officially proclaimed the 1990s the "Decade of the Brain." And indeed in the past nine years, we have seen an unprecedented explosion of information on how the human brain works. Thousands of research projects, books, magazine cover stories, and television specials regale us with new facts and figures, colorful PET scans, and at times, suspiciously simple ways to improve our memories, prevent Alzheimer's, and make our babies geniuses.

Our knowledge of brain functioning has been revolutionized. And many of the new findings have changed medical practice. We have a much better understanding of mental illnesses and the drugs that ameliorate them. Treatment for tumors, seizures, and other brain diseases and disorders has become much more successful.

But what about the educational applications of these new findings?

Have we learned enough to incorporate neuroscientific findings into our schools? Is it possible that the Decade of the Brain will usher in the Decade of Education?

Interpreting Brain Research for Classroom Practice

Brain science is a burgeoning new field, and we have learned more about the brain in the past 5 years than in the past 100 years. Nearly 90 percent of all the neuroscientists who have ever lived are alive today. Nearly every major university now has interdisciplinary brain research teams.

But almost all scientists are wary of offering prescriptions for using their research in schools. Joseph LeDoux from New York University and author of *The Emotional Brain* (1996) says, "There are no quick fixes. These ideas are very easy to sell to the public, but it's too easy to take them beyond their actual basis in science." Susan Fitzpatrick, a neuroscientist at the McDonnell Foundation, says scientists don't have a lot to tell educators at this point. She warns,

> Anything that people would say right now has a good chance of not being true two years from now because the understanding is so rudimentary and people are looking at things at such a simplistic level. (1995, p. 24)

Researchers especially caution educators to resist the temptation to

A child's brain at birth has all the brain cells, or neurons, that it will ever have.

From *Educational Leadership*, November 1998, pp. 8-13. Reprinted with permission of the Association for Supervision and Curriculum Development. © 1998 by ASCD. All rights reserved.

adopt policies on the basis of a single study or to use neuroscience as a promotional tool for a pet program. Much work needs to be done before the results of scientific studies can be taken into the classroom. The reluctance of scientists to sanction a quick marriage between neuroscience and education makes sense. Brain research

ways done. Others are causing us to take a closer look at educational practice.

Finding One

The brain changes physiologically as a result of experience. The environment in which a brain operates determines to a large degree the functioning ability of that brain.

structures are modified by the environment (Diamond & Hopson, 1998). Her research established the concept of neural plasticity—the brain's amazing ability to constantly change its structure and function in response to external experiences. A further finding that should please us all is that dendrites, the connections between brain

Babies don't talk one week, tie their shoes the next, and then work on their emotional development.

does not—and may never—tell us specifically what we should do in a classroom. At this point it does not "prove" that a particular strategy will increase student understanding. That is not currently the purpose of neuroscience research. Its purpose is to learn how the brain functions. Neuroscience is a field of study separate from the field of education, and it is unrealistic to expect brain research to lead directly to pedagogy. So how do we use the current findings?

We need to critically read and analyze the research in order to separate the wheat from the chaff. If educators do not develop a functional understanding of the brain and its processes, we will be vulnerable to pseudoscientific fads, inappropriate generalizations, and dubious programs.

Then, with our knowledge of educational practice, we must determine if and how brain research informs that practice. Educators have a vast background of knowledge about teaching and learning. This knowledge has been gained from educational research, cognitive science, and long experience. Given this knowledge base, educators are in the best position to know how the research does—or does not—supplement, explain, or validate current practices.

Although we must be cautious about many neuroscientific findings, a few are quite well established. Some validate what good educators have al-

Researchers agree that at birth, humans do not yet possess a fully operational brain. The brain that eventually takes shape is the result of interaction between the individual's genetic inheritance and everything he or she experiences. Ronald Kotulak, in his book *Inside the Brain* (1996), uses the metaphor of a banquet to explain the relationship between genes and the environment.

> The brain gobbles up the external environment through its sensory system and then reassembles the digested world in the form of trillions of connections which are constantly growing or dying, becoming stronger or weaker depending on the richness of the banquet. (p. 4)

The environment affects how genes work, and genes determine how the environment is interpreted. This is a relatively new understanding. It wasn't too many years ago that scientists thought the brain was immutable or fixed at birth. Scientists had known for some time that with a few specialized exceptions, a child's brain at birth has all the brain cells, or neurons, that it will ever have. Unlike tissue in most other organs, neurons do not regenerate, so researchers assumed that the brain you had at birth was the brain you were stuck with for life.

However, Marian Diamond and her colleagues at the University of California at Berkeley pioneered research in the mid-1960s showing that brain

cells, can grow at any age. Researchers have found this to be true in humans as well as in animals. Contrary to folk wisdom, a healthy older person is not necessarily the victim of progressive nerve cell loss and diminishing memory and cognitive abilities.

So our environment, including the classroom environment, is not a neutral place. We educators are either growing dendrites or letting them wither and die. The trick is to determine what constitutes an enriched environment. A few facts about the brain's natural proclivities will assist us in making these determinations.

1. The brain has not evolved to its present condition by taking in meaningless data; an enriched environment gives students the opportunity to make sense out of what they are learning, what some call the opportunity to "make meaning."

2. The brain develops in an integrated fashion over time. Babies don't talk one week, tie their shoes the next, and then work on their emotional development. An enriched environment addresses multiple aspects of development simultaneously.

3. The brain is essentially curious, and it must be to survive. It constantly seeks connections between the new and the known. Learning is a process of active construction by the learner, and an enriched environment gives students the opportunity to relate what they are learning to what

they already know. As noted educator Phil Schlechty says, "Students must do the work of learning."

4. The brain is innately social and collaborative. Although the processing takes place in our students' individual brains, their learning is enhanced when the environment provides them with the opportunity to discuss their thinking out loud, to bounce their ideas off their peers, and to produce collaborative work.

Finding Two

IQ is not fixed at birth.

This second finding is closely linked to the first. Craig Ramey, a University of Alabama psychologist, took on the daunting task of showing that what Diamond did with rats, he could do with children. His striking research (Ramey & Ramey, 1996) proved that an intervention program for impoverished children could prevent children from having low IQs and mental retardation.

Ramey has directed studies of early educational intervention involving thousands of children at dozens of research centers. The best programs, which started with children as young as six weeks and mostly younger than four months, showed that they could raise the infants' scores on intelligence tests by 15 to 30 percent. It is important to note that although IQ tests may be useful artifacts, intelligence is probably much more multifaceted. Every brain differs, and the subtle range of organizational, physiological, and chemical variations ensures a remarkably wide spectrum of cognitive, behavioral, and emotional capabilities.

Finding Three

Some abilities are acquired more easily during certain sensitive periods, or "windows of opportunity."

At birth, a child's cerebral cortex has all the neurons that it will ever have. In fact, in utero, the brain produces an overabundance of neurons, nearly twice as many as it will need. Beginning at about 28 weeks of prenatal development, a massive pruning of

Brain Fact
Enriching the Environment

Marian Diamond and her team of researchers at the University of California at Berkeley have been studying the impact of enriched and impoverished environments on the brains of rats. Diamond believes that enriched environments unmistakably influence the brain's growth and learning. An enriched environment for children, Diamond says,

■ Includes a steady source of positive emotional support;

■ Provides a nutritious diet with enough protein, vitamins, minerals, and calories;

■ Stimulates all the senses (but not necessarily all at once!);

■ Has an atmosphere free of undue pressure and stress but suffused with a degree of pleasurable intensity;

■ Presents a series of novel challenges that are neither too easy nor too difficult for the child at his or her stage of development;

■ Allows social interaction for a significant percentage of activities;

■ Promotes the development of a broad range of skills and interests that are mental, physical, aesthetic, social, and emotional;

■ Gives the child an opportunity to choose many of his or her efforts and to modify them;

■ Provides an enjoyable atmosphere that promotes exploration and the fun of learning;

■ Allows the child to be an active participant rather than a passive observer.

Diamond, M., & Hopson, J. (1998). *Magic trees of the mind: How to nurture your child's intelligence, creativity, and healthy emotions from birth through adolescence* (pp. 107–108). New York: Dutton.

neurons begins, resulting in the loss of one-third to one-half of these elements. (So we lose up to half our brain cells before we're born.) While the brain is pruning away excess neurons, a tremendous increase in dendrites adds substantially to the surface area available for synapses, the functional connections among cells. At the fastest rate, connections are built at the incredible speed of 3 billion a second. During the period from birth to age 10, the number of synaptic connections continues to rise rapidly, then begins to drop and continues to decline slowly into adult life.

Much credit for these insights into the developing brain must be given to Harry Chugani and Michael Phelps at the UCLA School of Medicine. Phelps co-invented the imaging technique called Positron Emission Tomography (PET), which visually depicts the brain's energy use. Using PET scans, Chugani has averaged the energy use of brains at various ages. His findings suggest that a child's

peak learning years occur just as all those synapses are forming (1996). Chugani states that not only does the child's brain overdevelop during the early years, but that during these years, it also has a remarkable ability to adapt and reorganize. It appears to develop some capacities with more ease at this time than in the years after puberty. These stages once called "critical periods" are more accurately described as "sensitive periods" or "windows of opportunity."

Probably the prime example of a window is vision. Lack of visual stimulation at birth, such as that which occurs with blindness or cataracts, causes the brain cells designed to interpret vision to atrophy or be diverted to other tasks. If sight is not restored by age 3, the child will be forever blind. . . . Similarly, the critical period for learning spoken language is totally lost by about age 10. If a child is born deaf, the 50,000 neural pathways that would normally activate the auditory cells remain silent, and the sound of the human voice, essential for learning language, can't get through. Finally, as the child grows older, the cells atrophy and the ability to learn spoken language is lost.

Not all windows close as tightly as those for vision and language development. Although learning a second language also depends on the stimulation of the neurons for the sounds of that language, an adult certainly can learn a second language and learn to speak it quite well. However, it is much more difficult to learn a foreign language after age 10 or so, and the language will probably be spoken with an accent. We might say that learning a second language is not a window that slams shut—it just becomes harder to open.

The implications of the findings regarding early visual, auditory, motor, cognitive, and emotional development are enormous. Indeed, in many places work has already begun to enrich prenatal and early childhood environments. One example is the application of the research with premature infants. Premature babies who are regularly touched in their incubators gain weight at twice the rate of those who are not touched. Preemies whose parents visit them regularly vocalize twice as much in the third week as babies who are visited infrequently or not at all.

The research findings on early development are in stark contrast with the current situation in society.

■ An estimated 12 percent of infants born in this country suffer significant reduction of their cognitive ability as a result of preterm birth; maternal smoking, alcohol use, or drug use in pregnancy; maternal and infant malnutrition; and postbirth lead poisoning or child abuse (Newman & Buka, 1997). Many of these factors could be eliminated with education programs for parents (or future parents). Twenty-five percent of all pregnant women receive no prenatal care.

■ The early years, which are most crucial for learning, receive the least emphasis in federal, state, and local programs. We spend at least seven times more on the elderly than we do on children from birth to age 5.

■ About half of all children in the United States are in full-time day care within the first year. Yet many day care centers not only are underfunded, but they are also staffed by untrained, low-paid workers and have too high an adult/child ratio. (Thirty-eight states do not require family child care providers to have *any* training prior to serving children.)

■ Our present system generally waits until children fall behind in school, then places them in special education programs. With intense early intervention, we could reverse or prevent some adverse effects. It is possible that the billions of dollars spent on special education services might be better spent on early intervention.

Finding Four

Learning is strongly influenced by emotion.

The role of emotion in learning has received a good deal of press in the past few years. Daniel Goleman's *Emotional Intelligence* (1995) and Joseph LeDoux's *The Emotional Brain* (1996) have been instrumental in increasing our understanding of emotion.

Emotion plays a dual role in human learning. First, it plays a positive role in that the stronger the emotion connected with an experience, the stronger the memory of that experience. Chemicals in the brain send a message to the rest of the brain: "This information is important. Remember it." Thus, when we are able to add emotional input into learning experiences to make them more meaningful and exciting, the brain deems the information more important and retention is increased.

In contrast, LeDoux has pointed out that if the emotion is too strong (for example, the situation is perceived by the learner to be threatening), then learning is decreased. Whether you call this "downshifting" or decreasing the efficiency of the rational thinking cortex of the brain, it is a concept with many implications for teaching and learning.

Expect More Findings

On the horizon are many more studies that may have implications for the education of the human brain from birth through old age. Current research areas include these:

■ The role of nutrition in brain functioning

■ How brain chemicals affect mood, personality, and behavior

■ The connection between the mind/brain and the body

Rather than passively wait for research findings that might be useful, educators should help direct the search to better understand how the brain learns. James McGaugh of the University of California at Irvine has suggested that we educators need to be more proactive and tell the scientists, "Here's what we need to know. How can you help us?"

Should the Decade of the Brain lead to an enlightened Decade of Education? Eventually, yes. Along with cognitive research and the knowledge base we already have, findings from the neurosciences can provide us with

---

The brain is essentially curious, and it must be to survive.

---

important insights into how children learn. They can direct us as we seek to enrich the school experience for all children—the gifted, the creative, the learning disabled, the dyslexic, the average students, and all the children whose capabilities are not captured by IQ or other conventional measures. We can help parents and other caregivers understand the effects of maternal nutrition and prenatal drug and alcohol use and the role of early interaction and enriched environments. Brain research can also offer valuable guidance to policymakers and school administrators as they strive to focus their priorities.

Does what we are learning about the brain matter? It must, because our children matter.

References

Chugani, H. T. (1996). *Functional maturation of the brain.* Paper presented at the Third Annual Brain Symposium, Berkeley, California.

Diamond, M., & Hopson, J. (1998). *Magic trees of the mind: How to nurture your child's intelligence, creativity, and healthy emotions from birth through adolescence.* New York: Penguin Putnam.

Fitzpatrick, S. (1995, November). Smart brains: Neuroscientists explain the mystery of what makes us human. *American School Board Journal.*

Goleman, D. (1995). *Emotional intelligence: Why it can matter more than IQ.* New York: Bantam.

Kotulak, R. (1996). *Inside the brain: Revolutionary discoveries of how the mind works.* Kansas City, MO: Andrews & McMeely.

LeDoux, J. (1996). *The emotional brain: The mysterious underpinnings of emotional life.* New York: Simon & Schuster.

Newman, L., & Buka, S. L. (1997). *Every child a learner: Reducing risks of learning impairment during pregnancy and infancy.* Denver, CO: Education Commission of the States.

Ramey, C. T., & Ramey, S. L. (1996). *At risk does not mean doomed.* National Health/Education Consortium Occasional Paper #4. Paper presented at the meeting of the American Association of Science, February 1996.

Pat Wolfe is an independent educational consultant. She can be reached at 555 Randolph St., Napa, CA 94559 (e-mail: wolfe@napanet.net).
Ron Brandt is Editor Emeritus of *Educational Leadership* and an independent educational consultant. He may be reached at 1104 Woodcliff Dr., Alexandria, VA 22308-1058 (e-mail:ronbrandt@erols.com).

THE MORAL CHILD

We're at ground zero in the culture wars: how to raise decent kids when traditional ties to church, school and community are badly frayed

Only in contemporary America could selecting a family anthology be considered a political act. On one cultural flank is famous Republican moralist William Bennett's bestselling *Book of Virtues,* a hefty collection of tales, fables and poems celebrating universal virtues such as courage, compassion and honesty. Side by side with the Bennett tome in many bookstores is Herbert Kohl and Colin Greer's *A Call to Character,* a similar assemblage of proverbs and stories organized around equally cherished values. No one could blame the casual browser for arbitrarily grabbing one or the other. But it's not a casual choice. These two volumes represent a fundamental and acrimonious division over what critics call the most pressing issue facing our nation today: how we should raise and instruct the next generation of American citizens.

The differences between the two volumes of moral instruction aren't even that subtle, once you're familiar with the vocabulary of America's culture war. Both agree on qualities of character like kindness and responsibility. But look deeper: Is unwavering patriotism more desirable than moral reasoning? Does discretion trump courage, or the other way around? Read the *Book of Virtues* to your children and they'll learn about valor from William Tell and Henry V at Agincourt. Read from *A Call to Character* and their moral instructors will be Arnold Lobel's decidedly unheroic but very human Frog and Toad. The former has sections devoted to work, faith and perseverance; the latter, playfulness, balance and adaptability. It's not just semantics or moral hairsplitting. These dueling miscellanies symbolize a much wider struggle for the hearts and minds of America's kids.

Beyond the hearth. Child rearing has always been filled with ambiguities. But while parents once riffled through their Dr. Spock and other how-to manuals for helpful perspectives on toilet training and fussy eaters, today the

WIMP OR BULLY?

Your 5-year-old has been in a fistfight. Although another child was clearly the aggressor, your son dominated the older boy in the end. You experience mixed feelings: pride that you son is not a wimp, but concern about the escalating use of violence to resolve childhood disputes.

EXPERTS' VIEW

This is a common dilemma, experts say, and one that genuinely has two sides. Parents should always try first to teach a child that there are lots of ways to resolve conflict harmoniously and that reason and compromise are more effective than duking it out. Kids should also be taught that the distinction between wimp and aggressor is a false one. But if the choice is being a victim or not, children need to learn to stand up for themselves. Says psychologist William Damon: "Even young children can handle some complexity. You may not use the words 'justifiable self-defense,' but kids can grasp the idea."

questions and concerns seem to have moved beyond the scope of child psychology and the familiar hearthside dilemmas. The issue for today's parents is how to raise decent kids in a complex and morally ambiguous world where traditional tethers to church, school and neighborhood are badly frayed. Capturing the heightened concerns of thousands of parents from around the country gathering at the Lincoln Memorial for this week's Stand for Children, one 41-year-old mother observes about raising her teenage daughter: "It's not just dealing with chores and curfews. That stuff's easy. But what do you do when the values you believe in are being challenged every day at the high school, the mall, right around the corner in your own neighborhood?"

It is a sign of how high the stakes have risen that both first lady Hillary Rodham Clinton and former Vice President Dan Quayle weighed in this year with new books on proper moral child rearing. Both are motivated by fear that the moral confusion of today's youth could be deleterious to our democracy, which draws its sustenance and vitality from new generations of competent and responsible citizens. There's a sense of desperation in current writing about moral parenting, a sense that, as one psychologist puts it, improper child rearing has become a "public health problem" requiring urgent attention. Some lawmakers and public officials are even agitating for creation of a national public policy on the cultivation of private character.

The perceived threat to the commonwealth varies, of course, depending on one's political perspective. Critics on the

From *U.S. News & World Report,* June 3, 1996, pp. 52–59. © 1996 U.S. News & World Report. Reprinted by permission.

right view moral relativity and indulgent parenting as the cause of today's moral confusion and call for the rediscovery of firmness, regimentation, deference and piety to counter our culture's decline. Those on the left are alarmed at what they see as a wave of simplistic nostalgia gaining force in the country: In their view, it is a bullying reformation designed to mold moral automatons incapable of genuine judgment or citizenship.

Morality's bedrock. The split is political, not scientific. Psychological understanding of moral development is actually quite sophisticated and consistent. For example, decades of research leave little doubt that empathy—the ability to assume another's point of view—develops naturally in the first years of life. Parents, of course, know this just from casual observation. Even infants show unmistakable signs of distress when another child is hurt or upset, and rudimentary forms of sympathy and helping—offering a toy to a distraught sibling, for example—can be observed in children as young as 1. Most psychologists who study empathy assume that the basic skill is biologically wired, probably created along with the bonds of trust that an infant forms with a caretaker, usually the mother. The task for parents is not so much a matter of teaching empathy as not quashing its natural flowering.

Building blocks. Empathy is the bedrock of human morality, the emotional skill required for the emergence of all other moral emotions—shame, guilt, pride and so forth. Almost every form of moral behavior imaginable—from doing chores responsibly to sacrificing one's life for a cause—is inconceivable without it. Yet empathy is not enough. A second crucial building block of morality is self discipline, and psychologists have some solid evidence about how this moral "skill" is nurtured.

Most parents tend to adopt one of three general "styles" of interacting with their kids, each style a different combination of three basic factors: acceptance and warmth (vs. rejection), firmness (vs. leniency) and respect for autonomy (vs. control). How parents combine these traits sends very different messages to their children, which over time are "internalized" in such character traits as self-esteem, self-control, social competence and responsibility—or, of course, in the absence of those traits.

There is little doubt about what works and what doesn't. In fact, says Temple University child psychologist Laurence Steinberg, author of a new study called *Beyond the Classroom,* extensive research over many years shows that parents who are more accepting and warm, firmer about rules and discipline and more supportive of their child's individuality produce healthier kids: "No research has ever suggested that children fare better when their parents are aloof than when they are accepting, when their parents are lenient rather than firm, or when their parents are psychologically controlling, rather than supportive of their psychological autonomy."

Psychologists call this ideal parenting style "authoritative" parenting, a middle ground between "autocratic" and "permissive" parenting, both of which tend to produce untoward consequences for children in terms of both competence and integrity. The need to control children appears to be especially damaging to self-discipline. "Parents who are high in control," Steinberg says, "tend to value obedience over independence. They are likely to tell their children that young people should not question adults, that their opinions count less because they are children, and so on. Expressions of individuality are frowned upon in these families and equated with signs of disrespect."

The best con men, of course, combine self-discipline with a keen ability to read others' thoughts and feelings. Morality requires more—specifically, the ability to think about such things as justice and fairness and ultimately to act on those thoughts. According to the late psychologist Lawrence Kohlberg of Harvard University, people pass through six fairly inflexible "stages" or moral reasoning, beginning with a childlike calculation of self-interest and ending with the embodiment of abstract principles of justice. The ability to think logically about right and wrong, Kohlberg believed, was essential to the development of complete moral beings: Moral habits and emotions alone, he argued, were inadequate for dealing with novel moral dilemmas or when weighing one value against another, as people often must do in real life.

Moral identity. Psychologists emphasize the importance of young children's "internalizing" values, that is, absorbing standards that are then applied in different times, places or situ-

SHAME AND RIDICULE

Your 6-year-old's teacher punishes him by making him wear a dunce cap. That strikes you as archaic and severe, but the teacher insists a bit of shame helps teach old-fashioned manners.

EXPERTS' VIEW

Psychologists no longer believe that shame and guilt are the stuff of neurosis. In fact, most now are convinced that morality cannot develop without these fundamental moral emotions. But public ridicule is more likely to produce humiliation and anger than healthy contrition. Parents should talk privately with the teacher to see if there are gentler and less demeaning ways to make misbehaving children feel shame.

ations. In a recently published study called *Learning to Care,* Princeton sociologist Robert Wuthnow argues that teenagers basically need to go through a second experience of internalization if they are to become caring adults. Just as young children absorb and integrate a rudimentary understanding of kindness and caring from watching adult models, adolescents need to witness a more nuanced form of caring, to absorb "stories" of adult generosity and self-sacrifice. That way, they see that involvement is a real possibility in a world where so much caring has been institutionalized.

Similarly, a recent study suggests that people who have chosen lives of lifelong, passionate commitment have had more opportunities than most people to develop appropriate trust, courage and responsible imagination. There is no such thing as a "Gandhi pill," Lesley College Prof. Laurent Parks Daloz and his colleagues write in the new book *Common Fire,* but there are commonly shared experiences: a parent committed to a cause, service opportunities during adolescence, cross-cultural experiences, a rich mentoring experience in young adulthood. Often, the authors conclude, the committed differ from the rest of us only by having more of these experiences, and deeper ones.

Force of habit. Of course, cultural battles rarely reflect the complexity of human behavior, and the current debate about proper moral child rearing has a black-and-white quality. As Bennett writes in his introduction to the *Book of Virtues,* moral education involves "explicit instruction, exhortation, and training. Moral education *must* provide training in good habits." But critics charge that such preoccupation with drill and habit suggests a dark and cynical view of human nature as a bundle of unsavory instincts that need constant squelching and reining in. In theology, it's called original sin; in psychological terms, it's a "behaviorist" approach, conditioning responses—or habits—which eventually become automatic and no longer require the weighing of moral options. The opposing philosophy—drawing from the romanticism of Jean Jacques Rousseau, psychology's "human potential" movement and the "constructivist" movement in education—emphasizes the child's natural empathy and untapped potential for reasoning.

The Clinton and Quayle volumes show how simplistic psychology can make for unsophisticated public philosophy. There's no question that the first lady's *It Takes a Village* is informed by an overriding respect for children as essentially competent beings who need nurturance to blossom. But critics see Clinton's optimism as dewy eyed and unrealistic, too much akin to the self-esteem movement and a "child centered" parenting style that allows kids to become morally soft. Quayle's *The American Family,* by contrast, endorses control and punishment as "a way to shape behavior toward respect and obedience." He notes approvingly that the five healthy families he studied reject the counsel of "prominent child experts," including the well-documented finding that spanking and other forms of physical coercion teach violence rather than values.

Quayle's analysis is only one of many calls to return to a time when children knew their proper place and society was not so disorderly. Perhaps the strongest prescription is *The Perversion of Autonomy* by psychiatrist Willard Gaylin and political theorist Bruce Jennings, both of New York's Hastings Center for Bioethics. The book is a gleeful celebration of the value of coercion. In the view of these authors, the manifest vulgarities of liberal society justify and demand a serious rollback of the civil rights era; for the good of society,

it follows, children require early and decisive flattening.

There is little question that the worst of New Age gobbledgook makes the cultural left an easy target for attack. One parent tells the story of when her 6-year-old was caught stealing at school. She met with the teacher, hoping together they could come up with a strategy to make it clear that stealing was unacceptable. But the teacher's response astonished her: "We don't use the word *stealing* here," she said. "We call it *uncooperative behavior.*" Few defend such foolish excesses of the self-esteem movement. But progressives argue they are aberrations used to attack liberal parenting and pedagogy. It's naive to focus on examples of indulgence, they argue, when if anything our culture is a child-hating culture, with family policies to match.

Classroom politics. This same ideological tug of war can be observed in the nation's schools, specifically in battles over the so-called character education movement. Only a few years old, the movement is fairly diverse, in some schools involving a specific packaged curriculum and reading materials, in others more of a philosophy or administrative style. But the general idea has captured the attention of the White House and Congress, both of which are searching for an appropriate federal role in promoting basic decency. Lawmakers

---

ORDER AND SQUALOR

Your 12-year-old daughter's bedroom is a pigsty. You worry that a disorderly room means a disorderly mind, but your husband says it's more important not to violate her personal space.

EXPERTS' VIEW

Experts are divided. Some come down firmly on the side of orderliness as an important habit and a lesson in family obligation. They dismiss the personal space argument as New Age nonsense. Others do not consider it a moral issue at all but an aesthetic one. Even adults differ: Some don't bother to make their beds, while others are fastidious. It's an issue for negotiation, which is a life skill that teenagers should learn.

---

have lent their symbolic support by endorsing "National Character Counts Week." The Department of Education has funded a few pilot programs and will soon fund a few more. And next week, President Clinton will address a joint White House-congressional conference on character building, the third such meeting sponsored by this administration.

Many states have also created character education requirements, and by conservative estimate, hundreds of schools and districts have adopted strategies for addressing morals and civic virtue. Precisely because of the diversity of philosophies that fall under the rubric "character education," experts say, parents need to be aware of what the term means in their own child's classroom.

For example, some schools have adopted conservative models that tend to emphasize order, discipline and courage—what Boston University educator Kevin Ryan labels the "stern virtues," as opposed to "soft" or easy virtues like compassion and self-esteem. Such programs don't shy away from unfashionable ideas like social control and indoctrination, says University of Illinois sociologist Edward Wynne, a guiding light to this approach and coauthor, with Ryan, of *Reclaiming Our Schools.* Wynne calls for a return to the "great tradition in education," that is, the transmission of "good doctrine" to the next generation. Because of the "human propensity for selfishness," Wynne encourages schools to use elaborate reward systems, including "ribbons, awards and other signs of moral merit." The model also emphasizes group sports and pep rallies as effective ways to elevate school spirit. Variations of this reward-and-discipline model emphasize drilling in a prescribed set of values, often focusing on a "virtue of the month."

Programs based on the stern virtues also tend to emphasize institutional loyalty and submission of the individual to the larger community. Ryan points to Roxbury Latin, a 350-year-old private boys' school in Boston, as an example of this approach. The school subscribes to an unambiguous set of Judeo-Christian values—honesty, courtesy and respect for others, according to the catalog. It attempts to inculcate these values through a classical curriculum, through mandatory, sermonlike "halls" and through formal and casual interac-

CODES AND CREATIVITY

Your son is dismissed from school because his pierced ear violates the dress code. You argue with the principal that the earring is a form of self-expression, but he insists societies need rules.

EXPERTS' VIEW

Some psychologists consider it unconscionable to place a child in the center of a culture war. The most crucial issue, they argue, is for parents and other authority figures to present kids with a united moral front. But psychologist Michael Schulman disagrees: "It could be an opportunity for a valuable lesson in choosing life's battles: Is this an important one? If so, what's the most effective strategy for social change?"

tions between teachers (called "masters") and students. No racial, ethnic or religious student organizations are permitted, in order to encourage loyalty to the larger school community. According to Headmaster F. Washington Jarvis, an Episcopal priest, Roxbury Latin's view of human nature is much like the Puritan founders': "mean, nasty, brutish, selfish, and capable of great cruelty and meanness. We have to hold a mirror up to the students and say, 'This is who you are. Stop it.'"

Roxbury Latin teaches kids to rein in their negative impulses not with harsh discipline, however, but with love and security of belonging. Displays of affection are encouraged, according to Jarvis, and kids are disciplined by being made to perform (and report) good deeds—a powerful form of behavior modification. Students are rebuked and criticized when they stray, but criticism is always followed by acts of caring and acceptance. Whenever a student is sent to Jarvis's office for discipline, the headmaster always asks as the boy leaves, "Do I love you?"

Ethical dilemmas. At the other end of the spectrum are character education programs that emphasize moral reasoning. These, too, vary a great deal, but most are derived at least loosely from the work of Kohlberg and other stage theorists. Strict Kohlbergian programs

tend to be highly cognitive, with students reasoning through hypothetical moral dilemmas and often weighing conflicting values in order to arrive at judgments of right and wrong. A classic Kohlbergian dilemma, for example, asks whether it's right for a poor man to steal medicine to save his dying wife. Even young children tend to justify dishonesty in this situation, but only adults do so based on a firmly held principle of what's unchallengeably right. Kohlbergian programs are also much more likely to have kids grapple with controversial social dilemmas, since it's assumed that the same sort of moral logic is necessary for citizens to come to informed decisions on the issues of the day—whether gay lifestyles ought to be tolerated in the U.S. Navy, for example.

Variations in programs on strict moral reasoning are generally based on a kind of "constructivist" model of education, in which kids have to figure out for themselves, based on real experiences, what makes the other person feel better or worse, what rules make sense, who makes decisions. Kids actively struggle with issues and from the inside out "construct" a notion of what kind of moral person they want to be. (Advocates of moral reasoning are quick to distinguish this approach from "values clarification," a 1960s educational fad and a favorite whipping boy of conservative reformers. Values clarification consisted of a variety of exercises aimed at helping kids figure out what was most important to them, regardless of how selfish or cruel those "values" might be. It's rarely practiced today.)

The Hudson school system in Massachusetts is a good example of this constructivist approach. The program is specifically designed to enhance the moral skills of empathy and self-discipline. Beginning in kindergarten, students participate in role-playing exercises, a series of readings about ethical dilemmas in history and a variety of community service programs that have every Hudson student, K through 12, actively engaged in helping others and the community. Environmental efforts are a big part of the program: Kindergartners, for instance, just completed a yearlong recycling project. The idea, according to Superintendent Sheldon Berman, is for children to understand altruism both as giving to the needy today and as self-sacrifice for future generations. By contrast, the conservative "Character

Education Manifesto" states explicitly: "Character education is *not* about acquiring the right *views*," including "currently accepted attitudes about ecology."

Needless to say, these philosophical extremes look very different in practice. Parents who find one or the other more appealing will almost certainly have different beliefs about human behavior. But the best of such programs, regardless of ruling philosophy, share in one crucial belief: that making decent kids requires constant repetition and amplification of basic moral messages. Both Roxbury Latin and Hudson, for example, fashion themselves as "moral communities," where character education is woven into the basic fabric of the school and reflected in every aspect of the school day.

Community voices. This idea is consistent with the best of moral development theory. According to Brown University developmental psychologist William Damon, author of *Greater Expectations,* "Real learning is made up of a thousand small experiences in a thousand different relationships, where you see all the facets of courage, caring and respect." Virtue-of-the week programs will never work, Damon contends, because they lack moral dimension and trivialized moral behavior. Children can handle moral complexity, he says, and sense what's phony. "Kids need a sense of purpose, something to believe in. Morality is not about prohibitions, things to avoid, be afraid of or feel guilty about."

MEDIA AND MORES

You allow your kids to watch certain R-rated videos, but you can't preview each one. Your 13-year-old argues: "I'm not going to become an ax murderer just because I watch a movie, Dad."

EXPERTS' VIEW

It's true he won't become an ax murderer, but he might absorb some distorted lessons about uncaring sexuality—if you're not around to discuss the differences between fantasy and reality. It's OK to question and reject social codes like movie ratings, psychologists say, but if you do, you must substitute meaningful discussion of sex, violence and censorship.

Building this sense of purpose is a task beyond the capacity of most families today. The crucial consistency of a moral message requires that kids hear it not only from their parents but from their neighbors, teachers, coach, the local policeman. Unfortunately, Damon says, few do. The culture has become so adversarial that the important figures in a child's life are more apt to be at one another's throats than presenting a unified moral front. Litigiousness has become so widespread that it even has a name, the "parents' rights movement." More than ever before, parents see themselves primarily as advocates for their children's rights, suing schools over every value conflict. In a New York case now making its way through the courts, for example, parents are suing because they object to the school district's community service requirement.

Moral ecology. The irony of postmodern parenting, writes sociologist David Popenoe in *Seedbeds of Virtue,* is that just when science has produced a reliable body of knowledge about what makes decent kids, the key elements are disintegrating: the two-parent family, the church, the neighborhood school and a safe, nurturing community. Popenoe and others advocate a much broader understanding of what it means to raise a

---

SMOKE AND MIRRORS

Despite your own youthful experimentation with drugs, you're worried about you teenager's fascination with today's drug culture. He claims he's embracing the values of the '60s.

EXPERTS' VIEW

This comes up a lot, now that children of the '60s are raising their own teenagers. It's crucial to be honest, but it's also fair to explain the social context and the spirit in which drugs were being used at the time. And it's OK to say it was a mistake—it wasn't the key to nirvana. Most experts suggest focusing on health effects and illegality rather than making it a moral issue.

---

moral child today—what communitarian legal theorist Mary Ann Glendon calls an "ecological approach" to child rearing, which views parents and family as just one of many interconnecting "seedbeds" that can contribute to a child's competency and character.

Hillary Clinton borrowed for her book title the folk wisdom, "It takes a village to raise a child." It's an idea that seems to be resonating across the political spectrum today, even in the midst of rough cultural strife. Damon, for example, ended his book with the inchoate notion of "youth charters," an idea that he says has taken on a life of its own in recent months. He has been invited into communities from Texas to New England to help concerned citizens identify shared values and develop plans for modeling and nurturing these values in newly conceived moral communities.

Americans are hungry for this kind of moral coherence, Damon says, and although they need help getting past their paralysis, it's remarkable how quickly they can reach consensus on a vision for their kids and community. He is optimistic about the future: "My great hope is that we can actually rebuilt our communities in this country around our kids. That's one great thing about America: people love their kids. They've just lost the art of figuring out how to raise them."

BY WRAY HERBERT WITH MISSY DANIEL IN BOSTON

Re-evaluating Significance of Baby's Bond With Mother

By SANDRA BLAKESLEE

Challenging a popular belief about human development, a researcher claims to have found that the security of a baby's attachment to its mother does not influence how well-adjusted that child will be later in life.

Events like divorce, disease and accidents are far more important in shaping a child's well-being at age 18 than any early bonding with its mother, said the researcher, Dr. Michael Lewis, a professor of pediatrics and psychiatry at the University of Medicine and Dentistry of New Jersey and director of the Institute for the Study of Child Development at the Robert Wood Johnson Medical School in New Brunswick.

The study is one of a number of research projects on attachment, a field that is gaining attention as experts debate what happens to infants and children when both mother and father work outside the home.

Dr. Lewis based his conclusion on a study of 84 children who were examined at age 1 in terms of maternal

An attack on the gold standard for understanding how babies and children develop

attachment—a popular measure of social adjustment and mental health—and again at age 18 in terms of adult attachment to family and friends.

Secure attachment in infancy did not protect children from being maladjusted at age 18, Dr. Lewis said, nor did insecure attachment in infancy predict trouble in adolescence. He reported his findings at a recent meeting of the International Society on Infant Studies in Atlanta and in a book "Altering Fate—Why the Past Does Not Predict the Future," published last year by the Guilford Press.

The new finding attacks the gold standard for understanding how babies and children develop: the so-called infant maternal attachment measure, which infers well-being from the reactions of babies who are temporarily separated then reunited with their mothers.

According to many experts in child development, how the baby reacts to the mother's return each time is critically important. In general, if the baby cries, goes to the mother and is comforted, the child is securely attached. If the baby ignores the mother and is ambivalent to her return or if the baby cries but refuses to be consoled, the baby is insecurely attached.

To the adherents of attachment theory, this little mini-drama speaks volumes about the child's psychological health and profoundly influences that child's developmental course.

Attachment theory is an offshoot of psychoanalysis and carries many of Sigmund Freud's ideas into modern practice, said Dr. Robert Cairns,

From *The New York Times*, August 4, 1998. © 1998 by The New York Times. Reprinted by permission.

director of the Center for Developmental Science at the University of North Carolina in Chapel Hill. It argues that early mother-infant relationships create "internal representations" in the baby's brain and that these shadows lay the foundation for psychological well-being and human personality throughout life. The mother is the critical figure. Early events are more primary than later events. Given these beliefs, the challenge became how to measure these "internal representations" in babies who cannot talk, Dr. Cairns said.

Figuring that behavior might imply something important about a baby's mind, researchers in the early 1970's devised a test called the Strange Situation. The test has many permutations but basically a mother and her 12-month-old baby enter a room in which they meet a stranger and find many interesting toys. After a few minutes, the mother leaves and the stranger plays with the baby.

After two minutes, the mother returns and the baby's behavior is observed. A little later, the mother leaves the child alone again, waits two minutes and comes back in.

The original goal was to find a measure that would, in five minutes, identify the structure of the course of human personality development, he said. The infant's external behavior is said to capture his or her internal model of the attachment relationship, Dr. Lewis said, "even though neglected and abused children often show secure attachment." Moreover, the nature of this early attachment emerges later in life, especially during stressful times.

A good attachment will protect you while a poor attachment will make you more vulnerable, he said.

This view now dominates infant and child psychiatry. The cardinal rule is that the mother-child relationship is vital for early life and determines subsequent social adjustment. Psychiatric literature on adolescence treats attachment as a stable individual characteristic, like brown eyes. Some theorists claim that adults

choose mates based on infant attachment status; insecurely attached individuals will seek securely attached people to balance out their weakness.

But life is not so simple, Dr. Lewis said. What happens to infants is important but the notion that our early reactions are frozen into the brain, unmalleable by later experience, is open to question. To see if early attachment correlates with later adjustment, Dr. Lewis found 84 children who had been evaluated at age 1—49 securely attached, 35 insecurely attached—and who were now seniors in high school. Each person was interviewed for an hour at home to measure adult attachment. Among other things, the teen-agers were asked to describe early relationships with their parents, to generate adjectives for each parent and provide memories to support the adjectives.

Interviews were scored by trained observers who examined how specific memories were integrated into a general understanding of the parent-child relationship. A teen-ager was deemed securely attached if he presented a coherent story about his relationship with his parents. A teen-ager was considered insecurely attached if that story was fragmented, ambivalent or incoherent.

Among securely attached infants, 57 percent were considered well-adjusted at age 18 and 43 percent were found to be maladjusted, Dr. Lewis said. Among insecure infants, 74 percent were considered secure at age 18 and 26 percent were believed to have remained insecure.

Dr. Lewis asserts that the critical factor in human development is not security of attachment at age 1 but subsequent experiences in family life. There are many critical periods in every child's life. Divorce played a primary role in their adjustment and "to understand a child's emotional and social development, you have to look at his current life," he said. He added: "We don't so much remember the past as we reconstruct it in the light of present events. Ac-

cidents and chance encounters are a major part of life. The task is always adaptation to the present."

The proponents of attachment theory, however, are not ready to give up on a method that in their view works. For example, Dr. Alan Sroufe, a leading attachment expert at the University of Minnesota in Minneapolis, conducted a long-term study several years ago and found that, in his sample, infant attachment can predict psychopathology at age 17. "I disagree with Mike Lewis," Dr. Sroufe said, "His study is weaker than ours and he used fewer children. I'm not surprised he

Do life's dramas at 1 play out at 18?

didn't find correlations. I also disagree with him on logical grounds. Your behavior is always a product of your history and your present circumstances."

Similarly, Dr. Jay Belsky, a professor of human development at Pennsylvania State University in University Park and another well-known proponent of attachment theory, argues that infant day care can disrupt attachment and may harm children in the long run. "To understand the present, you have to understand what the child brings to the circumstances," Dr. Belsky said. "Of course it matters how development proceeds, but what happens early in life makes a difference."

The debate is over how much of a difference. Critics of attachment theory, including Dr. Lewis, say that most researchers place far too much importance on what happens in the first year or two of life.

Some proponents of the theory even argue that critical mother- infant bonding begins at birth. "Years ago, I visited a program in Philadelphia to foster the social and emotional development of children of teen-aged inner-city mothers," Dr. Lewis said. "The program consisted of placing the naked newborn child on the naked belly of the mother, as if early bonding would somehow inoculate the child against all future problems."

Dr. Irving Lazar, a professor emeritus of child development at Vanderbilt University in Nashville, is even more critical of attachment theorists. "Of course babies need good mothers," he said.

"It's important to feel loved and secure. But the so-called attachment measure is ludicrous. The one-time observation of a baby's reaction to its mother's return has no meaningful consequences." All it does is make mothers feel guilty, he said.

Dr. Cairns said that animal studies mostly supported Dr. Lewis.

Studies of other mammals separated from their mothers, including the monkey experiments of Dr. Harry Harlow in which babies were raised without mothers, show no permanent damage to the deprived animals, he said. Dr. Harlow's monkeys treated their first-born babies "like basketballs" and that is what got reported, Dr. Cairns said, but babies born later to those same mothers were well-cared for.

The mothers adapted.

When pressed, people on both sides of the debate will say "of course both past and present are important," Dr. Cairns said, "but they really don't mean it." Many have entrenched ideological positions which, if confined to an ivory tower, might be amusing. These arguments, though, have important policy consequences for American society, he said.

If the first year of life is all-important, then why bother investing huge sums in later intervention programs? But if the first year of life is not that important, and it is the quality of your whole childhood that matters, how could we possibly change things?

Helping Children Become More Prosocial: Ideas for Classrooms, Families, Schools, and Communities

Alice S. Honig and Donna S. Wittmer

Part 1 of this review of strategies and techniques to enhance prosocial development focused on techniques that teachers and parents can use with individual children or small groups of children (see Wittmer & Honig, Encouraging Positive Social Development in Young Children, *Young Children* 49 [5]: 4–12). Part 2 offers suggestions for involving whole classrooms, entire school systems, parents, and communities in creating classroom and home climates for kindness, cooperation, generosity, and helpfulness.

Child-sensitive, high-quality care in classrooms promotes prosocial behaviors

If you thought so, you were right. Here is more information to back you up. Peaceful play and cooperation are more likely to occur when teachers set up developmentally appropriate classrooms (Bredekamp & Rosegrant 1992). Staff competence and years of teacher experience are significant factors in ensuring such quality care. In one research study the more highly trained and stable the preschool staff were, the *lower* were teacher-rated and observed preschool aggression scores, despite children's varying histories of full-time or part-time nonparental care during infancy and

Alice Sterling Honig, Ph.D., professor of child development at Syracuse University in Syracuse, New York, was program director for the Family Development Research Program and has authored numerous books, including Parent Involvement in Early Childhood Education *and* Playtime Learning Games for Young Children. *She directs the annual Syracuse Quality Infant/Toddler Caregiving Workshop.*

Donna Sasse Wittmer, Ph.D., is assistant professor in early childhood education at the University of Colorado in Denver. She has had extensive experience directing, training in, and conducting research in early childhood care and education programs.

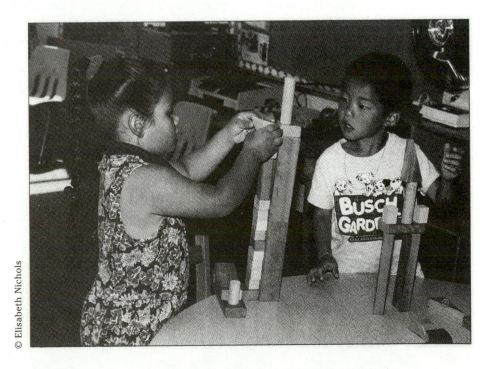

© Elisabeth Nichols

From *Young Children*, January 1996, pp. 62–70. © 1996 by the National Association for Education of Young Children. Reprinted by permission.

39

toddlerhood (Park & Honig 1991). In another study 4-year-olds in a constructivist classroom, given many opportunities for choices and autonomous construction of attitudes, principles, and social problem-solving strategies, showed higher social-cognitive skills than their peers from another preschool program with whom they played board games (DeVries & Goncu 1990).

Children in strongly adult-directed preschool classrooms engage in less prosocial behavior than do children in classrooms that encourage more child-initiated learning and interactions (Huston-Stein, Friedrich-Cofer, & Susman 1977). In a longitudinal study of 19-year-olds who had attended either a highly adult-directed preschool or a program that emphasized child initiations much more, the teenagers who had been in the latter program were more socially competent and had fewer juvenile delinquency convictions (Schweinhart, Weikart, & Larner 1986).

Howes and Stewart (1987) discovered that children who experience high-quality child care and supportive parents acquire the *ability to decode and regulate emotional signals in peer play.* Social sensitivity to others' cues and needs is a good predictor of positive peer relations. Unfortunately, the researchers also found that families who are the most stressed choose the lowest quality child care arrangements, are the most likely to change arrangements, and have children with the lowest levels of competence during social play with peers. A community resource-and-referral agency may be the best source of materials and information to help families recognize and choose high-quality child care and to inform parents about NAEYC accreditation.

Emphasize cooperation rather than competition

Every experienced preschool teachers surely wants young children to be prepared to succeed in their school learning careers. Competitive classrooms result in some children becoming tense, fearing failure, and becoming less motivated to persist at challenging tasks. In a cooperative-interaction classroom, the emphasis is on children working together to accomplish mutual goals (Aronson, Bridgeman, & Geffner 1978). Even toddlers can work together in cooperative play. For example, if each grasps the opposite end of a towel and both coordinate efforts, they can keep a beach ball bouncing on the towel.

Every child has an essential and unique contribution to make to class learning. One teaching tool has been called the "jigsaw technique" because the teacher provides each child with one piece of information about a lesson; then the children must work cooperatively with each other to learn all the material and information necessary for a complete presentation by the group (Aronson et al. 1978).

We have referred here only to a few studies emphasizing the positive outcomes of cooperative learning environments, but surely our readers have read about this in numerous books and articles in recent years!

Teach cooperative and conflict-resolution games and sports

Caregiver creativity in initiating group games and in devising conflict-resolution games promotes peace in the classroom (Kreidler 1984). New games and variations of traditional children's games and sports that encourage cooperation rather than competition facilitate prosocial interactions (Orlick 1982, 1985; Prutzman et al. 1988). When Musical Chairs is played so that each time a chair is taken away, the "leftover" child must find a lap to sit on rather than be forced out of the game, no child feels left out or a failure. Bos (1990) provides examples of such games. In Spider Swing one child sits on the lap of another, with legs hanging out the back of the swing. Bos calls games in which children play cooperatively together to create pleasure and fun "coaction." Why not try these and invent some of your own?

Of course, even more important than an occasional game is helping children live cooperatively in the classroom every day and resolve personal conflicts peaceably.

Set up classroom spaces and play materials to facilitate cooperative play

Arrangements of space and varieties of toys and learning materials affect whether children act more aggressively or cooperate more peacefully. A small, cluttered play area can lead to more tension and fights. A group seesaw, a tire-bouncer, or a nylon parachute encourage group cooperation because the children *need* each other to maximize their enjoyment.

In the research we reviewed, more prosocial responses were given by young children attending child care or nursery school programs when (1) a variety of age-appropriate materials were available and (2) space was arranged to accommodate groups of varying sizes (Holloway & Reichhart-Erickson 1988). Children who played with large hollow blocks and unit blocks in a large block area of their preschool learned and practiced positive social problem-solving skills rather than aggression (Rogers 1987). Yet, where preschoolers are crowded together in a narrow area with large blocks, there is greater pressure to use the blocks as missiles or pretend guns.

Classroom layout affect children's emotional security and sense of free choice in play. Combine your environmental design skills with your expertise in early childhood education to arrange class traffic patterns that maximize peaceful interactions. Think through the placement of clearly defined and well-supplied interest centers; provide unobstructed access to materials; give aesthetic attention to color and wall decorations; and decrease clutter. Arrange inviting spaces with soft cushions for children to nestle on when they need to calm down or rest when distressed. Your executive space-planning skills can promote more comfortable feelings conductive to a more harmonious, cooperative classroom climate.

Use bibliotherapy: Incorporate children's literature to enhance empathy and caring in daily reading activities

A growing number of preschool and primary teachers do use bibliotherapy. If you do not, you may find this a good time to begin!

Choose children's literature for prosocial themes and characters that provide altruistic models. *Two Good Friends* (by Judy Delton) is the charming story of how two friends—Bear, who is messy but a fine cook, and Duck, who is tidy but a poor cook—care for each other lovingly and generously. Dr. Seuss's Horton the Elephant is that kind of prosocial character in the books *Horton Hears a Who* and *Horton Hatches an Egg*. So is the king's young page boy in Seuss's *The King's Stilts*. And so is *The Little Engine That Could,* as she chugs courageously up and over a very tall mountain to bring toys to boys and girls. Sucking his thumb vigorously, one little boy listened enraptured as his caregiver read the story of the brave little engine who did not want to disappoint the children. The child kept nodding his head and whispering to himself, "That was very nice of her! That was very nice of her!"

McMath (1989) suggests asking open-ended questions that help children think about and understand the motives and actions of storybook characters. When skilled adults read stories that feature altruistic characters, they promote children's ability to grasp socioemotional motivations and motivate children to imitate empathic and helpful responses (Dreikurs, Grunwald, & Pepper 1982). Many publishers, such as the Albert Whitman Company, provide children's books that adults can read to young children to help them cope with and find adaptive solutions to disturbing personal concerns, such as living with family alcoholism, parental divorce, or domestic violence.

Actively lead group discussions on prosocial interactions

Some teachers focus on developing supportive classroom communities. Discussion of social interactions within the group is usually a central part of the curriculum in this kind of classroom.

Sharing increases among preschool children whose teachers give them explanations as to *why* sharing is important and *how* to share (Barton & Osborne 1978). Some second-grade teachers daily set aside brief classroom time to encourage children to discuss specific incidents in which they and their classmates were helpful and kind with one another. After one month, prosocial interactions increased about twofold among these children, compared with a randomly assigned group of control children (Honig & Pollack 1990).

As a teacher, you have learned a great deal about the individual interests and talents of your children. During show-and-tell circle times you can extend group discussion to increase children's awareness of *distributive justice*—how goods and benefits are distributed justly among people with varying needs, temperaments, talents, and troubles. Lively discussions can center around what is "fair" or not so fair. Children between 4 and 8 years old are busy learning rules for games and rules for social relations, and they are often concerned about fairness and who gets advantages. Yet, preschoolers are capable of realizing, for example, that at meal and snack times, rigid equality in distributing food would not be the best plan if one child habitually comes to school without breakfast and is very hungry.

Young children often protest if there is not strict equality in distributing goodies. Many a teacher or parent has heard the protest, "That's not fair. He got more than me!" Through discussions, children can move from a position of belief in strict equality in treat or toy distribution toward awareness of the concepts of *equity and benevolence*—that is, the idea that the special needs of other must be taken into account (Damon 1977).

Talk about taking turns and about *different* ways each child gets some special time or privilege, although not exactly the same as another receives. These talks can be especially helpful for preschoolers who are distressed because Mama is now nursing a new baby and seemingly gives lots more time and attention to the tiny new stranger. Caregiver kindness lies not only in providing extra nurturing for that preschooler during this difficult time but also in assisting all the children to think through issues of neediness and fairness. As you help children to learn about "turn taking" through group discussions, you increase their understanding of fairness. Although in some families it may be a new baby's turn to get special attention, such as nursing, preschoolers now get other kinds of special attention from parents, such as a story reading at bedtime or a change to help with cooking, a household repair job, or some other special activity in which a baby cannot participate.

Encourage social interaction between normally developing children and children with special needs

Teachers must initiate specific friendship-building strategies when atypical children in an inclusive classroom exhibit low-level prosocial skills. Activities to promote classroom friendship are available (Fox 1980; Smith 1982; Edwards 1986; Wolf 1986). Children with disabilities need your inventive interventions to learn how to make a friend, use positive and assertive techniques to enter a play group, and *sustain* friendly play bouts with peers (Honig & Thompson 1994). Promotion of specific friendship skills to enhance the social integration of typical and atypical children requires well-planned teacher strategies and initiatives. Prosocial interactions of children with disabilities may need a boost. Some typical preschoolers also may need a boost in their sensitivity to others' difficulties *and* competencies (Gresham 1981; Honig & McCarron 1990).

More than other children, a child with a disability may need help from classmates and the teacher or extra time to finish a project. If you are making preparations to create an inclusive classroom that integrates atypical and typical children, then class discussions about fairness become particularly urgent. Children will need to talk about and struggle with a new idea: strict equal apportionment according to work done may not be the kindest or most prosocial decision in special cases. If a child with cerebral palsy and marked difficulties in hand coordination finishes far fewer placemats than the other children in a class project, she or he has tried just as hard as the others and should receive the same share of any "profits" from the class craft sale.

Develop class and school projects that foster altruism

With the help of a caring teacher, children can think about and decide on a class project to help others (Solomon et al. 1988). Some classes prominently label and display a jar in which they put pennies to donate to hungry children or to families in need at holiday time. When the jar is full, children count the money and compose a joint class letter to the organization to which they are contributing. Other class projects can arise from children's suggestions during group discussion times about troubles that faraway or nearby children are having. Prosocial projects include cleaning up the schoolyard, writing as pen pals to children in troubled lands, collecting toys or food for individuals in need, and making friends with other people during visits to a home for the aged.

Your perceptive knowledge about individuals in the class is especially useful when you encourage each child to generate personal ideas for sharing kindness and caring in her or his own family. As a group, the children may

decide to draw their own "helping coupons." Each child creates a gift book with large, hand-drawn coupons. Every coupon promises a helpful act to a parent or family member. Some of the coupons could be "reading my baby sister a story," "setting the table," "sorting socks from the laundry basket into pairs," "sharing my toy cars with my brother," and "brushing my teeth all by myself while Papa puts the baby to bed." Young children dictate their helpful offers for you to write down and then illustrate the coupons with signs and pictures that remind them of what sharing or caring action their coupon represents. Children generously give the coupons to family members as personal gifts—promises of help.

Encourage cooperative in-classroom activities that require several children's joint productive efforts. Ideas include drawing a group mural, building a large boat or space station with blocks and Tinkertoys, planning and producing a puppet show, and sewing a yarn picture that has been outlined on both sides of burlap.

Move very young children with peers to the next age group

Toddlers adjust more positively to movement from one group to a slightly older group in center care when they move with peers. Howes (1987) found that children who stayed in the same child care center with the same peer group increased their proportion of complementary and reciprocal peer play more than did children who changed peer group within their center. Continuity of quality child care and continuity of peer group relationships are important in the development of a child's feelings of security and social competence. Consider security needs and friendship patterns rather than rigid age criteria in moving young children to a new classroom.

Arrange regular viewing of prosocial media and videogames

Viewing prosocial videos and television programs increases children's social contacts as well as fosters

smiling, praising, hugging (Coates, Pusser, & Goodman 1976), sharing, cooperating, turn taking, positive verbal/physical contact (Forge & Phemister 1987), and willingness to help puppies in need (Poulds, Rubinstein, & Leibert 1975). Regular viewing of prosocial television, particularly *Mister Rogers' Neighborhood,* has resulted in higher levels of task persistence, rule obedience, and tolerance of delayed gratification. Children from low-socioeconomic families who watched this program daily showed increased cooperative play, nurturance, and verbalization of feelings (Friedrich & Stein 1973). In contrast, children who were exposed to aggressive videogames donated less to needy children than did children who played prosocial videogames (Chambers 1987).

Invite moral mentors to visit the class

Damon (1988) urges teachers actively to recruit and involve *moral mentors* in the classroom. Invite individuals who have contributed altruistically to better the lives of others in the community to come in and talk about their lives and experiences. Children may be eager to nominate someone in their own family to tell about how they help others. Perhaps Aunt Esther visits a nursing home and livens up senior citizens' days. Perhaps Uncle Irving outfitted the family station wagon with a ramp so he can take people in wheelchairs to weekend ball games. Children learn to reframe their ideas about community helpfulness and personal generosity toward others in trouble if a special guest—a high school swimming star who volunteers as a coach for children with physical impairments, for example—comes to visit and talks about her or his experiences helping others.

Work closely with families for prosocial programming

Families need to know that prosocial interactions are an integral curriculum component of your child care program. As a practicing professional, you use your prosocial skills to support and affirm family members of each child in your classroom. And, of course, you know how your close contact with parents provides you with insight and more sensitive understanding of each child. Parents also need you to share your concern for and emphasis on prosocial classroom activities and goals. During informal greetings at the beginning of the day or at end-of-day pickup times, you may want to affirm how special each parent's role is in promoting care and concern for others at home (Barnett et al. 1980). Yarrow and colleagues (in Pines 1979) revealed that parents who exhibit tender concern when their very young children experience fright or upset and who firmly discourage aggressive actions to solve squabbles have children who show very early signs of concern and empathy for others' troubles. These personal examples of "baby altruism" persist into elementary school (Pines 1979).

In interviews 10 years after graduation from a program that emphasized caring and prosocial development in outreach with families as well as in high-quality group care, teenagers and their families reported that they felt more family support, closeness, and appreciation than did control youth. Compared with members of the control group, the adolescents also had far lower rates of juvenile delinquency (Lally, Mangione, Honig 1988).

Establish a parent resource lending library

Interested parents will appreciate being able to browse through prosocial articles in your child care facility. For example, make available a copy of Kobak's (1979) brief article on how she embeds caring and awareness of positive social interactions in all classroom activities, dialogues, and projects. Her concept of a *caring quotient* (CQ) classroom emphasizes the importance of children learning positive social interaction skills as well as intellectual (IQ) skills. Social problem solving by a class must take into consideration that the child whose problem is being brainstormed has to feel

that the class members *care* about him or her as they explore ways to resolve a problem, such as chronic truancy or a book borrowed from a teacher and never returned.

Convince parents of the importance of a specific focus on prosocial as well as cognitive curriculum through displays of brief, easy-to-read reports of research articles. The Abecedarian program provides powerful research findings (Finkelstein 1982). Children who had attended this infant and preschool program that emphasized cognitive development were 15 times more aggressive with kindergarten peers than a control group of children who had not been in child care or who had attended community child care. A prosocial curriculum was then instituted for future waves of children in the program; the difference in aggression between program children and their peers in kindergarten subsequently disappeared, according to later evaluations.

Promote a bias-free curriculum

A bias-free curriculum promotes more prosocial interactions among children despite multicultural differences in ethnicity, language, or family background (Derman-Sparks & the A.B.C. Task Force 1989). Emphasize how all children and adults feel better and get a fairer chance when others treat them courteously and kindly. Children who feel that others are *more,* rather than less, similar to themselves behave more prosocially toward them (Feshbach 1978). During class meeting times, children discover how much alike they are—in having special family members they feel close to, in enjoying a picnic or an outing with family, in playing with friends, and in wanting to feel safe, well-loved, and cared about.

Require responsibility: Encourage children to care for younger children and classmates who need extra help

Anthropologists, studying six different cultures, noted that when children help care for younger siblings and in-

teract with a cross-age variety of children in social groups in nonschool settings, then children feel more responsible for the welfare of the group and gain more skills in nurturing (Whiting & Whiting 1975).

Children should be given responsibility, commensurate with their abilities, to care for and help teach younger children or children who may need extra personal help in the classroom. In a long-term study of at-risk infants born on the island of Kauai, children who carried out such caring actions of *required helpfulness* were more likely 32 years later to be positively socially functioning as family members and as community citizens (Werner 1986).

Become familiar with structured curriculum packages that promote prosocial development

Complete program packages are available with materials and specific ideas as well as activities for enhancing prosocial behaviors in the classroom. Shure's (1992) daily lesson plans give step-by-step techniques for teaching how the feelings or wishes of one child may be the same or different from those of another child and how to challenge children to think of the consequences of their behaviors and to think up alternatives to inappropriate or hurtful behaviors in solving their social problems. *Communicating to Make Friends* (Fox 1980) provides 18 weeks of planned activities to promote peer acceptance. Dinkmeyer and Dinkmeyer's *Developing Understanding of Self and Others* (1982) provides puppets, activity cards, charts, and audiocassettes to promote children's awareness of others' feelings and social skills. The Abecedarian program instituted *My Friends and Me* (Davis 1977) to promote more prosocial development.

Arrange Bessell and Palomares's (1973) Magic Circle lessons so that children, each day during a safe, nonjudgmental circle time, feel *secure enough to share* their stories, feelings, and memories about times they have had troubles with others, times when they have been helped by others, and times when they have been thoughtful and caring on behalf of others.

Commercial sources also provide some materials that directly support teacher attempts to introduce peace programs and conflict-resolution programs in their classrooms (e.g., Young People's Press, San Diego). Sunrise Books (Provo, Utah) is a commercial source of book and video materials for teachers and parents to promote positive discipline and conflict resolution. One book by Nelson (n.d.) features the use of class meetings, a technique that builds cooperation, communication, and problem solving so that classmates' mutual respect and accountability increase.

Watkins and Durant (1992) provide pre-K to second-grade teachers with specific classroom techniques for prevention of antisocial behaviors. They suggest the right times to *ignore* inappropriate behavior and specify other situations when the teacher must use *control*. Teachers are taught to look for signs that they may actually be rewarding socially inappropriate behavior by their responses. The use of subtle, nonverbal cues of dress, voice control, and body language are recommended in order to promote children's more positive behaviors.

Implement a comprehensive school-based prosocial program that emphasizes ethical teaching

John Gatto, a recipient of the New York City Teacher of the Year award in 1990, admitted, "The children I teach are cruel to each other, they lack compassion for misfortune, they laugh at weakness, they have contempt for people whose need for help shows too plainly" (Wood 1991, 7).

Wood urges teachers to conceptualize a more ethical style of teaching that he calls "maternal teaching." He suggests that teachers develop a routine of morning meetings that involve greetings and cooperation, as in singing together. Children feel personally valued when they are greeted by

name as they enter a school. Classes can create rules of courtesy for and with each other, and the rules should be prominently posted. Wood urges teachers to "figure out a way to teach recess and lunch. . . . When children come in from recess, the teacher often can spend another half hour of instructional time sorting out the hurt feelings and hurt bodies and hurt stories she wasn't even there to see or hear" (1991, 8). Children can be taught the power of "please" and "thank you." Role playing helps them become aware of how hurtful name-calling and verbal put-downs are. You, of course, are a powerful positive model of social courtesies as you listen to each child's ideas and give each a turn to talk at mealtime and grouptime. Help children feel all-school ownership. Flowers and table-cloths in school lunchrooms can be incentives for making lunchtime a friendly and positive experience.

Brown and Solomon (1983) have translated prosocial research for application throughout school systems. In the California Bay Area, they implemented a comprehensive program in several elementary schools to increase prosocial attitudes and behavior among the children and their families. In the program the following occur:

1. Children from about age 6 onward, with adult supervision, take responsibility for caring for younger children.
2. Cooperative learning requires that children work with each other in learning teams within classes.
3. Children are involved in structured programs of helpful and useful activities, such as visiting the elderly or shut-ins, making toys for others, cleaning up or gardening in nearby parks and playgrounds.
4. Children of mixed ages engage in activities.
5. Children help with home chores on a regular basis with parental approval and cooperation.
6. Children regularly role-play situations in which they can experience feelings of being a victim *and* a helper.
7. The entire elementary school recognizes and rewards caring, helping, taking responsibility, and other prosocial

behaviors, whether they occur at home or at school.
8. Children learn about prosocial adult models in films, television, and their own community. The children watch for such models in the news media and clip newspaper articles about prosocially acting persons. They also invite such models to tell their stories in class.
9. Empathy training includes children's exposure to examples of animals or children in distress, in real life or staged episodes. They hear adults comment on how to help someone in trouble, and they watch examples of helpfulness.
10. Continuity and total saturation in a school program create a climate that *communicates prosocial expectations and supports children's learning and enacting prosocial behaviors* both at home and in school.

Train older children as peer mediators

In some New York City schools and elsewhere in the United States, the Resolving Conflict Creatively Program (RCCP) trains fifth-graders as peer mediators to move to situations of social conflict, such as a playground fight, and help the participants resolve their problems. RCCP rules mandate that each child in a conflict be given a chance by the peer mediators to describe and explain the problem from her or his viewpoint and to try to agree on how to settle the problem. Peer mediators are trained in nonviolent and creative ways of dealing with social conflicts (RCCP, 163 Third Avenue #239, New York, NY 10003).

Teachers of kindergarten and primary children may want to look into this. Think how much influence the "big kids" would have on *your* children!

Cherish the children: Create an atmosphere of affirmation through family/classroom/ community rituals

Loving rituals—such as a group greeting song that names and welcomes each child individually every

Suggested Books for Classroom Parents' Library

Box, B. 1990. *Together we're better: Establishing a coative learning environment.* Roseville, CA: Turn the Page Press.

Briggs, D. 1975. *Your child's self-esteem.* New York: Dolphin.

Crary, E. 1990. *Kids can cooperate: A practical guide to teaching problem solving.* Seattle, WA: Parenting Press.

Damon, W. 1988. *The moral child: Nurturing children's natural moral growth.* New York: Free Press.

Feshbach, N., & S. Feshbach. 1983. *Learning to care: Classroom activities for social and effective development.* Glenview, IL: Scott Foresman.

Finkelstein, N. 1982. Aggression: Is it stimulated by day care? *Young Children* 37 (6): 3–13.

Gordon, T. 1975. *Parent effectiveness training.* New York: Plume.

Honig, A. 1996. *Developmentally appropriate behavior guidance for infants and toddlers from birth to 3 years.* Little Rock, AR: Southern Early Childhood Association.

Kobak, D. 1970. Teaching young children to care. *Children Today* 8 (6–7): 34–35.

Orlick, T. 1985. *The second cooperative sports and games book.* New York: Pantheon.

Shure, M. 1994. *Raising a thinking child: Help your young child to resolve everyday conflicts and get along with others.* New York: Henry Holt.

Smith, C. 1993. *The peaceful classroom: 162 easy activities to teach preschoolers compassion and cooperation.* Mount Rainier, MD: Gryphon House.

Wolf, P., ed. 1986. *Connection: Friendship in the lives of young children and their teachers.* Redmond, WA: Exchange Press.

morning, or leisurely and soothing backrubs given at naptime in a darkened room—establish a climate of caring in the child care classroom.

College students who scored high on an empathy scale remembered their parents as having been empathic and affectionate when the students were younger (Barnett et al. 1980). Egeland and Sroufe (1981), in a series of longitudinal research studies, reported devastating effects from the lack of early family cherishing of infants and young children. (Of course, therapists' offices and prisons are full of people who were not loved in their early years.)

A warm smile or an arm around the shoulder lets a child know he or she is valued and cared for. Encourage children to tell something special about their relationship to a particular child on that child's birthday. Write down these birthday stories in a personal book for each child. An attitude of affirmation creates an environment in which children feel safe, secure, accepted, and loved (Salkowski 1991). Special holiday celebration times, such as Thanksgiving, Abraham Lincoln's birthday, Father's Day, and Mother's Day, offer opportunities to create ritual class activities and to illustrate ceremonies and appropriate be-

haviors for expressing caring and thankfulness.

Teachers are bombarded with books and articles about the importance of developing positive self-esteem in each child and how to attempt to instill it. Many of these sources contain important and helpful ideas (see Honig & Wittmer 1992).

Sometimes children come into care from such stressful situations that it is hard for them to control their own sadness and anger. One teacher uses a "Magic Feather Duster" to brush off troubles and upsets from children. A preschooler arriving in child care aggravated and upset announces, "Teacher, I think you better get the Magic Feather Duster to brush off all the 'bad vibes'!" After the teacher carefully and tenderly uses her magic duster, the child sighs, relaxes, and feels ready to enter into the atmosphere of a caring and peaceful classroom. Each teacher creates her or his own magic touches to help children feel secure, calm, and cooperative.

The more cherished a child is, the less likely he or she is to bully others *or* to be rejected by other children. The more nurturing parents and caregivers are—the more positive affection and responsive, empathic care they provide—the more positively chil-

dren will relate in social interactions with teachers, caring adults, and peers and in cooperating with classroom learning goals, as well.

References

Aronson, E., D. Bridgeman, & R. Geffner, 1978. Interdependent interactions and prosocial behavior. *Journal of Research and Development in Education* 12 (1): 16–27.

Aronson, E., C. Stephan, J. Sikes, N. Blaney, & M. Snapp. 1978. *The jigsaw classroom.* Beverly Hills, CA: Sage.

Barnett, M., J. Howard, L. King, & G. Dino. 1980. Empathy in young children: Relation to parents' empathy, affection, and emphasis on the feelings of others. *Developmental Psychology* 16: 243–44.

Barton, E. J., & J. G. Osborne. 1978. The development of classroom sharing by a teacher using positive practice. *Behavior Modification* 2: 231–51.

Bessell, H., & U. Palomares. 1973. *Methods in human development: Theory manual.* El Cajun, CA: Human Development Training Institute.

Bos, B. 1990. *Together we're better: Establishing a coactive learning environment.* Roseville, CA: Turn the Page Press.

Bredekamp, S., & T. Rosegrant, eds. 1992. *Reaching potentials: Appropriate curriculum and assessment for young children.* Vol. 1: Washington, DC: NAEYC.

Brown, D., & D. Solomon. 1983. A model for prosocial learning: An in-progress field study. In *The nature of prosocial development: Interdisciplinary theories and strategies,* ed. D. L. Bridgeman. New York: Academic.

Chambers, J. 1987. The effects of prosocial and aggressive videogames on children's donating and helping. *Journal of Genetic Psychology* 148: 499–505.

Coates, B., H. Pusser, & I. Goodman. 1976. The influence of "Sesame Street" and "Mr. Rogers' Neighborhood" on children's social behavior in the preschool. *Child Development* 47: 138–44.

Damon, W. 1977. *The social world of the child.* San Francisco, CA: Jossey-Bass.

Damon, W. 1988. *The moral child: Nurturing children's natural moral growth.* New York: Free Press.

Davis, D. E. 1977. *My friends and me.* Circle Pines, MN: American Guidance Service.

Derman-Sparks, L., & the A.B.C. Task Force 1989. *Anti-bias curriculum: Tools for empowering young children.* Washington, DC: NAEYC.

DeVries, R., & A. Goncu. 1990. Interpersonal relations in four-year-old dyads from constructivist and Montessori programs. In *Optimizing early child care and education,* ed. A. S. Honig, 11–28. London: Gordon & Breach.

Dinkmeyer, D., & D. Dinkmeyer, Jr. 1982. *Developing understanding of self and others (Rev. DUSO-R).* Circle Pines, MN: American Guidance Service.

Dreikurs, R., B. B. Grunwald, & F. C. Pepper. 1982. *Maintaining sanity in the classroom: Classroom management techniques.* New York: Harper & Row.

Edwards, C. P. 1986. *Social and moral development in young children: Creative approaches for the classroom.* New York: Teachers College Press.

Egeland, B., & A. Sroufe. 1981. Developmental sequelae of maltreatment in infancy. *Directions for Child Development* 11: 77–92.

Feshbach, N. 1978. Studies of empathetic behavior in children. In *Progress in experimental personality research,* Vol. 8, ed. B. Maher, 1–47. New York: Academic Press.

Finkelstein, N. 1982. Aggression: Is it stimulated by day care? *Young Children* 37 (6): 3–13.

Forge, K. L., & S. Phemister. 1987. The effect of prosocial cartoons on preschool children. *Child Study Journal* 17: 83–88.

Fox, L. 1980. *Communicating to make friends.* Rolling Hills Estates, CA: B. L. Winch.

Friedrich, L. K., & A. H. Stein. 1973. *Aggressive and prosocial television programs and the natural behavior of preschool children.* Monographs of the Society for Research in Child Development, vol. 38, issue 4, no. 151. Chicago: University of Chicago Press.

Gresham, F. 1981. Social skills training with handicapped children: A review. *Review of Educational Research* 51: 139–76.

Holloway, S. D., & M. Reichhart-Erickson. 1988. The relationship of day care quality to children's free-play behavior and social problem-solving skills. *Early Childhood Research Quarterly* 3: 39–53.

Honig, A., & P. McCarron. 1990. Prosocial behaviors of handicapped and typical peers in an integrated preschool. In *Optimizing early child care and education,* ed. A. S. Honig. London: Gordon & Breach.

Honig, A., & B. Pollack. 1990. Effects of a brief intervention program to promote prosocial behaviors in young children. *Early Education and Development* 1: 438–44.

Honig, A. S., & A. Thompson. 1994. Helping toddlers with peer entry skills. *Zero to Three* 14 (5): 15–19.

Honig, A. S., & D. S. Wittmer. 1992. *Prosocial development in children: Caring, sharing, and cooperating: A bibliographic resource guide.* New York: Garland Press.

Howes, C. 1987. Social competence with peers in young children: Developmental sequences. *Developmental Review* 7: 252–72.

Howes, C., & P. Stewart. 1987. Child's play with adults, toys, and peers: An examination of family and child care influences. *Developmental Psychology* 23 (8): 423–30.

Huston-Stein, A., L. Friedrich-Cofer, & E. Susman. 1977. The relation of classroom structure to social behavior, imaginative play, and self-regulation of economically disadvantaged children. *Child Development* 48: 908–16.

Kobak, D. 1979. Teaching children to care. *Children Today* 8 (6/7): 34–35.

Kreidler, W. 1984. *Creative conflict resolution.* Evanston, IL: Scott Foresman.

Lally, J. R., P. Mangione, & A. S. Honig. 1988. The Syracuse University Family Development Research Program: Long range impact of an early intervention with low-income children and their families. In *Parent education as early childhood interventions: Emerging directions in theory, research, and practice,* ed. D. Powell, 79–104. Norwood, NJ: Ablex.

McMath, J. 1989. Promoting prosocial behaviors through literature. *Day Care and Early Education* 17 (1): 25–27.

Nelson, J. n.d. *Positive discipline in the classroom featuring class meetings.* Provo, UT: Sunrise.

Orlick, T. 1982. *Winning through cooperation: Competitive insanity—cooperative alternatives.* Washington, DC: Acropolis.

Orlick, T. 1985. *The second cooperative sports and games book.* New York: Pantheon Press.

Park, K., & A. Honig. 1991. Infant child care patterns and later teacher ratings of preschool behaviors. *Early Child Development and Care* 68: 80–87.

Pines, M. 1979. Good samaritans at age two? *Psychology Today* 13: 66–77.

Poulds, R., E. Rubinstein, & R. Leibert. 1975. Positive social learning. *Journal of Communication* 25 (4): 90–97.

Prutzman, P., L. Sgern, M. L. Burger, & G. Bodenhamer. 1988. *The friendly classroom for a small planet: Children's creative response to conflict program.* Philadelphia: New Society.

Rogers, D. 1987. Fostering social development through block play. *Day Care and Early Education* 14 (3): 26–29.

Salkowski, C. J. 1991. Keeping the peace: Helping children resolve conflict through a problem-solving approach. *Montessori Life* (Spring): 31–37.

Schweinhart, L. J., D. P. Weikart, & M. B. Larner. 1986. Consequences of three curriculum models through age 15. *Early Childhood Research Quarterly* 1: 15–45.

Shure, M. 1992. *I can problem solve: An interpersonal cognitive problem-solving program.* Champaign, IL: Research Press.

Smith, C. A. 1982. *Promoting the social development of young children: Strategies and activities.* Palo Alto, CA: Mayfield.

Solomon, D., M. S. Watson, K. L. Delucci, E. Schaps, & V. Battistich. 1988. Enhancing children's prosocial behavior in the classroom. *American Educational Research Journal* 25 (4): 527–54.

Watkins, K. P., & L. Durant. 1992. *Complete early childhood behavior management guide.* West Nyack, NY: Center for Applied Research in Education.

Werner, E. 1986. Resilient children. In *Annual editions: Human development,* eds. H. E. Fitzgerald & M. G. Walraven. Sluice Dock, CT: Dushkin.

Whiting, B., & J. Whiting. 1975. *Children of six cultures: A psychocultural analysis.* Cambridge, MA: Harvard University Press.

Wittmer, D., & A. Honig. 1994. Encouraging positive social development in young children, Part 1. *Young Children* 49 (5): 4–12.

Wolf, P., ed. 1986. *Connecting: Friendship in the lives of young children and their teachers.* Redmond, WA: Exchange Press.

Wood, C. 1991. Maternal teaching: Revolution of kindness. *Holistic Education Review* (Summer): 3–10.

BEYOND LITTLETON

How Well Do You Know Your Kid?

The new teen wave is bigger, richer, better educated and healthier than any other in history. But there's a dark side, and too many parents aren't doing their job.

By Barbara Kantrowitz and Pat Wingert

JOCKS, PREPS, PUNKS, GOTHS, GEEKS. They may sit at separate tables in the cafeteria, but they all belong to the same generation. There are now 31 million kids in the 12-to-19 age group, and demographers predict that there will be 35 million teens by 2010, a population bulge bigger than even the baby boom at its peak. In many ways, these teens are uniquely privileged. They've grown up in a period of sustained prosperity and haven't had to worry about the draft (as their fathers did) or cataclysmic global conflicts (as their grandparents did). Cable and the Internet have given them access to an almost infinite amount of information. Most expect to go to college, and girls, in particular, have unprecedented opportunities; they can dream of careers in everything from professional sports to politics, with plenty of female role models to follow.

But this positive image of American adolescence in 1999 is a little like yearbook photos that depict every kid as happy and blemish-free. After the Littleton, Colo., tragedy, it's clear there's another dimension to this picture, and it's far more troubled. In survey after survey, many kids—even those on the honor roll—say they feel increasingly alone and alienated, unable to connect with their parents, teachers and sometimes even classmates. They're desperate for guidance, and when they don't get what they need at home or in school, they cling to cliques or immerse themselves in a universe out of their parents' reach, a world defined by computer games, TV and movies, where brutality is so common it has become mundane. The parents of Eric Harris and Dylan Klebold have told friends they never dreamed their sons could kill. It's an extreme case, but it has made a lot of parents wonder: do we really know our kids?

Many teens say they feel overwhelmed by pressure and responsibilities. They are juggling part-time jobs and hours of homework every night; sometimes they're so exhausted that they're nearly asleep in early-morning classes. Half have lived through their parents' divorce. Sixty-three percent are in households where both parents work outside the home, and many look after younger siblings in the afternoon. Still others are home by themselves after school. That unwelcome solitude can extend well into the evening; mealtime for this generation too often begins with a forlorn touch of the microwave.

In fact, of all the issues that trouble adolescents, loneliness ranks at the top of the list. University of Chicago sociologist Barbara Schneider has been studying 7,000 teenagers for five years and has found they spend an average of 3½ hours alone *every day*. Teenagers may claim they want privacy, but they also crave and need attention—and they're not getting it. Author Patricia Hersch profiled eight teens who live in an affluent area of northern Virginia for her 1998 book, "A Tribe Apart." "Every kid I talked to at length eventually came around to saying without my asking that they wished they had more adults in their lives, especially their parents," she says.

Loneliness creates an emotional vacuum that is filled by an intense peer culture, a critical buffer against kids' fear of isolation. Some of this bonding is normal and appropriate; in fact, studies have shown that the human need for acceptance is almost a biological drive, like hunger. It's especially intense in early adolescence, from about 12 to 14, a time of "hyper self-consciousness," says David Elkind, a professor of child development at Tufts University and author of "All Grown Up and No Place to Go." "They become very self-centered and spend a lot of time thinking about what others think of them," Elkind says. "And when they think about what others are thinking, they make the error of thinking that everyone is thinking about *them*." Dressing alike is a refuge, a way of hiding in the group. When they're 3 and scared, they cling to a security blanket; at 16, they want body piercings or Abercrombie shirts.

If parents and other adults abdicate power, teenagers come up with their own rules. It's "Lord of the Flies" on a vast scale. Bullying has become so extreme and so common that many teens just accept it as part of high-school life in the '90s. Emory University psychologist Marshall Duke, an expert on children's friendships, recently asked 110 students in one of his classes if any of them had ever been threatened in high school. To his surprise, "they all raised their hand." In the past, parents and teachers served as mediating forces in the classroom jungle. William Damon, director of the Stanford University Center for Adolescence, re-

Peril and Promise: Teens by the Numbers

They watch too much television, and their parents may not be around enough, but today's teenagers are committing fewer crimes, having fewer babies and generally staying out of serious trouble. Here's a look at who they are—and what they're up to:

Demographics

THE BREAKDOWN
Teenagers account for roughly 10 percent of the U.S. population.

Teens (13–19)

White
18,199,000   66%

Black
3,992,000   15

Hispanic
3,723,000   14

Asian, Pac. Islander
1,030,000   4

American Indian, Eskimo and Aleut
275,000   1

KIDS HAVING KIDS: A TREND ON THE DECLINE
The birthrate among teens has fallen dramatically, down 16 percent overall.

Birthrates for females 15–19

Percent change, ■ –20% or more   ▨ –5 to –14.9%
1991–97   ▦ –15 to –19.9%

PARENTS AT WORK
Parents work more, so their teenagers are often left unsupervised.

Families with employed parents

■ Both parents
▨ Single mother

1978 1988 1998

DROP IN CRIME
In 1997, kids were responsible for 17 percent of violent-crime arrests.

Arrests per 100,000 juveniles 10–17

Violent-crime rate

1980 85 90 95

Lifestyle

SEXUAL ACTIVITY
Almost one out of five teenagers is still a virgin by the age of 20.

Percentage of teens who have had sexual intercourse, 1995

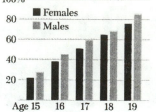

■ Females
▨ Males

Age 15 16 17 18 19

COOLEST BRANDS

Boys	Girls
Nike	Nike
Sony	adidas
Tommy Hilfiger	Tommy Hilfiger
Nintendo	The Gap
adidas	Old Navy

FAVORITE TV SHOWS

Boys	Girls
'The Simpsons'	'Dawson's Creek'
'South Park'	'Friends'
'MTV'	'7th Heaven'
'Home Improve.'	'The Simpsons'
'Friends'	'Buffy the V.S.'

LESS OF THE BAD STUFF: SMOKING, DRINKING AND DOING DRUGS
Today, teens say, they misbehave less than kids in the recent past. The percentage who, in the last 30 days, admit to having used …

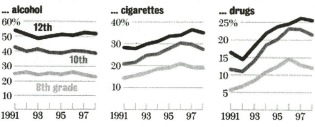

… alcohol   … cigarettes   … drugs

1991 93 95 97

calls writing a satirical essay when he was in high school about how he and his friends tormented a kid they knew. Damon got an "A" for style and grammar, but the teacher took him aside and told him he should be ashamed of his behavior. "That's what is supposed to happen," Damon says. "People are supposed to say, 'Hey, kid, you've gone too far here'." Contrast that with reports from Littleton, where Columbine students described a film class nonchalantly viewing a murderous video created by Eric Harris and Dylan Klebold. In 1999 this apparently was not remarkable behavior.

When they're isolated from parents, teens are also more vulnerable to serious emo-

tional problems. Surveys of high-school students have indicated that one in four considers suicide each year, says Dr. David Fassler, a child and adolescent psychiatrist in Burlington, Vt., and author of "Help Me, I'm Sad: Recognizing, Treating and Preventing Childhood and Adolescent Depression." By the end of high school, many have actually tried to kill themselves. "Often the parents or teachers don't realize it was a suicide attempt," he says. "It can be something ambiguous like an overdose of nonprescription pills from the medicine cabinet or getting drunk and crashing the car with suicidal thoughts."

Even the best, most caring parents can't protect their teenagers from all these problems, but involved parents can make an enormous difference. Kids do listen. Teenage drug use (although still high) is slowly declining, and even teen pregnancy and birthrates are down slightly—largely because of improved education efforts, experts say. More teens are delaying sex, and those who are sexually active are more likely to use contraceptives than their counterparts a few years ago.

In the teenage years, the relationship between parents and children is constantly evolving as the kids edge toward independence. Early adolescence is a period of transition, when middle-school kids move from one teacher and one classroom to a different teacher for each subject. In puberty, they're moody and irritable. "This is a time

when parents and kids bicker a lot," says Laurence Steinberg, a psychology professor at Temple University and author of "You and Your Adolescent: A Parents' Guide to Ages 10 to 20." "Parents are caught by surprise," he says. "They discover that the tricks they've used in raising their kids effectively during childhood stop working." He advises parents to try to understand what their kids are going through; things do get better. "I have a 14-year-old son," Steinberg says, "and when he moved out of the transition phase into middle adolescence, we saw a dramatic change. All of a sudden, he's our best friend again."

IN MIDDLE ADOLESCENCE, ROUGHLY THE first three years of high school, teens are increasingly on their own. To a large degree, their lives revolve around school and their friends. "They have a healthy sense of self," says Steinberg. They begin to develop a unique sense of identity, as well as their own values and beliefs. "The danger in this time would be to try to force them to be something you want them to be, rather than help them be who they are." Their relationships may change dramatically as their interests change; in Schneider's study, almost three quarters of the closest friends named by seniors weren't even mentioned during sophomore year.

Late adolescence is another transition, this time to leaving home altogether. "Par-

Online

HOOKED UP
47% of teens are using the computer to go online this year.

Percentage of teens who go online

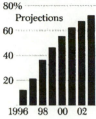

Projections

80%
60
40
20

1996 98 00 02

WHAT DO THEY DO?
They keep up with each other—and what's out there.

Top 10 activities

E-mail	83%
Search engine	78
Music sites	59
General research	58
Games	51
TV/movie sites	43
Chat room	42
Own Web page	38
Sports sites	35

EVERY MOVE THEY MAKE
With age comes online freedom. Here's how parents say they monitor their kids while they're on the Net.

	Age 11–15	16–18
Sit with them while online	38%	9%
Kids can log on only with an adult	34	5
Mainly use for online games	28	15
Limit hours for kids' use	47	21
Know which Web sites kids can visit	68	43
Kids are online whenever they want	54	75
Use the Net more than watching TV	19	22

ents have to be able to let go," says Steinberg, and "have faith and trust that they've done a good enough job as parents that their child can handle this stuff." Contrary to stereotypes, it isn't mothers who are most

Home life

PASSING THE HOURS
Kids spend more time partying than studying each week. They also like tube time.

Activity	percentage of teens/hours	
Watching TV	98%	11.0
Listening to CDs, tapes, etc.	96	9.9
Doing chores	84	4.1
Studying	59	3.7
Going to parties	58	4.0
Going to religious functions	51	2.5
Working at a regular paid job	32	4.7

WHAT WERE WE TALKING ABOUT?
Parents and kids both say they're discussing important life issues.

Issue discussed	parents/kids	
Alcohol/drugs	98%	90%
How to handle violent situations	83	80
Basic facts of reproduction	76	80
AIDS	78	75

● **85%** of teens said that **Mom** cares 'very much' about them. **58%** said the same about **Dad**.

● **25%** of teens said that their **mom** is 'always' **home** when they return from school. **10%** said their **dad** was.

● Do parents let teenagers make their own decisions about weekend **curfew**? **66%** said no.

● How much are teens '**understood**' by their family members? **35%** said 'quite a bit.'

SPENDING HABITS
Teens average just under $100 in total weekly spending.

Weekly spending
■ Allowance ▨ Own

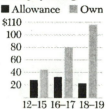

$110
100
80
60
40
20

12–15 16–17 18–19

RESEARCH BY BRET BEGUN. SOURCES: CENSUS BUREAU; BLS; NAT'L CENTER FOR JUVENILE JUSTICE; NCHS; TEENAGE RESEARCH UNLIMITED; MONITORING THE FUTURE STUDY, UNIV. OF MICHIGAN; KAISER FAMILY FOUNDATION; NAT'L LONGITUDINAL STUDY OF ADOLESCENT HEALTH; JUPITER COMMUNICATIONS; GREENFIELD ONLINE; THE ALAN GUTTMACHER INST.

likely to mourn in the empty nest. They're often relieved to be free of some chores. But Steinberg says that fathers "suffer from thoughts of missed chances."

That should be the ultimate lesson of tragedies like Littleton. "Parents need to share what they really believe in, what they really think is important," says Stanford's Damon. "These basic moral values are more important than math skills or SATs." Seize any opportunity to talk—in the car, over the

breakfast table, watching TV. Parents have to work harder to get their points across. Ellen Galinsky, president of the Families and Work Institute, has studied teenagers' views of parents. "One 16-year-old told us, 'I am proud of the fact that [my mother] deals with me even though I try to push her away. She's still there'." So pay attention now. The kids can't wait.

With Anne Underwood

Out of the Mouths of Babes

Voices of At-Risk Adolescents

KORYNNE TAYLOR-DUNLOP and MARCIA M. NORTON

Professional educators and public figures have had much to say in an attempt to educate us in the dynamics of family systems, addiction, and abuse and their impact on the group identified as "at-risk adolescents." The media has been quite graphic in its depiction of children who rear themselves when parents fail them. Newspapers, television, and radio outlets are frequently consumed with stories of crime, disease, poverty, loss of hope, and the absence of heroes.

In the past, dropout theory has linked dropping out with student's background. Over time, the concept of dropping out has evolved into the concept of at-risk, which focuses on the *potential* for dropping out. Dropping out is an event in a long series of life stresses. All students are at risk, but for some students, at a certain point, the risk becomes simply too high.

In addition to being confronted with background obstacles, students experience negative forces in the schools themselves. Those forces or impediments include the lack of intrinsic rewards, teacher obsession with covering curriculum, technical definitions of knowledge, mechanical perceptions of success, and a lack of variety in teaching styles.

Nearly everyone, from politicians to teaching professionals, has had something to say about how to help those students walk across "the bridge to the twenty-first century," but the voice that has consistently been missing from the dialogue is that of the adolescents. An in-depth ethnographic study of eleven at-risk young women, aged 15 to 17, was recently conducted at a high school in a middle class neighborhood in New York State. Two of the girls were in an alternative education program; the remainder were students in the regular program. The three Latino, two Caucasian, and six African American students participated in focus groups, individual interviews, and small group meetings. Data collection included school profile information and shadowing.

Three primary themes emerged: the young women's desire to have adults communicate with them in a non-hurtful way, to have what they learned be meaningful, and to be talked *with* instead of *at*. The intended outcomes of the study were (1) to develop recommendations that would guide school officials in building and sustaining a caring school community and (2) to develop a program that promoted self-esteem.

Persons Perceived as Caring

When the eleven young women were asked whom they turn to when they have a problem and why they turn to that person, they identified remarkably few people. That was also true when they were asked who keeps them in school. The school security guards, a guidance counselor, a female in the community who once had been at risk and since has "made it," a best friend, and a few professional

Korynne Taylor-Dunlop is an assistant professor in the Division of Education, Department of Counseling and Human Services, at Indiana University—South Bend. Marcia M. Norton is a professor in the Department of Educational Administration at the State University of New York at New Paltz.

From *The Clearing House*, May/June 1997, pp. 274–275. Reprinted with permission of the Helen Dwight Reid Educational Foundation. Published by Heldref Publications, 1319 Eighteenth St., NW, Washington, DC 20036-1802. © 1997.

staff members were perceived as the students' primary sources of support. That finding is in accord with Goodman (1995): "For all the reams of research and the endless social jargon, the current troubled state of children in America can be summed up pretty much in one sentence. There aren't enough caring adults in their lives. Most of the adults that children now see live inside of a television set" (79).

When probed, some of the students identified peers and cousins as the caring persons in their lives, primarily because those persons listened and could relate to them:

> My cousin. My cousin can relate to it. She listens and gives good advice, even if I don't like to hear it.

> Friends, no adults, I can't talk to my parents, they don't listen, their way that's it. They throw things back in my face. Friends give good advice. Friends understand more—like about a guy, they are going through the same thing.

The school security guards are often the first person to whom the girls turn:

> Last week I was so upset, Alvin, the security guard, took me to Claire [a female security guard]. My best friend, she is in the hospital for depression [for the third time]. I can talk to Claire, and she can relate. She has good advice.

A few students perceived one counselor, one administrator, and a few teachers to be the persons they turn to when they have a problem:

> Mr. Manilow [a counselor]—I'm cool with him. Dr. Angelou [the assistant principal], she tells me education is important, she helps me out. She wants me to write a book about my life and having babies.

The counselor had been instrumental in acquiring baby clothes for that student, giving her a car seat, and enrolling her in a parenting program. He has also begun researching colleges that have accommodations for teen parents so that she can consider going to college.

In another case, caring behavior on the part of an administrator was interpreted by a student as noncaring. The student had been sexually abused by various family members. She told the assistant principal about the abuse; the assistant principal, together with a counselor, then filed the mandated report to Child Protective Services and attempted to get the student to agree to counseling. She refused. The student commented:

> My English teacher. I just feel close to her. She's always asking me if I'm O.K. Dr. Angelou—I used to like her. But, I told her about a big problem. She told the school, I didn't like that. She betrayed me. I didn't know she'd tell.

Sadly, there were a few students who felt there was no one they either would or could turn to:

> Nobody. I don't trust nobody. I mostly leave it inside. I'm never going to change.

Myself. I keep problems for myself or write in my journal. Myself is the one person I can trust. You never know who will turn on you.

Uncaring People and Situations

When asked to describe noncaring behaviors exhibited by adults in the school, the students engaged in various nonverbal behaviors that indicated their stress or upset. They hugged their bodies, rocked rhythmically, rubbed their eyes, twirled their hair, or put an arm on the chair or around the shoulder of the person who was speaking. A few students engaged in inappropriate laughter due to their lack of comfort. Finally, one said,

> Mr. Godfrey, I hate him so much. He says he can't help you. I went to him the other day and cried and cried. He said nothing, didn't even give me a tissue. My friend was treated the same way. The school has the attitude of "why do I have to bother with them [us]?" It's easier that way for them. The security guards are caring and friendly, they say go to class, stay out of trouble.

A few students focused on teachers in general:

> Teachers should act like they care. But they just want you in and out.

> Everybody should get together. Like the Alternative Education program. Because it's a small group, the teachers have you deal with your problems in small group. Everybody is a friend. I really like it. Teachers have you make all the decisions.

> They should talk to you more and try to help you more.

> We should get equal attention but they make no effort. They focus on the good kids, they don't reach out. My math teacher treats me like dirt. I'm either embarrassed or ignored. I was told in front of the whole class that I failed my test. There should be more respect. Don't throw it in my face.

The students were sensitive to adult attitudes and the ways they are expressed:

> People catch an attitude. The security guard, Delila, is always angry. I can't stand her. She's always talking about people, she's a phony.

> People who scream at me. It's their attitude, tone of voice. Their tone of voice says they are looking down at you.

In response to a question about how the school could become more like a family, one student said,

> The school is so segregated. It bothers me. I want everyone to get along. It is impossible for it to happen. Everyone doesn't want to listen.

Race and ethnicity were considered of major importance to the at-risk students. "It's the real issue," said one. Other students elaborated on how deep the feelings go:

Black, white and Spanish don't mix much. Black don't mix much. Black don't mix at all. You only stay with non-blacks if they are from when you were a little kid. The white kids in class say they can't do the work with these kids [us] in the class.

There are lots of racial fights. Latin, African American. The school is not really trying to make it come together. If anything they try to keep everyone separate. There is a lot of animosity and they do nothing about it.

Racism! I was shocked when I moved here. The whites are favored, the blacks and Hispanics are always wrong.

Supportive Links

Sykes (1990) pointed out that a personality, rather than a technique, a skill, or knowledge, was most important in touching the lives of students. Students remembered teachers' human qualities—their "personality and style, passion and caring, even their eccentricities" (79–80).

Supportive adult links were described in the following ways:

Teachers who care tell me not to go to the Alternative Education Program, that I am too bright. They tell me I can do a lot better. Some teachers really help you.

My counselor calls me down, checks in with me, takes me out to lunch. He says, "How are you doing, how's my daughter?" He knows it's hell with my schoolwork.

They talk to you seriously. They don't yell, like some do. They reach you.
They ask if I'm O.K., they conference with you. They say, "Is your homework done?" They let you know they really want you to pass.

When we asked the students to describe a time that they needed help or information and to whom they went, one student responded:

I need help every day with my work. I ask people at home. There is an older lady, and sometimes I stay at her house. She helps me with my work.

The student had developed a relationship with a neighbor while baby-sitting for the woman's child. The woman serves as both a role model and a safe haven for the student, who lives with her grandfather and mother. The student's mother spends most of her time on the street and the grandfather sexually abused the mother. The student intimated that she is able to fend off her grandfather by escaping to her neighbor's house. The student continued:

No one at school helps me. There are places to get help in school but I have no off periods to go there.

Spending time with friends, which is age appropriate, seemed to be the preferred activity of the young women in the study. Activities centered around going to each other's houses, talking on the phone, talking about their lives. Some spent time at the local teen center; others

went to the local ice cream store and to the mall. Sports, which play a major role for some, represent both a skill and a way to pay for college.

Destructive Links

Those people whom the young people perceive as destructive links were described by them as lacking maturity and creating fear in the student. There was a consensus of opinion that one female security guard was a destructive link:

There is one security guard, Delila. The things she says to you! Delila doesn't like [a female student]. Delila should be more mature, but instead she wants to fight [the student]. Delila, her attitude is bad, she should know [the student] is a little girl. Delila has her own kids and she is twenty-eight to thirty years old. She shouldn't be like that.

Some teachers were cited as failing to be supportive links:

They tell me to come for extra help, and when I get there no one is there and they change the room around and don't tell you where it is.
Teachers have a bad attitude, they say, "I get paid if you pass or don't pass."
They don't pay attention to me, so I don't pay attention to them. I can see through them.

The guidance office received mixed reviews. Only one of the counselors was seen as consistently helpful, approachable, and available to the students:

Mr. Manilow is very helpful. He is looking for colleges where I can bring my daughter. He has helped me realize I can go far away to school even though I have a baby.

I needed information about the Alternative Education program. Mr. Manilow got me the application. He told me I had to wait until January. Working in the Alternative Education Program you do better, there are small classes. They pay attention to me individually. Not like here where there are about 120 kids in some classes.

One of the students responded very negatively about the guidance office:

They are no help. It's the last place I'd go for anything. I hate going there.

When we asked her why, she responded:

Most of the black students are told as freshmen that it's hopeless, helpless for college. That they should just hold on to staying in high school.

Another student had a different reason for not going to the guidance office:

Mainly because of Mr. Godfrey. The secretaries have an attitude. Mr. Godfrey is always in a power struggle. He needs everything his own way. He talks down to me and my parents. He is negative in general, talks down to all the parents. You won't believe what he said to my parents when they talked to him about putting me in the Alternative Education program. He said, "Well, that is mostly for the minorities in this school."

When the students were asked what single thing they would change to improve the school's culture and strengthen the sense of caring, their responses were expressed in a variety of ways, but the message remained the same:

More black kids, teachers. More kids I can relate to.

Get everybody together whether Spanish or black. Do something that everyone participates in.

To determine if a sense of membership exists in the school, we asked if the school is like a family.

No, it's little families—of kids.

Not to me, not a family but different levels of work areas, houses.

It's not like a family because of the cafeteria. Spanish are in one door, black in another door, white on the other side of the cafeteria. If you go out with a black guy, Spanish guys mind that. They talk about you if you do. If you are hanging out with a white person, they talk about you. They say you are turning white . . . a wannabe.

When we asked if there were celebrations or activities that attempted to bring the various cultures together, the uniform answer was no.

Adults Who Help Keep At-Risk Adolescents in School

The at-risk young women at this high school are staying in school by various means of support—role models, heroes, a significant teacher or counselor, and each other. In some cases, they attribute their ability to stay in school solely to their own determination.

Keeping an at-risk student in school sometimes requires the intervention of adults who have skills in networking, exploring resources, and putting strategies in place:

I was pregnant eight months ago. I asked the nurse what to do. She suggested child development classes. Mr. Manilow enrolled me in the Teen Pregnancy Program at another school. We [the student, the nurse, and Mr. Manilow] and a person at the Teen Pregnancy Program discussed how to be a responsible mother, how having to raise a child is, protective sex, labor.

The questions pertaining to whom students saw as successful or as heroes yielded disturbing results. Several students responded in a similar way to this one:

I have no heroes, not even when I was little.

On the brighter side:

Bill Cosby, he's a black person, he made it, rich, stayed together, no one put him down, he's very intelligent.

An older woman I know, she's a teacher, she went to school, supports herself, nobody to help.

Role of the Family and Home

Thirty years of research show that 90 percent of school achievement is determined by how often a child attends school, how much reading is done at home, and how much television a child watches. Studies also show that parental involvement is more important to academic success that the family's income level. Some of the barriers to involvement by parents at the school in this study were described by Boger (1989):

Parents who are underinvovled in their child's education do not lack interest. They have not been afforded the appropriate opportunities, encouragement and support. For many parents, there are several factors that present barriers to involvement in traditional home-school activities: school practices that do not accommodate the growing diversity of the families they serve; parent time and child care constraints; negative experience with schooling; lack of support for cultural diversity; and primacy of basic survival needs. (3)

For some students, school was a safe haven from the psychological and physical harm found at home. We spent many hours with one student before she shared that

I don't tell anyone my problems. I'll only tell you what I want you to know.

After several probes and a lengthy silence, she continued,

[Kids should] ask for help. Try to get someone. Encourage them. Talk to them, ask how they are doing in school. There is no one in my house. I live with my grandfather. *There is no one* there to say, Lucinda, go to school! My grandfather is seventy-four. No one says, go to school, I am on my own. Sometimes I think about moving in with a neighbor, but I don't know, I can't leave my grandfather by himself. But I need someone to take care of *me!* Things are not working out. If it wasn't for [an older woman], I wouldn't be in school.

A few responses indicated that the family system was a weak link in the lives of the young women, particularly with regard to spending time together. One student saw her father once a month, and another student reported that the family members were home at the same time but they did not really sit and talk:

Dinner is the only time I spend with my family. Watching T.V. during dinner.

There were similar responses to the question of what the students would tell families whose children were having difficulty in school. The responses centered on the importance of asking an adolescent why she said or did this or that, being involved, knowing what is going on at school, and talking to the teachers and counselors as well as to the student:

Work with the children. Don't let go. Have hope that they will do well. Help them, talk to them, talk to someone, if they are messing up. Don't say, "I'll forget about you." There is hope.

Pay more attention, ask how is she doing once in a while. Spend more time with her.

See what the problem is. Is something bothering her? Like me, my parents didn't even know I was doing bad. Ask are the kids trying to do what should be done.

One student cited her mother's words of wisdom as a positive influence on a sibling:

My sister was having trouble, my mother did good for her. My mother helped her and said, "You have to learn, it's important or you won't get anywhere." You have to keep reminding the person. Homework, do your homework all the time.

A few students admitted that their parents exhibited a lack of interest in the success or failure of them or a sibling:

My mother is sick and tired of going through problems with my brother. It is up to us to make it. Whether we do or we don't.

My mother doesn't even care. When I show her that I got good grades she says, "Yeah, O.K." If I come home and leave my bookbag on the floor and never move it, she doesn't say, "Did you do your homework?"

[Parents need to] see what's wrong with school. Why doesn't the student like going? Fix the problem. No matter what, fix it. Parents need to find out about homework, but don't pressure too much. My mother nags me sometimes. Parents need to find out about why that specific class is the problem.

In some cases, what may actually be parents' cultural and language barriers to helping students were perceived as evidence of parents not caring for the student:

If you want success, support them totally. My parents don't even know the school curriculum, they are Spanish. So I am by myself. I'm the mother and the father. Mine don't know what's going on. It's always been that way.

Why Students Say They Stay in School

Students reported coming to school for their favorite courses (art and math were the most popular). The students' criteria for a favorite course appeared to depend on the amount of self-expression they could achieve in the class, whether it offered practical application, and whether the subject matter came to them easily, giving them a feeling of mastery or being smart.

One of the impediments to keeping these students in school seems to be the school's revolving door detention/suspension policy. Mann (1986) asserted that the most difficult of the high school's clientele "serendipitously solve the institution's problem by disap-

pearing" (314). A student demonstrated familiarity with this practice:

At [the high school] you cut, you get suspended, you cut, you get suspended. Soon you get so far away from the work that you can't pass. Then you are sixteen and you are dropped out. You're not doing nothing, you're failing, there's no point, you drop out.

The nature, enormity, and tension of the problems with which these students cope make it surprising that they actually come to school and that any learning occurs at all. They named the problems that work against their staying in school, such as:

My brother is in jail.

How problems at home affect school work. I don't want to do nothing. I can see.

Whether or not to be in school. I get lazy and don't go. I need someone to attach to, someone my age, older, black.

Boys. I love my baby's father. We went through a lot of fighting. He hit me while I was pregnant. But we are still together. I was mean when I was pregnant. I hit him, I spit on him. He went to jail after the baby was born. He stole a car. He's out and things are much better now. Babies, sex, relationships.

The students' consensus was that there should be more of what we were doing during the study, that is, meeting with students to discuss their feelings and opinions. One student seemed to speak for the others when she said

I like this group. It helps my feeling inside. I don't like to keep feelings inside, otherwise I blow up.

Summary

Research on successful secondary schools cites four characteristics of such schools: shared values, a sense of belonging, a sense of school membership, and academic engagement (Goodlad 1984; Wehlage 1989). Engagement requires intention, concentration, and commitment by students and staff. As with school membership, the degree of engagement is highly dependent on the institution's contribution to the equation that produces learning. Engagement is a result of interaction between the students, teachers, and curriculum.

Above all, the young women in the study sought and appreciated institutional caring and authentic learning. Students in the Alternative Education Program, who had self-selected into the program, seemed to be more secure in the feeling that teachers saw them as persons, made time for them, and in general, cared for them as people. Overall, the students perceived teachers who were attentive, respectful, helpful, and good at listening as being caring and concerned about the students' social and academic welfare.

Racism was a major theme for the black, Latino, and Caucasian students. The students indicated through their responses that they felt bias from adults as well as from the various ethnic groups of students in the school. Female students did not seem to perceive distinctions or discrimination based on gender.

Achieving understanding and reaching constructive solutions requires putting aside "if only" thinking: if only the kids were the way they used to be, if only families were intact, if only there were more money to hire counselors (Paterson, Purky, and Parker 1986). Schools need to help at-risk students interpret the life they are living. Decisions must be made on how schools are going to teach students the competencies they want them to have, the roles the students can play in reconstructing their neighborhoods, and how the students can change their community. Parallel to this must be the reconstructing of the educational delivery system to meet the needs of all students.

REFERENCES

Boger, J. 1989. The school development program's parents' program: An ecological approach to parent involvement. (Unpublished training material)

Ekstrom, R. B., M. E. Goertz, J. M. Pollack, and D. A. Rock. 1986. Who drops out of high school and why? Findings from a national study. *Teachers College Record* 87 (3): 356–73.

Goodlad, J. I. 1984. *A place called school: Prospects for the future.* New York: McGraw-Hill.

Mann, D. 1986a. Can we help dropouts? Thinking about doing the undoable. *Teachers College Record* 87 (3): 307–23.

———. 1986b. Dropout prevention: Getting serious about programs that work. *NASSP Bulletin* 70 (489): 66–73.

Newmann, F. M., and G. G. Wehlage. 1993. Five standards of authentic instruction. *Educational Leadership* 50 (7): 8–12.

Sykes, G. 1990. Fostering teacher professionalism in schools. In *Restructuring schools: The next generation of educational reform,* edited by R. F. Elmore et al., 59–96. San Francisco: Jossey-Bass.

Wehlage, G. G. 1983. *Effective programs for the marginal high school student.* Bloomington, Ill.: Phi Delta Educational Foundation.

Wehlage, G. G., R. A. Rutter, N. Lesko, and R. R. Fernandez. 1989. *Reducing the risk: Schools as communities of support.* Philadelphia: Falmer Press, Taylor and Francis.

Unit Selections

Key Points to Consider

❖ What are some of the issues raised regarding the Individuals with Disabilities Education Act? What information should parents and teachers of disabled students seek in order to best serve their needs?

❖ Who are the gifted and talented? How can knowledge of their characteristics and learning needs help to provide them with an appropriate education?

❖ What cultural differences exist in our society? How can teacher expectations affect the culturally or academically diverse child? How would multicultural education help teachers deal more effectively with these differences?

❖ What are some of the criticisms concerning multicultural programs?

DUSHKINONLINE **Links**   **www.dushkin.com/online/**

These sites are annotated on pages 4 and 5.

The Equal Educational Opportunity Act for All Handicapped Children (Public Law 94-142) gives disabled children the right to an education in the least-restrictive environment, due process, and an individualized educational program that is specifically designed to meet their needs. Professionals and parents of exceptional children are responsible for developing and implementing an appropriate educational program for each child. The application of these ideas to classrooms across the nation at first caused great concern among educators and parents. Classroom teachers whose training did not prepare them for working with the exceptional child expressed negative attitudes about mainstreaming. Special resource teachers also expressed concern that mainstreaming would mitigate the effectiveness of special programs for the disabled and would force cuts in services. Parents feared that their children would not receive the special services they required because of governmental red tape and delays in proper diagnosis and placement.

It has been more than two decades since the implementation of P.L. 94-142, which was amended by the Individuals with Disabilities Education Act (IDEA) in 1991 and introduced the term "inclusion." Inclusion tries to ensure that disabled children will be fully integrated within the classroom. Many of the above concerns have been studied by psychologists and educators, and their findings have often influenced policy. For example, research has indicated that inclusion is more effective when regular classroom teachers and special resource teachers work cooperatively with disabled children.

The articles concerning the educationally disabled confront many of these issues. In "Taking Inclusion into the Future," the authors discuss the most recent reauthorized Individuals with Disabilities Act, and Susan Lei Lani Stewart presents "Good Questions to Ask: When a Child with a Developmental Delay Joins Your Class."

Other exceptional children are the gifted and talented. These children are rapid learners who can absorb, organize, and apply concepts more effectively than the average child. They often have IQs of 140 or more and are convergent thinkers (i.e., they give the correct answer to teacher or test questions). Convergent thinkers are usually models of good behavior and academic performance, and they respond to instruction easily; teachers generally value such children and often nominate them for gifted programs. There are other children, however, who do not score well on standardized tests of intelligence because their thinking is more divergent (i.e., they can imagine more than one answer to teacher or test questions). These gifted divergent thinkers may not respond to traditional instruction. They may become bored, respond to questions in unique and disturbing ways, and appear uncooperative and disruptive. Many teachers do not understand these unconventional thinkers and fail to

identify them as gifted. In fact, such children are sometimes labeled as emotionally disturbed or mentally retarded because of the negative impressions they make on their teachers. Because of the differences between these types of students, a great deal of controversy surrounds programs for the gifted. Such programs should enhance the self-esteem of *all* gifted and talented children, motivate and challenge them, and help them realize their creative potential. The two articles in the subsection on gifted children consider the characteristics of giftedness, and they explain how to identify gifted students and provide them with an appropriate education.

The third subsection of this unit concerns student diversity. Just as labeling may adversely affect the disabled child, it may also affect the child who comes from a minority ethnic background where the language and values are quite different from those of the mainstream culture. The term "disadvantaged" is often used to describe these children, but it is negative, stereotypical, and apt to result in a self-fulfilling prophecy whereby teachers perceive such children as incapable of learning. Teachers should provide academically and culturally diverse children with experiences that they might have missed in the restricted environment of their homes and neighborhoods. Rita Dunn, in "The Goals and Track Record of Multicultural Education," takes issue with some aspects of multicultural programs while other articles in this section address these individual differences and suggest strategies for teaching these diverse children.

Exceptional and Culturally Diverse Children

Dorothy Kerzner Lipsky and Alan Gartner

Taking Inclusion into the Future

The recently reauthorized Individuals with Disabilities Education Act reinforces the view that inclusion is the best way to educate our students with disabilities. But we still have far to go to make sure all students are given fair opportunities to learn together.

To improve education for children with disabilities, we cannot address special education by itself. Rather, we must look toward educational restructuring—changing the nature and practice of education in general, not just education called "special." The reauthorized Individuals with Disabilities Education Act (IDEA) reflects these needs and propels them further.

Until 1975, with the passage of the Education of All Handicapped Children Act, children with disabilities were not ensured what was a right of their nondisabled siblings and peers, the right to attend public schools. The 1975 law granted a "free appropriate public education" to all children, regardless of the nature or severity of their handicap. In the two decades since then, the U.S. public education system has provided students with that access, an achievement unparalleled anywhere in the world. As such, it both marks what schools can do and provides a basis for what still needs to be done—educational outcomes of high quality for all students.

Special Education, Both Separate and Unequal

Too often in the past, providing access meant that students with disabilities were served in separate special education classes and programs—despite the 1975 law's "least restrictive environment" (LRE) mandate. This mandate required that students with disabilities be educated to the maximum extent with children who were not disabled, and that students with disabilities be removed from regular classes only when they could not be educated in a regular setting with supplementary aids and support services. After more than two decades, the most recent data from the U.S. Department of Education reports that 55 percent of children with disabilities, ages 6 through 21, are not fully included in regular classes. This, despite the fact that more than 71 percent of the five million students with disabilities, ages 6 through 21, served through IDEA in the 1995–96 school year had the least severe impairments—learning disabilities (51 percent) and speech or language impairments (20 percent) (*U.S. Department of Education*, 1997, Tables II–6).

Throughout the 1980s and into the current decade, the experience of students with disabilities, their parents, and their teachers is that a dual system of education fails all students, primarily those with disabilities, in terms of student learning, drop-out rates, graduation rates, participation in postsecondary education and training, and community living (see Lipsky &

Gartner, 1997). The most recent federal study reports that the graduation rate for students with disabilities was 57 percent,[1] as compared with 76 percent for students without disabilities (*U.S. Department of Education*, 1997, p. IV-11).

Longitudinal studies and research findings confirmed the experience of students, parents, and teachers that the separate system was flawed and unequal; this led to many championing a new inclusive design. This model holds to several principles: students are more alike than different; with effective educational practices, schools can educate well and together a wide range of students with better outcomes for all; and separation is costly, a civil rights violation, and a cause for limited outcomes for students with disabilities.

IDEA 1997

Similar beliefs motivated the administration and Congress to reauthorize the federal law. Culminating a two-year process, the reauthorized IDEA emphasizes two major principles: The education of students with disabilities should produce outcomes akin to those expected for students in general, and students with disabilities should be educated with their nondisabled peers. These features are expressed in

From *Educational Leadership,* October 1998, pp. 78-81. © 1998 by the Association for Supervision and Curriculum Development. All rights reserved. Reprinted by permission.

the law's "findings" section, its implementation provisions, and the funding provisions as they concern inclusive education. Although the reauthorization does not mention "inclusive education" (nor had previous laws), one might think of IDEA 1997 as the *Inclusion Development* and *Expansion Act.*

Findings: Congress asserted that the education of students with disabilities would be more effective by "having high expectations for students and ensuring their success in the general curriculum. . . ."; "[ensuring] that special education can become a service for such children rather than a place where they are sent. . . ."; and "providing incentives for whole-school approaches. . . ." The House and Senate Committee reports that accompany the law highlight the primary purpose of the new Act: to go beyond access to the schools and to secure for every child an education that actually yields successful educational results.

Implementation: Two sets of requirements will have direct consequences for students: student evaluation requirements and instruction and assessment requirements. In determining a student's classification and special needs, schools must consider whether factors other than disability will affect the student's performance. Specifically, the law states that a student may not be identified as disabled if the determining factor is inadequacy of instruction in reading or math. In other words, if the failure lies in the school's services, then the remedy is not labeling the student but fixing the school's program.

IDEA consistently reinforces the expectation that a student with a disability will be educated in the general education environment. For example, if a student is or may be participating in the general education program, the individual education program (IEP) team must include a general education teacher. If the child is currently in a general education classroom, the classroom teacher is to be a member of the IEP team. This brings to the IEP process someone familiar with the general education curriculum,

which will be the basis of the student's program. And since the IEP meeting is supposed to be a decision-making event in which parents also participate, a school might be vulnerable to a legal challenge if it fails to include a general education teacher.

Further, should the school system propose that a child with a disability not participate with nondisabled students in academic, extracurricular, or nonacademic activities, it must justify such nonparticipation. In other words, supplemental aids and support services in the general education environment and in the curriculum should be considered the norm; schools must justify and explain exclusion in any of these areas. Only then may they consider other placements.

Schools must develop performance goals drawn from general classroom students for all students with disabilities. They then must develop performance indicators to assess achievement of these goals, with necessary adaptations and modifications. The school's and district's public reports must incorporate the results of performance. This is a requirement for all schools and covers all students.

Funding: States must change their funding formulas for supporting local school districts by removing incentives for placing students in more (rather than less) restrictive environments. This will require changes in all but a handful of states. Additionally, the previous provision that IDEA funds may not be used to benefit nondisabled students has been rescinded. Further, given that general education teachers will be a major role in providing services to students with disabilities, IDEA personnel-preparation funds may be used to train them. Indeed, in language accompanying the

appropriations bills, Congress has emphasized that the substantial new funds must be used for such activities.

Implementing Inclusive Education Programs

In the implementation of the new federal mandate, a growing body of experience can guide practice. Over a two-year period, the National Center on Educational Restructuring and Inclusion (NCERI) surveyed school districts identified by each chief state school officer as implementing inclusive education programs (*NCERI,* 1994, 1995). The reports from nearly 1,000 school districts provide a basis for understanding the factors necessary for successful implementation.

Inclusion goes beyond returning students who have been in separate placements to the general education classroom. It incorporates an end to labeling students.

These are congruent with the findings of a Working Forum on Inclusive Schools, convened by 10 national organizations (*Council for Exceptional Children,* 1995) and reported in an Association for Supervision and Curriculum Development publication (Thousand & Villa, 1995).

The NCERI study identified seven factors for the successful implementation of inclusive education:

1. *Visionary leadership.* This leadership can come from many sources, including school superintendents, building administrators, teachers, parents, school board members, disability advocates, and universities. Whatever the initial impetus for inclusive education programs, all stakeholders must ultimately take responsibility for the outcome.

2. *Collaboration.* The process of inclusive education involves three types of collaboration: between general and special educators, between classroom practitioners and providers of related services, and between those

involved in student evaluation and program development (that is, the IEP team) and classroom practitioners. Each group needs time for collaboration.

3. *Refocused use of assessment.* Schools must replace the traditional screening for separate special education programs with more authentic assessment that addresses student strengths as well as needs and that provides useful guidance for classroom practitioners. Schools must develop and use adapted methods to assess student knowledge. They must question the use of traditional measures of potential (such as IQ tests) and opt for curriculum-based assessment.

4. *Support for staff and students.* School staff must have time to work together and have effective professional development programs. Staff development should be sensitive to the needs of adult learners and involve

with special needs into the general education environment can provide preventive services for some students and enhanced learning opportunities for others, thereby making inclusive education no more costly over time. However, districts that continue to operate under a dual system will be more costly.

6. *Parental involvement.* Because parental involvement is essential, schools report creative approaches to make parents an integral part of the school community. This goes well beyond the procedural due process requirements of the law. For example, in New York City's Community School District 22, pairs of general and special education parents have been instructed about the basis of inclusive education and its benefits for all students.

7. *Effective program models, curriculum adaptations, and instructional practices.* There is no single model of

about individualizing instruction. However, after a year of collaboration, both report greater knowledge and comfort in these areas. They use many of the same instructional strategies in the inclusive education classroom that are effective for students in general classrooms. These include cooperative learning, hands-on learning, peer and cross-age tutoring and support models, instruction based on students' multiple intelligences, classroom technology, and paraprofessionals and classroom assistants (not "Velcroed" to the individual child but serving the whole class).

As Congress pointed out in the reauthorized IDEA, special education should be understood as a service, not a place. Thus, a student (labeled either special or general education) may receive services in a variety of settings or groups. Though not a legal term, inclusion is best expressed in the student who is on the regular register, attends homeroom with her or his peers, participates equally in all school activities, receives instruction suited to her or his needs, is held to the school's common standards, and receives the same report card as other students. As a New York City Public Schools superintendent stated, "Inclusion is about 'ownership.' They are all our students."

As a New York City Public Schools superintendent stated, "Inclusion is about 'ownership.' They are all our students."

more than one-shot experiences. Support for students should include the full panoply of supplemental aids and services that the law mandates, such as curriculum modifications; alternative instructional strategies; adapted assessment measures; and procedures, technology, and roles for paraprofessionals and other support personnel.

5. *Appropriate funding levels and formulas.* Data from school districts about special education funding are limited and difficult to compare. School districts reporting in the *National Study* (NCERI, 1994, 1995) indicate that although there are initial start-up costs for planning and professional development activities, a unitary system over time is not more expensive than separate special education. Funds that follow the student

inclusion. Most common is the pairing of a general and a special education teacher to work together in an inclusive classroom with general and special education students. At one middle school, a special education teacher and his or her class become part of the team. In other settings, a special education teacher serves as a consultant to several general education teachers, in whose classes students with disabilities are included. Increasingly, districts are seeking teachers who are dual licensed and, thus, can themselves teach inclusive classrooms.

Special education teachers often report their lack of knowledge about the general education curriculum, whereas general education teachers often report their lack of knowledge

The Future of Inclusive Education

As Edmonds (1979) declared two decades ago concerning the education of minority students, we know how to provide effective education at the school level, but we have yet to do so on a districtwide basis. So, too, with inclusive education. We have numerous pilot programs and, increasingly, whole-school approaches for inclusion. However, inclusion as yet remains largely a separate initiative, parallel to, rather than integrated within, broad school reforms. Some of the national reforms, especially Slavin's Success for All, Levin's Accelerated Schools, Sizer's Coalition of Essential Schools, Comer's School

Development, and Wang's Community for Learning, incorporate inclusive models (Wang, Haertel, & Walberg, 1998).

Beyond these efforts, other factors are conducive to the expansion of inclusive education. They include the success of inclusive education programs; the now firm legal mandate to educate students with disabilities with their non-disabled peers, especially the requirement that their performance be included in school and district performance reports; public concern for the costs of separate programs that do not serve students with disabilities well; and the growing insistence from parents not only that their children with disabilities be served in the public schools, but also that their children's education be of high quality, preparing them to participate as full and contributing members of an inclusive society. These changes need to occur in more than just school. Commensurate changes must occur in the universities, in the workplace, and in the community.

Inclusion goes beyond returning students who have been in separate placements to the general education classroom. It incorporates an end to labeling students and shunting them out of the regular classroom to obtain needed services. It responds to Slavin's call for "neverstreaming" by establishing a refashioned mainstream, a restructured and unified school system that serves all students together.

[1]This figure exaggerates the total in that it includes not only those students with disabilities who received a standard diploma but also those who received a modified diploma, or a certificate of completion or who "age out."

References

Council for Exceptional Children. (1995). *Creating schools for all our students: What twelve schools have to say.* Reston, VA: Author.

Edmonds, R. (1979). Some schools work and more can. *Social Policy, 9*(5), 26–31.

Lipsky, D., & Gartner, A. (1997). *Inclusion and school reform: Transforming America's classrooms.* Baltimore: Paul H. Brookes.

National Center on Educational Restructuring and Inclusion. (1994). *National study of inclusive education.* New York: Author.

U.S. Department of Education. (1997). *Nineteenth annual report to Congress on the implementation of the Individuals with Disabilities Education Act.* Washington, DC: Author.

Thousand, J. S., & Villa, R. A. (1995). Managing complex change toward inclusive schooling. In R. A. Villa & J. S. Thousand (Eds.), *Creating an inclusive school* (pp. 51–79). Alexandria, VA: ASCD.

Wang, M. C., Haertel, G. D., & Walberg, H. J. (1998). Models of reform: A comparative guide. *Educational Leadership, 55*(7), 66–71.

Dorothy Kerzner Lipsky is Director of the National Center on Educational Restructuring and Inclusion, the Graduate School and University Center, the City University of New York, 33 West 42nd St., New York, NY 10036-8099. **Alan Gartner** is Professor at the City University of New York.

Good Questions to Ask: When a Child with a Developmental Delay Joins Your Class

Susan Lei Lani Stewart

It is always a challenge for a teacher when a child with a developmental delay joins the class. The challenge may be positive and yet overwhelming.

In my own early experience of teaching young children, although I was excited to draw children with developmental delays into the class, I often felt overwhelmed by what I did not know. Traditional questions asked of parents upon their child's enrollment did not always provide the information I needed to truly include the child with a developmental delay.

For example, whether a child has a medical diagnosis of Down syndrome or an educational assessment of a developmental delay, it is critical that the teacher consider the *uniqueness* of the child. While chil-

dren with Down syndrome may have some similar characteristics, each child has individual strengths and needs. A simple diagnosis can never capture the whole individual child.

Today teachers and caregivers have a wealth of resources they can access when a child with a developmental delay joins their class. It is important to tap these resources, but unless the teacher has used or heard about the resources before, obtaining information and support can be daunting.

The questions to ask parents and specialists (that follow) are a good place to begin. These questions have emerged from my experiences in teaching young children with disabilities and delays in community preschools.

From questions to answers

Building relationships with specialists in the community will have a great impact on a teacher's program. Specialists can serve as resources for particular concerns and can refer the teacher or caregiver to

literature or to others with specialized knowledge. Tapping into these resources the educator expands her ability to work with all children competently and confidently.

In areas of the United States that are remote or have few specialists, it is possible for the early childhood educator and caregiver to access helpful information by other means. Each state has an Interagency Coordinating Council (ICC) for the care and education of infants and young children with disabilities. Teachers can contact their state departments of education, health, or welfare to locate area representatives. They can use the Internet to communicate with specialists from other areas.

All of us must Read! Read! but beware, for each author has a particular bent, and information may not be based in research or theory.

Asking questions and seeking answers can seem overwhelming. However, a teacher builds a strong foundation of knowledge that she can employ in her classroom, which in turn makes teaching more pleasurable and effective.

Susan Lei Lani Stewart, Ph.D., is an assistant professor of education and director of the birth to kindergarten program at Salem College in Winston-Salem, North Carolina. As a preschool teacher, Susan included children with delays and disabilities in her classroom.

Reprinted with permission from *Young Children*, September 1999, pp. 25-27. © 1999 by the National Association for the Education of Young Children.

Questions to Ask Parents

It is important to remember that parents respond to disabilities in numerous ways. Sensitivity to the family and respect are critical in fostering a positive parent-preschool relationship. Some parents may not wish to share this information with you.

1. Does your child have any medical or physical issues we should know about so that we can protect him or her from harm while at school?

Many disabling conditions have secondary issues that impact the care and education of young children with developmental delays. For example, some children with Down syndrome have *atlanto-axial subluxation,* a condition causing instability of a neck joint and having implications for physical activity.

2. Is your child eligible for special services through the school district?

This information allows the teacher to determine if there is someone with whom she may consult regarding the child's strengths, needs, and behaviors. If a child is eligible for special services through the public school system, the child will have a service coordinator and will receive services from a multidisciplinary team (MDT) of professionals.

Generally, children who have developmental delays and are between the ages of three and five receive special services through the local school district (or the lead educational agency). Infants and toddlers who have developmental delays may receive services through the local school district or through another agency such as mental health.

3. Does your child have an Individualized Family Service Plan (IFSP) or an Individualized Education Plan (IEP)?

The child who is eligible for special services must have an IFSP or IEP, authorized in the 1997 Amendments to the Individuals with Disabilities Education Act (IDEA). These plans, which guide the intervention services for individual children, are created and carried out by the MDT (i.e., service coordinator, teacher, therapists, family, and other specialists as needed).

The information contained in an IFSP or IEP outlines the strengths of the child, areas in which the child needs additional support, specific goals for the child, how and when the goals are to be met, who will work with the child to meet those goals, how often the child will receive specific services and who will pay for those services, the location in which services will be provided (with a preference for the most natural environment), and plans for the child's transition from one program to the next program. These plans can help the teacher make adjustments in the classroom environment or curriculum to support and facilitate the development of individual children.

4. Are there any services (medical, educational, or therapeutic) that your child is receiving outside of the school district that you think we should know about?

If the parent is comfortable sharing this information, it can be beneficial for the teacher to know what different services therapists or interventionists are providing the child and family so as not to work at cross purposes. Information from therapists and interventionists can help teachers more fully include a child in the class and enable them to support the intervention efforts through classroom activities and experiences.

5. What are your expectations for your child in this class?

Although we often assume that parental desires and expectations are a driving force of the IFSP/IEP, parents may have unwritten expectations about their child's performance in the classroom. Unexpressed expectations may lead to parental dissatisfaction with the preschool experience. In offering parents an opportunity to express their expectations, the teacher implies an honest discussion of the feasibility of meeting parental desires within the preschool environment, creating a parent-teacher relationship built on trust rather than unrealistic expectations and unmet desires.

Ideally the teacher and care provider should be part of the team of professionals acting in the interests of a child who has been identified as eligible to receive special services. For various reasons, at times a team member is overlooked in the process of planning for a child's specialized services or connecting in the information loop. Prepared with questions such as these, the teacher can become an informed and productive team member.

Questions to Ask Specialists

Confidentiality is essential for the protection of the family! Teachers should ask only specific questions of a specialist about a particular child when they have been given written permission by parents. Even if it means that a teacher could serve the child better with more knowledge about what occurs beyond the classroom, respect for the family's right to privacy is imperative.

1. What should I know about this child so that I can effectively involve her in my class and keep her from harm?

Specialists who have previously worked with a child are likely aware of strategies that are particularly effective for that child. Specialists are often trained to see environments with different eyes, which makes them a valuable resource to the teacher for information about adjusting the classroom environment to the unique needs of the individual.

2. May I get a copy of the IFSP or IEP?

When teachers are part of a child's support team, they should have a copy of the child's IFSP/IEP in their files. If the teacher is not currently a part of the child's team, she may want to request of the family that she be included so as to support the child's growth and development while in her care.

3. What are the expectations for this child in my class?

The IFSP/IEP should state explicitly what goals and objectives the child is to work on in particular settings. Professionals, like parents, may also have unwritten expectations about the child's performance in the classroom. It is helpful for teachers to know those expectations and address them appropriately.

4. As the teacher, what are the expectations of me in this child's IFSP/IEP?

If intervention is to occur in the classroom, the IFSP/IEP should state explicitly the expected role of the child's teacher. Teachers may be expected to assist the child in achieving goals and objectives, track the child's progress, assess his skills, and evaluate how well the program is supporting the child's progress toward the goals established in the IFSP/IEP.

A teacher may not be expected to work specifically with the child on his goals, but to welcome specialists into the classroom to work with the child or schedule her day to accommodate pullout services in a separate room. The variations on these themes are many. A teacher being clear at the outset as to her roles and responsibilities can prevent a lot of confusion and uncomfortable situations.

5. What can I do in the classroom to support outside intervention efforts?

If a child receives intervention services only in environments other than the classroom, the teacher can also support the child's use of new and developing skills under the guidance of the intervention specialists. Even if the classroom is not considered the primary site of intervention, all of the child's environments should work in tandem to support her growth and development so that she has multiple opportunities to practice and refine her skills.

6. How can I deal with [mention a specific concern]?

Since children typically spend a large portion of their day in preschool or child care, teachers have the opportunity to observe a child from a broad perspective and inform team members of their observations. A teacher is likely to have many questions about a child's behavior that have not been addressed previously by other team members. It may be that others have not observed the child exhibiting specific behaviors that concern the teacher.

Specialists who have worked with many different children, however, may support the teacher greatly in investigating the behaviors further and provide helpful suggestions on addressing the behaviors. Sometimes a behavior warrants specialized intervention. In any case, teachers should not hesitate to ask. Their action may alert the team to a significant concern, ease the teachers' own minds, build up their professional repertoires of teaching skills, and/or support the growth and development of the child—all valid reasons to ask questions.

Resources

Council for Exceptional Children
1920 Association Drive
Reston, VA 22091-1589
800-328-0272, TDD: 703-264-9449
http://www.cec.sped.org
Division for Early Childhood:
http://www.dec-sped.org
Young Exceptional Children
The Division for Early Childhood of the Council for Exceptional Children—
303-620-4576
1444 Wazee Street, Suite 230
Denver, CO 80202

For further reading

Allred, K.W., R. Briem, & S.J. Black. 1998. Collaboratively addressing needs of young children with disabilities. *Young Children* 53 (5): 32–36.

Chandler, P. 1994. *A place for me: Including children with special needs in early care and education settings.* Washington, DC: NAEYC.

Murphy, D.M. 1997. Parent and teacher plan for the child. *Young Children* 52 (4): 32–36.

Olson, J., C.L. Murphy, & P.D. Olson. 1999. Readying parents and teachers for the inclusion of children with disabilities: A step-by-step process. *Young Children* 54 (3): 18–22.

Tertell, E.A., S.M. Klein, & J.L. Jewett, eds. 1998. *When teachers reflect: Journeys toward effective, inclusive practice.* Washington, DC: NAEYC.

Wolery, M., P.S. Strain, & D.B. Bailey. 1992. Reaching potentials of children with special needs. In *Reaching potentials: Appropriate curriculum and assessment for young children*, S. Bredekamp & T. Rosegrant eds. Vol. 1, 92–111. Washington, DC: NAEYC.

Wolery, M., & J.S. Wilbers, eds. 1994. *Including children with special needs in early childhood programs.* Washington, DC: NAEYC.

Meeting the Needs of Gifted Learners in the Early Childhood Classroom

Brooke Walker,
Norma Lu Hafenstein,
and Linda Crow-Enslow

In one corner of an early childhood classroom, there is a cave constructed of brown butcher paper. Stalactites and stalagmites fabricated from iridescent cellophane hang from the roof of the cave. A model of a volcano, painted in bright colors, graces the window. The parts of the volcano are labeled: magma, lava, crater, crust, and ash. Inside the volcano are "gems" fashioned from glitter that sparkles when the sun shines through the window. Hanging from the classroom ceiling is a large model of the earth with the interior parts labeled: crust, mantle, outer core, and inner core. Stories written or dictated by the children, titled "When I Went to the Center of the Earth," decorate the walls.

Fifteen children, ages three and four, are engrossed in many different learning-center activities designed around the theme The Earth, their present integrated-thematic unit. In the block center three children build ramps to roll their rocks down. Brian exclaims as he knocks down a ramp, "An earthquake struck and broke my ramp."

In the math center Sarah separates rocks into sets of eight. Steven is adding up his rocks: "One plus four is five," he counts as he writes the answer in his equation book. In the science center Patty sorts rocks into "soft" and "hard" piles. George and Sally are weighing rocks on a scale, then graphing results with a teacher's help. In the art center two children create sand paintings while two others paint "pet rocks." In the language center Peter writes different rock words to put in his "Can Can," a small can

containing slips of paper with unit words on them: earth, cave, rock, mantle, plate, volcano, fault, crust, lava, fossil, core.

True learning in early childhood occurs when children involve themselves in a variety of developmentally appropriate learning experiences presented in an interdisciplinary manner. Effective early childhood teachers continually adapt and expand these experiences to respond to the individual needs of the children in their classrooms.

The vignettes above describe activities in a classroom in which an integrated-thematic curriculum has been designed to meet the needs of young gifted children. To develop an appropriate curriculum for these children, early childhood teachers need an understanding of the characteristics that distinguish such children from their peers and ways to differentiate the curriculum to address their educational needs.

Today the concept of giftedness is expanding beyond the traditional emphasis on general academic prowess (Nutall, Romero, & Kalesnick 1992). Research with preschoolers is pinpointing capabilities that may be the building blocks of giftedness in differentiated areas such as science, art, and music (Goldsmith & Feldman 1985; Wexler-Sherman, Gardner, & Feldman 1988). Recognizing this, Nutall, Romero, and

From *Young Children*, January 1999, pp. 32-36. © 1999 by the National Association for the Education of Young Children (NAEYC). Reprinted by permission.

There are many types of giftedness. A person can be musically gifted, artistically gifted, athletically gifted, and so on. This article is about intellectually gifted children.

Kalesnick (1992) propose the following definition for gifted children:

> Gifted children are those showing sustained evidence of advanced capability relative to their peers in general academic skills and/or in more specific domains (music, art, science, etc.) to the extent that they need differentiated educational programming. (p. 302)

Characteristics of young intellectually gifted children

Labeling children is not a preferred method of dealing with differences; however, it is sometimes necessary in order to provide children with appropriate educational programming. Although there are always differences among children (Barbour 1992), research has demonstrated that as a group, young gifted children possess characteristics that distinguish them from their peers in the areas of cognitive, affective, and physical development.

In their cognitive development, young gifted children may demonstrate a high level of language development, an accelerated pace of thought, the ability to generate original ideas and solutions, a sensitivity to learning, and the ability to synthesize and think abstractly (Roedell, Jackson, & Robinson 1980; Hollinger & Kosak 1985; Lewis & Michaelson 1985; Parke & Ness 1988; VanTassel-Baska 1988; Lewis & Louis 1991).

These children's attention spans and interests often differ from the norm. They are able to concentrate for comparatively long periods of time on subjects that interest them. In many cases they develop "passion" areas in which they are intensely interested (Parke & Ness 1988).

There may be discrepancies between physical and intellectual development (Roedell 1990). Motor skills, often fine-motor, lag behind cognitive and conceptual abilities (Webb & Kleine 1993). Young gifted children may see in their mind's eye what they want to draw or construct, but their motor skills do not allow them to achieve their goal (Webb 1994).

In their affective development, young gifted children often have an evaluative approach to themselves and others. They attempt to organize people and things in a search for consistency and justice. They may invent complex games and try to organize their playmates (Webb 1994).

Young gifted children are often very sensitive to their emotions and those of others (Schetky 1981). They are more aware of the world around them, of their place in it, and of the relationships between people and places, time and spaces. Their mature vocabularies and ideas and frequently uneven development make them vulnerable to social isolation if they lack interaction with children of similar abilities.

These children are still preschoolers developmentally, however, and their curriculum needs to emphasize exploration, manipulation, and play (Parke & Ness 1988). As Riley notes,

> Much of the knowledge children absorb is best acquired by exploration in the real world where they may freely, actively, construct their vision of reality, rather than be passively instructed about it. (1974, 139)

Young children learn by observing what happens when they interact with materials and people. Development of their skills is achieved through hands-on learning (Piaget & Inhelder 1969).

Developing curriculum to meet the needs of high-ability young children

While young gifted children need developmentally appropriate activities similar to those of their same-age peers, their unique characteristics dictate the need for curriculum differentiation. Children with advanced abilities require opportunities to be exposed to and use the vocabulary and concepts typically used by much older children. They need to study subjects in depth because they have unusually keen powers to make con-

Photo courtesy of the authors

nections and perceive relationships. Curriculum should be individualized to meet their high levels of ability in particular domains.

An integrated-thematic curriculum can be adapted to meet the needs of young gifted children while also meeting the needs of the other children in the classroom. It is an enrichment tool in the highest sense. It provides children with an intellectual framework not available when studying only one content area and exposes them to many ideas not covered in traditional curricula (Van-Tassel-Baska 1988). The children described at the beginning of the article enjoy learning complex vocabulary such as magma, lava, and crust. However, their learning activities such as building a ramp with blocks or comparing soft and hard rocks are experiential and hands-on.

Providing depth

The first step in developing an integrated-thematic curriculum appropriate for young gifted children is to select an overarching theme around which to organize the year of study. The theme provides children with the opportunity to see and understand relationships while they explore concepts in depth.

For instance, teachers in our early childhood classroom example selected the theme "The Magic School Bus Explores My World and Beyond." It is based on the Magic School Bus series of books in which the children "ride" in a magic school bus through their different units of study. Month by month children explore a variety of social studies and science units that relate to the overall theme. Teachers select units that are rich in content and appeal to young children. Within each unit, all disciplines are represented in developmentally appropriate and meaningful ways.

In our example four units were chosen to express the exploration theme: The Human Body, The Earth, The World of the Imagination, and Rainforests. The units become mean-

ingful as the children participate in creating unit-related environments in the classroom—during the rainforest unit the children made life-size replicas of plants, trees, and animals that live and grow in the rainforest.

Providing connections between the disciplines

In *Interdisciplinary Curriculum: Design and Implementation,* Jacobs (1989) writes that one disadvantage of integrated curriculum is that it can suffer from the "potpourri" approach: units may become samplings of knowledge without incorporating the different disciplines and skills to be covered. Teachers can avoid this problem by employing a web such as the one on the next page titled "Design for an In-Depth Integrated Unit."

When teachers design activities and lessons using this structure, they attend to each of the disciplines and to the connections between them. The web contains opportunities for higher-level thinking and creativity. Maker (1982) includes higher-level thinking skills as essential elements in a curriculum for high-ability children. Gifted learners also have a very high potential for creative activity and should begin developing that potential as early as possible (Clark 1997).

Guiding *inquiry questions* provide a framework for the experiences in which the children engage. These types of questions provide a focus for children's exposure to key ideas and themes within and across domains of knowledge (VanTassel-Baska 1988). For example, the guiding inquiry questions for the human body unit in The Magic School Bus Explores My

World and Beyond theme include the following:

1. What are the systems in the body?
2. How do they work together?
3. How does what I do affect my body?
4. How do I care for my body?

Additionally, inquiry questions lend personal meaning to the study. In answering unit questions, children are encouraged to explore how their learning relates to them personally. The last two questions address this issue specifically: "How does what I do affect my body?" and "How do I care for my body?"

"How to Develop an In-Depth Integrated Unit" is a complete web that builds on the basic skills and disciplines, using a variety of specialized activities relating to the human body, the chosen unit of study.

Providing opportunities to address content at different levels

Besides providing young gifted children with occasions to explore topics in depth and make connections between disciplines, a meaningful curriculum needs to furnish children with opportunities to address content at many different levels.

Individualizing means recognizing and allowing for differences in development, understanding, approach to learning, and interests when teachers plan activities so that there is sufficient variety to meet the needs and interests of each child (Dodge & Colker 1992). In the case of young gifted children, individualizing means making sure that

Curriculum should always be created so that high-ability and low-ability children, children with special needs, and children with special gifts can individually find it challenging and achievable.

children are allowed to develop their abilities even though they are working at a level above what is considered age or grade appropriate.

Consider the example of Adam. When Adam entered an early childhood program at age three, he could read at a third-grade level. Participating with the class in learning to recognize the letters of the alphabet would have been frustrating to Adam and inhibiting to his development. Teachers designed an individualized reading program for Adam in which he read books appropriate for him during times when other children were learning their letters. He was allowed to write his own stories in the writing center and read them to the class.

Individualization can be accomplished in both learning-center and group activities.

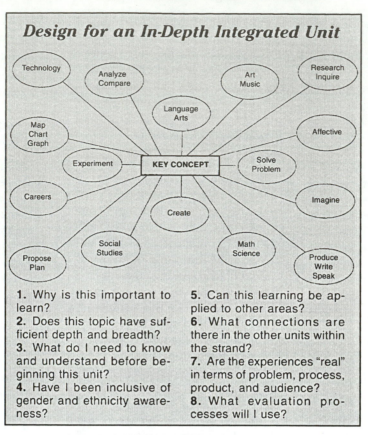

Design for an In-Depth Integrated Unit

1. Why is this important to learn?
2. Does this topic have sufficient depth and breadth?
3. What do I need to know and understand before beginning this unit?
4. Have I been inclusive of gender and ethnicity awareness?
5. Can this learning be applied to other areas?
6. What connections are there in the other units within the strand?
7. Are the experiences "real" in terms of problem, process, product, and audience?
8. What evaluation processes will I use?

of skill and concept development. Some of the learning-center activities presented during the human body unit include

- comparing animal bones with replicas of human bones,
- dictating or writing stories that include facts about bodies,
- weighing fruits and vegetables and graphing their differences,
- using spaghetti and meatballs to do math problems,
- creating self-portraits,
- creating skeletons from Popsicle sticks, and
- counting the number of tiles needed to equal the length of the small intestine.

Learning-center activities address different levels of ability. While one child chooses to use spaghetti and meatballs to practice counting, another child may use them to add and subtract. Some children read their stories to a teacher or a parent volunteer, while others dictate stories. A child gifted in music might write a song to fit the unit.

While all good preschool programs include choice in activities, offering activities that address the highest level of skills of the children in the class ensures that the learning needs of all children are met.

Learning-center activities

Learning centers encourage both autonomy and self-control. They allow

children to take responsibility for their own learning and engage in activities that interest them (Isbell 1995). Teachers can design learning centers to meet the needs of young gifted children by generating activities that challenge the children's highest level

Group activities

Group activities provide the opportunity for children to develop a classroom community and learn content that is unfamiliar to all of them. During the human body unit, the children role-played blood cells passing through the heart and lungs, sang songs about the body parts, dissected animal organs (with adult help), and acted out organ functions.

The children's interests help to guide the unit of study. If a class is

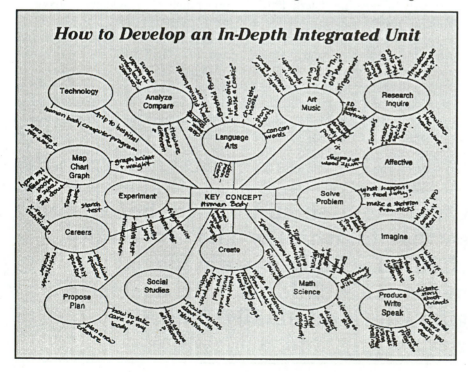

How to Develop an In-Depth Integrated Unit

Curriculum for high-ability children should never be shallowly show-offy. Curriculum for any child should be meaningful.

particularly interested in the senses, for example, more time may be spent on this topic than on others. Guest speakers and field trips are interesting to all children and provide enrichment to the curriculum for young gifted learners.

In summary

All children have unique patterns of development, individual interests, and needs. Many gifted young children, however, share some common characteristics and needs in the cognitive, physical, and social and emotional domains. An integrated-thematic curriculum, which is appropriate for all early childhood learners, can be adapted to meet gifted children's needs by providing opportunities for in-depth study and concept development. Individualizing activities to meet children's highest level of ability will ensure that high-ability young children's educational needs are met.

References

Barbour, N. B. 1992. Early childhood gifted education: A collaborative perspective. *Journal for the Education of the Gifted* 15 (2): 145–62.

Clark, B. 1997. *Growing up gifted.* 5th ed. Upper Saddle River, NJ: Prentice Hall.

Dodge, D. T., & L. J. Colker. 1992. *The creative curriculum for early childhood.* 3d ed. Mt. Rainier, MD: Gryphon House. (ERIC Document No. ED 342 487).

Goldsmith, L. T., & D. H. Feldman. 1985. Identifying gifted children: The state of the art. *Pediatric Annals* 14 (10): 709–16.

Hollinger, C., & S. Kosak. 1985. Early identification of the gifted and talented. *Gifted Child Quarterly* 29 (4): 168–71.

Isbell, R. 1995. *The complete learning center book: An illustrated guide for 32 different learning centers.* Brooklyn, NY: Gryphon.

Jacobs, H. H. 1989. The growing need for interdisciplinary curriculum content. In *Inter-disciplinary curriculum: Design and implementation,* ed. H. H. Jacobs, 13–24. Alexandria, VA: Association for Supervision and Curriculum Development.

Lewis, M., & B. Louis. 1991. Young gifted children. In *Handbook of gifted education,* eds. N. Colangelo & G. Davis, 365–81. Needham Heights, MA: Allyn & Bacon.

Lewis, M., & L. Michaelson. 1985. The gifted infant. In *The psychology of gifted children: Perspectives on development and education,* ed. J. Freeman, 35–57. New York: Wiley.

Maker, C. J. 1982. *Teaching models in the education of the gifted.* Rockville, MD: Aspen.

Nutall, E. V., I. Romero, & J. Kalesnick. 1992. *Assessing and screening preschoolers: Psychological and educational dimensions.* Needham Heights, MA: Allyn & Bacon.

Parke, B., & T. Ness. 1988. Curricular decision making for the education of young children. *Gifted Child Quarterly* 32 (1): 196–99.

Piaget, J., & B. Inhelder. 1969. *The psychology of the child.* New York: Basic.

Riley, S. S. 1974. Some reflections on the value of children's play. In *Providing the best for young children,* eds. J. McCarthy & C. R. May, 138–45. Washington, DC: NAEYC.

Roedell, W. C. 1990. *Nurturing giftedness in young children.* Report No. EDO-EC-90. Reston, VA: Council for Exceptional Children. (ERIC Document No. ED 321 492).

Roedell, W., N. Jackson, & H. Robinson. 1980. *Gifted young children.* New York: Teachers College Press.

Schetky, D. H. 1981. The emotional and social development of the gifted child. *Gifted Child Today* 4 (3): 2–4.

Webb, J. T. 1994. *Nurturing social-emotional development of gifted children.* Report No. EDO-EC-93-10. Reston, VA: Council for Exceptional Children. (ERIC Document Reproduction Service No. ED 372 554).

Webb, J. T., & P. A. Kleine. 1993. Assessing gifted and talented children. In *Testing young children,* eds. J. Culbertson & D. Willis, 383–407. Austin, TX: Pro-Ed.

Wexler-Sherman, C., H. Gardner, & D. H. Feldman. 1988. A pluralistic view of early assessment: The Project Spectrum approach. *Theory into Practice* 27 (1): 77–83.

VanTassel-Baska, J. 1988. Curriculum for the gifted: Theory, research, and practice. In *Comprehensive curriculum for gifted learners,* eds. J. VanTassel-Baska, J. Feldhusen, K. Seeley, G. Wheately, L. Silverman, & W. Foster, 1–17. Needham Heights, MA: Allyn & Bacon.

For Further Reading

Bredekamp, S., & C. Copple, eds. 1997. *Developmentally appropriate practice in early childhood programs.* Rev. ed. Washington, DC: NAEYC.

Foster, S. M. 1993. Meeting the needs of gifted and talented preschoolers. *Children Today* 22 (3): 23–30.

James, R., & L. Johnson. 1991. The preschool/primary gifted child. *Journal for the Education of the Gifted* 14 (3): 56–63.

Kitano, M. 1989. The K–3 teacher's role in recognizing and supporting young gifted children. *Young Children* 44 (3): 57–63.

Smutny, J. F., K. Veenker, & S. Veenker. 1989. *Your gifted child: How to recognize and develop the special talents in your child from birth to age seven.* New York: Ballantine.

Whitmore, J. R. 1986. *Intellectual giftedness in young children: Recognition and development.* New York: Haworth.

Wolfle, J. 1989. The gifted preschooler: Developmentally different, but still three or four years old. *Young Children* 44 (3): 41–48.

Brooke Walker, M.A., *has taught at the Ricks Center for Gifted Children in Denver, Colorado, for seven years. She has made presentations on the education and development of young gifted children at state and national conferences. Her research has been published in* Gifted Child Quarterly, Roeper Review, *and* Research in Middle Level Education Quarterly.

Norma Lu Hafenstein, Ph.D., *is founder and director of the Ricks Center for Gifted Children. She consults throughout the country on giftedness and has works published in* Gifted Child Quarterly, Roeper Review, *and* Research in Middle Level Education Quarterly.

Linda Crow-Enslow, M.A., *has taught early childhood education for eight years and has presented the gifted education curriculum model used in the early childhood classrooms at state and national conferences.*

How All Middle-Schoolers Can Be "Gifted"

By Jay A. McIntire
From *NASSP Bulletin*

As much as we would like students not to compare themselves based on school success, grades, or other measures of achievement, they must do so to fulfill their identity formation task. They will compare themselves on any criterion that occurs to them. Instead of fighting this comparison, we should take advantage of it.

Middle-level schools, by expanding the use of certain positive aspects frequently associated with gifted education programs, can greatly increase the positive identity messages students receive. This increases the chances for students to develop identities with positive feelings and self-perceptions with respect to school and their ability to succeed in school.

Students who participate in gifted education programs receive several messages that allow them to affiliate and discriminate themselves in ways that lead to an identity based on positive traits. Perhaps the most powerful message is that the student can achieve success in school and through school. Anything educators do to provide such messages to the maximum number of students should be encouraged.

Positive influences of gifted education participation on identity formation include the following: sets students apart from peers (distinction); provides group membership (affiliation); provides positive identity message; may prove self-fulfilling; may result in an improved match between instructional level and instruction received.

Unfortunately, participation in gifted education can also result in identity messages that are confusing or might even undermine healthy identity formation. The same distinction from peers that may be positive for some can be negative for others. If the distinction is not only from most peers, but from all one's friends from various group affiliations, identification of a gift or talent can lead to identity confusion or underachievement. Some students, parents, and teachers also confuse identified high potential with increased value or even outright superiority. This is less often a problem among students than among the adults involved.

Negative influences of gifted education participation on identity formation include the following: sets students apart from peers; can be confused with increased value or worth; group membership is not equitably available; lacks connotation of effort; may set unrealistic expectations; may be seen as one-size-fits-all; high, flat profile may be identity challenge.

For many reasons, all of which must be overcome, almost all systems for identifying outstanding potential have been relatively unsuccessful in recognizing ability among members of certain minorities, individuals from economically stressed homes and communities, and students with disabilities. Thus, any positive messages (not to mention educational opportunities) are not evenly distributed.

Another equity problem is seen in some poorly designed gifted programs that treat all students the same, rather than matching differentiated learning experiences to areas of demonstrated need. Such programs not only undermine the development of talent, but deny students the opportunity to benefit from distinctions between themselves and their gifted peers based on areas of strength, interest, or other factors.

Gifted education programs also can give unintended negative identity messages to students who do not participate in them. This is especially

Reprinted from *The Education Digest,* May 1998, pp. 57–61, Ann Arbor, Michigan.

common in schools whose gifted education programs are not sufficiently rigorous. In these cases, many students rightly say, "I could do that."

Identity Messages

If every child was gifted at something, which obviously is not the case, what identity messages would be provided by gifted education? It would be impossible for gifted programs to be one-size-fits-all, so a wide variety of individually matched programs would be provided for developing a vast range of gifts and talents. This would provide each student with a strength-based identity message while giving them group affiliation with others whose recognized potential was in a related or similar area.

Few gifted children have outstanding potential in the limited subjects covered by traditional curricula. If schools devoted time to providing in-depth learning opportunities in many more areas, we could identify and provide programs and positive identity messages for far more students with outstanding potential.

A small town once had a dance studio. Although a large number of students received positive identity messages from their experiences at this studio after school and on weekends, these achievements were rarely recognized or taken advantage of in school. Some students thought of themselves as failures in school, but successes in dance. If the school had provided resources relating to dance, some of these early adolescents would have received the message that excellence in dance was appreciated by the school and that school could contribute to dance excellence.

Middle-level schools can increase the number of students for whom school seems relevant by recognizing excellence being developed outside school and fostering these developments through school. When a student is gifted and talented at home but learning-disabled or failing at school, the discrepancy may be due to a disconnect between the limited curricular options in school and the unlimited options offered by life.

Although administrators and team members already have scheduling nightmares, making space in the schedule for long-term development of individual student expertise would allow all students to receive the positive identity messages associated with students in gifted education. Such strength-based school models are becoming more common in recent school reforms. By making the development of expertise an expectation for each student, both positive group affiliation and individual distinction become possible.

Defining Broadly

It is hard to imagine an early adolescent who is recognized as the school's expert on a subject feeling incapable of learning or succeeding in high school and beyond. A feeling of expertise, when applied to any endeavor, is bound to contribute to identity development. Is expertise possible for every student (or even most)? Yes, if expertise is defined broadly.

The goal of a middle-level school should not be to develop expertise on an adult scale, but to assist each student in learning something that is unique among their school peers. By using the school's resources and expertise and the natural curiosity and interest of each student, and by providing time and support for hard work over an extended period, schools could make the production of in-house experts a central part of their missions.

Essential middle-level features such as teaming, advisory, flexible block scheduling, and curricular choices are well-suited to the development of individual expertise. Service learning and problem-based learning determined by student choice are also well-suited to such an educational focus.

A middle school devoted to maximizing positive identity formation would be an "expert factory." With a quality staff and three years of a couple hours a week devoted to the understanding of expertise and the development of experts, there would be few students leaving for high school who did not believe they could learn and succeed.

What are requirements for the development of expertise through school? Expert performance relies on a long-term, positive interaction between a student's basic skills, abilities, interests, creativity, and prior experiences, on the one hand, and a school's context (environment, peers, culture, expectations, etc.), curriculum, teachers, teaching, leadership, and creativity.

The resulting experts from different expert factories probably would have different characteristics. Developing a definition of expertise and a set of criteria for demonstrating expertise would involve the staff, parents, and students. To demonstrate expertise before graduation, a student might need to document, via portfolio, numerous learning skills applied to their chosen area. Most portfolio standards for middle-level expertise probably would require the gathering of information using multiple sources, including demonstration of the use of reading and computer technology. Most would require communicating one's expertise through at least two modes. The possibilities are almost endless.

Would all experts have skills that seem alike in the end? Absolutely not. One student might develop expertise as a flutist; reading, listening, performing, learning the basics of how waves in air result in sound, and assisting with flute lessons for beginners might all be part of a portfolio. A second student, experiencing developmental delays, but with a favorite dog, might choose to become the school's expert on beagles.

A third student might choose to explore certain areas of mathematics, including calculus. While such study might be beyond the interest and capability of most middle-level students, it is unlikely that the student developing calculus expertise would know as much about the flute or about beagles as the students who focused on those areas.

Positive Signs for All

By making the development of unique expertise a goal and an expectation for each student in the school, each one could gain positive identity messages and learning opportunities currently provided only to students in quality gifted education programs. Using such a focus, a middle-level school could increase the number of students receiving positive identity messages relating to school; increase the responsibility of each student for their education; increase the recognition of individual, family, and cultural values and interests; increase the level of challenge for each student; and increase learning for each student.

Gifted students would also benefit from such a system. Any differentiation of their curriculum, even outside the hours set aside for developing expertise, would be consistent with the school's overall mission. These students would continue to feel distinct based on the expertise they would be developing, but this challenging and identity-affirming experience would be shared by every student, providing for affiliation needs. The positive identity formation aspects of gifted education would be maintained without the negatives.

Implementing an expert development program would not supplant any aspect of curriculum currently provided. Such a program would not obviate the need for differentiating some curriculum for many gifted students, although it probably would for some.

To summarize, middle-level schools are uniquely able to help early adolescents develop healthy, positive identities that include an understanding that they can achieve success in at least some aspect of school and that school has something to contribute to their developing areas of personal interest. One way schools might approach this goal would be to promote the development of individual expertise.

To develop and recognize individual expertise, schools would need to vastly increase breadth of areas in which excellence is recognized, valued, and developed; become more aware of individual students' interests and goals;

create a school climate in which expertise is accepted and expected; provide time and resources to the development of expertise; develop criteria students would need to document their expertise; and make developing expertise the mission, moto, and culture of the school.

Schools that develop experts would also see such positive outcomes as:

- Increased teacher appreciation and understanding of individual student strengths;
- An achievement orientation in each student;
- Diminished confusion between excellence and personal value;
- Awareness in each student that he or she can excel at something, given careful selection, quality education, and hard work over a period of time;
- Higher personal expectations and aspirations;

- Increased school understanding of personal, familial, and cultural values and interests; and
- Increased student input and responsibility.

Best of luck in developing the identities of your incoming middle-level students. You can do it. After all, you are the expert!

Jay A. McIntire is Policy Specialist, Council for Exceptional Children, 1920 Association Drive, Reston, Virginia 20191. Condensed from NASSP Bulletin, *82 (February 1998), 110–18. Published by National Association of Secondary School Principals, from which related educational materials are available by contacting NASSP, 1904 Association Drive, Reston, Virginia 20191 (phone: 703-860-0200).*

Rita Dunn

The Goals and Track Record of Multicultural Education

Paying attention to the varied learning styles of all students will do more to accomplish the goals of multicultural education than misguided programs that often divide children.

Because multicultural education is a volatile political issue—one with articulate proponents and antagonists on both sides—the research on this topic needs to be examined objectively. Many practices that schools promote make little sense in terms of how multiculturally diverse students learn. Thus, we need to examine the data concerning how poor achievement has been reversed among culturally diverse students in many schools.

What Is Multicultural Education?

Multicultural education originated in the 1960s as a response to the long-standing policy of assimilating immigrants into the melting pot of our dominant American culture (Sobol 1990). Over the past three decades, it has expanded from an attempt to reflect the growing diversity in American classrooms to include curricular revisions that specifically address the academic needs of students. In recent years, it has been distorted by some into a movement that threatens to divide citizens along racial and cultural lines (Schlessinger 1991). Generally, multicultural education has focused on two broad goals: increasing academic achievement and promoting greater sensitivity to cultural differences in an attempt to reduce bias.

Increasing Academic Achievement

Efforts intended to increase the academic achievement of multicultural groups include programs that (1) focus on the research on culturally based learning styles as a step toward determining which teaching styles or methods to use with a particular group of students; (2) emphasize bilingual or bicultural approaches; (3) build on the language and culture of African- or Hispanic-American students; and (4) emphasize math and science specifically for minority or female students (Blanks 1994). Programs in each of these categories are problematic.

■ *Culturally based learning styles.* So long as such programs include rea-

Photo courtesy of St. John's University's Center for the Study of Learning and Teaching Styles

Twenty percent of students in every culture are tactual learners—children who begin concentrating on new and difficult information by manipulating resources with their hands.

From *Educational Leadership,* April 1997, pp. 74–77. © 1997 by the Association for Supervision and Curriculum Development. All rights reserved. Reprinted by permission.

Photo courtesy of St. John's University's Center for the Study of Learning and Teaching Styles

At least 20 percent of all students in every culture are kinesthetic learners who cannot sit in their seats for very long; they learn by *doing* rather than by listening or reading.

sonable provisions for language and cultural differences, they can help students make the transition into mainstream classes. In that sense, they may be considered similar to other compensatory programs that are not multicultural in their emphasis. As a researcher and advocate of learning styles, however, I would caution against attempting to identify or respond to so-called cultural learning styles. Researchers have clearly established that there is no single or dual learning styles for the members of any cultural, national, racial, or religious group. A single learning style does not appear even within a family of four or five (Dunn and Griggs 1995).

■ *Bilingual or bicultural approaches.* Attention to cultural and language differences can be done appropriately or inappropriately. Bi- and trilingualism in our increasingly interdependent world are valuable for, and should be required of, all students. An emphasis on bilingualism for only non-English-speaking children denies English-speaking students skills required for successful interactions internationally. Today, many adults need to speak several languages fluently and to appreciate cultural similarities and differences to succeed in their work.

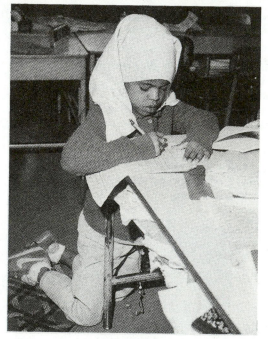

Photo courtesy of the Lafayettee Academy

Another problem arises in those classrooms in which bilingual teachers speak English ungrammatically and haltingly. Such teachers provide a poor model for non-English-speaking children, who may remain in bilingual programs for years, unable to make the transition into English-speaking classes. Ultimately, this impairs the ability of these children to move into well-paying professions and careers—the ultimate goal of most of their parents.

■ *Selective cultural programs.* Building on the language and culture of selected groups and not of others sug-

gests bias and bigotry. Parents should teach their children to appreciate and respect their native cultures; schools should teach children to appreciate and respect all cultures. If the need exists to expand attention to more cultures, let us do that. But let us stop promoting one culture over another with the inevitable result of dividing our children and diminishing their sense of belonging to the dominant culture that is uniquely American—intentionally a combination of the best of all its citizens.

■ *Minority- and gender-based grouping for math and science.* Emphasizing math and science specifically for minority or female students may be based on good intentions, but it ignores the fact that minority students and female students all learn differently from one another and differently from their counterparts—whether those be high- or low-achieving classmates. Providing resources and methods that help all students learn rapidly and well should be the focus for teaching math and science—and every other subject. Are there not males and majority students who fail those subjects? The answer is to change how those subjects are taught, not to isolate certain groups and teach them as though they all have the same style of learning.

Sensitizing Ourselves to Social Agendas

Some multicultural education programs are specifically designed to increase cultural and racial tolerance and reduce bias. These are intended to restructure and desegregate schools, increase contact among the races, and encourage minorities to become teachers; and they lean heavily on cooperative learning (Banks 1994). Sleeter and Grant (1993) describe these programs as emphasizing human relations, incorporating some compensatory goals and curricular revisions to emphasize positive contributions of ethnic and cultural groups, and using learning styles to enhance students' achievement and reduce racial tensions.

Some of these programs emphasize pluralism and cultural equity in American society as a whole, seeking to apply critical thinking skills to a critique of racism and sexism. Others emphasize multilingualism or examine issues from viewpoints other than those of the dominant culture.

In my judgment, these focuses are more political than educational or social. Critical thinking is a requirement for all—not a select few. In addition, whose thinking prevails in these programs, and what are their credentials? Being a minority member or having taken a course does not automatically make a person proficient in teaching minority or female students, or in critiquing social issues. Political debate is helpful to developing young minds; one-sided, preconceived viewpoints are not.

Curriculum and Multicultural Achievement

In the debate over New York's "Children of the Rainbow" curriculum, the ideas of multicultural education captured almost daily headlines. Opponents argued that curriculum change would not increase student achievement, whereas proponents insisted that culturally diverse students performed poorly in school because they could not relate to an American curriculum.

Drew, Dunn, and colleagues (1994) tested how well 38 Cajun students and 29 Louisiana Indian students, all poor achievers, could recall story content and vocabulary immediately and after a delay. Their recall differed significantly when they were instructed with (1) traditional versus multisensory instructional resources and (2) stories in which cultural relevance matched and mismatched students' identified cultural backgrounds. Each subject was presented with four story treatments (two culturally sensitive and two dominant American) and tested for recall immediately afterward and again one week later. The findings for Cajun subjects indicated significant differences between instructional treatments, with greater recall in each multisensory instructional condition—Cultural-Immediate, Cultural-Delayed, American-Immediate, and American-Delayed. The main effect of instructional treatment for Louisiana Indian subjects was significant as well. Recall scores were even higher when they used multisensory materials for American stories. No significant main effect emerged for test interval with either group.

> **What determined whether students mastered the content was how the content was taught, not the content itself.**

This study demonstrated that what determined whether students mastered the content was *how* the content was taught, not the content itself. The culturally sensitive curriculum did not produce significantly higher achievement for these two poorly achieving cultural groups; the methods that were used did.

Teaching Methods and Multicultural Achievement

Other studies of teaching methods revealed even more dramatic results. Before being taught with methods that responded to their learning styles, only 25 percent of special education high school students in a suburban New York school district had passed the required local examinations and state competency tests to receive diplomas. In the first year of the district's learning styles program (1987–88), that number increased to 66 percent. During the second year, 91 percent of the district's special education students were successful, and in the third year, the results remained constant at 90 percent—with a greater ratio of "handicapped" students passing state competency exams than regular education students (Brunner and Majewski 1990).

Two North Carolina elementary principals reported similarly impressive gains as a result of their learning styles programs. In an impoverished, largely minority school, Andrews (1990) brought student scores that had consistently been in the 30th percentile on the California Achievement Tests to the 83rd percentile over a three-year period by responding to students' learning styles. Shortly thereafter, Stone (1992) showed highly tactual, learning disabled (LD) elementary school students how to learn with Flipp Chutes, Electroboards,

Task Cards, and Pic-A-Holes while seated informally in rooms where levels of light matched their style preferences. The children were encouraged to study either alone, with a classmate or two, or with their teacher—based on their learning style strength. Within four months, those youngsters had achieved four months' reading gains on a standardized achievement test—better than they ever had done previously and as well as would have been expected of children achieving at normal levels.

Many professional journals have reported statistically higher scores on standardized achievement and attitude tests as a result of learning style teaching with underachieving and special education students (Dunn, Bruno, Sklar, Zenhausem, and Beaudry 1990; Dunn, Griggs, Olson, Gorman, and Beasley 1995; Klavas 1993; Lemmon 1985; Perrin 1990; Quinn 1993). Indeed, a four-year investigation by the U.S. Office of Education that included on-site visits, interviews, observations, and examinations of national test data concluded that the Dunn and Dunn Learning Styles Model was one of only a few strategies that had had a positive effect on the achievement of special education students throughout the nation (Alberg, Cook, Fiore, Friend, and Sano 1992).

What Have We Learned?

Research documents that underachieving students—whether they are from other cultures or from the dominant U.S. culture—tend to learn differently from students who perform well in our schools (Dunn and Griggs 1995; Milgram, Dunn, and Price 1993). As indicated in the examples cited earlier, schools with diverse populations reversed academic failure when instruction was changed to complement the children's learning style strengths.

In our book, *Multiculturalism and Learning Style* (Dunn and Griggs 1995), my coauthor and I summarize research findings on each of the major cultural groups in the United States—African Americans, Asian Americans, European Americans, Hispanic Americans, and Native Americans. The research clearly shows that there is no such thing as a cultural group style. There are cross-cultural and intracultural similarities and differences among all peoples. Those differences are enriching when understood and channeled positively.

Given this information, I believe it is unwise for schools with limited budgets to support multicultural education in addition to—and apart from—regular education. Instead, schools need to make their instructional delivery systems responsive to how diverse students learn (Dunn 1995).

Educational programs should not separate young children from one another. Any separation becomes increasingly divisive over time and is likely to produce the opposite of what multicultural education is intended to accomplish. Segregated children begin to feel different from and less able than the larger groups of children they see—but are apart from. These feelings can lead to emotional insecurity and a dislike of others.

The United States was founded as a nation intended to absorb people from many nations. Monocultural education in the guise of multicultural education offends the cornerstone of those intentions. The melting pot concept does not diminish one's heritage. It unites the strengths of many cultures into a single, stronger blend of culture to reflect the best of all.

References

Alberg, J., L. Cook, T. Fiore, M. Friend, and S. Sano. (1992). *Educational Approaches and Options for Integrating Students with Disabilities: A Decision Tool*. Triangle Park, N.C.: Research Triangle Institute.

Andrews, R. H. (July-September 1990). "The Development of a Learning Styles Program in a Low Socioeconomic, Underachieving North Carolina Elementary School." *Journal of Reading, Writing, and Learning Disabilities International* 6, 3: 307–314.

Banks, J. A. (1994). *An Introduction to Multicultural Education*. Boston: Allyn and Bacon.

Brunner, C. E., and W. S. Majewski (October 1990). "Mildly Handicapped Students Can Succeed with Learning Styles." *Educational Leadership* 48, 2: 21–23.

Drew, M., R. Dunn, P. Quinn, R. Sinatra, and J. Spiridakis. (1994). "Effects of Matching and Mismatching Minority Underachivers with Culturally Similar and Dissimilar Story Content and Learning Style and Traditional Instructional Practices." *Applied Educational Research Journal* 8, 2: 3–10.

Dunn, R., J. Bruno, R. I. Sklar, R. Zenhausern, and J. Beaudry. (May-June 1990). "Effects of Matching and Mismatching Minority Developmental College Students' Hemispheric Preferences on Mathematics Scores." *Journal of Educational Research* 83, 5: 283–288.

Dunn, R., S. A. Griggs, J. Olson, B. Gorman, and M. Beasley. (1995). "A Meta-Analytic Validation of the Dunn and Dunn Research Learning Styles Model." *Journal of Educational Research* 88, 6: 353–361.

Dunn, R. (1995). *Educating Diverse Learners: Strategies for Improving Current Classroom Practices*. Bloomington, Ind.: Phi Delta Kappa.

Dunn, R., and S. A. Griggs. (1995). *Multiculturalism and Learning Styles: Teaching and Counseling Adolescents*. Westport, Conn: Praeger Publishers, Inc.

Klavas, A. (1993). "In Greensboro, North Carolina: Learning Style Program Boosts Achievement and Test Scores." *The Clearing House* 67, 3: 149–151.

Lemmon, P. (1985). "A School Where Learning Styles Make a Difference. *Principal* 64, 4: 26–29.

Milgram, R. M., R. Dunn, and G. E. Price, eds. (1993). *Teaching and Counseling Gifted and Talented Adolescents: An International Learning Style Perspective*. Westport, Conn.: Praeger Publishers, Inc.

Perrin, J. (October 1990). "The Learning Styles Project for Potential Dropouts." *Educational Leadership* 48, 2: 23–24.

Quinn, R. (1993). "The New York State Compact for Learning and Learning Styles." *Learning Styles Network Newsletter* 15, 1: 1–2.

Schlessinger, A., Jr. (1991). "Report of the Social Studies Syllabus Review Committee: A Dissenting Opinion." In *One Nation, Many Peoples: A Declaration of Cultural Independence*, edited by New York State Social Studies Review and Development Committee. New York: Author.

Sleeter, C. E., and C. A. Grant. (1993). *Making Choices for Multicultural Education: Five Approaches to Race, Class, and Gender*. 2nd ed. New York: Merrill.

Sobol, T. (1990). "Understanding Diversity." *Educational Leadership* 48, 3: 27–30.

Stone, P. (November 1992). "How We Turned Around a Problem School." *Principal* 71, 2: 34–36.

Rita Dunn is Professor, Division of Administrative and Instructional Leadership, and Director, Center for the Study of Learning and Teaching Styles, St. John's University, Grand Central and Utopia Parkways, Jamaica, NY 11439. She is the author of 17 books, including ASCD's *How to Implement and Supervise Learning Style Programs* (1996).

Multiculturalism at a Crossroads

By John Gallagher
From *Middle Ground*

LINCOLN, Nebraska, might seem an unlikely place to find a diverse population of students, but anyone who enters Charles Culler Middle School quickly forgets stereotypes about homogeneity in the American heartland. The school is 35% minority, with significant numbers of Hispanic, African-American, and Asian students. One in 10 is learning English as a second language.

All student course work reflects contributions of a multicultural society. Seventh-graders read African literature and study world history from the perspective of the different people who have shaped it. Students from other countries help teach the intricacies of mathematical equations to their U.S.-born peers, who in turn help them improve their English. And teachers and administrators make a conscious effort to practice tolerance for diversity. "You live it every day," says Culler Principal Ross Dirks. "I feel strongly that this is important."

Active involvement of teachers and students in expanding the curriculum is a hallmark of effective multicultural education, proponents claim, calling it valuable to prepare students for a changing world. In the best cases, success stems as much from the lessons adults teach outside the classroom as from the curriculum they follow inside.

Dirks tells teachers that "By the year 2010, if the demographics are correct, a white majority may no longer be a fact of life in America. That's the world your kids will live in. They have to have knowledge about the way other people live."

Yet few issues spark as much controversy nationally as multicultural education. The term has become a regular salvo in political skirmishes, shorthand for the anxiety various groups feel about affirmative action, political correctness, and homosexuality.

Critics of multicultural education, including historian Arthur Schlesinger and former U.S. Civil Rights Commissioner Linda Chavez, say it violates basic social principles, such as the vision of America as a melting pot for generations of immigrants. Multiculturalism, they contend, stresses our differences, not common bonds, driving us apart instead of bringing us together. Other critics call it a cover for indoctrinating students in liberal political ideologies.

"Multiculturalism is still a put-off word for much of the population," says Bob Green, principal of Shea Middle School, in Phoenix, Arizona. "I think the definition of it needs to be brought out more, because it's really a basic way to address inequities and various conflicts in our nation. We're talking about equal access to education and equal opportunities."

Those who criticize multicultural education as divisive largely miss the point, writer Michael Dirda argues: By its nature, multiculturalism emphasizes links between different peoples. Thus, an integrated curriculum would expose students to the works of Homer and show them how he influenced Virgil, who influenced Dante, who influenced T. S. Eliot. Students would learn African and Asian folklore and mythology in addition to stories about the Norse Gods. Teachers might mix in the poetry of Tu Fu and Scheherazade's *The Arabian Nights* with lessons on Grimm's fairy tales or *Don Quixote*.

"In truth, most multicultural curricula are based on simple justice and common sense: Our schools are heavily Hispanic, Asian, and African American," says Dirda. "If we teach material relating to these cultures, we may capture the enthusiasm of these frequently disadvantaged students, as well as impart some useful insights to kids from other backgrounds. Ultimately, anyone should be able to sympathize with the plights of Jane Austen's heroines or the feelings of Richard Wright's Bigger Thomas. After all, the essence of being human lies in that old phrase 'our common humanity.' "

Five Features

James Banks, University of Washington professor of education and an expert on multicultural education, believes discussions of this issue will help determine the nation's future. The challenge is teaching adolescents to have a flexible, not narrow, view of the world around them. To Banks, multicultural education represents much more than adding a few topics to the curriculum. He considers it an intervention strategy, not a program that can be stuffed into an existing syllabus. He believes schools with a rich multicultural focus share five characteristics:

- Content integration—expanding the curriculum to acknowledge the experiences and contributions of diverse groups.
- Knowledge construction—helping students understand how people create beliefs based on their heritage and experiences, a reflection of what Banks calls "their own cultural biographies."
- Pedagogy—using strategies that lead to higher achievement for students of color. For example, studies show Latino and African-American students learn more working in cooperative groups.

Reprinted from *The Education Digest*, April 1998, pp. 22–28, Ann Arbor, Michigan.

- Prejudice reduction—helping students develop more positive attitudes about people of different races and ethnicities.
- An empowering school culture—examining the impact of school policies, such as academic tracking and discipline referrals, on students from different backgrounds.

So far, Banks says, few schools embracing multicultural education meet all five goals. They tend to focus on one plank or the other, he says.

"We're stuck in the multicultural moments," agrees Howard Miller, associate professor of Middle School and Literacy Education at Lincoln University. Lots of teachers and schools "are very careful about having posters and lots of books in the library that represent different cultures, but they don't do anything with them."

Some schools are moving in the right direction by evaluating the entire educational experience to see if it fits comfortably under the large umbrella of multiculturalism. At Shea, minority students receive special math counseling because administrators found their poor skills were preventing many from attending college. Green, who conducts multicultural-education workshops around the country, says educators must ask themselves hard questions about their commitment to diversity: "What's in the curriculum? What are the teaching strategies? What do we do administratively to provide opportunities for kids? How do we conduct ourselves within our school atmosphere."

Unwanted Soul-Searching

Such soul-searching is not what everyone has in mind. Some educators still see multiculturalism as all about boosting achievement of poor, black students. Not only does this lump together black students from a wide range of backgrounds; it ignores interests of other racial and ethnic groups. Educators who view multiculturalism this narrowly deny the diversity of people within, not just among, various communities.

"What they think about is, 'How do you teach a black kid?'" says Salvario Mungo, associate professor of education at Illinois State University. "I tell them that a black kid living in Evanston, Illinois, and a black kid living in East St. Louis are going to be different."

Textbooks also can restrict multicultural emphasis. Although many experts believe textbook publishers have significantly improved their lessons to more accurately reflect the diversity of America, they acknowledge continued limitations.

"Our textbooks are certainly written from a bias," says Susan Baird, a teacher at Ashland Middle School, in Ashland, Oregon. "Even when they try to patch on a good piece on Sojourner Truth, or some other prominent person of non-Anglo culture, it's still by and large male and white."

The bigger problem may be the inclination to tack multiculturalism onto the school calendar. Advocates say it should not be limited to a "heroes and holidays" program in which teachers mention a prominent African-American scientist in passing or a short lesson about Mexico's Independence Day. For multiculturalism to work, they say, it must be infused throughout the curriculum.

"That's where multiculturalism has gotten a black eye." Green says. "We tried too many 'Tacos on Tuesday' programs, or black African weeks, and said, 'We served that well.'"

Reducing multiculturalism to such celebrations, or even displaying inclusive photos or posters around the school, may make some educators feel good. But such facile attempts rarely help students respect diversity. These efforts also can have negative repercussions. "Members of the minority culture are offended at the one-day display," Miller says. You (also) raise the prejudice of people who say, 'Why don't we have a white history month or German-American history month?' You create a mess for yourself."

Nebraska is our only state with a mandate to teach multicultural education in all schools. Yet, even with the law behind them, Nebraska teachers have a tough job meeting goals of multicultural education. Weak administrative support can quash good intentions.

Schools can meet the letter of the law without really addressing the intent, says Bill Lopez, a middle-level instructor at the University of Nebraska's School of Education and a former middle-school teacher. When preparing his mostly white college students to lead the classrooms of tomorrow, Lopez tries to help them understand the forms racism can take and the way language relates to different cultures. He also stresses the importance of reflecting multiple perspectives when teaching significant historical events.

"The first thing I have teachers think about is what the characteristics are of a multicultural teacher," he says. "I try to do it in a constructive way, but generally, I push them toward the idea that a multicultural teacher has a vision not only of what they need to be but what they want their students to be."

Flowchart

Lopez offers a flowchart for making a multicultural middle school: Identify the players; form the multicultural committee; determine the community needs; determine the multicultural approach(es) wanted; develop a multicultural plan; determine the characteristics each player should have, based on the approach and plan; determine how to assess the characteristics each player has or should have; develop an initial inservice plan for all players, including motivational strategies; assess where the players are; develop additional inservice programs based on the assessments; provide ongoing support for players; and provide for regular review and assessment of how the plan is being implemented.

Meanwhile, the Nebraska Department of Education (NDE) offers ideas on designing and developing staff competencies, noting that effective multicultural education depends on staff who work directly with children in each school. NDE says some competencies that staff should develop in increasing their effectiveness in multicultural instruction include:

1. Recognize their personal feelings, attitudes, and perceptions as part of their cultural norms and bias.
2. Recognize the value of ethnic and cultural diversity as a basis for societal enrichment, cohesiveness, and survival.
3. Know in teachable detail about the experiences, viewpoints, and needs of various cultural groups.
4. Acquire sensitivity to words and actions insulting or hurtful to various minority groups.
5. Demonstrate through instruction and classroom or school environment how people of various groups, cultures, and backgrounds can communicate effectively and work cooperatively.
6. Use knowledge and experience of multicultural issues in selection, evaluation, and revision of instructional materials that are unbiased, factual, and complete in treating minority groups.

7. Conceptualize and describe the development of the United States as a multidimensional society of ethnic and cultural diversity where diversity has been an asset and prejudice has been a destructive force in economics, cooperation, and public policy.

Such suggestions notwithstanding, teachers and principals who have been cautious about adopting multicultural education can find some justification for moving slowly. The issue has prompted many local controversies, including the 1997 firing of Patsy and Nadine Cordova, two sisters who taught in Vaughn Junior and Senior High School in Vaughn, New Mexico. Given wide discretion and regular approval by the school administration in their choice of curricular materials, the Cordovas tried to integrate Chicano history and culture into their classes, which were more than 90% Hispanic.

Relevance

"Why didn't somebody teach me about Chicano history?" Nadine asks. "I don't want my students to walk away and say, 'No one ever tried to teach me.' At least they know I tried to teach them something relevant."

In 1996, school administrators started censoring the Cordovas' lessons. Superintendent Arthur Martinez sent Nadine a letter stating that she was teaching "racial intolerance" and "a biased political agenda." Another time, he told the teachers their classes were "preoccupied with colonizers" and taught children "that Mexicans are noble and honorable while Spanish and Anglos are greedy and hurtful people." Such lessons, he argued, acted "to place a giant chip on their fragile shoulders."

The Cordovas denied the charges, but tension between the teachers and the school district escalated until they lost their jobs. At Martinez's request, the Chief of Police escorted the sisters from the school. The Cordovas have filed a lawsuit challenging their dismissal.

Even the most carefully calibrated attempts to expand multicultural education can run into problems. Susan Baird notes that some topics she discusses in class—such as world religions—occasionally upset parents and students. She says she works hard to be sensitive to those concerns, which often reduces tension. As a result, religion has "become pretty comfortable and easy to talk about" in her class.

Students and parents have been less open-minded about homosexuality. Victoria Forrester, a sixth-grade teacher at Amelia Earhart Elementary School, in Alameda, California, almost lost her job after she spent seven minutes in class discussing the April 1997 episode of the television series, *Ellen*, in which Ellen Degeneres acknowledged that both she and her TV character were lesbians.

Forrester seized the opportunity, generated by a student's praise for the episode, to talk generally about the importance of people sticking up for themselves. But a parent complained Forrester violated his right to prevent his daughter from hearing conversations about homosexuality. The local school board cleared Forrester, but the state Commission on Teacher Credentialing is reviewing the parent's complaint for possible action.

Parental objections don't present the only difficulties for teachers committed to multicultural education. Colleagues also can pour cold water on their ideas.

Dirks, the Lincoln principal, says he met strong resistance from teachers at the school where he previously worked, which served a largely white and middle-class population of students and staff: "It was a really closed community. When teachers asked me, 'Why are we doing this,' it really frustrated me because they didn't see the bigger part of the world. They weren't totally closed to it, but they felt it was more like one of those silly projects from the central office."

Tackling Tough Issues

Perhaps there is no way to avoid controversy in multicultural programs. Indeed, some educators believe it's wrong to try. Diluting a program to diminish debate is a disservice to students who need to grapple with tough social issues.

"If you're going to be concerned about multicultural education, you're not going to be in the business of avoiding controversy," says Lincoln University's Howard Miller. "You need to face it head on. You need to openly discuss controversial issues and let kids know they are indeed controversial. You should, in fact, design some of your program around that very fact."

Ultimately, students might be the best allies of multiculturalism. With their interest in justice and fairness, middle-schoolers in particular can learn to appreciate the need for all people to be accepted in society.

"Middle school kids think they can fix the world, and they're going to do it right now," Baird says. "It's wonderful. I would never tell them that it may take them a little longer."

John Gallagher is a freelance writer based in Brooklyn, New York. Condensed from Middle Ground, *1 (February 1998), 10–14, 42. Used with permission of National Middle School Association, from which subscriptions to* Middle Ground *are available by contacting NMSA, 2600 Corporate Exchange Dr., Ste. 370, Columbus, Ohio 43231 (phone: 800–528–NMSA).*

Voices and Voces:
Cultural and Linguistic Dimensions of Giftedness

by Ellen Riojas Clark and Virginia Gonzalez

It can be hard to recognize abilities in young language-minority students. Parent and teacher evaluations in conjunction with alternative assessments can capture these students' capabilities.

They are language-minority, low socioeconomic status (SES) kids. Can they be gifted? In what ways? What methods should be used to assess them? In an effort to establish the importance of identifying both linguistic and cultural giftedness in this group, two case studies look at the interaction of cognition, language, and culture—through a holistic lens of appropriate alternative assessments. Teachers' and parents' views are incorporated with dual-language testing to capture capabilities that might otherwise remain hidden. Results will show why all of these measures are necessary to get an accurate picture of the children's abilities.

We use the terms *voices* and *voces* (Spanish for *voices*) to offer a critical reflective view of the assessment of language-minority children who are gifted, and also to propose an alternative assessment model for measuring cultural nonverbal dimensions of giftedness. As part of our study of cultural and linguistic giftedness, we consider the need to establish a dialogue between cultures, in which mainstream *voices* and minority *voces* communicate their particular world views, philosophies, and ethnic identities envisioned within their social and ethnic groups. We will also argue that evaluators need to become advocates for language-minority children.

The term *voices* will be used to represent the mainstream school culture's interpretation of linguistic giftedness, illustrated by the classroom teachers' descriptions of the children's abilities. We define *voices* as: 1) the documentation of quantitative products such as scores on

Ellen Riojas Clark, Ph.D., is an associate professor, Division of Bilingual/Bicultural Studies, University of Texas at San Antonio.
Virginia Gonzalez, Ph.D., is an associate professor, Educational Curriculum & Instruction Department, Texas A&M University, College Station, Texas.

VOICES
TABLE
EDUCATED
COOPERATIVE

standardized intelligence tests, which are highly influenced by language and learning, and 2) the interpretation of children's behaviors and the selection of performance standards that guide the curriculum-based or traditional views of giftedness, focusing only on logico-mathematical academic abilities. In contrast, the term *voces* will be used to represent the minority community interpretation of cultural giftedness, illustrated by the parents' descriptions of their children's socioemotional abilities. We define *voces* as cultural manifestations of giftedness expressed in various verbal and nonverbal forms.

The following two case studies examine the role of dominant-language assessment on the identification of linguistic giftedness and cultural factors on nonverbal giftedness.

Cultural Factors and Giftedness

As noted by Dundes, a familial environment, regardless of SES and cultural-linguistic background, is vitally important because it educates its members in the culture

 From *Educational Horizons*, Fall 1998, pp. 41-47. © 1998 by Ellen Riojas Clark and Virginia Gonzalez. Reprinted by permission.

of the home and the group and " . . . insures conformity to the accepted cultural norms and continuity from generation to generation."[1] Frasier indicated that giftedness could be expressed through different cultural and linguistic representations in low-SES children.[2] Later on, he noted that minority children do receive stimulation representative of their sociocultural environment.[3] That is, the cultural experience of minority gifted children began to be considered by researchers who tried to portray the diversity of the *voces* expressed by these children and their families. These minority *voces* are illustrated in the parents' descriptions of the two children's verbal and nonverbal giftedness presented in this article.

We have finally come to understand that minority families can nurture their children's giftedness in a culturally rich manner.

In addition, several authors have discussed the methodological problems related to the sociocultural nature of defining and measuring intelligence. For example, Darder stated, " . . . IQ testing is unable to function as a fair measurement of innate intelligence, because its primary concern is directly linked to a relative ranking of people based on criteria derived solely from the values of a selective cultural system."[4] In a previous paper, the authors noted that Hispanic mothers described their sons' giftedness using the Spanish phrases *es un niño bien educado* (literal translation: is a well-educated boy) to describe their sons' outstanding behaviors in culturally appropriate situations. Hispanic parents might also use the term *malcriado* (literal translation: ill bred) in opposition to *bien educado*, to tell their children that their behavior is inappropriate and will reflect badly on the family.[5] Thus, Hispanic gifted children (as described by their parents) can analyze a situation, determine the appropriate behavior, and perform in an exemplary manner that will reflect well on self and family.

Contemporary ethnic researchers emphasize the need to value and celebrate the diverse expressions of giftedness. We have finally come to understand that minority families can nurture their children's giftedness in a culturally rich manner. The following two case studies present a portrait of the cultural and linguistic dimensions of giftedness by using an alternative developmental assessment model.

Case studies—Oscar and Alberto

Two case studies are analyzed in this article: 1) Oscar, a 6-year-old Spanish monolingual child and 2) Alberto,

a 5-year-old bilingual Spanish-English child. Pseudonyms are used for both children in order to protect their identities. The boys were attending a bilingual kindergarten classroom when they were referred for assessment for possible giftedness by their teachers. Background information was collected using the Home Language Survey[6] and the Parents' and Teachers' Ratings of Cognitive, Linguistic, and Social Skills.[7]

The families and home environments of the two children are similar. Oscar and Alberto both came from low-SES, traditional, intact, Hispanic families that provided secure, well-structured, and stable environments for the children. That is, in spite of limited economic resources, these families provided a nurturing home environment. In both families, mothers and fathers were present in the household; both mothers were housewives and both fathers held blue collar jobs. None of the parents had much formal schooling; they had attended the *escuela secundaria* (the equivalent of a junior high school in the United States). The parents of both children were immigrants from Mexico, and both children were born in the U.S. Oscar's parents have resided here for fifteen years; Alberto's parents for four. Both families lived in a low-SES Hispanic *barrio* in a middle-sized city near the Mexican border.

Both Oscar and Alberto were the youngest of three children. Spanish was used as the primary language in each home and both sets of parents noted a recent increase of English use, indicating the influence of schooling on both children's language abilities.

We believe that including parents and teachers enriches assessment, because they are "experts" in daily life behaviors in natural settings, and they are also social agents for the development of language-minority children.

Alternative development assessment model

An "ethnic-researcher" developmental approach including nonverbal and verbal tasks and stimuli representing both minority and majority cultures and languages as the major component for accurately identifying cultural and linguistic giftedness in bilingual children was used to evaluate Oscar and Alberto.[8] During early childhood, individuals acquire language as a tool for thinking. Research has shown that minority children perform at higher cognitive developmental levels in nonverbal than in verbal tasks.[9] Current research indicates the need to use alternative assessments across contexts by multiple informants for language-minority children.[10] We believe that including parents and teachers enriches assessment, because they are "experts" in daily life behaviors in natural settings, and they are also social agents for the development of language-minority children. Thus, following these recommendations, the two case studies presented here use alternative measures that have a strong data-driven base:

1. Home Language Survey
2. Parents' and Teachers' Ratings of Children's Cognitive, Linguistic, and Social Abilities
3. Qualitative Use of English and Spanish Tasks
4. Cartoon Conservation Scales

Standardized tests used as comparison measures:

1. Language Assessment Scales (LAS)
2. Test of Nonverbal Intelligence-2 (TONI-2)

A **home language survey,** as well as parent and teacher ratings were used to get a clearer picture of the children's abilities. Parents were asked to: 1) rate their and their children's Spanish and English proficiency; 2) rate the frequency of use of Spanish and English at home; 3) provide the ages of the children in the home; and 4) provide background information for both parents.[11] **Parents' and teachers' ratings** involve describing the child's linguistic and cognitive abilities both at home and school, including selecting descriptors of the child's abilities and writing additional comments.[12]

QUEST in Spanish and English was chosen because it reliably explains verbal and nonverbal concept formation in bilingual children as a two-way universal and culturally-linguistically bound process influenced by cognition, culture, and language. Based on this model, five verbal and nonverbal classification tasks (labeling, defining, sorting, verbal justification of sorting, and category clue) were designed to assess bilingual children's general and linguistic-gender conceptual processes.[13]

The **Cartoon Conservation Scale** (CCS) includes Piagetian tasks with drawings done in a "comic-book" format providing concrete images. Each item involves a story that the child finishes in a way that she or he thinks "makes it true." The structure of the CCS presents eight conservation subscales: number, substance, length, distance, egocentricity, horizontality of water, volume or displacement of water, and probability.[14]

Results: A Comparison of Oscar and Alberto
Parents' Assessments

Parents' descriptions of their children's cognitive, linguistic, and social abilities are based on the parents' rating scales. The parents' *voces* describe the cultural dimensions of their gifted children's cognitive, linguistic, and social skills using terms conveying a different meaning in Spanish than the literal translation in English—expressing differences between the Hispanic and mainstream American cultures. Despite these differences, these minority parents also valued education and the attainment of academic goals in their children.

When Oscar's parents described his cognitive and linguistic abilities, they used Spanish. A translated version of their descriptions is: "My son is very intelligent. He is always asking about something that is new to him, he wants it explained very well and then he never forgets it, . . . once a story is read to him he can retell the story and doesn't forget any details, . . . he learns everything very rapidly, and has great abilities." Oscar's parents used the expression in Spanish *"es un niño ejemplar"* to describe his cognitive abilities. A literal translation of this Spanish expression is "he is an example of a child," but in Spanish the cultural connotation is that "the child has an outstanding social behavior that shows maturity and wiseness." In describing Oscar's linguistic abilities, his parents stated that speaking to him was like speaking with an adult. The child's problem-solving abilities were described in terms of his adult-like speech and reasoning. Oscar's parents reported that he gave them advice in how to face problematic household situations; a translation of their description is: "Mami, when you have a problem you must always be patient." In addition, Oscar's parents described him as an imaginative and independent child who liked to do puzzles and drawings, had good writing skills, and enjoyed reading.

The interpersonal skills of being cooperative, independent, and able to understand social rules were used by Alberto's parents also as examples of his gifted problem-solving abilities.

Alberto's parents described their son's cognitive abilities using Spanish: *"Mi hijo es* (My son is) *atrevido* (risk-taker), *intenso* (intense), *curioso* (witty), *persistente* (persistent), *listo* (quick), *inteligente* (studious, applied), *laborioso* (hard-worker) *y* (and) *sabio* (wise)." The translation of some Spanish terms into English indicates a variation in connotative meanings, such as in the word *inteligente.* Alberto's parents described his cognitive abilities as very advanced for his chronological age: "He is observant, and has a long attention span; he is good in math; he likes to do puzzles, and takes apart things and puts them back together again; and he has good navigating skills." They perceived Alberto's willingness to help solve problems as adult-like behavior because he analyzed situations, determined what needed to be done, and did it without being asked. Alberto's parents described his social and interpersonal skills in Spanish: "*Mi hijo es* (My son is) *simpático* (charming), *empático* (sentimental), *cooperativo* (cooperative), *abierto* (open-minded), *servicial* (helpful), *sano* (moral), *amistoso* (friendly), *considerado* (considerate), *seguro* (confident), *impulsivo* (sure), *y respetuoso* (respectful). *Es un niño ejemplar* (he is an example of a child)." The interpersonal skills of being cooperative, independent, and able to understand social rules were used by Alberto's parents also as examples of his gifted problem-solving abilities.

Teachers' Assessments

Teachers' descriptions of the children's cognitive, linguistic, and social abilities were collected using the teachers' rating scales. They implement the curriculum endorsed by the mainstream school culture, and because of this they represent the *voices* in their descriptions of the children's abilities. But teachers cannot divorce themselves from their cultural identities, reflected in the strategies, methodologies, and educational philosophies that they choose to endorse. Due to this individual choice, teachers also represent the *voces* in their descriptions of the children's abilities.

Oscar's teacher reported that he had good reasoning skills in math and he problem-solved using math manipulatives. She talked about Oscar's motivation for learning, mentioning that he was "very knowledgeable in many areas" and that "he showed excitement in putting puzzles together without the outline." She explained Oscar's "very expanded vocabulary" as the result of his family travel experiences and his ability to relate knowledge from his real-world experience to classroom activities. When playing, she described him as creative and independent; and when working with others, she described him as a leader who "organizes groups," and as a responsible child who volunteered for cleaning up in the classroom without being told.

Alberto's teacher described him as eager to learn, intrinsically motivated, persistent, and committed to finishing tasks. His teacher also mentioned that Alberto liked to assemble things and draw, and had good problem-solving skills. Like his parents, his teacher mentioned Alberto's advanced language skills as exemplified by his large vocabulary and very good story-telling skills. His teacher considered Alberto to be independent, very helpful, cooperative, caring, friendly, observant, thoughtful, talkative, and adventurous.

Alternative Assessments
Oscar's QUEST performance (in Spanish)

Oscar performed at a concrete level in nonverbal tasks, and at a functional level in verbal tasks. Even though Oscar could: 1) not label all the items, he could still define them verbally at a concrete level; and 2) sort

items nonverbally at the concrete level, he could not articulate the reasons why he had grouped the objects into categories and subcategories. Thus, we conclude that Oscar showed nonverbal cultural giftedness, but did not show linguistic giftedness.

Alberto's QUEST performance (in Spanish and English)

Alberto's performance in English was much lower than in Spanish, demonstrating the effect of assessing a minority child in his first language and culture on his verbal and nonverbal cognitive development. His performance was also higher for animal than for food items, which represented different cultural and linguistic possible categorizations. Based on Alberto's metalinguistic and concrete performance in QUEST in Spanish, he was diagnosed as culturally and linguistically gifted.

CCS performance

The subscales passed by Oscar and Alberto in Spanish were conservation of number and length, horizontality, and probability. In addition, Oscar passed the scale of volume, and Alberto passed the scale of egocentricity, both in Spanish. Both children's performance at the concrete level indicated advanced cognitive development.

> **Therefore, not only the language used in testing is important, but also the cultural stimuli and perspectives used to interpret their performance.**

Standardized Test Performance

On the **Test of Nonverbal Intelligence** (TONI-2),[15] Oscar's score indicated average intelligence; Alberto's score indicated superior intelligence. Both Oscar's scores (4 in Spanish and 1 in English) on the **Language Assessment Scales**[16] and his teacher's language ratings, indicated that he was Spanish monolingual. Alberto was found to be bilingual, but also Spanish-dominant, based upon his scores on the LAS (4 in Spanish and 2 in English) and his similar parents' and teachers' ratings.

Discussion and Conclusions
Gifted or Not?

Can a monolingual, minority, low-SES child be gifted? Oscar's case indicates "yes," the child can be culturally or nonverbally gifted as evidenced by alternative developmental measures (QUEST and CCS) administered in Spanish. Oscar's case shows that nonverbal cultural giftedness is *not* associated with the degree of bilingualism, but with the degree of sensitivity of alternative assessments to measure minority cultural representations influencing cognition. Therefore, not only the language used in testing is important, but also the cultural stimuli and perspectives used to interpret their performance. As for Alberto, we discovered that he shows not only nonverbal but also verbal giftedness in Spanish as evidenced by QUEST and CCS. Our analysis of Alberto's case leads us to be positive about the stimulating role of not only two cultures but also two languages on cognitive development.

Both case studies also show that nonverbal cultural giftedness in language-minority children cannot be measured by nonverbal standardized intelligence tests. Moreover, there were also differences between both children's performance in nonverbal and verbal tasks in QUEST Spanish and the TONI-2. Within a developmental perspective, these differences may indicate that cognition results from the dynamic interaction between internal and external factors. Thus, it is possible that Alberto was positively influenced by being bilingual because he was more intelligent nonverbally than Oscar, who was only monolingual Spanish. Then, these two children presented differences in their range of cognitive developmental potential, and also in how cultural and linguistic factors contributed to the actualization of their potentials.[17]

The Home Environment

Several researchers have noted the important role of the family in offering mentoring and support to minority children in order to be successful in the mainstream educational environment. For instance, Van Tassel-Baska pointed out that it is not only what economic resources are present in the family that have been traditionally associated with parental occupation and educational level, but what coping strategies low-SES at-risk children are able to learn from supportive positive role models in their families. He found that African-American and Asian-American adolescents who had been identified as gifted and succeed academically in school, had "families which served as a major source of encouragement and influence . . . [and] . . . had at least one parent who was dominant and monitored the child's progress through school very closely."[18] For these adolescents, the support of extended family members was important (usually the maternal grandmother) because they transmitted positive values, provided guidance, and nurtured their self-concept and self-esteem.[19]

By analyzing the home environments of both children, we see that both fathers self-reported that they were proficient in English, and both mothers self-reported that they were limited English-proficient. Even though primarily Spanish was used to communicate in both households, only Alberto started to learn English; Oscar remained monolingual Spanish. Thus, we believe that

individual differences precede cultural and linguistic differences, and that any language-minority child is first an individual and then a member of a particular linguistic and cultural community.

Based on these cases, it seems that: 1) a monolingual child can be culturally or nonverbally gifted; 2) the level of nonverbal cognitive development influences the rate and amount of first- and second-language acquisition; and 3) cultural and linguistic factors do not affect every child in the same manner given individual differences.

> *However, the Hispanic voces of the parents described giftedness also as a socially and emotionally mature behavior expressed by their children in appropriate contexts of their minority culture.*

Voces and *voices:* **Integrating parents' and teachers' perspectives**

We found both similarities and differences between the teachers' and the parents' descriptions of the cognitive, linguistic, and social abilities of the two cases. The teachers' *voices* representing the school mainstream culture coincided with the parents' *voces* when they were describing giftedness as an advanced verbal and logico-mathematical intelligence. However, the Hispanic *voces* of the language-minority children's parents described giftedness also as a socially and emotionally mature behavior expressed by their children in appropriate contexts of their minority culture.

Lay people from the majority culture also have the tendency to emphasize successful behaviors in a real-life sociocultural context when describing "intelligent" individuals.[20] In contrast, Sternberg also found that "experts," professionals trained in psychology, defined intelligence using the traditional scholastic aptitude skills measured by standardized IQ tests referring only to the verbal and logico-mathematical domains of intelligence.[21] There is an interesting relationship between CCS, QUEST, and the parents' and teachers' views of the children. CCS and QUEST results show that the children were operating at higher cognitive developmental levels for their ages. The parents' view of their children is that they were gifted because their "adult-like" behaviors were at a higher developmental level. The teachers' view of the children emphasized their academic skills and logico-mathematical developmental abilities.

Integrating the teachers' *voices* and the minority parents' *voces* in this study builds on the concept of exploring the potential of cross-cultural benefits and resources advocated by Serpell.[22] We have also learned that children from low-SES households whose family members provide adequate emotional nurturing, transmit positive educational values, and celebrate their academic success, do function as empathic role models and mentors.

In conclusion, we believe that cultural and linguistic giftedness does exist among minority monolingual or unbalanced bilingual children, but we can only observe its psychological expressions in behaviors measured through sensitive alternative assessments like QUEST and CCS. We want to advocate the need to give language-minority children and their parents the opportunity to express their *voces*. Our view of giftedness is enhanced and elaborated by the perspectives of the *voces* of minority homes, communities, and people in interaction with the traditional *voices* of our mainstream American school culture.

1. A. Dundes, *The Study of Folklore* (New Jersey: Prentice Hall, 1965), 2, 294, 297.
2. M.M. Frasier, "The Identification of Gifted Black Students: Developing New Perspectives," *Journal for the Education of the Gifted* 10, no. 3. (1987): 155–180.
3. M.M. Frasier, Disadvantaged and Culturally Diverse Gifted Students," *Journal for the Education of the Gifted* 14, no. 3 (1991): 234–245.
4. A. Darder, *Culture and Power in the Classroom: A Critical Foundation for Bicultural Education* (New York: Bergin & Garvey, 1991).
5. V. Gonzalez and E.R. Riojas-Clark, "Folkloric and Historical Dimensions of Giftedness," in V. Gonzalez, ed., *Language and Cognitive Development in Second Language Learning: Educational Implications for Children and Adults* (Needham Heights, Mass.: Allyn & Bacon, 1999), 1–18.
6. V. Gonzalez, "A Model of Cognitive, Cultural, and Linguistic Variables Affecting Bilingual Spanish/English Children's Development of Concepts and Language," doctoral dissertation (Austin, Tex.: The University of Texas at Austin, ERIC Document Reproduction Service No. ED 345 562, 1991).
7. V. Gonzalez, "A Model of Cognitive, Cultural, and Linguistic Variables Affecting Bilingual Spanish/English Children's Development of Concepts and Language," *Hispanic Journal of Behavioral Sciences* 16, no. 4 (1994): 396–421.
8. V. Gonzalez and T.D. Yawkey, "The Assessment of Culturally and Linguistically Diverse Students: Celebrating Change," *Educational HORIZONS* 73, no. 1, (1993): 41–49.
9. Gonzalez, "A Model of Cognitive, Cultural, and Linguistic Variables," 1991; Gonzalez, "A Model of Cognitive, Cultural, and Linguistic Variables," 1994; and V. Gonzalez, P. Bauerle, and M. Felix-Holt, "Theoretical and Practical Implications of Assessing Cognitive and Language Development in Bilingual Children with Qualitative Methods," *The Bilingual Research Journal* 20, no. 1 (1996): 93–131.
10. J. Cummins, "Interdependence of First-and-Second-Language Proficiency in Bilingual Children," in E. Bialystock, ed., *Language Processing in Bilingual Children* (Cambridge, England: Cambridge University Press, 1991), 70–89; J.W. Oller, Jr., "Challenged Bilinguals," *NABE NEWS* 17, no. 4 (1994): 15–16, 18; R.J. Samuda, "Towards Nondiscriminatory Assessment: Principles and Applications," in R.J. Samuda, et al., eds., *Assessment and Placement of Minority Students* (Toronto, Canada: C. J. Hogrefe, 1991), 173–189; and J.S. Renzulli, "The National Research Center on the Gifted and Talented: The Dream, the Design, and the Destination," *Gifted Child Quarterly* 35, no. 2 (1991): 73–80.
11. Gonzalez, "A Model of Cognitive, Cultural, and Linguistic Variables," 1991.
12. M. Fleming, et al., *Parents' and Teachers' Ratings of Minority Children's Cognitive, Linguistic, and Social Abilities* (Tucson, Ariz.: The University of Arizona and Tucson Independent School District, 1992).
13. Gonzalez, "A Model of Cognitive, Cultural, and Linguistic Variables," 1991; Gonzalez, "A Model of Cognitive, Cultural, and Linguistic Variables," 1994; and V. Gonzalez, *Cognition, Culture, and Language in Bilingual Children: Conceptual and Semantic Development* (Bethesda, Md.: Austin & Winfield, 1995).
14. E.A. De Avila, *Cartoon Conservation Scales (CCS)* (San Antonio, Tex.: Stephen Jackson & Associates, 1976).
15. L. Brown, R.J. Sherbenou, and S.K. Johnsen, *Test of Nonverbal Intelligence-2 (TONI-2)* (Austin, Tex.: Pro-Ed, 1990).
16. E. A. De Avila and S. E. Duncan, *The Language Assessment Scales (LAS)* (Monterey, Calif.: CTB/McGraw-Hill, 1986).
17. Gonzalez and Yawkey, "Assessment of Culturally and Linguistically Diverse Students."
18. J. Van Tassel-Baska, "The Role of the Family in the Success of Disadvantaged Gifted Learners," *Journal for the Education of the Gifted* 13, no. 1 (1989): 22–36.
19. Ibid.
20. R.J. Sternberg, *Beyond IQ: A Triarchic Theory of Human Intelligence* (New York: Cambridge University Press, 1984).
21. Ibid.
22. R. Serpell, "Assessment Criteria for Severe Intellectual Disability in Various Cultural Settings," *International Journal of Behavioral Development* 11, no. 1 (1988): 117–144.

Unit Selections

Key Points to Consider

❖ Compare and contrast the different approaches to learning. What approach do you think is best, and why? What factors are important to your answer (e.g., objectives, types of students, setting, personality of the teacher)?

❖ What teaching strategies could you use to promote greater student retention of material? What are good ways to attract and keep students' attention? Must a teacher be an "entertainer"? Why or why not?

❖ How can a teacher promote positive self-esteem, values, character, caring, and attitudes? How are they related to cognitive learning? How much emphasis should be put on cultivating character or positive student interactions? How would you create a "caring" classroom? Discuss whether or not this would interfere with achievement of cognitive learning targets.

❖ If you wanted to create a constructivist classroom in the subject area and/or grade in which you want to teach, what would the classroom look like? What would you emphasize, and how would your actions reflect construcivist principles and research on intelligence?

DUSHKIN ONLINE Links   www.dushkin.com/online/

23. **Education Week on the Web**
   http://www.edweek.org
24. **Online Internet Institute**
   http://www.oii.org
25. **Teachers Helping Teachers**
   http://www.pacificnet.net/~mandel/
26. **The Teachers' Network**
   http://www.teachnet.org

These sites are annotated on pages 4 and 5.

Learning can be broadly defined as a relatively permanent change in behavior or thinking due to experience. Learning is not a result of change due to maturation. Changes in behavior and thinking of students result from complex interactions between their individual characteristics and environmental factors. A continuing challenge in education is understanding these interactions so that learning can be enhanced. This unit focuses on approaches within educational psychology that represent different ways of viewing the learning process and related instructional strategies. Each approach to learning emphasizes a different set of personal and environmental factors that influence certain behaviors. While no one approach can fully explain learning, each is a valuable contribution to our knowledge about the process.

The discussion of each learning approach includes suggestions for specific techniques and methods of teaching to guide teachers in understanding student behavior and in making decisions about how to teach. The articles in this section reflect a recent emphasis on applied research conducted in schools, research on the brain, and on constructivist theories. The relatively large number of articles on information processing/cognitive learning and instruction, as opposed to behaviorism, also reflects a change in emphasis. Behaviorism, however, remains important in our understanding of learning and instruction.

Researchers have recently made significant advances in understanding the way our minds work. Information processing refers to the way that the mind receives sensory information, stores it as memory, and recalls it for later use. This procedure is basic to all learning, no matter what teaching approach is taken, and we know that the method used in processing information determines to some extent how much and what we remember. The essays in the first subsection present some of the fundamental principles of brain functioning, information processing and cognition, human intelligence, and styles of thinking.

For years, behaviorism was the best-known approach to learning. Most practicing and prospective teachers are familiar with concepts such as classical conditioning, reinforcement, and punishment, and there is no question that behaviorism has made significant contributions to understanding learning. But behaviorism has also been subject to much misinterpretation, in part because it seems so simple. In fact, the effective use of behaviorist principles is complex and demanding, as debate presented in the articles in the second subsection points out.

Humanistic/social psychological learning emphasizes the affective, social, moral, and personal development of students. Humanistic learning involves acceptance of the uniqueness of each individual, stressing character, feelings, values,

and self-worth. To the humanist, learning is not simply a change in behavior or thinking; learning is also the discovery of the personal meaning of information. Social psychology is the study of the nature of interpersonal relationships in social situations. In education, this approach looks at teacher-pupil relationships and group processes to derive principles of interaction that affect learning. Two articles in this section examine the application of humanistic/social psychological principles. One focuses on self-esteem while the other examines character education, morals, and values.

Instructional strategies are the teacher behaviors and methods of conveying information that affect learning. Teaching methods or techniques can vary greatly, depending on objectives, group size, types of students, and personality of the teacher. For example, discussion classes are generally more effective for enhancing thinking skills than are individualized sessions or lectures. For the final subsection, four articles have been selected that show how teachers can use principles of cognitive psychology and intelligence in their teaching. The first article emphasizes the importance of an appropriate classroom environment that will encourage and support students' thinking. Strategies to promote learning through the use of cognitive maps and study guides as well as effective approaches to using technology are summarized, while the article by Fogarty shows how constructivist classrooms can be created based on recent research on intelligence.

Learning and Instruction

Brain Basics:
Cognitive Psychology and Its Implications for Education

Richard L. Bucko

The human brain is a unique creation composed of a hundred billion neurons connected by trillions of synapses. For millennia, people have asked how this three-pound mass of soft tissue inside the human skull performs such tasks as writing letters, solving problems, and contemplating the universe. These questions are now finding answers through recent findings about the way the human brain works. The general field of study is known as cognitive science. When applied to the study of human cognition, it is known as cognitive psychology. When applied to the field of education, it is known as brain-based learning. Brain-based learning may be the most important influence on the way we teach since the first school was founded.

Knowledge of brain-based learning will be essential to educators of the future because good teaching requires an understanding of how the brain receives, processes, and produces information. As our understanding of cognitive psychology grows, learning problems will be addressed analytically, with an understanding of the damage to connections that causes these problems. Brain-based learning can be the foundation of pragmatic future education reform based on clear evidence of how children learn.

This article will address key research findings about brain research, the thinking skills movement, popular literature on the brain, and implications for schools.

Key Findings about Brain Functions

Three technological innovations are now allowing neuroscientists to analyze and observe the connection between the various areas of the brain. First, neural imaging allows researchers to observe the inner workings of the brain. As subjects see colors or words, various areas of the brain light up on imaging screens. Different brain regions can be observed handling letters of the alphabet, numbers, tastes, and smells. In a bilingual person, one area will handle one language while another deals with the second language.

Second, molecular biology is revealing the operations of genes and molecules inside brain cells. One example is from the work of Eric Kandel at Columbia University. He discovered a short string of chemical molecules, called CREB, which serves as a switch to turn certain genes in the brain on and off. CREB is needed to change short-term memory into long-term memory. As we age,

Richard L. Bucko is Principal of George C. Baker School in Moorestown Township Public Schools, New Jersey (enrollment 2,800). Dr. Bucko has published and presented in the area of effective instruction, and his study of the subject of brain-based learning is a continuation of his interest in this area.

From *ERS Spectrum*, Summer 1997, pp. 20–25. © 1997 by Educational Research Service. Reprinted by permission.

CREB is less plentiful, a fact that may partially explain memory loss as we enter later years. Even the sense of smell is managed by over 1,000 genes controlling neurons that respond to various smells, connecting these odors to associated behaviors, memories, and thoughts (Flam 1996).

Third, computers have given us an exact way to think about information processing by helping us to learn how processing is localized.

The convergence of brain scans, molecular biology, and computers has opened the way for researchers to localize the regions where different concepts are stored and to observe how these regions are joined together in thought and consciousness (Hilts 1995).

The Way the Brain Works—

The wiring of the brain is far more complex than the most powerful supercomputer. We have billions of neurons and many more supporting cells within the confines of our heads. One amazing finding is that the physical structure of these cells changes as they respond to the environment and experience. When confronted with changes to our surroundings or new experiences, brain cells grow or shrink and new thread-like connections between neurons are established, or old ones are strengthened. If a person is blinded, for example, the other sensory portions of the brain will become stronger.

Today, brain researchers consider the brain to be organized in both a focal and diffuse manner, depending on what functions are being addressed. Basic sensory and motor functions are controlled by specific areas, while higher mental functions involve a constellation of areas across the brain.

Complex thinking requires memory applications from several locations. It may involve visual or auditory memories, concept identification, and language usage. All of this occurs while other portions of the brain are aware of sensations of feeling, temperature, visual stimuli, sounds, and possibly tangential thoughts—and all the while that thinker's brain is responsible for maintaining balance while walking and chewing gum. This is what is meant by the term *parallel processing*, the ability of the brain to perform many tasks at once.

Human speech has provided a rich area for the study of the way information travels through the brain. An incredible array of "category deficits" in human thinking arise from damage to the brain. Examples include people whose overall functioning is normal but who cannot recall the names of animals; people who can write words but not numbers; and people who can recognize faces of loved ones but cannot say their names. The range extends from unnoticeable gaps to an almost complete inability to understand language.

When studied in detail, in many patients and with the assistance of imaging equipment, the various disabilities give us a good picture of how the brain organizes and manipulates information. For example, damage to a particular part of the back of the brain can cause a person to fail to recognize categorical relationships such as a violin as a musical instrument, or robin as a bird, or any other individuals as belonging to particular categories.

After more than a century of study, cases like this have allowed researchers to tentatively identify about 20 categories that the brain uses to organize knowledge. These include plants, animals, body parts, colors, numbers, verbs, facial expressions, and sounds. There are certainly many more (Hilts 1995).

In mapping emotions, opposites such as happiness and sadness are not registered in the same place in the brain. They entail different and independent patterns of activity in different locations. Because happiness and sadness involve separate brain areas, we can have bittersweet emotions, such as when we fondly think of a deceased loved one.

In a memory, connections are made to areas of the brain that may control memory of visual images, odors, sounds, and certain words. This is a vital point for educators. Connections between the various brain areas are the foundation of thinking and knowing. Connections allow us to put two or more memory images together. These images may be of sounds, sights, ideas, or emotions. The ability to *associate* or *connect* these images stored in different areas of the brain allows us to be "smart." By connecting these images at the speed of electricity, we are able to create a simple thought, such as "I am going to take the dog out," or a more complex one, such as "It is my wife's birthday—it will make her happy if I send her flowers." We will address the implications for the classroom shortly.

Levels of Brain Function—

There is value in identifying the three levels of brain function that are addressed in a school or workplace. The nature of the organization of brain functions and their connections to one another form the *first* level of brain performance, known as neurological development. The *second* level is subskill performance. This requires the connections of several parts of the brain that are required to perform the *third*, or skill level. For example, eye-hand coordination, visual integration, and cognitive recall are subskills required to perform the skill of writing; all of these subskills contribute to writing performance.

When we think of skill performance in analytical terms, we can become more effective teachers who systematically analyze the performance of individual students. The learning difficulties or strengths of the individual are affected by developmental levels and relative strengths within a skill or subskill.

Male/Female Differences—

Yes, there are differences in the structure of male and female brains. One example is the larger size of the corpus callosum (a structure that joins the left and right hemispheres) in females. Another is the tendency of female brains to develop in a rather uniform manner, while male brains do not.

Differences in brain organization appear to result in variations in cognitive abilities. Most significantly, it is generally true that females tend to be more fluent than males in the use of language, and males tend to be better at spatial analysis. Less definite research indicates that boys excel in mathematical ability and tend to be more aggressive than females. Efforts to explain sex differences tend to focus on one or more of the following: different brain organization, hormonal effects on cerebral function, genetic sex-linkage, maturation rate, and environment (Kolb and Whishaw 1996).

The sex-based concept of left-brain dominance (highly verbal, logical thinker and basically rational) verses right brain dominance (less verbal, spatial memory strength, and intuitive processor), is receiving little support in the recent research. It is, at best, inconclusive. Each hemisphere relies heavily on the other, thereby producing a synergy that cannot be separated. According to Renate and Geoffrey Caine (1991), "schools should provide the opportunity to develop all abilities even as we continue to prefer some over others" (p. 34).

The Thinking Skills Movement

As John Dewey pointed out in the 1930s, thinking can be done well or badly, and good thinking, like good manners, can be taught. Thinking occurs in the formation of beliefs, and in making decisions and solving problems. If good thinking can be taught, it can have far-reaching applications well beyond the classroom.

Since 1956, Bloom's *Taxonomy of Educational Objectives* has provided one of the fundamental frameworks for teachers to teach thinking skills in the classroom. Writers and workshop presenters use this well-organized structure for the teaching of thinking. Bloom's Taxonomy was a notable effort—but it has not been borne out by the last few decades of research on cognitive processes (Hart 1986).

Some Bloom advocates try to adapt the taxonomy to current brain research. Adapting Bloom's model of higher and lower forms of cognition to classroom instruction may have some merit, but other approaches to developing thinking, language, and metacognitive processing seem to have more potential.

Through the 1980s, "thinking skills" was a key buzzword in teacher training. Prominent theorists included Perkins, Costa and Adler. D. N. Perkins wrote of intelligence as the combination of *Power* (natural ability/IQ), *Tactics* (thinking strategy) and *Content* combining to form *Intelligence*. Thus,

Intelligence = Power + Tactics + Content

The "unnaturalness of good thinking" required that thinking be taught in a variety of ways. Perkins described "thinking frames" or tactics/strategies that enhance intelligence.

In 1980, the Association for Supervision and Curriculum Development published a compilation of the works of various authors entitled *Developing Minds*. Edited by Arthur Costa, the book presented useful ways to enhance thinking in such content areas as writing, reading, science, and math. It included 18 articles by 18 different authors on programs for teaching thinking.

Hundreds of additional books and articles added to the vast array of materials about teaching thinking. But all of this activity took place with no clear idea of how the mind received, processed, or produced information.

It is interesting how little we have heard in recent years about "thinking skills." Is it no longer important, or was it void of valid content? Is the vacuum of knowledge about the brain being filled by meaningful and applicable cognitive research?

As early as 1986, Mortimer Adler was one of the few voices presenting an alternative view about teaching thinking. He supported content-based instruction that involved reading, writing, measuring, testing, and trying to draw conclusions. When practical thinking applications were applied to content instruction, meaningful thinking instruction took place. This approach is supported today through research that tells us that making connections with the brain is the key to long-term memory and the ability to apply classroom learning in other contexts.

For centuries, humans have recognized the importance of quality thinking. What has changed in recent years is the advance of technology that has enabled researchers to study, even to observe, what takes place when we think. It is interesting, but not surprising, that some of the foremost thinkers about thinking during the 1980s (Hart 1986) have become leaders in the application of the science of cognition and brain-based learning.

The Recent Brain Literature

Since the early 1980s, there have been a number of books on best-seller lists that have used findings about the brain as subject matter that has fascinated millions of readers. Two books by Oliver Sacks, *The Man Who Mistook His Wife for a Hat* (1987) and *An Anthropologist on Mars* (1995) depict unusual case studies of behavioral abnormalities caused by neurological damage. This seems to have a fascination for many readers.

Howard Gardner documented the concept that the brain possesses many forms of intelligence in his 1983 book *Frames of Mind*. By the 1990s, the concept of multiple intelligence had caught on in many schools. His book and its variants continued selling in the popular market. Educators are familiar with his important theory that there are at least seven intelligences: mathematical, musical, kinesthetic, linguistic, spatial, intrapersonal, and interpersonal. A strength in one does not predict a strength in another. Gardner's Harvard-based research was state-of-the-art and played a strong role in raising the consciousness of educators toward the importance of learning more about the brain. Like the popular books previously mentioned, it also raised the interest level of the general public.

The *Triarchic Mind* followed in 1988 with a description of three forms of intelligence. Robert Sternberg presented his "triarchic theory" of intelligence using three manifestations: 1) the internal world of the individual, which is the traditional view of intelligence, 2) the relationship of that intelligence to the environment around us, and 3) the relationship of intelligence to experiences we have had since the time we were born.

Emotional Intelligence (1995), by Daniel Goleman, is a serious look at the importance of those factors not measured on an IQ test. Goleman argues that our view of intelligence is far too narrow. He uses brain and behavioral research to demonstrate the factors involved when people of high IQ fail at life and those of modest IQ do extremely well. Emotional intelligence includes persistence, impulse control, enthusiasm, empathy, and social awareness.

In line with the current interest in character education, the recent book *Moral Intelligence* (1997), by Robert Coles, again uses the term intelligence in a title. Coles makes the point that during the elementary school years the child becomes a moral creature—it is the time when the conscience is, or is not, created.

These important years are the time when the malleable mind is being formed. Children are eager to absorb the world that is placed around them—the good or the bad, the moral or the immoral. The brain is a sponge during these young years when it is capable of gaining vast amounts of information. Too often our society forgets that the early years are the most important time to direct our efforts in school and at home. It is the fortunate child who is nurtured in both.

Although his work has focused on educational disabilities, Melvin Levine has been a guiding light to educators on the role of brain function. As a researcher, pediatrician, and professor at the University of North Carolina, he has been able to develop his ideas about how the developing brain functions. As a lecturer and as the author of several books, most notably, *Educational Care* (1994), he has been able to extend his influence to many schools.

Educational Care provides a guide for parents and teachers to collaborate in the management of children with school-related problems. Through the development of diagnostic instruments that integrate neurological, behavioral, and developmental findings, he has been able to better understand the workings of a child's mind and plan better ways to teach those with educational difficulties.

Applications in Education

Learning and Memory—

Cognitive psychologists have identified two separate types of memory systems. The "what" memory system holds facts such as faces, names, and dates. The "how-to" memory preserves skills such as reading or sewing. Memories of both types are stored in the short-term holding area behind the forehead where they remain for a few moments. Some of these memories are converted to long-term storage that may last for years. "What" memory tends to fade quickly, but "how-to" memory can last a lifetime (Hilts 1995).

Conversion of short-term into long-term memory involves the growth of new connections between neurons. Certain memory-enhancing strategies, such as repetition and association, are effective ways of growing connections between neurons. Actual changes to the brain occur—the size of a brain area grows or shrinks, depending on experience and practice. Memory is generally considered to be a five-step process: 1) acquisition, 2) registration, 3) storage, 4) access, 5) transfer.

Thematic instruction provides connections among storage areas of the brain, therefore reinforcing memory through dispersal. The more areas that are "touched" by the stimulus, the greater the probability of long-term retention.

Cooperative learning also provides connections to other parts of the brain through integration with other content topics or through social interaction.

Opportunities to think and speak about a topic, as well as to listen and do hands-on activities, will also enhance the probability of long term retention.

Creation of many strong connections between areas of the brain provides the key to memory enhancement. As Gardner would say, this is influenced by an individual's strength in the specific area of intelligence being addressed. The important point for educators is that the brain's *thinking* function involves retaining information and connecting the information storage locations when necessary.

John Bruer makes a strong case for the relevance of prior knowledge in his 1993 book *Schools for Learning*. A good teacher will consciously use an "anticipatory set" (capture students' attention and relate the topic to prior knowledge), because the way we understand and remember new material depends on how it relates to what we already know. Learning is an active process as well as a constructive one. Our brains make sense of what we experience by actively connecting it with prior knowledge.

The Learning Environment—

The emotional condition of one's mind can have a great influence on the brain's ability to retain information. If the learner's mind is stressed by fear and anxiety, maximum learning cannot occur. Too much of the mind's energy and attention is expended on the emotion and not on the intended learning. When divorce, peer pressure, the birth of a sibling, or other stress-causing circumstances occur, learning suffers.

Climate is a term often used to describe the character and culture of a school. A pleasant, academic orientation enhances the mind's readiness to accept and retain information. Friendly classmates, pleasant surroundings, gentle colors, cleanliness, and abundant classical music are possible ingredients of a healthy learning climate.

Far too little effort is spent in creating school environments that increase the ability to learn. The classroom is often a very unnatural environment. School typically requires long hours of attention in a sitting position—a task far more difficult for some than others.

Success for an adult in a home or work setting generally does not require being in one chair or room for an extended time. In those settings, social interaction, motivation, and energy, as well as a variety of other task-specific skills, are essential. Teaching, for example, requires energy, motivation, verbal and interpersonal skills, as well as the ability to use effective instructional strategies. Yet, the degree to which such skills are recognized and used to the greatest advantage during a typical school day is generally minimal.

The Mind/Body Connection—

Sometimes we forget that the brain benefits from care of the entire body. Good nutrition and exercise are fundamental to optimum school performance. Aerobic activity feeds the brain with oxygen and glucose—essential to increasing nerve connections. Children who exercise regularly do better in school according to many studies.

Getting more physical activity into the school day is a challenge, but it can be achieved through large-group music aerobics, class recess that involves significant activity, and gym classes that involve real movement.

Classroom learning benefits from added activity. Physical movement involving lesson content enhances brain function and learning. Studies have found that young children learn subtraction faster and retain it longer when it is presented in a variety of forms, including physical activity such as moving classmates as numbers in an equation or calculating comparable distances or times for outdoor runs.

Music and the Arts—

Like physical education classes, music and the arts can be powerful forces in the effort to create learning connections. Plato said that music "is a more potent instrument than any other for education." He was prescient in his understanding that music trains the brain for advanced forms of thinking.

In a recent University of California study, two groups of three year olds were the subject of a unique experiment. One group took piano lessons and sang daily in chorus. The other did not have music as part of their curriculum. After eight months, the musical group performed far better on a puzzle completion task (Blakeslee 1995). This skill could translate into better math and engineering skills.

Studies such as this support the belief that early music training may improve a child's ability to reason. While it may not be practical to provide students with daily classes with a music teacher, playing classical music during quiet work times in class and in the hallways can significantly increase student exposure.

The possibilities for the integration of history, math, and language into music, art, and drama are endless. Classroom dramatizations, the use of geometry in art, and other cross-curricular possibilities are only limited by the teacher's imagination.

Summary

The neurological system of each student contains a variety of skill strengths and weaknesses that influence school performance. The task is to think of the brain as an organ for learning and to match instruction and the learning environment to the way that the brain most effectively gathers and retains information.

The following practices, some of which are already used in many classrooms, can help us attune schooling to what brain-based learning research tells us:

- Use a wide variety of instruction geared toward different types of intelligence.
- Incorporate movement into instructional activities.
- Make greater use of instructional strategies that build connections among the different brain functions, such as thematic instruction and cooperative learning.
- Do more to promote students' physical fitness.
- Stress the importance of early music training to enhance children's cognitive skills, and integrate music into other subject areas.
- Create pleasant, relaxed classroom environments through pleasing colors, classical music, and cleanliness.
- Relate new topics to students' prior knowledge in order to strengthen their long-term memory of content.
- Teach critical thinking skills by applying them to content instruction through reading, writing, measuring, testing, and trying to draw conclusions.

Schools have been slow to implement instruction that reflects what we know about the brain and learning. There are many reasons—inertia, the fear of taking a chance, lack of time to reflect on and plan for change, and difficulties in communicating to educators what *does* make a difference.

Change in education is notoriously slow. Wisely, we don't want to be reckless with our children. But as more and more evidence supports the power of understanding cognitive psychology, we are on the eve of a learning revolution that could change our schools for the better.

References

Adler, Mortimer. (1986). "Why Critical Thinking Programs Won't Work." *Education Week* (September 17, 1986).

Blakeslee, Sandra. (1995). *New York Times (Science Times)*, May 16, 1995: C1.

Bloom, Benjamin et al. (1956). *Taxonomy of Educational Objectives: The Classification of Educational Goals.* New York: Longmans Green.

Bruer, John T. (1993). *Schools for Learning.* Cambridge, MA: MIT Press.

Caine, Renate and Geoffrey Caine. (1991). *Making Connections: Teaching and the Human Brain.* Alexandria, VA: Association for Supervision and Curriculum Development.

Coles, Robert. (1997). *The Moral Intelligence of Children.* New York: Random House.

Costa, Arthur L., editor. (1985). *Developing Minds* Alexandria, VA: Association for Supervision and Curriculum Development.

Flam, Faye. (1996). "Tracking Down Thoughts." *The Philadelphia Inquirer* (May 20, 1996): E-3.

Gardner, Howard (1983). *Frames of Mind.* New York: Basic Books.

Gardner, Howard. (1995). "Reflections on Multiple Intelligences." *Phi Delta Kappan* (November 1995).

Goleman, Daniel. (1995). *Emotional Intelligence.* New York: Bantam Books.

Hart, Leslie A. (1986). "A Response: All Thinking Paths Lead to the Brain." *Educational Leadership* (May 1986).

Hilts, Phillip. (1995). "Brain's Memory System Comes Into Focus." *The New York Times* (May 30, 1995): C1.

Kolb, Bryan and Ian Q. Whishaw. (1996). *Fundamentals of Human Neuropsychology.* W. H. Freeman and Co.

Levine, Melvin. (1987). *Developmental Variation and Learning Disorders.* Boston, MA: Educators Publishing Service.

Levine, Melvin. (1994). *Educational Care.* Boston, MA: Educators Publishing Service.

Perkins, D. N. (1986). "Thinking Frames." *Educational Leadership* (May, 1986).

Sacks, Oliver. (1987). *The Man Who Mistook His Wife For a Hat.* New York: Harper Perennial.

Sacks, Oliver. (1995). *An Anthropologist on Mars.* New York: Vintage Books.

Sternberg, Robert J. (1988). *The Triarchic Mind.* New York: Viking.

In Search of . . . Brain-Based Education

BY JOHN T. BRUER

The "In Search of . . ." television series is no way to present history, Mr. Bruer points out, and the brain-based education literature is not the way to present the science of learning.

WE HAVE almost survived the Decade of the Brain. During the 1990s, government agencies, foundations, and advocacy groups engaged in a highly successful effort to raise public awareness about advances in brain research. Brain science became material for cover stories in our national newsmagazines. Increased public awareness raised educators' always simmering interest in the brain to the boiling point. Over the past five years, there have been numerous books, conferences, and entire issues of education journals devoted to what has come to be called "brain-based education."

Brain-based educators tend to support progressive education reforms. They decry the "factory model of education," in which experts create knowledge, teachers disseminate it, and students are graded on how much of it they can absorb and retain. Like many other educators, brain-based educators favor a constructivist, active learning model. Students should be actively engaged in learning and in guiding their own instruction. Brain enthusiasts see neuroscience as perhaps the best weapon with which to destroy our outdated factory model.[1] They argue that teachers should teach for meaning and understanding. To do so, they claim, teachers should create learning environments that are low in threat and high in challenge, and students

---

JOHN T. BRUER is president of the James S. McDonnell Foundation, St. Louis.

From *Phi Delta Kappan*, May 1999, pp. 649-657. © 1999 by John T. Bruer. Reprinted by permission.

THE DANGER WITH MUCH OF THE BRAIN-BASED EDUCATION LITERATURE IS THAT IT BECOMES EXCEEDINGLY DIFFICULT TO SEPARATE THE SCIENCE FROM THE SPECULATION.

should be actively engaged and immersed in complex experiences. No reasonable parent or informed educator would take issue with these ideas. Indeed, if more schools taught for understanding and if more teachers had the resources to do so, our schools would be better learning environments.

However, there is nothing new in this critique of traditional education. It is based on a cognitive and constructivist model of learning that is firmly rooted in more than 30 years of psychological research. Whatever scientific evidence we have for or against the efficacy of such educational approaches can be found in any current textbook on educational psychology.[2] None of the evidence comes from brain research. It comes from cognitive and developmental psychology; from the behavioral, not the biological, sciences; from our scientific understanding of the mind, not from our scientific understanding of the brain.

To the extent that brain-based educators' recipe for school and classroom change is well grounded in this behavioral research, their message is valuable. Teachers should know about short- and long-term memory; about primacy/recency effects; about how procedural, declarative, and episodic memory differ; and about how prior knowledge affects our current ability to learn. But to claim that these are "brain-based" findings is misleading.

While we know a considerable amount from psychological research that is pertinent to teaching and learning, we know much less about how the brain functions and learns.[3] For nearly a century, the science of the mind (psychology) developed independently from the science of the brain (neuroscience). Psychologists were interested in our mental functions and capacities—how we learn, remember, and think. Neuroscientists were interested in how the brain develops and functions. It was as if psychologists were interested only in our mental software and neuroscientists only in our neural hardware. Deeply held theoretical assumptions in both fields supported a view that mind and brain could, and indeed should, be studied independently.

It is only in the past 15 years or so that these theoretical barriers have fallen. Now scientists called cognitive neuroscientists are

beginning to study how our neural hardware might run our mental software, how brain structures support mental functions, how our neural circuits enable us to think and learn. This is an exciting and new scientific endeavor, but it is also a very young one. As a result we know relatively little about learning, thinking, and remembering at the level of brain areas, neural circuits, or synapses; we know very little about how the brain thinks, remembers, and learns.

Yet brain science has always had a seductive appeal for educators.[4] Brain science appears to give hard biological data and explanations that, for some reason, we find more compelling than the "soft" data that come from psychological science. But seductive appeal and a very limited brain science database are a dangerous combination. They make it relatively easy to formulate bold statements about brain science and education that are speculative at best and often far removed from neuroscientific fact. Nonetheless, the allure of brain science ensures that these ideas will often find a substantial and accepting audience. As Joseph LeDoux, a leading authority on the neuroscience of emotion, cautioned educators at a 1996 brain and education conference, "These ideas are easy to sell to the public, but it is easy to take them beyond their actual basis in science."[5]

And the ideas are far-ranging indeed. Within the literature on the brain and education one finds, for example, that brain science supports Bloom's Taxonomy, Madeline Hunter's effective teaching, whole-language instruction, Vygotsky's theory of social learning, thematic instruction, portfolio assessment, and cooperative learning.

The difficulty is that the brain-based education literature is very much like a docudrama or an episode of "In Search of . . ." in which an interesting segment on Egyptology suddenly takes a bizarre turn that links Tutankhamen with the alien landing in Roswell, New Mexico. Just where did the episode turn from archaeological fact to speculation or fantasy? That is the same question one must constantly ask when reading about brain-based education.

Educators, like all professionals, should be interested in knowing how basic research, including brain science, might contribute to improved professional practice. The danger

with much of the brain-based education literature, as with an "In Search of . . ." episode, is that it becomes exceedingly difficult to separate the science from the speculation, to sort what we know from what we would like to be the case. If our interest is enhancing teaching and learning by applying science to education, this is not the way to do it. Would we want our children to learn about the Exodus by watching "In Search of Ramses' Martian Wife"?

We might think of each of the numerous claims that brain-based educators make as similar to an "In Search of . . ." episode. For each one, we should ask, Where does the science end and the speculation begin? I cannot do that here. So instead I'll concentrate on two ideas that appear prominently in brain-based education articles: the educational significance of brain laterality (right brain versus left brain) and the claim that neuroscience has established that there is a sensitive period for learning.

Left Brain, Right Brain: One More Time

"Right Brain versus left brain" is one of those popular ideas that will not die. Speculations about the educational significance of brain laterality have been circulating in the education literature for 30 years. Although repeatedly criticized and dismissed by psychologists and brain scientists, the speculation continues.[6] David Sousa devotes a chapter of *How the Brain Learns* to explaining brain laterality and presents classroom strategies that teachers might use to ensure that both hemispheres are involved in learning.[7] Following the standard line, the *left hemisphere* is the logical hemisphere, involved in speech, reading, and writing. It is the analytical hemisphere that evaluates factual material in a rational way and that understands the literal interpretation of words. It is a serial processor that tracks time and sequences and that recognizes words, letters, and numbers. The right hemisphere is the intuitive, creative hemisphere. It gathers information more from images than from words. It is a parallel processor well suited for pattern recognition and spatial reasoning. It is the hemisphere that recognizes faces, places, and objects.

According to this traditional view of laterality, left-hemisphere-dominant individuals tend to be more verbal, more analytical, and better problem solvers. Females, we are told, are more likely than males to be left-hemisphere dominant. Right-hemisphere-dominant individuals, more typically males, paint and draw well, are good at math, and deal with the visual world more easily than with the verbal. Schools, Sousa points out, are overwhelmingly left-hemisphere places in which left-hemisphere-dominant individuals, mostly girls, feel more comfortable than right-hemisphere-dominant individuals, mostly boys. Hemispheric dominance also explains why girls are superior to boys in arithmetic —it is linear and logical, and there is only one correct answer to each problem—while girls suffer math anxiety when it comes to the right-hemisphere activities of algebra and geometry. These latter disciplines, unlike arithmetic, are holistic, relational, and spatial and also allow multiple solutions to problems.

Before we consider how, or whether, brain science supports this traditional view, educators should be wary of claims about the educational significance of gender differences in brain laterality. There are tasks that psychologists have used in their studies that reveal gender-based differences in performance. Often, however, these differences are specific to a task. Although males are superior to females at mentally rotating objects, this seems to be the only spatial task for which psychologists have found such a difference.[8] Moreover, when they do find gender differences, these differences tend to be very small. If they were measured on an I.Q.-like scale with a mean of 100 and a standard deviation of 15, these gender differences amount to around five points. Furthermore, the range of difference within genders is broad. Many males have better language skills than most females; many females have better spatial and mathematical skills than most males. The scientific consensus among psychologists and neuroscientists who conduct these studies is that whatever gender differences exist may have interesting consequences for the scientific study of the brain, but they have no practical or instructional consequences.[9]

Now let's consider the brain sciences and how or whether they offer support for some of the particular teaching strategies Sousa recommends. To involve the right hemisphere in learning, Sousa writes, teachers should encourage students to generate and use mental imagery: "For most people, the left hemisphere specializes in coding information verbally while the right hemisphere codes information visually. Although teachers spend much time talking (and sometimes have their students talk) about the learning objective, little time is given to developing visual cues." To ensure that the left hemisphere gets equal time, teachers should let students "read, write, and compute often."[10]

What brain scientists currently know about spatial reasoning and mental imagery provides counterexamples to such simplistic claims as these. Such claims arise out of a folk theory about brain laterality, not a neuroscientific one.

Here are two simple spatial tasks: 1) determine whether one object is above or below another, and 2) determine whether two objects are more or less than one foot apart. Based on our folk theory of the brain, as spatial tasks both of these should be right-hemisphere tasks. However, if we delve a little deeper, as psychologists and neuroscientists tend to do, we see that the information-processing or computational demands of the two tasks are different.[11] The first task requires that we place objects or parts of objects into broad categories—up/down or left/right— but we do not have to determine how far up or down (or left or right) one object is from the other. Psychologists call this *categorical* spatial reasoning. In contrast, the second task is a spatial *coordinate* task, in which we must compute and retain precise distance relations between the objects.

Research over the last decade has shown that categorical and coordinate spatial reasoning are performed by distinct subsystems in the brain.[12] A subsystem in the brain's *left* hemisphere performs categorical spatial reasoning. A subsystem in the brain's *right* hemisphere processes coordinate relationships. Although the research does point to differences in the information-processing abilities and biases of the brain hemispheres, those differences are found at a finer level of analysis than "spatial reasoning." It makes no sense to claim that spatial reasoning is a right-hemisphere task.

Based on research like this, Christopher Chabris and Stephen Kosslyn, leading researchers in the field of spatial reasoning and visual imagery, claim that any model of brain lateralization that assigns conglomerations of complex mental abilities, such as spatial reasoning, to one hemisphere or the other, as our folk theory does, is simply too crude to be scientifically or practically useful. Our folk theory can neither explain what the brain is doing nor generate useful predictions about where novel tasks might be computed in the brain.[13] Unfortunately, it is just such a crude folk theory that brain-based educators rely on when framing their recommendations.

Visual imagery is another example. From the traditional, folk-theoretic perspective, generating and using visual imagery is a right-hemisphere function. Generating and using visual imagery is a complex operation that involves, even at a crude level of analysis, at least five distinct mental subcomponents: 1) to create a visual image of a dog, you must transfer long-term visual memories into a temporary visual memory store; 2) to determine if your imagined dog has a tail, you must zoom in and identify details of the image; 3) to put a blue collar on the dog requires that you add a new element to your previously generated image; 4) to make the dog look the other way demands that you rotate your image of the dog; and 5) to draw or describe the imagined dog, you must scan the visual image with your mind's eye.

There is an abundance of neuroscientific evidence that this complex task is not confined to the right hemisphere. There are patients with brain damage who can recognize visual objects and draw or describe visible objects normally, yet these patients cannot answer questions that require them to generate a mental image. ("Think of a dog. Does it have a long tail?") These patients have long-term visual memories, but they cannot use those memories to generate mental images. All these patients have damage to the rear portion of the left hemisphere.[14]

Studies on split-brain patients, people who have had their two hemispheres surgically disconnected to treat severe epilepsy, allow scientists to present visual stimuli to one hemisphere but not the other. Michael Gazzaniga and Kosslyn showed split-brain patients a lower-case letter and then asked the patients whether the corresponding capital letter had any curved lines.[15] The task required that the patients generate a mental image of the capital letter based on the lower-case letter they had seen. When the stimuli were presented to the patients' left hemispheres, they performed perfectly on the task. However, the patients made many mistakes when the letter stimuli were presented to the right hemisphere. Likewise, brain-imaging studies of normal adult subjects performing imagery tasks show that both hemispheres are active in these tasks.[16] Based on all these data, brain scientists have concluded that the ability to generate visual imagery depends on the left hemisphere.

One of the most accessible presentations of this research appears in *Images of Mind,* by Michael Posner and Mark Raichle, in which they conclude, "The common belief that creating mental imagery is a function of the right hemisphere is clearly false."[17] Again, different brain areas are specialized for different tasks, but that specialization occurs at a finer level of analysis than "using visual imagery." Using visual imagery may be a useful learning strategy, but if it is useful it is not because it involves an otherwise underutilized right hemisphere in learning.

The same problem also subverts claims that one hemisphere or the other is the site of number recognition or reading skills. Here is a simple number task, expressed in two apparently equivalent ways: What is bigger, two or five? What is bigger, 2 or 5? It involves recognizing number symbols and understanding what those symbols mean. According to our folk theory, this should be a left-hemisphere task. But once again our folk theory is too crude.

Numerical comparison involves at least two mental subskills: identifying the number names and then comparing the numerical magnitudes that they designate. Although we seldom think of it, we are "bilingual" when it comes to numbers. We have number words—e.g., *one, two*—to name numbers, and we also have special written symbols, Arabic numerals—e.g., 1, 2. Our numerical bilingualism means that the two comparison questions above place different computational demands on the mind/brain. Using brain-recording techniques, Stanislaus Dehaene found that we identify number words using a system in the brain's left hemisphere,

THE FUNDAMENTAL PROBLEM WITH THE RIGHT-BRAIN VERSUS LEFT-BRAIN CLAIMS IN THE EDUCATION LITERATURE IS THAT THEY RELY ON INTUITIONS AND FOLK THEORIES ABOUT THE BRAIN.

but we identify Arabic numerals using brain areas in both the right and left hemispheres. Once we identify either the number words or the Arabic digits as symbols for numerical quantities, a distinct neural subsystem in the brain's right hemisphere compares magnitudes named by the two number symbols.[18]

Even for such a simple number task as comparison, both hemispheres are involved. Thus it makes no neuroscientific sense to claim that the left hemisphere recognizes numbers. Brain areas are specialized, but at a much finer level than "recognizing numbers." This simple task is already too complex for our folk theory to handle. Forget about algebra and geometry.

Similar research that analyzes speech and reading skills into their component processes also shows that reading is not simply a left-hemisphere task, as our folk theory suggests. Recognizing speech sounds, decoding written words, finding the meanings of words, constructing the gist of a written text, and making inferences as we read all rely on subsystems in both brain hemispheres.[19]

There is another different, but equally misleading, interpretation of brain laterality that occurs in the literature of brain-based education. In *Making Connections,* Renate Caine and Geoffrey Caine are critical of traditional "brain dichotomizers" and warn that the brain does not lend itself to such simple explanations. In their view, the results of research on split brains and hemispheric specialization are inconclusive—"both hemispheres are involved in all activities"—a conclusion that would seem to be consistent with what we have seen in our brief review of spatial reasoning, visual imagery, number skills, and reading.

However, following the folk theory, they do maintain that the left hemisphere processes parts and the right hemisphere processes wholes. In their interpretation, the educational significance of laterality research is that it shows that, within the brain, parts and wholes always interact. Laterality research thus provides scientific support for one of their principles of brain-based education: the brain processes parts and wholes simultaneously. Rather than number comparison or categorical spatial reasoning, the Caines provide a more global example: "Consider a

poem, a play, a great novel, or a great work of philosophy. They all involve a sense of the 'wholeness' of things and a capacity to work with patterns, often in timeless ways. In other words, the 'left brain' processes are enriched and supported by 'right brain' processes."[20]

For educators, the Caines see the two-brain doctrine as a "valuable metaphor that helps educators acknowledge two separate but simultaneous tendencies in the brain for organizing information. One is to reduce information to parts; the other is to perceive and work with it as a whole or a series of wholes."[21] Effective brain-based educational strategies overlook neither parts nor wholes, but constantly attempt to provide opportunities in which students can make connections and integrate parts and wholes. Thus the Caines number among their examples of brain-based approaches whole-language instruction,[22] integrated curricula, thematic teaching, and cooperative learning.[23] Similarly, because we make connections best when new information is embedded in meaningful life events and in socially interactive situations, Lev Vygotsky's theory of social learning should also be highly brain compatible.[24]

To the extent that one would want to view this as a metaphor, all I can say is that some of us find some metaphors more appealing than others. To the extent that this is supposed to be an attempt to ground educational principles in brain science, the aliens have just landed in Egypt.

Where did things go awry? Although they claim that laterality research in the sense of hemispheric localization is inconclusive, the Caines do maintain the piece of our folk theory that attributes "whole" processing to the right hemisphere and "part" processing to the left hemisphere. Because the two hemispheres are connected in normal healthy brains, they conclude that the brain processes parts and wholes simultaneously. It certainly does—although it probably is not the case that wholes and parts can be so neatly dichotomized. For example, in visual word decoding, the right hemisphere seems to read words letter by letter—by looking at the parts—while the left hemisphere recognizes entire words—the visual word forms.[25]

But again, the parts and wholes to which the brain is sensitive appear to occur at quite a fine-grained level of analysis—categories versus coordinates, generating versus scanning visual images, identifying number words versus Arabic digits. The Caines' example of part/whole interactions—the left-hemisphere comprehension of a text and the right-hemisphere appreciation of wholeness—relates to such a highly complex task that involves so many parts and wholes at different levels of analysis that it is trivially true that the whole brain is involved. Thus their appeal to brain science suffers from the same problem Kosslyn identified in the attempts to use crude theories to understand the brain. The only brain categories that the Caines appeal to are parts and wholes. Then they attempt to understand learning and exceedingly complex tasks in terms of parts and wholes. This approach bothers neither to analyze the brain nor to analyze behaviors.

The danger here is that one might think that there are brain-based reasons to adopt whole-language instruction, integrated curricula, or Vygotskian social learning. There are none. Whether or not these educational practices should be adopted must be determined on the basis of the impact they have on student learning. The evidence we now have on whole-language instruction is at best inconclusive, and the efficacy of social learning theory remains an open question. Brain science contributes no evidence, pro or con, for the brain-based strategies that the Caines espouse.

The fundamental problem with the right-brain versus left-brain claims that one finds in the education literature is that they rely on our intuitions and folk theories about the brain, rather than on what brain science is actually able to tell us. Our folk theories are too crude and imprecise to have any scientific, predictive, or instructional value. What modern brain science is telling us—and what brain-based educators fail to appreciate—is that it makes no scientific sense to map gross, unanalyzed behaviors and skills—reading, arithmetic, spatial reasoning—onto one brain hemisphere or another.

Brains Like Sponges: The Sensitive Period

A new and popular, but problematic, idea found in the brain-based literature is that there is a critical or sensitive period in brain development, lasting until a child is around 10 years old, during which children learn faster, easier, and with more meaning than at any other time in their lives. David Sousa presented the claim this way in a recent commentary in *Education Week,* titled "Is the Fuss About Brain Research Justified?"

As the child grows, the brain selectively strengthens and prunes connections based on experience. Although this process continues throughout our lives, it seems to be most pronounced between the ages of 2 and 11, as different development areas emerge and taper off.... These so-called "windows of opportunity" represent critical periods when the brain demands certain types of input to create or consolidate neural networks, especially for acquiring language, emotional control, and learning to play music. Certainly, one can learn new information and skills at any age. But what the child learns during that window period will strongly influence what is learned after the window closes.[26]

In a recent *Educational Leadership* article, Pat Wolfe and Ron Brandt prudently caution educators against any quick marriage between brain science and education. However, among the well-established neuroscientific findings about which educators can be confident, they include, "Some abilities are acquired more easily during certain sensitive periods, or 'windows of opportunity.'" Later they continue, "During these years, [the brain] also has a remarkable ability to adapt and reorganize. It appears to develop some capacities with more ease at this time than in the years after puberty. These stages once called 'critical periods' are more accurately described as 'sensitive periods' or 'windows of opportunity.'"[27] Eric Jensen, in *Teaching with the Brain in Mind,* also writes that "the brain learns fastest and easiest during the school years."[28]

If there were neuroscientific evidence for the existence of such a sensitive period, such evidence might appear to provide a biological argument for the importance of elementary teaching and a scientific rationale for redirecting resources, restructuring curricula, and reforming pedagogy to take advantage of the once-in-a-lifetime learning opportunity nature has given us. If teachers could understand when sensitive periods begin and end, the thinking goes, they could structure curricula to take advantage of these unique windows of opportunity. Sousa tells of an experienced fifth-grade teacher who was upset when a mother asked the teacher what she was doing to take advantage of her daughter's windows of opportunity before they closed. Unfortunately, according to Sousa, the teacher was unaware of the windows-of-opportunity research. He warns, "As the public learns more about brain research through the popular press, scenes like this are destined to be repeated, further eroding confidence in teachers and in schools."[29]

This well-established neuroscientific "finding" about a sensitive period for learning originated in the popular press and in advocacy documents. It is an instance where neuroscientists have speculated about the implications of their work for education and where educators have uncritically embraced

that speculation. Presenting speculation as fact poses a greater threat to the public's confidence in teachers and schools than does Sousa's fifth-grade teacher.

During 1993, the *Chicago Tribune* ran Ron Kotulak's series of Pulitzer-Prize-winning articles on the new brain science. Kotulak's articles later appeared as a book titled *Inside the Brain: Revolutionary Discoveries of How the Mind Works.* Kotulak, an esteemed science writer, presented the first explicit statement that I have been able to find on the existence of a sensitive period between ages 4 and 10, during which children's brains learn fastest and easiest.[30] Variations on the claim appear in the Carnegie Corporation of New York's 1996 publication, *Years of Promise: A Comprehensive Learning Strategy for America's Children,* and in *Building Knowledge for a Nation of Learners,* published by the Office of Educational Research and Improvement of the U.S. Department of Education.[31]

A report released in conjunction with the April 1997 White House Conference on Early Brain Development stated, "[B]y the age of three, the brains of children are two and a half times more active than the brains of adults—and they stay that way throughout the first decade of life.... This suggests that young children—particularly infants and toddlers—are biologically primed for learning and that these early years provide a unique window of opportunity or prime time for learning.[32]

If the sensitive period from age 4 to age 10 is a finding about which educators can be confident and one that justifies the current fuss about brain science, we would expect to find an extensive body of neuroscientific research that supports the claim. Surprisingly, brain-based enthusiasts appeal to a very limited body of evidence.

In Kotulak's initial statement of the sensitive-period claim, he refers to the brain-imaging work of Dr. Harry Chugani, M.D., at Wayne State University: "Chugani, whose imaging studies revealed that children's brains learned fastest and easiest between the ages of 4 and 10, said these years are often wasted because of lack of input."[33]

Years of Promise, the Carnegie Corporation report, cites a speech Kotulak presented at a conference on Brain Development in Young Children, held at the University of Chicago on 13 June 1996. Again referring to Chugani's work, Kotulak said that the years from 4 to about 10 "are the wonder years of learning, when a child can easily pick up a foreign language without an accent and learn a musical instrument with ease."[34] *Years of Promise* also cites a review article published by Dr. Chugani that is based on remarks he made at that Chicago conference.[35] *Rethinking the Brain,* a report based on the Chicago conference, also cites the same sources, as does the U.S. Department of Education document. What's more, Wolfe, Brandt, and Jensen also cite Chugani's work

in their discussions of the sensitive period for learning.

A 1996 article on education and the brain that appeared in *Education Week* reported, "By age 4, Chugani found, a child's brain uses more than twice the glucose that an adult brain uses. Between the ages 4 and 10, the amount of glucose a child's brain uses remains relatively stable. But by age 10, glucose utilization begins to drop off until it reaches adult levels at age 16 or 17. Chugani's findings suggest that a child's peak learning years occur just as all those synapses are forming."[36]

To be fair, these educators are not misrepresenting Chugani's views. He has often been quoted on the existence and educational importance of the sensitive period from age 4 until age 10.[37] In a review of his own work, published in *Preventive Medicine,* Chugani wrote:

> The notion of an extended period during childhood when activity-dependent [synapse] stabilization occurs has recently received considerable attention by those individuals and organizations dealing with early intervention to provide "environmental enrichment" and with the optimal design of educational curricula. Thus, it is now believed by many (including this author) that the biological "window of opportunity" when learning is efficient and easily retained is perhaps not fully exploited by our educational system.[38]

Oddly, none of these articles and reports cite the single research article that provides the experimental evidence that originally motivated the claim: a 1987 *Annals of Neurology* article.[39] In that 1987 article, Chugani and his colleagues, M. E. Phelps and J. C. Mazziota, report results of PET (positron emission tomography) scans on 29 epileptic children, ranging in age from five days to 15 years. Because PET scans require the injection of radioactive substances, physicians can scan children only for diagnostic and therapeutic purposes; they cannot scan "normal, healthy" children just out of scientific curiosity. Thus the 1987 study is an extremely important one because it was the first, if not the only, imaging study that attempted to trace brain development from infancy through adolescence.

The scientists administered radioactively labeled glucose to the children and used PET scans to measure the rate at which specific brain areas took up the glucose. The assumption is that areas of the brain that are more active require more energy and so will take up more of the glucose. While the scans were being acquired, the scientists made every effort to eliminate, or at least minimize, all sensory stimulation for the subjects. Thus they measured the rate of glucose uptake when the brain was (presumably) not

NEITHER CHUGANI, HIS CO-AUTHORS, NOR OTHER NEUROSCIENTISTS HAVE STUDIED HOW QUICKLY OR EASILY 5-YEAR-OLDS LEARN AS OPPOSED TO 15-YEAR-OLDS.

engaged in any sensory or cognitive processing. That is, they measured resting brain-glucose metabolism.

One of their major findings was that, in all the brain areas they examined, metabolic levels reached adult values when children were approximately 2 years old and continued to increase, reaching rates twice the adult level by age 3 or 4. Resting glucose uptake remained at this elevated level until the children were around 9 years old. At age 9, the rates of brain glucose metabolism started to decline and stabilized at adult values by the end of the teenage years. What the researchers found, then, was a "high plateau" period for metabolic activity in the brain that lasted from roughly age 3 to age 9.

What is the significance of this high plateau period? To interpret their findings, Chugani and his colleagues relied on earlier research in which brain scientists had counted synapses in samples of human brain tissue to determine how the number and density of synaptic connections change in the human brain over our life spans. In the late 1970s, Peter Huttenlocher of the University of Chicago found that, starting a few months after birth and continuing until age 3, various parts of the brain formed synapses very rapidly.[40] This early, exuberant synapse growth resulted in synaptic densities in young children's brains that were 50% higher than the densities in mature adult brains. In humans, synaptic densities appear to remain at these elevated levels until around puberty, when some mechanism that is apparently under genetic control causes synapses to be eliminated or pruned back to the lower adult levels.

With this background, Chugani and his colleagues reasoned as follows. There is other evidence suggesting that maintaining synapses and their associated neural structures accounts for most of the glucose that the brain consumes. Their PET study measured changes in the brain's glucose consumption over the life span. Therefore, they reasoned, as the density and number of synapses wax and wane, so too does the rate of brain-glucose metabolism. This 1987 PET study provides important indirect evidence about brain development, based on the study of living brains, that corroborates the direct evidence based on counting synapses in samples of brain tissue taken from patients at autopsy. In the original paper, the scientists stated an important conclusion: "Our findings support the commonly accepted view that brain maturation in humans proceeds at least into the second decade of life."[41]

However, if you read the 1987 paper by Chugani, Phelps, and Mazziota, you will not find a section titled "The Relationship of Elevated Brain Metabolism and Synaptic Densities to Learning." Neither Chugani nor any of his co-authors have studied how quickly or easily 5-year-olds learn as opposed to 15-year-olds. Nor have other neuroscientists studied what high synaptic densities or high brain energy consumption means for the ease, rapidity, and depth of learning.

To connect high brain metabolism or excessive synaptic density with a critical period for learning requires some fancy footwork—or maybe more accurately, sleight of hand. We know that from early childhood until around age 10, children have extra or redundant synaptic connections in their brains. So, the reasoning goes, during this high plateau period of excess brain connectivity, "the individual is given the opportunity to retain and increase the efficiency of connections that, through repeated use during a critical period, are deemed to be important, whereas connections that are used to a lesser extent are more susceptible to being eliminated."[42] This, of course, is simply to assume that the high plateau period is a critical period.

Linking the critical period with learning requires an implicit appeal to another folk belief that appears throughout the history of the brain in education literature. This common assumption is that periods of rapid brain growth or high activity are optimal times, sensitive periods, or windows of opportunity for learning.[43] We get from Chugani's important brain-imaging results to a critical period for learning via two assumptions, neither of which is supported by neuroscientific data, and neither of which has even been the object of neuroscientific research. The claim that the period of high brain connectivity is a critical period for learning, far from being a neuroscientific finding about which educators can be confident, is at best neuroscientific speculation.

Chugani accurately described the scientific state of affairs in his *Preventive Medicine* review. He *believes,* along with some educators and early childhood advocates, that there is a biological window of opportunity when learning is easy, efficient, and easily retained. But there is no neuroscientific evidence to support this belief. And where there is no scientific evidence, there is no scientific fact.

Furthermore, it would appear that we have a considerable amount of research ahead of us if we are to amass the evidence for or against this belief. Neuroscientists have little idea of how experience before puberty affects either the timing or the extent of synaptic elimination. While they have documented that the pruning of synapses does occur, no reliable studies have compared differences in final adult synaptic connectivity with differences in the experiences of individuals before puberty. Nor do they know whether the animals or individuals with greater synaptic densities in adulthood are necessarily more intelligent and developed. Neuroscientists do not know if prior training and education affect either loss or retention of synapses at puberty.[44]

Nor do neuroscientists know how learning is related to changes in brain metabolism and synaptic connectivity over our lifetimes. As the developmental neurobiologist Patricia Goldman-Rakic told educators, "While children's brains acquire a tremendous amount of information during the early years, most learning takes place after synaptic formation stabilizes."[45] That is, a great deal, if not most, learning takes place after age 10 and after pruning has occurred. If so, we may turn into efficient general learning machines only after puberty, only after synaptic formation stabilizes and our brains are less active.

Finally, the entire discussion of this purported critical period takes place under an implicit assumption that children actually do learn faster, more easily, and more deeply between the ages of 4 and 10. There are certainly critical periods for the development of species-wide skills, such as seeing, hearing, and acquiring a first language, but critical periods are interesting to psychologists because they seem to be the exception rather than the rule in human development. As Jacqueline Johnson and Elissa Newport remind us in their article on critical periods in language learning, "In most domains of learning, skill increases over development."[46]

When we ask whether children actually do learn more easily and meaningfully than adults, the answers we get are usually anecdotes about athletes, musicians, and students of second languages. We have not begun to look at the rate, efficiency, and depth of learning across various age groups in a representative sample of learning domains. We are making an assumption about learning behavior and then relying on highly speculative brain science to explain our assumption. We have a lot more research to do.

So, despite what you read in the papers and in the brain-based education literature, neuroscience has *not* established that there is a sensitive period between the ages of 4 and 10 during which children learn more quickly, easily, and meaningfully. Brain-based educators have uncritically embraced neuroscientific speculation.

The pyramids were built by aliens—to house Elvis.

A February 1996 article in *Newsweek* on the brain and education quoted Linda Darling-Hammond: "Our school system was invented in the late 1800s, and little has changed. Can you imagine if the medical profession ran this way?"[47] Darling-Hammond is right. Our school system must change to reflect what we now know about teaching, learning, mind, and brain. To the extent that we want education to be a research-based enterprise, the medical profession provides a reasonable model. We can only be thankful that members of the medical profession are more careful in applying biological research to their professional practice than some educators are in applying brain research to theirs.

We should not shrug off this problem. It is symptomatic of some deeper problems about how research is presented to educators, about what educators find compelling, about how educators evaluate research, and about how professional development time and dollars are spent. The "In Search of . . ." series is a television program that provides an entertaining mix of fact, fiction, and fantasy. That can be an amusing exercise, but it is not always instructive. The brain-based education literature represents a genre of writing, most often appearing in professional education publications, that provides a popular mix of fact, misinterpretation, and speculation. That can be intriguing, but it is not always informative. "In Search of . . ." is no way to present history, and the brain-based education literature is not the way to present the science of learning.

1. Renate Nummela Caine and Geoffrey Caine, Making *Connections: Teaching and the Human Brain* (New York: Addison-Wesley, 1994); idem, "Building a Bridge Between the Neurosciences and Education: Cautions and Possibilities," *NASSP Bulletin*, vol. 82, 1998, pp. 1–8; Eric Jensen, *Teaching with the Brain in Mind* (Alexandria, Va.: Association for Supervision and Curriculum Development, 1998); and Robert Sylvester, *A Celebration of Neurons* (Alexandria, Va.: Association for Supervision and Curriculum Development, 1995).

2. See, for example, Michael Pressley and C. B. McCormick, *Advanced Educational Psychology for Educators*, Researchers, and Policymakers (New York: HarperCollins, 1995).

3. John T. Bruer, *Schools for Thought: A Science of Learning in the Classroom* (Cambridge, Mass.: MIT Press, 1993); and idem, "Education and the Brain: A Bridge Too Far," *Educational Researcher*, November 1997, pp. 4–16.

4. Susan F. Chipman, "Integrating Three Perspectives on Learning," in Sarah L. Friedman, Kenneth A. Klivington, and R. W. Peterson, eds., *The Brain, Cognition, and Education* (Orlando, Fla.: Academic Press, 1986), pp. 203–32.

5. *Bridging the Gap Between Neuroscience and Education: Summary of a Workshop Cosponsored by the Education Commission of the States and the Charles A. Dana Foundation* (Denver: Education Commission of the States, 1996), p. 5.

6. Chipman, op. cit.; Howard Gardner, *Art, Mind, and Brain: A Cognitive Approach to Creativity* (New York: Basic Books, 1982); Mike Rose, "Narrowing the Mind and Page: Remedial Writers and Cognitive Reductionism," *College Composition and Communication*, vol. 39, 1988, pp. 267–302; and Jerre Levy, "Right Brain, Left Brain: Fact and Fiction," *Psychology Today*, May 1985, p. 38.

7. David A. Sousa, *How the Brain Learns: A Classroom Teacher's Guide* (Reston, Va.: National Association of Secondary School Principals, 1995).

8. M. C. Linn and A. C. Petersen, "Emergence and Characterization of Sex Differences in Spatial Ability: A Meta-Analysis," *Child Development*, vol. 56, 1985, pp. 1470–98.

9. Sally Springer and Georg Deutsch, *Left Brain, Right Brain* (New York: W. H. Freeman, 1993).

10. Sousa, pp. 95, 99.

11. Christopher F. Chabris and Stephen M. Kosslyn, "How Do the Cerebral Hemispheres Contribute to Encoding Spatial Relations?," *Current Directions in Psychology*, vol. 7, 1998, pp. 8–14.

12. Ibid.

13. Ibid.

14. Martha Farah, *Visual Agnosias* (Cambridge, Mass.: MIT Press, 1991).

15. Stephen M. Kosslyn et al., "A Computational Analysis of Mental Image Generation: Evidence from Functional Dissociations in Split-Brain Patients," *Journal of Experimental Psychology: General*, vol. 114, 1985, pp. 311–41.

16. Stephen M. Kosslyn et al., "Two Types of Image Generation: Evidence for Left and Right Hemisphere Processes," *Neuropsychologia*, vol. 33, 1995, pp. 1485–1510.

17. Michael I. Posner and Mark E. Raichle, *Images of Mind* (New York: Scientific American Library, 1994), p. 95.

18. Stanislaus Dehaene, "The Organization of Brain Activations in Number Comparison," *Journal of Cognitive Neuroscience*, vol. 8, 1996, pp. 47–68.

19. Mark Jung Beeman and Christine Chiarello, "Complementary Right- and Left-Hemisphere Language Comprehension," *Current Directions in Psychology*, vol. 7, 1998, pp. 2–7.

20. Caine and Caine, p. 37.

21. Ibid., p. 91.

22. Ibid., pp. 9, 48, 91.

23. Ibid., pp. 127–30.

24. Ibid., pp. 47–48.

25. Beeman and Chiarello, op. cit.

26. David A. Sousa, "Is the Fuss About Brain Research Justified?," *Education Week*, 16 December 1998, p. 35.

27. Pat Wolfe and Ron Brandt, "What Do We Know from Brain Research?," *Educational Leadership*, November 1998, p. 12.

28. Jensen, p. 32.

29. Sousa, "Is the Fuss About Brain Research Justified?," p. 35.

30. Ronald Kotulak, *Inside the Brain: Revolutionary Discoveries of How the Mind Works* (Kansas City: Andrews McMeel, 1996), p. 46.

31. *Years of Promise: A Comprehensive Learning Strategy for America's Children* (New York: Carnegie Corporation of New York, 1996), pp. 9–10; and Office of Educational Research and Improvement, *Building Knowledge for a Nation of Learners* (Washington, D.C.: U.S. Department of Education, 1996).

32. Rima Shore, *Rethinking the Brain: New Insights into Early Development* (New York: Families and Work Institute, 1997), pp. 21, 36.

33. Kotulak, p. 46.

34. Ronald Kotulak, "Learning How to Use the Brain," 1996, available on the Web at http://www.newhorizons.org/ofc_21cliusebrain.html.

35. Harry T. Chugani, "Neuroimaging of Developmental Nonlinearity and Developmental Pathologies," in R. W. Thatcher et al., eds., *Developmental Neuroimaging* (San Diego: Academic Press, 1996), pp. 187–95.

36. Debra Viadero, "Brain Trust," *Education Week*, 18 September 1996, pp. 31–33.

37. *Better Beginnings* (Pittsburgh: Office of Child Development, University of Pittsburgh, 1997); A. DiCresce, "Brain Surges," 1997, available on the Web at www.med.wayne.edu/wmp97/brain.htm; and Lynell Hancock, "Why Do Schools Flunk Biology?," *Newsweek*, 19 February 1996, pp. 58–59.

38. Harry Chugani, "A Critical Period of Brain Development: Studies of Cerebral Glucose Utilization with PET," *Preventive Medicine*, vol. 27, 1998, pp. 184–88.

39. Harry T. Chugani, M. E. Phelps, and J. C. Mazziota, "Positron Emission Tomography Study of Human Brain Function Development," *Annals of Neurology*, vol. 22, 1987, pp. 487–97.

40. Peter R. Huttenlocher, "Synaptic Density in Human Frontal Cortex—Developmental Changes of Aging," *Brain Research*, vol. 163, 1979, pp. 195–205; Peter R. Huttenlocher et al., "Synaptogenesis in Human Visual Cortex—Evidence for Synapse Elimination During Normal Development," *Neuroscience Letters*, vol. 33, 1982, pp. 247–52; Peter R. Huttenlocher and Ch. de Courten, "The Development of Synapses in Striate Cortex of Man," *Human Neurobiology*, vol. 6, 1987, pp. 1-9; and Peter R. Huttenlocher and A. S. Dabholkar, "Regional Differences in Synaptogenesis in Human Cerebral Cortex," *Journal of Comparative Neurology*, vol. 387, 1997, pp. 167-78.

41. Chugani, Phelps, and Mazziota, p. 496.

42. Chugani, "Neuroimaging of Developmental Nonlinearity," p. 187.

43. Herman T. Epstein, "Growth Spurts During Brain Development: Implications for Educational Policy and Practice," in S. Chall and A. F. Mirsky, eds., *Education and the Brain* (Chicago: University of Chicago Press, 1978), pp. 343-70; and Chipman, op. cit.

44. Patricia S. Goldman-Rakic, Jean-Pierre Bourgeois, and Pasko Rakic, "Synaptic Substrate of Cognitive Development: Synaptogenesis in the Prefrontal Cortex of the Nonhuman Primate," in N. A. Krasnegor, G. R. Lyon, and P. S. Goldman-Rakic, *Development of the Prefrontal Cortex: Evolution, Neurobiology, and Behavior* (Baltimore: Paul H. Brooks, 1997), pp. 27-47.

45. *Bridging the Gap*, p. 11.

46. Jacqueline S. Johnson and Elissa L. Newport, "Critical Period Effects on Universal Properties," *Cognition*, vol. 39, 1991, p. 215.

47. Hancock, p. 59.

The First Seven . . . and the Eighth

A Conversation with Howard Gardner

Human intelligence continues to intrigue psychologists, neurologists, and educators. What is it? Can we measure it? How do we nurture it?

Kathy Checkley

Howard Gardner's theory of multiple intelligences, described in Frames of Mind *(1985), sparked a revolution of sorts in classrooms around the world, a mutiny against the notion that human beings have a single, fixed intelligence. The fervor with which educators embraced his premise that we have multiple intelligences surprised Gardner himself. "It obviously spoke to some sense that people had that kids weren't all the same and that the tests we had only skimmed the surface about the differences among kids," Gardner said.*

Here Gardner brings us up-to-date on his current thinking on intelligence, how children learn, and how they should be taught.

How do you define intelligence?

Intelligence refers to the human ability to solve problems or to make something that is valued in one or more cultures. As long as we can find a culture that values an ability to solve a problem or create a product in a particular way, then I would strongly consider whether that ability should be considered an intelligence.

First, though, that ability must meet other criteria: Is there a particular representation in the brain for the ability? Are there populations that are especially good or especially impaired in an intelligence? And, can an evolutionary history of the intelligence be seen in animals other than human beings?

I defined seven intelligences (see box) in the early 1980s because those intelligences all fit the criteria. A decade later when I revisited the task, I found at least one more ability that clearly deserved to be called an intelligence.

That would be the naturalist intelligence. What led you to consider adding this to our collection of intelligences?

Somebody asked me to explain the achievements of the great biologists, the ones who had a real mastery of taxonomy, who understood about different species, who could recognize patterns in nature and classify objects. I realized that to explain that kind of ability, I would have to manipulate the other intelligences in ways that weren't appropriate.

So I began to think about whether the capacity to classify nature might be a separate intelligence. The naturalist ability passed with flying colors. Here are a couple of reasons: First, it's an ability we need to survive as human beings. We need, for example, to know which animals to hunt and which to run away from. Second, this ability isn't restricted to human beings. Other animals need to have a naturalist intelligence to survive. Finally, the big selling point is that brain evidence supports the existence of the naturalist intelligence. There are certain parts of the brain particularly dedicated to the recognition and the naming of what are called "natural" things.

How do you describe the naturalist intelligence to those of us who aren't psychologists?

From *Educational Leadership*, September 1997, pp.8-13. © 1997 by the Association for Supervision and Curriculum Development. All rights reserved. Reprinted by permission.

The naturalist intelligence refers to the ability to recognize and classify plants, minerals, and animals, including rocks and grass and all variety of flora and fauna. The ability to recognize cultural artifacts like cars or sneakers may also depend on the naturalist intelligence.

Now, everybody can do this to a certain extent—we can all recognize dogs, cats, trees. But, some people from an early age are extremely good at recognizing and classifying artifacts. For example, we all know kids who, at age 3 or 4, are better at recognizing dinosaurs than most adults.

Darwin is probably the most famous example of a naturalist because he saw so deeply into the nature of living things.

Are there any other abilities you're considering calling intelligences?

Well, there may be an existential intelligence that refers to the human inclination to ask very basic questions about existence. Who are we? Where do we come from? What's it all about? Why do we die? We might say that existential intelligence allows us to know the invisible, outside world. The only reason I haven't given a seal of approval to the existential intelligence is that I don't think we have good brain evidence yet on its existence in the nervous system—one of the criteria for an intelligence.

You have said that the theory of multiple intelligences may be best understood when we know what it critiques. What do you mean?

The standard view of intelligence is that intelligence is something you are born with; you have only a certain amount of it; you cannot do much about how much of that intelligence you have; and tests exist that can tell you how smart you are. The theory of multiple intelligences challenges that view. It asks, instead,

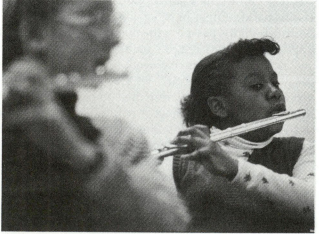
© Susie Fitzhugh

"Given what we know about the brain, evolution, and the differences in cultures, what are the sets of human abilities we all share?"

My analysis suggested that rather than one or two intelligences, all human beings have several (eight) intelligences. What makes life interesting, however, is that we don't have the same strength in each intelligence area, and we don't have the same amalgam of intelligences. Just as we look different from one another and have different kinds of personalities, we also have different kinds of minds.

This premise has very serious educational implications. If we treat everybody as if they are the same, we're catering to one profile of intelligence, the lan-

School matters, but only insofar as it yields something that can be used once students leave school.

guage-logic profile. It's great if you have that profile, but it's not great for the vast majority of human beings who do not have that particular profile of intelligence.

Can you explain more fully how the theory of multiple intelligences challenges what has become known as IQ?

The theory challenges the entire notion of IQ. The IQ test was developed about a century ago as a way to determine who would have trouble in school. The test measures linguistic ability, logical-mathematical ability, and, occasionally, spatial ability.

What the intelligence test does not do is inform us about our other intelligences; it also doesn't look at other virtues like creativity or civic mindedness, or whether a person is moral or ethical.

We don't do much IQ testing anymore, but the shadow of IQ tests is still with us because the SAT—arguably the most potent examination in the world—is basically the same kind of disembodied language-logic instrument.

The truth is, I don't believe there is such a general thing as scholastic aptitude. Even so, I don't think that the SAT will fade until colleges indicate that they'd rather have students who know how to use their minds well—students who may or may not be good test takers, but who are serious, inquisitive, and know how to probe and problem-solve. That is really what college professors want, I believe.

Can we strengthen our intelligences? If so, how?

We can all get better at each of the intelligences, although some people will improve in an intelligence area more readily than others, either because biology gave them a better brain for that intelligence or because their culture gave them a better teacher.

Teachers have to help students use their combination of intelligences to be successful in school, to help them learn whatever it is they want to learn, as well as what the teachers and society believe they have to learn.

Now, I'm not arguing that kids shouldn't learn the literacies. Of course they should learn the literacies. Nor am I arguing that kids shouldn't learn the disciplines. I'm a tremendous champion of the disciplines. What I argue against is the notion that there's only one way to learn how to read, only one way to learn how to compute, only one way to learn about biology. I think that such contentions are nonsense.

It's equally nonsensical to say that everything should be taught seven or eight ways. That's not the point of the MI theory. The point is to realize that any topic of importance, from any discipline, can be taught in more than one way. There are things people need to know, and educators have to be extraordinarily imaginative and persistent in helping students understand things better.

A popular activity among those who are first exploring multiple intelligences is to construct their own intellectual profile. It's thought that when teachers go through the process of creating such a profile, they're more likely to recognize and appreciate the intellectual strengths of their students. What is your view on this kind of activity?

My own studies have shown that people love to do this. Kids like to do it, adults like to do it. And, as an activity, I think it's perfectly harmless.

I get concerned, though, when people think that determining your intellectual profile—or that of someone else—is an end in itself.

You have to use the profile to understand the ways in which you seem to learn easily. And, from there, determine how to use those strengths to help you become more successful in other endeavors. Then, the profile becomes a way for you to understand yourself better, and you can use that understanding to catapult yourself to a better level of understanding or to a higher level of skill.

How has your understanding of the multiple intelligences influenced how you teach?

As long as you can lose one ability while others are spared, you cannot just have a single intelligence.

My own teaching has changed slowly as a result of multiple intelligences because I'm teaching graduate students psychological theory and there are only so many ways I can do that. I am more open to group work and to student projects of various sorts, but even if I wanted to be an "MI professor" of graduate students, I still have a certain moral obligation to prepare them for a world in which they will have to write scholarly articles and prepare theses.

Where I've changed much more, I believe, is at the workplace. I direct research projects and work with all kinds of people. Probably 10 to 15 years ago, I would have tried to find people who were just like me to work with me on these projects.

I've really changed my attitude a lot on that score. Now I think much more in terms of what people are good at and in putting together teams of people whose varying strengths complement one another.

How should thoughtful educators implement the theory of multiple intelligences?

Although there is no single MI route, it's very important that a teacher take individual differences among kinds very seriously. You cannot be a good MI teacher if you don't want to know each child and try to gear how you teach and how you evaluate to that particular child. The bottom line is a deep interest in children and how their minds are different from one another, and in helping them use their minds well.

Now, kids can be great informants for teachers. For example, a teacher might say, "Look, Benjamin, this obviously isn't working. Should we try using a picture?" If Benjamin gets excited about that approach, that's a pretty good clue to the teacher about what could work.

The theory of multiple intelligences, in and of itself, is not going to solve anything in our society, but linking the multiple intelligences with a curriculum focused on understanding is an extremely powerful intellectual undertaking.

When I talk about understanding, I mean that students can take ideas they learn in school, or anywhere for that matter, and apply those appropriately in new situations. We know people truly understand something when they can represent the knowledge in more than one way. We have to put understanding up front in school. Once we have that goal, multiple intelligences can be a terrific handmaiden because understandings involve a mix of mental representations, entailing different intelligences.

People often say that what they remember most about school are those learning experiences that were linked to real life. How does the theory of multiple intelligences help connect learning to the world outside the classroom?

The theory of multiple intelligences wasn't based on school work or on tests. Instead, what I did was look at the world and ask, What are the things that people do in the world? What does it mean to be a surgeon? What does it mean to be a politician? What does it mean to be an artist or a sculptor? What abilities do you need to do those things? My theory, then, came from the things that are valued in the world.

So when a school values multiple intelligences, the relationship to what's valued in the world is patent. If you cannot easily relate this activity to something that's valued in the world, the school has probably

© Susie Fitzhugh

lost the core idea of multiple intelligences, which is that these intelligences evolved to help people do things that matter in the real world.

School matters, but only insofar as it yields something that can be used once students leave school.

The Intelligences, in Gardner's Words

■ Linguistic intelligence is the capacity to use language, your native language, and perhaps other languages, to express what's on your mind and to understand other people. Poets really specialize in linguistic intelligence, but any kind of writer, orator, speaker, lawyer, or a person for whom language is an important stock in trade highlights linguistic intelligence.

■ People with a highly developed logical-mathematical intelligence understand the underlying principles of some kind of a causal system, the way a scientist or a logician does; or can manipulate numbers, quantities, and operations, the way a mathematician does.

■ Spatial intelligence refers to the ability to represent the spatial world internally in your mind—the way a sailor or airplane pilot navigates the large spatial world, or the way a chess player or sculptor represents a more circumscribed spatial world. Spatial intelligence can be used in the arts or in the sciences. If you are spatially intelligent and oriented toward the arts, you are more likely to become a painter or a sculptor or an architect than, say, a musician or a writer. Similarly, certain sciences like anatomy or topology emphasize spatial intelligence.

■ Bodily kinesthetic intelligence is the capacity to use your whole body or parts of your body—your hand, your fingers, your arms—to solve a problem, make something, or put on some kind of a production. The most evident examples are people in athletics or the performing arts, particularly dance or acting.

■ Musical intelligence is the capacity to think in music, to be able to hear patterns, recognize them, remember them, and perhaps manipulate them. People who have a strong musical intelligence don't just remember music eas-

ily—they can't get it out of their minds, it's so omnipresent. Now, some people will say, "Yes, music is important, but it's a talent, not an intelligence." And I say, "Fine, let's call it a talent." But, then we have to leave the word *intelligent* out of *all* discussions of human abilities. You know, Mozart was damned smart!

■ Interpersonal intelligence is understanding other people. It's an ability we all need, but is at a premium if you are a teacher, clinician, salesperson, or politician. Anybody who deals with other people has to be skilled in the interpersonal sphere.

■ Intrapersonal intelligence refers to having an understanding of yourself, of knowing who you are, what you can do, what you want to do, how you react to things, which things to avoid, and which things to gravitate toward. We are drawn to people who have a good understanding of themselves because those people tend not to screw up. They tend to know what they can do. They tend to know what they can't do. And they tend to know where to go if they need help.

■ Naturalist intelligence designates the human ability to discriminate among living things (plants, animals) as well as sensitivity to other features of the natural world (clouds, rock configurations). This ability was clearly of value in our evolutionary past as hunters, gatherers, and farmers; it continues to be central in such roles as botanist or chef. I also speculate that much of our consumer society exploits the naturalist intelligences, which can be mobilized in the discrimination among cars, sneakers, kinds of makeup, and the like. The kind of pattern recognition valued in certain of the sciences may also draw upon naturalist intelligence.

How can teachers be guided by multiple intelligences when creating assessment tools?

We need to develop assessments that are much more representative of what human beings are going to have to do to survive in this society. For example, I value literacy, but my measure of literacy should not be whether you can answer a multiple-choice question that asks you to select the best meaning of a paragraph. Instead, I'd rather have you read the paragraph and list four questions you have about the paragraph and figure out how you would answer those questions. Or, if I want to know how you can write, let me give you a stem and see whether you can write about that topic, or let me ask you to write an editorial in response to something you read in the newspaper or observed on the street.

The current emphasis on performance assessment is well supported by the theory of multiple intelligences. Indeed, you could not really be an advocate of multiple intelligences if you didn't have some dissatisfaction with the current testing because it's so focused on short-answer, linguistic, or logical kinds of items.

MI theory is very congenial to an approach that says: one, let's not look at things through the filter of a short-answer test. Let's look directly at the performance that we value, whether it's a linguistic, logical, aesthetic, or social performance; and, two, let's never pin our assessment of understanding on just one particular measure, but let's always allow students to show their understanding in a variety of ways.

You have identified several myths about the theory of multiple intelligences. Can you describe some of those myths?

One myth that I personally find irritating is that an intelligence is the same as a learning style. Learning styles are claims about ways in which individuals purportedly approach everything they do. If you are planful, you are supposed to be planful about everything. If you are logical-sequential, you are supposed to be logical-sequential about everything. My own research and observations suggest that that's a dubious assumption. But whether or not that's true, learning styles are very different from multiple intelligences.

Multiple intelligences claims that we respond, individually, in different ways to different kinds of content, such as language or music or other people. This is very different from the notion of learning style.

You can say that a child is a visual learner, but that's not a multiple intelligences way of talking about things. What I would say is, "Here is a child who very easily represents things spatially, and we can draw upon that strength if need be when we want to teach the child something new."

Another widely believed myth is that, because we have seven or eight intelligences, we should create seven or eight tests to measure students' strengths in each of those areas. That is a perversion of the theory. It's re-creating the sin of the single intelligence quotient and just multiplying it by a larger number. I'm personally against assessment of intelligences unless such a measurement is used for a very specific learning purpose—we want to help a child understand her history or his mathematics better and, therefore, want to see what might be good entry points for that particular child.

What experiences led you to the study of human intelligence?

It's hard for me to pick out a single moment, but I can see a couple of snapshots. When I was in high school, my uncle gave me a textbook in psychology. I'd never actually heard of psychology before. This textbook helped me understand color blindness. I'm color blind, and I became fascinated by the existence of plates that illustrated what color blindness was. I could actually explain why I couldn't see colors.

Another time when I was studying the Reformation, I read a book by Erik Erikson called *Young Man Luther* (1958).[1] I was fascinated by the psychological motivation of Luther to attack the Catholic Church. That fascination influenced my decision to go into psychology.

The most important influence was actually learning about brain damage and what could happen to people when they had strokes. When a person has a stroke, a certain part of the brain gets injured, and that injury can tell you what that part of the brain does. Individuals who lose their musical abilities can still talk. People who lose their linguistic ability still might be able to sing. That understanding not only brought me into the whole world of brain study, but it was really the seed that led ultimately to the theory of multiple intelligences. As long as you can lose one ability while others are spared, you cannot just have a single intelligence. You have to have several intelligences.

---

1. See Erik Erikson, *Young Man Luther* (New York: W. W. Norton, 1958).

Howard Gardner is Professor of Education at Harvard Graduate School of Education and author of, among other books, *The Unschooled Mind: How Children Think and How Schools Should Teach* (1991). He can be reached at Roy B. Larsen Hall, 2nd Floor, Appian Way, Harvard Graduate School of Education, Cambridge, MA 02138. **Kathy Checkley** is a staff writer for *Update* and has assisted in the development of ASCD's new CD-ROM, *Exploring Our Multiple Intelligences,* and pilot online project on multiple intelligences.

ABILITY AND EXPERTISE

It's Time to Replace the Current Model of Intelligence

BY ROBERT J. STERNBERG

BILLY HAS an IQ of 121 on a standardized individual intelligence test, and Jimmy has an IQ of 94 on the same test. What do these scores, and the difference between them, mean? The conventional answer to this question is that they represent a kind of intellectual predestination: The two children possess inborn gifts that are relatively fixed and will, to a large extent, predict their future achievement. So no one will be surprised if Billy goes on to do well in high school and gets into a good college—or if Jimmy barely gets through school and ends up with a minimum-wage job—because that's what this familiar and widely accepted model of human intelligence would lead us to expect.

But a scientific model is just a way of fitting together pieces of information and things we have observed into

Robert J. Sternberg is IBM Professor of Psychology in the Department of Psychology at Yale University. His areas of specialization are human abilities and cognition. A long version of this article appeared in **Educational Researcher**, *April 1998.*

a pattern that makes sense. It does not represent the certain or only way of arranging the pieces, and models can be and often are modified or even discarded when we make new discoveries or look at what we know in new ways. This happened, for example, in the early seventeenth century, when the Ptolemaic model of the solar system, in which all the heavenly bodies were said to revolve around the earth, was replaced by the Copernican, sun-centered, model of the solar system.

Many psychologists now question the simple identification of IQ with ability, which the old model of human intelligence posits. They believe that abilities are too broad and too complex to be measured by the kind of IQ test that Billy and Jimmy took. They also believe that environment and genetics play a part and, furthermore, that abilities are not a fixed quantity: They can be modified by education and experience. I'd like to propose a further, and important, building block for this new model of human intelligence—namely that the difference in Billy's and Jimmy's IQ scores simply means that the two children are at a different stage in developing the expertise measured by the IQ test. Furthermore, I suggest

From the Spring 1999 issue of the *American Educator*, pp. 10-13, 50-51. Reprinted by permission of the *American Educator*, the quarterly journal of the American Federation of Teachers, and Robert J. Sternberg.

that people who study abilities and those who study expertise are really talking about the same thing. What we are measuring when we administer a Wechsler Intelligence Scale for Children (WISC) or an Iowa Test of Basic Skills (ITBS) or an SAT are the same. They are not different in kind but only in the point at which we are measuring them.

In the Eye of the Beholder

When we give an achievement test, we accept the idea that we are testing a form of expertise, but this is equally true when we administer an IQ test. What differs is the level of expertise we measure and, probably more important, the way we perceive what we are measuring. The familiar IQ/ability model creates a certain expectation: that one kind of accomplishment (IQ test scores) will predict—and, in fact, lead to—another kind of accomplishment (grades or scores on achievement tests). And of course we also use different words to describe the two kinds of accomplishment.

But this way of looking at the two kinds of test scores is a familiar convenience rather than a psychological reality. Solving problems on a verbal-analogies test or a test of mathematical problem solving, which are supposed to test a child's abilities, calls for expertise just the way so-called achievement tests do: You can't do well on these so-called tests of ability without knowing the vocabulary or having some familiarity with problem-solving techniques. The chief difference between ability and achievement tests is not what they measure but the point at which they measure it. IQ and other tests of ability are, typically, administered early in a child's school career, whereas various indications about school performance, such as grades or achievement test scores, are collected later. However, all of the various kinds of assessments are of the same kind, psychologically. They all test—to some extent—what you know and how well you can use it. What distinguishes ability tests from the other kinds of assessments is how the ability tests are used (usually, predictively), rather than what they measure. There is no qualitative distinction.

But if the distinction between what these tests measure does not exist, how do we come to make it? The answer is a complicated story, but the principal reason is historical accident. Briefly, the two kinds of testing were developed separately and used on different groups of people. IQ/ability testing, which originated in Alfred Binet's testing of young children, focused on exceptionally low levels of performance and came to be viewed primarily as predictive. Early studies of expertise were done with adults. They focused on exceptionally high

levels of performance and came to be viewed as measures of achievement.

The Traditional Model

According to the traditional model of fixed individual differences, the capabilities that a child inherits interact with the child's environment to produce, at an early age, a relatively fixed potential for achievement. Children fulfill this potential to a greater or lesser degree. Thus, if a child who scores well on ability tests does well in school, we say he is living up to his potential. If, as sometimes happens, his achievement does not match his test scores, we call him an *underachiever*—or if the kid confounds expectations by working hard and doing well, he gets the label of *overachiever*. Ironically, ability test scores are considered a better indicator of what a child can achieve (or should achieve) than what the child actually does. A test of verbal analogies, in this view, might actually tell us more about a person's verbal abilities than the person's comprehension of the reading he or she does in everyday life; or a test of mathematical problem-solving skills might be viewed as more informative than the mathematical problem solving the person does on the job.

According to this model, the more intelligent students (that is, the ones with higher IQs) do better in school. As a result, they are likely to attend selective colleges, go on to professional schools, and eventually get well-paying jobs and enjoy other forms of success. The less intelligent do worse in school and may drop out. At best, they probably have to be satisfied with low-status credentials that reflect hard work rather than ability, and their role in the labor market is to fill the jobs that the more intelligent people don't want to do.

This is the view Richard Herrnstein and Charles Murray present in *The Bell Curve* (1994), and as people who have read the book will remember, it assigns African Americans as a group to the status of an underclass, based on the average "potential" of group members displayed in IQ and other ability tests. Herrnstein and Murray's use of the traditional model has occasioned a great deal of controversy. However, the view of IQ as fixed and determinant is, unfortunately, consistent with many current educational practices and common views about intellectual competence.

Developing Expertise

The idea that abilities are a form of developing expertise offers a more flexible and optimistic view of human capabilities, and one that is more in line with what we are discovering about human intelligence. Children become experts in the skills needed for success on ability tests in much the same ways that they become experts in doing anything else—through a combination of genetic endowment and experience (Ericsson, 1996). To do well on a test, a child needs to acquire, store, and learn how to use at least two kinds of knowledge: explicit knowledge of a domain and implicit or tacit knowledge of a field. Knowledge of a domain is subject-matter knowledge: In American history, for example, it would be the facts, trends, and major ideas about the political, economic, and social development of our country. Implicit knowledge is the kind of knowledge one needs to be successful in a field but which is not part of the subject matter and often is not even talked about. For example, in American history, the role of the Federalist Papers in the shaping of the U.S. Constitution would be explicit knowledge; how to use the library or Internet to research an essay about the Federalist Papers and how to take and organize notes and carry the paper through successive drafts to completion would be implicit knowledge.

Tests measure both explicit and implicit knowledge: knowledge of the subject matter and knowledge about how to take a test. This is as true of ability tests as it is of achievement tests. A verbal-analogies test, for example, measures explicit knowledge of vocabulary and a student's ability to reason with this knowledge, but the test also measures implicit knowledge of how to take a test. Thus, the student has to work within certain time limits and choose the best answer from a list of answers no one of which is exactly right.

To translate the gaining of expertise on test-taking into procedural terms, students need

- direct instruction in how to solve test-like problems—usually this takes place in school;
- practice in solving such problems, again usually in academic contexts;
- an opportunity to watch others, such as teachers or other students, solve test-like problems;
- practice thinking about such problems, sometimes mentally simulating what to do when confronting them;
- rewards for successful solutions (good grades, praise from teachers, other kinds of recognition), thereby reinforcing such behavior.

The difference between Billy's score of 121 and Jimmy's 94 also reflects a number of personal and cultural factors, and they do not all pertain to what we usually consider expertise. For example, the two boys may possess different degrees of "test-wiseness," that is, understanding the tricks of taking tests (Millman, Bishop, and Ebel, 1965; Bond and Harman, 1994). They may feel differing levels of anxiety and/or alertness on the day they are tested, and this would probably show itself in their scores. Cultural differences between them may lead to different attitudes about the importance of doing well on a test, particularly one that clearly does not "count." Most important of all, the boys may be at different levels of developing expertise in the skills that the test measures.

Individual Differences

But saying that IQ tests and other assessments of ability are testing the same thing as achievement tests and that the expertise revealed is not fixed should not be taken to mean that everybody has the same intellectual capacity. The difference in expertise that Billy and Jimmy reveal on their IQ tests may indicate an underlying difference in their capacities. However, IQ tests do not directly measure these differences and neither do any of the other ways in which we currently seek to measure ability (see, for example, Vygotsky, 1978). Individual differences in developing expertise result in much the same way as in most kinds of learning: from (a) the rate of learning (which can be caused by the amount of direct instruction received, the amount of problem solving done, the amount of time and effort spent in thinking about problems, and so on); and from (b) the asymptote of learning—that is, the limit set by ability to what a student can ultimately achieve, given unlimited training. This limit, or asymptote, can be caused by differences in numbers of schemas—the networks of information on various subjects stored in our memories—the organization of schemas, efficiency in using schemas, and so on (see Atkinson, Bower, and Crothers, 1965). For example, children can learn how to solve the various kinds of mathematical problems found in tests of mathematical abilities, whether through regular schooling, a special course, or through assimilation of everyday experience. When they learn, they will learn at different rates, and reach different asymptotes. Ultimately the differences represent genetic and environmental factors that are interacting in ways that we cannot now measure.

Various Kinds of Expertise

As I've already noted, the so-called ability tests typically come earlier in a student's school career than the various types of achievement tests, but what IQ tests measure is not psychologically prior. Achievement tests might just as well be used to predict scores on ability tests—and sometimes they are, as for instance, when school officials try to predict a student's college admissions test scores on the basis of the student's grades. When we look at the test of abilities as though they are psychologically prior, we are confusing the order in which students usually take these tests with some kind of psychological ordering. But in fact, our temporal ordering implies no psychological ordering at all. The recent change in the meaning of the acronym *SAT* (from Scholastic Aptitude Test to Scholastic Assessment Test) reflects the recognition that what was called an aptitude test measures more than just "aptitude"—indeed, it hints at the interchangeability of the two kinds of tests. Nevertheless, the SAT is still widely used as an ability test, and the SAT-II, which more directly measures subject-matter knowledge, as a set of achievement tests.

Tests that claim to measure ability through questions employing vocabulary, reading comprehension, verbal analogies, arithmetic problem solving, and the like are all, in part, tests of achievement. Even abstract-reasoning tests measure achievement in dealing with geometric symbols, which is a skill taught in Western schools (Laboratory of Comparative Human Cognition, 1982). Indeed, if we examine the content of ability tests, it is clear that they measure achievement that the students taking the test should have accomplished several years back. We could just as well use academic performance to predict ability-test scores. The problem with the traditional model is not that it proposes a correlation between ability tests and other forms of achievement. That undoubtedly exists. It is rather the traditional model's proposing that the capacities measured by the tests *cause* later success—or failure—instead of merely preceding it.

An Illusion of Causality

The notion that success on ability tests predicts success in many other areas gains credibility from the fact that some of the skills or qualities that make people more expert at taking tests are also likely to make them successful in other aspects of life in our culture. Taking a test, say, of verbal or figural analogies, or of mathematical problem solving, typically requires skills such as (a) puzzling out what someone else wants (here, the person who wrote the test), (b) command of English vocabulary, (c) reading comprehension, (d) allocation of limited time, (e) sustained concentration, (f) abstract reasoning, (g) quick thinking, (h) symbol manipulation, and (i) suppression of anxiety and other emotions that can interfere with test performance. These skills are also part of what is required for successful performance in school and in many kinds of job performance. Thus, an expert test-taker is likely also to have skills that will be involved in other kinds of expertise as well, such as expertise in getting high grades in school.

To the extent that the expertise required for one kind of performance overlaps with the expertise required for another kind of performance, there will be a correlation between performances. However, the expertise that ability tests measure is not the cause of school or job expertise; it is itself an expertise that overlaps with school or job expertise. Differences in test scores, academic performance, and job performance are all effects of different levels of expertise.

The New Model

The notion of *developing* expertise means that people are constantly in the process of developing expertise when they work within a given domain. Individuals can differ in rate and asymptote of development. However, the main constraint in achieving expertise is not some fixed prior level of capacity, of the kind measured by IQ tests. It is the degree to which students are purposefully engaged in working and teachers in helping them. This involves direct instruction, active participation, role modeling, and reward.

The model of developing expertise has five key elements: metacognitive skills, learning skills, thinking skills, knowledge, and motivation. The elements all influence one another, both directly and indirectly. For example, learning leads to knowledge, but knowledge facilitates further learning.

1. Metacognitive skills. Metacognitive skills refer to students' understanding and control of their own learning. These skills would include what a student knows about writing papers or solving arithmetic word problems, both in regard to the steps that are involved and how these steps can be executed effectively (Sternberg 1985, 1986, 1988; Sternberg and Swerling, 1996).

2. Learning skills. Learning skills are sometimes divided into explicit learning, which occurs when we make an effort to learn, and implicit learning, which occurs when we simply pick up information without any particular effort. Examples of learning skills are distinguishing relevant from irrelevant information; putting together the relevant information; and relating new information to information already stored in memory (Sternberg, 1985, 1986).

3. Thinking skills. There are three main sets of thinking skills. Critical (analytical) thinking skills include analyzing, critiquing, judging, evaluating, comparing and contrasting, and assessing. Creative thinking skills include creating, discovering, inventing, imagining, supposing, and hypothesizing. Practical thinking skills include applying, using, and practicing (Sternberg, 1985, 1986, 1994,

1997). They are the first step in translating thought into real-world action.

4. Knowledge. There are two main kinds of knowledge that are relevant in academic learning. Declarative knowledge is of facts, concepts, principles, laws, and the like. It is "knowing that." Procedure knowledge is of procedures and strategies. It is "knowing how." Of particular importance is procedural tacit knowledge, which involves knowing how the system in which one is operating functions (Sternberg, Wagner, Williams & Horvath, 1995).

5. Motivation. There are a number of different kinds of motivation, and in one or another of its forms, motivation is probably indispensable for school success. Without it, the student never even tries to learn (McClelland, 1985; McClelland, Atkinson, Clark, and Lowell, 1976; Bandura, 1977, 1996; Amabile, 1996; Sternberg and Lubart, 1996).

6. Context. All of the elements discussed above are characteristics of the learner. However, it is a mistake to assume, as conventional tests usually do, that factors external to the student's mastery of the material play no part in how well the student does on a test. Such contextual factors include whether the student is taking the test in his or her native language, whether the test emphasizes speedy performance, the importance to the student of success on the test, and the student's familiarity with the kinds of material on the test.

Novices—beginning learners—work toward expertise through deliberate practice. But this practice requires an interaction of all five of the key elements in the model. At the center, driving the elements, is motivation. Without it, nothing happens. Motivation drives metacognitive skills, which in turn activate learning and thinking skills, which then provide feedback to the metacognitive skills, enabling the student's level of expertise to increase (see also Sternberg, 1985). The declarative and procedural knowledge acquired through the extension of the thinking and learning skills also results in these skills being used more effectively in the future.

All of these processes are affected by, and can in turn affect, the context in which they operate. For example, if a learning experience is in English but the learner has only limited English proficiency, his or her learning will be inferior to that of someone with more advanced English language skills. Or if material is presented orally to someone who is a better visual learner, that individual's performance will be reduced. Eventually, as the five elements influence one another, the student reaches a kind of expertise at which he or she becomes a reflective practitioner who is able to consciously use a certain set of skills. But expertise occurs at many levels. The expert first-year graduate or law student, for example, is still a far cry from the expert professional. People thus cycle through many times, on the way to successively higher levels of expertise.

Implications for the Classroom

The model of abilities as a form of developing expertise has a number of immediate implications for education, in general, and classroom practice, in particular.

First, teachers and all who use ability and achievement tests should stop distinguishing between what the two kinds of tests assess. The measurements are not different in kind but only in the point at which they are being made.

Second, tests measure *achieved* levels of developing expertise. No test—of abilities or anything else—can specify the highest level a student can achieve.

Third, different kinds of assessments—multiple-choice, short answer, performance-based, portfolio—complement one another in assessing multiple aspects of developing expertise. There is no one "right" kind of assessment.

Fourth, instruction should be geared not just toward imparting a knowledge base, but toward developing reflective analytical, creative, and practical thinking with a knowledge base. Students learn better when they think to learn, even when their learning is assessed with straightforward multiple-choice memory assessments (Sternberg, Torff, and Grigorenko, 1998).

The model I've proposed here views students as novices who are capable of becoming experts in a variety of areas. The traditional model, which posits fixed individual differences—and typically bases the kind of instruction a student gets on these differences—holds many students back from attaining the expertise they are capable of. It is true that for various reasons (including, perhaps, genetic as well as environmentally based differences), not all individuals will reach the same ultimate level of expertise. But they should all be given the opportunity to reach new levels of competence well beyond what they, and in some cases, others may think possible. The fact that Billy and Jimmy have different IQs tells us something about differences in what they now do. It does not tell us anything about what ultimately they will be able to achieve.

References

Amabile, T. M. (1996). *Creativity in context.* Boulder, CO: Westview.

Atkinson, R. C., Bower, G. H., & Crothers, E. J. (1965). *An introduction to mathematical learning theory.* New York: John Wiley & Sons.

Bandura, A. (1977). Self-efficacy: Toward a unifying theory of behavioral change. *Psychological Review,* 84, 181–215.

Bandura, A. (1996). *Self-efficacy: The exercise of control.* New York: Freeman.

Bond, L., & Harman, A. E. (1994). Test-taking strategies. In R. J. Sternberg (Ed.), *Encyclopedia of human intelligence* (Vol. 2, pp. 1073–1077). New York: Macmillan.

Ericsson, A. (Ed.) (1996). *The road to excellence.* Mahwah, NJ: Erlbaum.

Herrnstein, R. J., & Murray, C. (1994). *The bell curve.* New York: Free Press.

Laboratory of Comparative Human Cognition (1982). Culture and intelligence. In R. J. Sternberg (Ed.), *Handbook of human intelligence* (pp. 642–719). New York: Cambridge University Press.

McClelland, D. C. (1985). *Human motivation.* New York: Scott Foresman.

McClelland, D. C., Atkinson, J. W., Clark, R. A., & Lowell, E. L. (1976). *The achievement motive.* New York: Irvington.

Millman, J., Bishop, H., & Ebel, R. (1965). An analysis of test-wiseness. *Educational and Psychological Measurement, 25,* 707–726.

Sternberg, R. J. (1985). *Beyond IQ: A triarchic theory of human intelligence.* New York: Cambridge University Press.

Sternberg, R. J. (1986). *Intelligence applied.* Orlando, FL: Harcourt Brace College Publishers.

Sternberg, R. J. (1988). *The triarchic mind: A new theory of human intelligence.* New York: Viking-Penguin.

Sternberg, R. J. (1994). Diversifying instruction and assessment. *The Educational Forum, 59*(1), 47–53.

Sternberg, R. J. (1997). *Successful intelligence.* New York: Plume.

Sternberg, R. J., & Lubart, T. I. (1995). *Defying the crowd: Cultivating creativity in a culture of conformity.* New York: Free Press.

Sternberg, R. J., & Lubart, T. I. (1996). Investing in creativity. *American Psychologist, 51,* 677–688.

Sternberg, R. J., & Spear-Swerling, L. (1996). *Teaching for thinking.* Washington, DC: APA Books.

Sternberg, R. J., Torff, B., & Grigorenko, E. L. (1998). Teaching triarchically improves school achievement. *Journal of Educational Psychology, 90,* 374–384.

Sternberg, R. J., Wagner, R. K., Williams, W. M., & Horvath, J. (1995). Testing common sense. *American Psychologist, 50,* 912–927.

Vygotsky, L. S. (1978). *Mind in society: The development of higher psychological processes.* Cambridge, MA: Harvard University Press.

This work was supported by the U.S. Office of Educational Research and Improvement (Grant R206R50001), but this support does not imply endorsement of positions taken or conclusions reached.

CAUTION— PRAISE CAN BE DANGEROUS

By Carol S. Dweck

THE SELF-ESTEEM movement, which was flourishing just a few years ago, is in a state of decline. Although many educators believed that boosting students' self-esteem would boost their academic achievement, this did not happen. But the failure of the self-esteem movement does not mean that we should stop being concerned with what students think of themselves and just concentrate on improving their achievement. Every time teachers give feedback to students, they convey messages that affect students' opinion of themselves, their motivation, and their achievement. And I believe that teachers can and should help students become high achievers who also feel good about themselves. But how, exactly, should teachers go about doing this?

In fact, the self-esteem people were on to something extremely important. Praise, the chief weapon in their armory, is a powerful tool. Used correctly it can help students become adults who delight in intellectual challenge, understand the value of effort, and are able to deal with setbacks. Praise can help students make the most of the gifts they have. But if praise is not handled properly, it can become a negative force, a kind of drug that, rather than strengthening students, makes them passive and dependent on the opinion of others. What teachers—and parents—need is a framework that enables them to use praise wisely and well.

Carol S. Dweck is a professor of psychology at Columbia University, who has carried out research on self-esteem, motivation, and academic achievement for thirty years. Her new book, Self-Theories: Their Role in Motivation, Personality, and Development, *was just published by The Psychology Press.*

Where Did Things Go Wrong?

I believe the self-esteem movement faltered because of the way in which educators tried to instill self-esteem. Many people held an intuitively appealing theory of self-esteem, which went something like this: Giving students many opportunities to experience success and then praising them for their successes will indicate to them that they are intelligent. If they feel good about their intelligence, they will achieve. They will love learning and be confident and successful learners.

Much research now shows that this idea is wrong. Giving students easy tasks and praising their success tells students that you think they're dumb.[1] It's not hard to see why. Imagine being lavishly praised for something you think is pretty Mickey Mouse. Wouldn't you feel that the person thought you weren't capable of more and was trying to make you feel good about your limited ability?

But what about praising students' ability when they perform well on challenging tasks? In such cases, there would be no question of students' thinking you were just trying to make them feel good. Melissa Kamins, Claudia Mueller, and I decided to put this idea to the test.

Mueller and I had already found, in a study of the relationship between parents' beliefs and their children's expectations, that 85 percent of parents thought they needed to praise their children's intelligence in order to assure them that they were smart.[2] We also knew that many educators and psychologists thought that praising children for being intelligent was of great benefit. Yet in almost 30 years of research, I had seen over and over that children who had maladaptive achievement patterns were already obsessed with their intelligence—and with proving it to others. The children worried about how smart they looked and feared that failing at some task—

From the *American Educator*, Spring 1999, pp. 4-9. © 1999 by Carol S. Dweck. Reprinted by permission.

even a relatively unimportant one—meant they were dumb. They also worried that having to work hard in order to succeed at a task showed they were dumb. Intelligence seemed to be a label to these kids, a feather in their caps, rather than a tool that, with effort, they could become more skillful in using.

In contrast, the more adaptive students focused on the process of learning and achieving. They weren't worried about their intelligence and didn't consider every task a measure of it. Instead, these students were more likely to concern themselves with the effort and strategies they needed in order to master the task. We wondered if praising children for being intelligent, though it seemed like a positive thing to do, could hook them into becoming dependent on praise.

Praise for Intelligence

Claudia Mueller and I conducted six studies, with more than 400 fifth-grade students, to examine the effects of praising children for being intelligent.[3] The students were from different parts of the country (a Midwestern town and a large Eastern city) and came from varied ethnic, racial, and socioeconomic backgrounds. Each of the studies involved several tasks, and all began with the students working, one at a time, on a puzzle task that was challenging but easy enough for all of them to do quite well. After this first set, we praised one-third of the children for their *intelligence*. They were told: "Wow, you got x number correct. That's a really good score. You must be smart at this." One-third of the children were also told that they got a very good score, but they were praised for their *effort*: "You must have worked really hard." The final third were simply praised for their *performance*, with no comment on why they were successful. Then, we looked to see the effects of these different types of praise across all six studies.

We found that after the first trial (in which all of the students were successful) the three groups responded similarly to questions we asked them. They enjoyed the task equally, were equally eager to take the problems home to practice, and were equally confident about their future performance.

In several of the studies, as a followup to the first trial, we gave students a choice of different tasks to work on next. We asked whether they wanted to try a challenging task from which they could learn a lot (but at which they might not succeed) or an easier task (on which they were sure to do well and look smart).

The majority of the students who had received praise for being intelligent the first time around went for the task that would allow them to keep on looking smart. Most of the students who had received praise for their effort (in some studies, as many as 90 percent) wanted the challenging learning task. (The third group, the students who had not been praised for intelligence or effort, were right in the middle and I will not focus on them.)

These findings suggest that when we praise children for their intelligence, we are telling them that this is the name of the game: Look smart; don't risk making mistakes. On the other hand, when we praise children for the effort and hard work that leads to achievement, they want to keep engaging in that process. They are not diverted from the task of learning by a concern with how smart they might—or might not—look.

The Impact of Difficulty

Next, we gave students a set of problems that were harder and on which they didn't do as well. Afterwards, we repeated the questions we had asked after the first task: How much had they enjoyed the task? Did they want to take the problems home to practice? And how smart did they feel? We found that the students who had been praised for being intelligent did not like this second task and were no longer interested in taking the problems home to practice. What's more, their difficulties led them to question their intelligence. In other words, the same students who had been told they were smart when they succeeded now felt dumb because they had encountered a setback. They had learned to measure themselves from what people said about their performance, and they were dependent on continuing praise in order to maintain their confidence.

In contrast, the students who had received praise for their effort on the easier task liked the more difficult task just as much even though they missed some of the problems. In fact, many of them said they liked the harder problems even more than the easier ones, and they were even more eager to take them home to practice. It was wonderful to see.

Moreover, these youngsters did not think that the difficulty of the task (and their relative lack of success) reflected on their intelligence. They thought, simply, that they had to make a greater effort in order to succeed. Their interest in taking problems home with them to practice on presumably reflected one way they planned to do this.

Thus, the students praised for effort were able to keep their intellectual self-esteem in the face of setbacks. They still thought they were smart; they still enjoyed the challenge; and they planned to work toward future success. The students who had been praised for their intelligence received an initial boost to their egos, but their view of themselves was quickly shaken when the going got rough. As a final test, we gave students a third set of problems that were equal in difficulty to the first set—the one on which all the students had been successful. The results were striking. Although all three groups had performed equally well on the first trial, the students who had received praise for their intelligence (and who had been discouraged by their poor showing on the second trial) now registered the worst performance of the three groups. Indeed, they did significantly worse than they had on the first trial. In contrast, students who were praised for working hard performed the best of the three groups and significantly better than they had originally. So the different kinds of praise apparently affected not just what students thought and felt, but also how well they were able to perform.

Given what we had already seen, we reasoned that when students see their performance as a measure of their intelligence, they are likely to feel stigmatized when they perform poorly and may even try to hide the fact. If, however, students consider a poor performance a temporary setback, which merely reflects how much effort they have put in or their current level of skill, then it will not be a stigma. To test this idea, we gave students the opportunity to tell a student at another school about the task they had just completed by writing a brief description on a prepared form. The form also asked them to report their score on the second, more difficult trial.

More than 40 percent of the students who had been praised for their intelligence lied about their score (to improve it, of course). They did this even though they were reporting their performance to an anonymous peer whom they would never meet. Very few of the students in the other groups exaggerated their performance. This suggests that when we praise students for their intelligence, failure becomes more personal and therefore more of a disgrace. As a result, students become less able to face and therefore deal with their setbacks.

The Messages We Send

Finally, we found that following their experiences with the different kinds of praise, the students believed different things about their intelligence. Students who had received praise for being intelligent told us they thought of intelligence as something innate—a capacity that you just had or didn't have. Students who had been praised for effort told us they thought of intelligence more in terms of their skills, knowledge, and motivation—things over which they had some control and might be able to enhance.

And these negative effects of praising for intelligence were just as strong (and sometimes stronger) for the high-achieving students as for their less successful peers. Perhaps it is even easier to get these youngsters invested in looking smart to others. Maybe they are even more attuned to messages from us that tell them we value them for their intellects.

How can one sentence of praise have such powerful and pervasive effects? In my research, I have been amazed over and over again at how quickly students of all ages pick up on messages about themselves—at how sensitive they are to suggestions about their personal qualities or about the meaning of their actions and experiences. The kinds of praise (and criticism) students receive from their teachers and parents tell them how to think about what they do—and what they are.

This is why we cannot simply forget about students' feelings, their ideas about themselves and their motivation, and just teach them the "facts." No matter how objective we try to be, our feedback conveys messages about what we think is important, what we think of them, and how they should think of themselves. These messages, as we have seen, can have powerful effects on many things including performance. And it should surprise no one that this susceptibility starts very early.

Melissa Kamins and I found it in kindergarten children.[4] Praise or criticism that focused on children's personal traits (like being smart or good) created a real vulnerability when children hit setbacks. They saw setbacks as showing that they were bad or incompetent— and they were unable to respond constructively. In contrast, praise or criticism that focused on children's strategies or the efforts they made to succeed left them hardy, confident, and in control when they confronted setbacks. A setback did not mean anything bad about them or their personal qualities. It simply meant that something needed to be done, and they set about doing it. Again, a focus on process allowed these young children to maintain their self-esteem and to respond constructively when things went wrong.

Ways of Praising

There are many groups whose achievement is of particular interest to us: minorities, females, the gifted, the underachieving, to name a few. The findings of these studies will tell you why I am so concerned that we not try to encourage the achievement of our students by praising their intelligence. When we worry about low-achieving or vulnerable students, we may want to reassure them they're smart. When we want to motivate high-achieving students, we may want to spur them on by telling them they're gifted. Our research says: Don't do that. Don't get students so invested in these labels that they care more about keeping the label than about learning. Instead of empowering students, praise is likely to render students passive and dependent on something they believe they can't control. And it can hook them into a system in which setbacks signify incompetence and effort is recognized as a sign of weakness rather than a key to success.

This is not to say that we shouldn't praise students. We can praise as much as we please when they learn or do well, but should wax enthusiastic about their strategies, not about how their performance reveals an attribute they are likely to view as innate and beyond their control. We can rave about their effort, their concentration, the effectiveness of their study strategies, the interesting ideas they came up with, the way they followed through. We can ask them questions that show an intelligent appreciation of their work and what they put into it. We can enthusiastically discuss with them what they learned. This, of course, requires more from us than simply telling them that they are smart, but it is much more appreciative of their work, much more constructive, and it does not carry with it the dangers I've been describing.

What about the times a student really impresses us by doing something quickly, easily—and perfectly? Isn't it appropriate to show our admiration for the child's ability? My honest opinion is that we should not. We should not be giving students the impression that we place a high value on their doing perfect work on tasks that are easy for them. A better approach would be to apologize for wasting their time with something that was too easy, and move them to something that is more challenging. When students make progress in or master that more challenging work, that's when our admiration—for their efforts—should come through.

A Challenging Academic Transition

The studies I have been talking about were carried out in a research setting. Two other studies[5] tracked students with these different viewpoints in a real-life situation, as they were making the transition to junior high school and during their first two years of junior high. This is a point at which academic work generally becomes more demanding than it was in elementary school, and many students stumble. The studies compared the attitudes and achievement of students who believed that intelligence is a fixed quantity with students who believed that they could develop their intellectual potential. We were especially interested in any changes in the degree of success students experienced in junior high school and how they dealt with these changes. For the sake of simplicity, I will combine the results from the two studies, for they showed basically the same thing.

First, the students who believed that intelligence is fixed did indeed feel that poor performance meant they were dumb. Furthermore, they reported, in significantly greater numbers than their peers, that if they did badly on a test, they would seriously consider cheating the next time. This was true even for students who were highly skilled and who had a past record of high achievement.

Perhaps even worse, these students believed that having to make an effort meant they were dumb—hardly an attitude to foster good work habits. In fact, these students reported that even though school achievement was very important to them, one of their prime goals in school was to exert as little effort as possible.

In contrast to the hopelessly counterproductive attitude of the first group, the second group of students, those who believed that intellectual potential can be developed, felt that poor performance was often due to a

lack of effort, and it called for more studying. They saw effort as worthwhile and important—something necessary even for geniuses if they are to realize their potential.

So once again, for those who are focused on their fixed intelligence and its adequacy, setbacks and even effort bring a loss of face and self-esteem. But challenges, setbacks, and effort are not threatening to the self-esteem of those who are concerned with developing their potential; they represent opportunities to learn. In fact, many of these students told us that they felt smartest when things were difficult; they gained self-esteem when they applied themselves to meeting challenges.

What about the academic achievement of the two groups making the transition to junior high school? In both studies, we saw that students who believed that intelligence was fixed and was manifest in their performance did more poorly than they had in elementary school. Even many who had been high achievers did much less well. Included among them were many students who entered junior high with high intellectual self-esteem. On the other hand, the students who believed that intellectual potential could be developed showed, as a group, clear gains in their class standing, and many blossomed intellectually. The demands of their new environment, instead of causing them to wilt because they doubted themselves, encouraged them to roll up their sleeves and get to work.

These patterns seem to continue with students entering college. Research with students at highly selective universities found that, although they may enter a situation with equal self-esteem, optimism, and past achievement, students respond to the challenge of college differently: Students in one group by measuring themselves and losing confidence; the others by figuring out what it takes and doing it.[6]

Believing and Achieving

Some of the research my colleagues and I have carried out suggests that it is relatively easy to modify the views of young children in regard to intelligence and effort in a research setting. But is it possible to influence student attitudes in a real-life setting? And do students become set in their beliefs as they grow older? Some exciting new research shows that even college students' views about intelligence and effort can be modified—and that these changes will affect their level of academic achievement.[7] In their study, Aronson and Fried taught minority students at a prestigious university to view their intelligence as a potentiality that could be developed through hard work. For example, they created and showed a film that explained the neural changes that took place in the brain every time students confronted difficulty by exerting effort. The students who were instructed about the relationship between intelligence and effort went on to earn significantly higher grades than their peers who were not. This study, like our intelligence praise studies, shows that (1) students' ideas about their intelligence can be influenced by the messages they receive, and (2) when these ideas change, changes in performance can follow.

But simply getting back to basics and enforcing rigorous standards—which some students will meet and some will not—won't eliminate the pitfalls I have been describing. This approach may convey, even more forcefully, the idea that intelligence is a gift only certain students possess. And it will not, in itself, teach students to value learning and focus on the *process* of achievement or how to deal with obstacles. These students may, more than ever, fear failure because it takes the measure of their intelligence.

A Different Framework

Our research suggests another approach. Instead of trying to convince our students that they are smart or simply enforcing rigorous standards in the hopes that doing so will create high motivation and achievement, teachers should take the following steps: first, get students to focus on their potential to learn; second, teach them to value challenge and learning over looking smart; and third, teach them to concentrate on effort and learning processes in the face of obstacles.

This can be done while holding students to rigorous standards. Within the framework I have outlined, tasks are challenging and effort is highly valued, required, and rewarded. Moreover, we can (and must) give students frank evaluations of their work and their level of skill, but we must make clear that these are evaluations of their current level of performance and skill, not an assessment of their intelligence or their innate ability. In this framework, we do not arrange easy work or constant successes, thinking that we are doing students a favor. We do not lie to students who are doing poorly so they will feel smart: That would rob them of the information they need to work harder and improve. Nor do we just give students hard work that many can't do, thus making them into casualties of the system.

I am not encouraging high-effort situations in which students stay up studying until all hours every night, fearing they will displease their parents or disgrace themselves if they don't get the top test scores. Pushing students to do that is not about valuing learning or about orienting students toward developing their potential. It is about pressuring students to prove their worth through their test scores.

It is also not sufficient to give students piles of homework and say we are teaching them about the importance of effort. We are not talking about quantity here but about teaching students to seek challenging tasks and to engage in an active learning process.

However, we as educators must then be prepared to do our share. We must help students acquire the skills they need for learning, and we must be available as constant resources for learning. It is not enough to keep harping on and praising effort, for this may soon wear thin. And it will not be effective if students don't know *how* to apply their effort appropriately. It is necessary that we as educators understand and teach students how to engage in processes that foster learning, things like task analysis and study skills.[8]

When we focus students on their potential to learn and give them the message that effort is the key to learning, we give them responsibility for and control over their achievement—and over their self-esteem. We acknowledge that learning is not something that someone gives students; nor can they expect to feel good about themselves because teachers tell them they are smart. Both learning and self-esteem are things that students achieve as they tackle challenges and work to master new material.

Students who value learning and effort know how to make and sustain a commitment to valued goals. Unlike some of their peers, they are not afraid to work hard; they know that meaningful tasks involve setbacks; and they know how to bounce back from failure. These are lessons that cannot help but serve them well in life as well as in school.

These are lessons I have learned from my research on students' motivation and achievement, and they are things I wish I had known as a student. There is no reason that every student can't know them now.

Endnotes

1. Meyer, W. U. (1982). Indirect communications about perceived ability estimates. *Journal of Educational Psychology, 74,* 888–897.
2. Mueller, C. M., & Dweck, C. S. (1996). Implicit theories of intelligence: Relation of parental beliefs to children's expectations. Paper presented at the Third National Research Convention of Head Start, Washington, D.C.
3. Mueller, C. M., & Dweck, C. S. (1998). Intelligence praise can undermine motivation and performance. *Journal of Personality and Social Psychology; 75,* 33–52.
4. Kamins, M., & Dweck, C. S. (1999). Person vs. process praise and criticism: Implications for contingent self-worth and coping. *Developmental Psychology.*
5. Henderson, V., & Dweck, C. S. (1990). Achievement and motivation in adolescence: A new model and data. In S. Feldman and G. Elliott (Eds.), *At the threshold: The developing adolescent.* Cambridge, MA: Harvard University Press; and Dweck, C. S., & Sorich, L. (1999). Mastery-oriented thinking. In C. R. Snyder (Ed.). *Coping.* New York: Oxford University Press.
6. Robins, R. W. & Pals, J. (1998). Implicit self-theories of ability in the academic domain: A test of Dweck's model. Unpublished manuscript, University of California at Davis; and Zhao, W., Dweck, C. S., & Mueller, C. (1998). Implicit theories and depression-like responses to failure. Unpublished manuscript, Columbia University.
7. Aronson, J., & Fried, C. (1998). Reducing stereotype threat and boosting academic achievement of African Americans: The role of conceptions of intelligence. Unpublished manuscript, University of Texas.
8. Brown, A. L. (1997). Transforming schools into communities of thinking and learning about serious matters. *American Psychologist, 52,* 399–413.

Constructivist Theory in the Classroom

Internalizing Concepts through Inquiry Learning

MARY M. BEVEVINO, JOAN DENGEL, and KENNETH ADAMS

Why should I care about Rwanda?
How does the Malaysian conflict concern me? How will it apply to my life?
World War I? Nobody's even alive from that conflict!
Why do we have to learn this stuff?

Every social studies teacher has heard these or similar student questions and complaints. What lies behind the fact that some students see so little value in learning about social studies? Teachers point out that students have trouble applying and transferring knowledge, that they do not have enough problem-solving skills, or that they do not understand the importance of what they are asked to learn. Students frustrate us when they cannot integrate previously learned and new concepts, even more so when they take absolutely no interest in our attempts to guide them into problem-solving practice.

Teachers can make learning meaningful when they employ activities that call on students to use their prior knowledge and experiences to construct their own frames of thought (Johnson et al. 1996). Through such inquiry learning approaches, we put students into situations that demand critical thinking and encourage the internalizing of major concepts. Inquiry activities also give students the opportunity to express, confront, and analyze preconceptions and misconceptions in an active, nonthreatening way. In this article, we explore the learning-cycle inquiry model, as outlined in figure 1.

Mary M. Bevevino is a professor of education, Joan Dengel is an associate professor of education, and Kenneth Adams is an associate professor of education, all at Edinboro University of Pennsylvania.

Constructing Knowledge through Inquiry Learning

Planning the Learning Cycle

The learning cycle is an inquiry approach originating with the Science Curriculum Improvement Study (Trowbridge and Bybee 1990). Robert Karplus and his colleagues based the learning cycle format on Piaget's cognitive development principles. Students "learn through their own involvement and action. . . . The goal is to allow students to apply previous knowledge, develop interests, and initiate and maintain a curiosity toward the materials at hand" (Trowbridge and Bybee 1990, 306).

Using the learning cycle format, the teacher can create a series of activities that are personally meaningful for students and give students opportunities to practice critical thinking skills. A simplified version of the plan outlined here can be completed in one class period; this plan is particularly useful in a ninety-minute class, but it can also be constructed to extend over several class periods.

In this inquiry format, the students first tackle a teacher-created problematic situation by conceptualizing questions, constructing hypotheses, and reaching consensus on solutions.

Next, they discuss and debate their proposed solutions with the class. Finally, they apply their contextualized insights to an important historical issue, researching and analyzing events and societal conditions of the time, proposing solutions to the controversial issue, and deciding on the best solutions. In the activities described here, students come to a consensus about mutually beneficial and workable alternatives to armed conflict.

From *The Clearing House*, May/June 1999, pp. 275-278. © 1999 by Heldref Publications, 1319 Eighteenth St., NW, Washington, DC 20036-1802. Reprinted by permission.

The Teacher's Duties

During this inquiry-based set of activities, the teacher sets the stage and selects the student groups that will participate in the activities. The teacher decides the issue to be studied, selects the activities, gives the directions, and sets up the problematic situations. He or she acts as a catalyst, encouraging students to propose hypotheses and to analyze the validity of previously gained personal and academic knowledge. By offering suggestions for problem solving and for shaping the learning cycle itself, he or she also encourages the students to reflect on the process. The teacher's job is to nurture divergent solutions and to help students to recognize and expand their ability to think critically. In *Piaget for Educators* (1990), Bybee observed that

[m]any educators are confronted with the task of facilitating development from concrete to formal levels of thought. To do so requires educators to understand the major differences between the two stages. Since both concrete and formal periods are concerned with logical thought, what are some basic differences between the periods? There are two differences. In the formal operational period, mental action no longer requires actual objects, events, or situations. For . . . students [at the concrete level], the realm of the real is possible. For formal students, the realm of the possible is real. (135)

Because any inquiry-based strategy is a complicated style of learning, the learning cycle format is not one to be used every day. For the teacher, planning a series of flexible activities requires a complex set of decisions. This learning format should be used when a complicated, controversial historical issue is to be studied, when the issue is crucial to course content, and when the teacher wants the students to construct their own knowledge. The maturity level and prior knowledge of the students are also considerations when choosing a specific historical issue (Clark and Starr 1991).

The plan described here targets the issue of conflict, specifically in the context of World War I; the problems

---

FIGURE 1
The Learning Cycle

Phase 1: Exploration	Students address a problem, make hypotheses, and predict solutions.
Phase 2: Discussion and Presentation of New Content	Students and the teacher discuss the result of Phase 1; the teacher introduces new concepts through a mini lecture.
Phase 3: Application and Expansion	Students use knowledge gained from Phases 1 and 2 to address a new problem.

FIGURE 2
Logic and Mutual Benefit Tests

The Logic Test:	All proposed solutions to the problem must rest on factual evidence, previous knowledge and experience, and logical reasoning; emotional responses unsubstantiated by logical decision making will not be allowed.
The Mutual Benefit Test:	Any solution must be agreed upon by all members of the group and must show evidence of some degree of benefit for all members of the group.

---

and conditions leading to war; and alternatives to armed conflict. To have the students consider the issue, the teacher first employs the concept of the family structure as a microcosmic example of the large-scale balance of power clashes leading up to the outbreak of World War I. The roles in Phase 1 are appropriate for juniors and seniors because students at that level generally have experience as wage earners and as consumers, have siblings or have friends who do, and are usually involved in both concrete and abstract thinking processes.

Phase 1: Exploration

The first phase demands that the students use prior knowledge and experience to solve a problem or series of problems. Students are clustered into groups of four to carry out a simulation game in which the students in each group act as siblings. The game encourages the students to experience conflict and come to consensus regarding balance of power, territorial allocations, work, and economic resources. In other words, it allows a complicated issue to be explored in a simplified way. Martorella (1991) noted that simulations "enable many students to relate easily to and become highly interested in a problem that they might not otherwise take very seriously. Furthermore, they allow students to assume control over their own learning and to be less dependent on the teacher" (225). The teacher structures the exploration by preparing a simulation that examines the concepts to be developed throughout the learning cycle.

To set up a simulation that will illustrate conflicts over territory, employment, economic resources, and balance of power, the teacher assigns roles to each of the four members of the group; the roles are defined as any combination of brothers and sisters, aged 17, 13, 9, and 5, who live with their parents in a two-bedroom apartment. Using the logic and mutual benefit guidelines (figure 2), the brothers and sisters must come to consensus on three problems: allocation of space, assignment of work, and allocation of economic resources.

This simulation should generate varying levels of controversy as the students recognize that their own ideas, needs, opinions, and conclusions are not necessarily compatible with those of others in the group. Students gain practice in engaging in and resolving controversy—essential skills for citizens in a democratic society. Each person in the group works for positive compromise that will permit the members to move forward with the most benefit to each (Martorella 1991).

Phase 2: Discussion and Presentation of New Content

Phase 2 of this learning cycle has three main components:

- The students share their proposed solutions.
- The students describe the conflicts they experienced in their groups and the strategies they used to come to consensus.
- The teacher introduces new content relative to the historical issue that then will be analyzed in Phase 3.

The second phase uses guided discussion and the lecture format to examine student solutions to the simulation game. The class also discusses the group dynamics that they have just experienced. These discussions require "the greatest attention and guidance on the teacher's part to ensure productive and meaningful results" (Martorella 1991, 224). This phase thus begins with each group reporting its solutions to the three problems while the teacher outlines the elements of each group's solutions on the board (thereby creating a visual display of the acceptability of divergent solutions). Each solution is scrutinized by the class according to the logic and mutual benefit tests. The teacher then poses questions that explore the conflicts that can arise when people decide on territorial problems, employment and work, and economic concerns. He or she asks the students about the dynamics of the group decision-making progress, pointing out that power can be used to benefit or disrupt group decision making. The teacher addresses the shifting of the balance of power within each group and the personalities in the groups and their impact on the struggle to reach consensus.

The use of the learning cycle can clarify students' thought processes and correct their misconceptions. The students have the opportunity to explain to argue, and to debate their ideas. "This process can result in disequilibrium and the possibility of developing more adequate concepts and patterns of reasoning" (Trowbridge and Bybee 1990, 306). The discussion period in Phase 2 requires the highest levels of critical thinking as students respond to open-ended teacher questions "that call for the application of individual values, that encourage personal input, and that require the student to make decisions related to attitudes, outlooks, and personal beliefs" (Mumford 1991,

194). The teacher encourages the development of student frames of thinking with questions such as the following:

- Why did you divide your room in that manner?
- What factors led you to decide on that arrangement?
- What must you be illustrating about your beliefs concerning the roles of smaller children in a family?
- What power struggles did you face during the attempt to reach consensus?
- What did those struggles reveal about the use of power in family decision making?
- How did the arrangement made by your group conform to the mutual benefit test?
- What is the value of applying the logic and mutual benefit tests to family decision making?
- How do those tests help to balance out the effect of power on your family's decision-making process?

Such questions help the students make connections, pursue logical thought processes, and recognize how their individual values, attitudes, and personal beliefs shape their decisions.

Using the lecture format, the teacher then introduces concepts such as territorialism, expansionism, employment, wages, economic and natural resource factors, tilting the balance of power, the struggle for economic dominance of power, and mediation strategies. He or she then draws parallels between the family controversy microcosm and the macrocosmic controversies that lead to worldwide conflict, at the same time introducing concepts related to conflict between nations, such as imperialism, nationalism, industrial growth, colonialism, and militarism. The teacher explains how historical antecedents influence personalities and events (figure 3). He or she also reviews treaties made prior to the war, demonstrating the interactions and shifting relationships that occurred among the affected nations (figure 4).

FIGURE 3
Historical Antecedents of World War I

1389	The Ottoman Empire conquers Serbia.
1850–1914	Europe experiences the pinnacle of nationalism.
1862–1890	Bismarck dominates European affairs.
1890	Kaiser Wilhelm ascends to power, demanding that Bismarck resign.
1912	Serbia gains independence from Turkish rule, yet many Serbs live in territories (e.g., Bosnia) ruled by Austria-Hungary.
1914	Archduke Ferdinand is assassinated on June 28.

FIGURE 4
Treaties Showing Interactions and Shifting Relationships of Nations Prior to World War I

1881	Bismarck signs an alliance with Austria-Hungary and Russia.
1882	The Triple Alliance of Germany, Austria-Hungary, and Italy is formed.
1894	Wilhelm reaffirms the alliance with Austria-Hungary and Italy but excludes Russia.
1894	France and Russia sign an alliance creating a rival block.
1904	France signs the *Entente Cordiale* with Great Britain, leading to close military and diplomatic ties.
1907	Great Britain signs an alliance with Russia.
1905–1911	Competition for colonies brings Germany and France to the brink of war.
1912	Balkan states attack the Ottoman Empire.

Phase 3: Application and Expansion

Phase 3 of the learning cycle requires the students to apply the knowledge, skills, and insights acquired in Phases 1 and 2 to a new situation or to creatively extend their knowledge into new areas of exploration. It also challenges misconceptions and assists students in the expansion of their preconceptual understanding of selected concepts.

This particular plan calls for students with newfound insights to analyze conditions and events occurring in Germany, France, and England from 1900 to 1913 related to territorialism, employment, availability of economic and natural resources, personalities, and attempts at mediation. The students' goal is to determine the causes for World War I.

Pondering these issues, small groups of students engage in research to create a composite picture of the major powers, describing their national agendas nationalistic divisiveness, colonial expansion into Africa and the Pacific Islands; the dynamics among the nations; and each country's perception of its own power, reputation, and competitiveness. After the groups present their composite descriptions to the class, the analysis of divergent solutions begins. In their small groups, students must come up with viable alternative solutions that meet the logic and mutual benefit tests, solutions that might have been employed to resolve the conflicts related to territory, employment, economics, and balance of power that precipitated the outbreak of international armed conflict in 1914. As a final activity, each group proposes its alternative solutions. The students and teacher discuss each proposal, analyzing its strengths and possible weaknesses. The learning cycle ends with the whole class coming to a consensus as to the best solutions offered.

Conclusion

Inquiry lessons that encourage students to develop their own frames of thought are complicated and time consuming to plan but extremely effective in the classroom. They give teachers a way to personalize and contextualize the great forces of history in such a manner that students can relate the importance of a historical issue to their own lives. Thus, learning about history becomes a personally interesting and deeply internalized experience.

REFERENCES

Bybee, R. W. 1990. *Piaget for educators.* 2nd ed. Prospect Heights, Ill.: Waveland Press.

Clark, L. H., and I. S. Starr. 1991. *Secondary and middle school teaching methods.* 6th ed. New York: Macmillan.

Johnson, J. A., V. L. Dupuis, D. Murial, G. E. Hall, and D. M. Gollnick. 1996. *Introduction to the foundations of American education.* 3rd ed. Boston: Allyn and Bacon.

Martorella, P. H. 1991. *Teaching social studies in middle and secondary schools.* New York: Macmillan.

Trowbridge, L. W., and R. W. Bybee. 1990. *Becoming a secondary school science teacher* Columbus: Merrill.

SUGGESTED READINGS

Boorstin, D., and B. M. Kelley. 1990. *A history of the United States since 1861.* Englewood Cliffs, N.J.: Prentice-Hall.

Ellis, E. G., and A. Esler. 1997. *World history: Connections to today.* Englewood Cliffs, N.J.: Prentice-Hall.

Henson, K. T. 1993. *Methods and strategies for teaching in secondary and middle schools.* 2nd ed. White Plains, N.Y,: Longman.

Johnson, D. W., and R. T. Johnson. 1988. Critical thinking through structured controversy. *Educational Leadership* 45:58–64.

Kim, E. C., and R. D. Kellough. 1991. *A resource guide for secondary school teaching: Planning for competencies.* 5th ed. New York: Macmillan.

Levine, J. M. 1989. *Secondary instruction: A manual for classroom teaching.* Boston: Allyn and Bacon.

The Challenges of Sustaining a Constructivist Classroom Culture

BY MARK WINDSCHITL

Illustration by John Berry

Mr. Windschitl sees articulating these challenges as a significant step in helping educators create and sustain a classroom culture that values diversity in learning and offers a new vision of the roles of teachers and learners—the culture of constructivism.

M S. HUGHES' sixth-grade classroom is a noisy place, and if you come to visit you may have a hard time finding her. Today, students are clustered in small groups, bent over note cards and diagrams they have assembled in order to determine whether they can

MARK WINDSCHITL is an assistant professor of curriculum and instruction in the College of Education, University of Washington, Seattle.

From *Phi Delta Kappan*, June 1999, pp. 751-755. © 1999 by Phi Delta Kappa International, Inc. Reprinted by permission.

design a habitat that can support Australian dingoes and marmosets.

The students have just participated in three days of discussion and reading about interrelationships among mammals. They are divided into four groups, each of which has negotiated with Ms. Hughes to devise a complex problem to work on that reflects their interests and abilities. One group chose a design problem: creating a habitat for a lo-

A growing number of teachers are embracing the fundamental ideas of constructivist learning—that their students' background knowledge profoundly affects how they interpret subject matter and that students learn best when they apply their knowledge to solve authentic problems, engage in "sense-making" dialogue with peers, and strive for deep understanding of core ideas rather than recall of a laundry list of facts.

prerequisite to offering support for the classroom teacher.

In this article, I characterize and categorize these challenges and describe the kinds of administrative support necessary to create and sustain a culture of constructivist teaching in schools. First, however, it is necessary to examine constructivism as a philosophy on which a systemic classroom culture can be based rather than to view it as a set of dis-

Constructivism is a culture— not a fragmented collection of practices.

cal zoo that will support at least three kinds of mammals naturally found in the same geographic area.

The students are now engaged for the next two weeks on this project. They find and share dozens of resources, many of which are spread out on tables and on the floor around the room. Allen brings to class a video he shot at the zoo last week so that everyone can see what different habitats look like. Michelle loads a CD-ROM on mammals that she brought from home, and James donates one of his mother's landscape architecture books for ideas on how to diagram spaces and buildings.

During the next two weeks, these students will develop an understanding of how mammal species interact with one another, cope with the environment, and follow the natural cycles of reproduction. Concepts such as "competition for resources" and "reproductive capacity"—whose definitions in other classes might have been memorized—arise instead from a meaningful and multifaceted context. These concepts are built on the experiences of the students and are essential, interconnected considerations in the success of the habitat design. This is one of the many faces of the constructivist classroom.

Unfortunately, much of the public conversation about constructivism has been stalled on its philosophical contrasts with more traditional approaches to instruction. Constructivists have offered varying descriptions of how classrooms can be transformed, usually framed in terms of these contrasts. And although these descriptions have prompted educators to reexamine the roles of teachers, the ways in which students learn best, and even what it means to learn, the image of what is possible in constructivist classrooms remains too idealized.

To all the talk about theory, educators must add layers of dialogue about real classroom experiences and concerns about those experiences. An essential part of this dialogue is the articulation of the pedagogical, logistical, and political challenges that face educators who are willing to integrate constructivism into their classroom practice. The new discourse shifts the emphasis from comparisons between constructivism and traditional instruction to the refinement of constructivist practices in real classrooms. This frank conversation about challenges is equally valuable for sympathetic administrators—being informed and reflective about these issues is a necessary

crete instructional practices that may be inserted into the learning environment whenever necessary. The challenges I describe here are challenges precisely because they cause us to reconsider and dare us to change the comfortable (and often unstated) norms, beliefs, and practices of the classroom culture we are so familiar with. Constructivism is more than a set of teaching techniques; it is a coherent pattern of expectations that underlie new relationships between students, teachers, and the world of ideas.

Constructivism as Culture

Constructivism is premised on the belief that learners actively create, interpret, and reorganize knowledge in individual ways. These fluid intellectual transformations occur when students reconcile formal instructional experiences with their existing knowledge, with the cultural and social contexts in which ideas occur, and with a host of other influences that serve to mediate understanding. With respect to instruction, this belief suggests that students should participate in experiences that accommodate these ways of learning. Such experiences include problem-based learning, inquiry activities, dialogues with peers and teachers that encourage making sense of the subject matter, exposure to multiple sources of information, and opportunities for students to demonstrate their understanding in diverse ways.

However, before teachers and administrators adopt such practices, they should understand that constructivism cannot make its appearance in the classroom as a set of isolated instructional methods grafted on to

take root or when familiar norms of behavior are transformed into new patterns of teacher/student interaction.[1] By contrast, if discrete practices that have been associated with constructivism (cooperative learning, performance assessments, hands-on experiences) are simply inserted as special activities into the regular school day, then it remains business as usual for the students. Teachers and students do not question their vision of learning, no one takes risks, and hardly a ripple is felt.

are more likely to be guided not by instructional theories but by the familiar images of what is "proper and possible" in classroom settings.[5]

Unfortunately, the signs and symbols of teacher-centered education and learning by transmission, which are likely to be a part of teachers' personal histories, persist in classrooms today.[6] In this environment, it is assumed that the more quiet and orderly the classrooms are, the more likely it is that learning is taking place. Individual desks face the front

Crafting instruction based on constructivism is not as straightforward as it seems.

otherwise traditional teaching techniques. Rather, it is a culture—a set of beliefs, norms, and practices that constitute the fabric of school life. This culture, like all other cultures, affects the way learners can interact with peers, relate to the teacher, and experience the subject matter. The children's relationships with teachers, their patterns of communication, how they are assessed, and even their notion of "what learning is good for" must all be connected, or the culture risks becoming a fragmented collection of practices that fail to reinforce one another. For example, the constructivist belief that learners are capable of intellectual autonomy must coincide with the belief that students possess a large knowledge base of life experiences and have made sense out of much of what they have experienced. These beliefs are linked with the practice of problem-based learning within relevant and authentic contexts and with the norm of showing mutual respect for one another's ideas in the classroom.

Portraying the constructivist classroom as a culture is important because many challenges for the teacher emerge when new rituals

Throughout this article then, challenges become apparent when we question the fundamental norms of the classroom—the images and beliefs we hold of teachers and students, the kinds of discourse encouraged in the classroom, the way authority and decision making are controlled, and even what "counts" as learning. I begin with a subtle but powerful influence on classroom instruction.

Images of Teaching: The Chains That Bind Us

Most of us are products of traditional instruction; as learners, we were exposed to teacher-centered instruction, fact-based subject matter, and a steady diet of drill and practice.[2] Our personal histories furnish us with mental models of teaching, and these models of how we were taught shape our behavior in powerful ways. Teachers use these models to imagine lessons in their classrooms, develop innovations, and plan for learning.[3] These images serve to organize sets of beliefs and guide curricular actions.[4] Teachers

of the room, where the teacher occupies a privileged space of knowing authority; students work individually on identical, skill-based assignments to ensure uniformity of learning. Value statements are embedded everywhere in this environment.

Constructivist teachers envision themselves emerging boldly from the confines of this traditional classroom culture, but the vision first requires critical reflection. Teachers must ask themselves, "Is my role to dispense knowledge or to nurture independent thinkers? How do I show respect for the ideas of the students? Am I here to learn from the students?" Teachers must struggle to develop a new, well-articulated rationale for instructional decisions and cannot depend on their previous teaching or learning experiences for much help in shaping their choice of methods; shifting the centers of authority and activity in accordance with this rationale requires persistence. For example, teachers can be uncomfortable with their apparent lack of control as students engage with their peers during learning activities and may be unwilling to allow supervisors who visit the classroom to observe this kind of environment. Teachers may reconsider their ideas of student-centered learning in favor of conforming to the more traditional images of the teacher as the hub of classroom discourse and attention.[7]

New Demands on the Teacher

Constructivist instruction, especially that which is based on design tasks or problem solving, places high demands on the teacher's subject-matter understanding. The teacher must not only be familiar with the principles underlying a topic of study but must also be prepared for the variety of ways these principles can be explored.

For example, if students are studying density in science class, the teacher must support the understanding of one group of students who want to approach the concept from a purely abstract, mathematical perspective as they construct tables, equations, and graphs to develop their knowledge. In this case, the teacher must understand these different representations of information and how they are interrelated. Another group of students may plan to recount the story of the Titanic, emphasizing the role that density played in the visibility of the iceberg, the ballast of the ship, and the sinking itself. Here, the teacher must be intellectually agile, able to apply his or her mathematical understanding of density to a real-life, inevitably more complex situation.

Teachers in different subject areas may allow students varying degrees of latitude in exploring content and will differ in how they accept student "constructions" of core curricular ideas. Mathematics is characterized by rule-based propositions and skills that may be open to discovery via many experiential pathways. Most forms of mathematics problems, however, have only one right answer. And if students are allowed to explore problems by their own methods,

teachers may find it difficult to see exactly how the students are making sense of the problem-solving process—not all constructions are created equal. Science and social studies present the same challenges, although science is less axiomatic than mathematics, and the issues explored in social studies are open to wider interpretation. Dealing with the "correctness" of student constructions is an ongoing concern, and the arguments have barely been introduced here, but reflection on these issues helps teachers develop a critical awareness of disciplinary "truths" and the viability of various ways of knowing the world.

In addition to the necessity for flexible subject-matter knowledge, constructivism places greater demands on teachers' pedagogical skill. Crafting instruction based on constructivism is not as straightforward as it seems. Educators struggle with how specific instructional techniques (e.g., lecture, discussion, cooperative learning, problem-based learning, inquiry learning) fit into the constructivist model of instruction. Regardless of the particular techniques used in instruction, students will always construct and reorganize knowledge rather than simply assimilate information from teachers or textbooks. The question is not whether to use lecture or discussion, but how to use these techniques to complement rather than dominate student thinking. For example, constructivist principles suggest that students should experience the ideas, phenomena, and artifacts of a discipline before being exposed to formal explanations of them. Students might begin units of instruction in science class by manipulating a pendulum, in math class by constructing polygons, or in social studies by reading letters from Civil War battlefields. Only after these experiences do teachers and students together suggest terminology, explanations, and conceptual organization.

Even though designing instruction is important, constructivist teaching is less about the sequencing

of events and more about responding to the needs of a situation.[8] Teachers must employ a sophisticated range of strategies to support individual students' understandings as they engage in the problem-based activities that characterize constructivist classrooms. These strategies include scaffolding, in which the task required of the learner is strategically reduced in complexity; modeling, in which the teacher either thinks aloud about or acts out how she would approach a problem; and coaching, guiding, and advising, which are loosely defined as providing learners with suggestions of varying degrees of explicitness.[9] The teacher is challenged to select the proper strategy and implement it with skill.

Problem-based activities exemplify another core value of the constructivist culture—collaboration. Students are witness to and participate in one another's thinking. Learners are exposed to the clear, cogent thinking of some peers as well as to the inevitable meandering, unreflective thought of others. Students do require training to function effectively in these groups.[10] However, even with training, many capable students are simply not interested in helping their peers, and negative consequences of group work—such as bickering, exclusion, and academic freeloading—are common.[11] These consequences can be minimized if the teacher is familiar with the principles of cooperative learning. And so, having students work together requires that the teacher have additional competencies in cooperative learning strategies and management skills particular to decentralized learning environments.

A final pedagogical challenge involves independent student projects. Depending on the degree of structure the teacher imposes in a classroom, students will have some latitude in choosing problems or design projects that relate to the theme under study. Often, students determine with the teacher suitable criteria for problems and for evidence of learning. Negotiation about criteria prompts questions such as: Is the problem meaningful? Important to the discipline? Complex enough? Does it relate to the theme under study? Does it require original thinking and interpretation, or is it simply fact finding? Will the resolution of this problem help us acquire the concepts and principles fundamental to the theme under study? Because curricular materials are often filled with prepared questions and tasks, teachers seldom have occasion to introduce their students to this idea of "problems about problems." Clearly, teachers must develop their own ability to analyze problems by reflecting on the nature of the discipline and refining their ideas through extended dialogue with colleagues and experiences with students.

Logistical and Political Challenges

Effective forms of constructivist instruction call for major changes in the curriculum, in scheduling, and in assessment.[12] When students are engaged in problem solving and are allowed to help guide their own learning, teachers quickly find that this approach outgrows the 50-minute class period. This situation often means that the teacher will have to negotiate with administrators and other teachers about the possibilities of block scheduling and integrating curricula. If teachers can team with partners from other subject areas, they can extend the length of their class periods and develop more comprehensive themes for study that bridge the worlds of science, social studies, math, and the arts.

The purpose of integrated curricula and extended class periods is to allow students to engage in learning activities that will help them develop deep and elaborate understandings of subject matter. These understandings may be quite different in nature from student to student. Thus there is a need for forms of assessment that allow students to demonstrate what they know and

that connect with rigorous criteria of excellence. These are not the paper-and-pencil, objective tests in which learners recognize rather than generate answers or create brief responses to questions in which they have little personal investment. Rather, students are required to produce journals, research reports, physical models, or performances in the forms of plays, debates, dances, or other artistic representations. Assessing these products and performances requires well-designed, flexible rubrics to maintain a link between course objectives and student learning. Designing these rubrics (through negotiation with students) builds consensus about what "purpose" means in a learning activity, about the nature of meaningful criteria, and about how assessments reflect the efficacy of the teacher as a promoter of understanding.

The final and perhaps most politically sensitive issue confronting teachers is that the diversity of understandings emerging from constructivist instruction does not always seem compatible with state and local standards. For example, student groups engaged in science projects on photosynthesis may have radically different approaches to developing their understanding of this phenomenon. One group may choose to focus on chemical reactions at the molecular level while another group may examine how oxygen and carbon dioxide are exchanged between animals and plants on a global scale. These two groups will take disconcertingly divergent paths to understanding photosynthesis.

This kind of project-based learning must be skillfully orchestrated so that, however students choose to investigate and seek resolutions to problems, they will acquire an understanding of key principles and concepts as well as the critical thinking skills that are assessed on standardized tests. Proponents of project-based learning have demonstrated that these kinds of learning outcomes are entirely possible.[13] Artful guidance by the teacher notwithstanding, it

can be unsettling for teachers to reconcile the language of "objectives, standards, and benchmarks" with the diversity of understandings that emerge in a constructivist classroom.

Conclusions and Recommendations

How does a school community support the instructional expertise, academic freedom, and professional collaboration necessary to sustain a constructivist culture? First, a core group of committed teachers must systematically investigate constructivism in order to understand its principles and its limitations. The ideas behind constructivism seem intuitive and sensible, but teachers and administrators must go beyond the hyperbole and the one-shot-workshop acquaintance with constructivism. Interested faculty members should conduct a thorough reading campaign, and at least one or two teachers should extend their experience by participating in advanced workshops, attending classes, and witnessing how constructivist cultures operate in other schools. Stipends and released time can be provided for a cadre of lead teachers to attend classes, do extra reading, adapt curriculum, and offer their own workshops to fellow teachers. Workshop topics could include the constructivist implementation of cooperative learning, scaffolding techniques, problem-based learning, or multifaceted assessment strategies.

The faculty members must openly discuss their beliefs about learners and about their roles as teachers. If these beliefs are left unexamined or unchallenged, then individuals have feeble grounding for their personal philosophies. Just as problematically then, everyone operates on different, untested assumptions. And all decisions about curriculum, instruction, and assessment are built on such assumptions.

Personal philosophies of education are particularly important when constructivism is used to furnish underlying principles—important because constructivism means risk taking and a divergence from business as usual. Sooner or later, teachers will be asked, "Why do you teach that way?" Whatever form that question takes, teachers must be able to justify the choices they make. This task will not be as intimidating if the teacher has mindfully linked the aspects of his or her constructivist philosophy to the various dimensions of classroom experience and to the larger goals of education.

The process of making these beliefs explicit can also strengthen teachers' resolve to move beyond the traditional images of what is proper and possible in the classroom. It can make clear to them the characteristics and limitations of the system that encouraged images of teachers as dispensers of information and students as passive recipients of knowledge. Accordingly, teachers must try to arrive at a new vision of their role. This vision must include serving as a facilitator of learning who responds to students' needs with a flexible understanding of subject matter and a sensitivity to how the student is making sense of the world.

Teachers and their principals must be prepared to go on record with these beliefs in discussions with parent groups and the school board. Educators should always have a rationale for what and how they teach; however, because constructivism is so contrary to historical norms, it is even more important in this case that the rationale be well founded, coherent, and applicable to the current school context. Community members will undoubtedly be suspicious of teaching methods that are so different from the ones they remember as students and that sound too much like a laissez-faire approach to learning.

Administrators must also take the lead in supporting a "less is more" approach. The compulsion to cover material is antithetical to the aim of constructivist instruction—the deep and elaborate understanding of selected core ideas. Textbooks, which are often the de facto curriculum, have become encyclopedic, and administrators should make teachers feel secure about using a variety of other resources. They should also provide funds to purchase alternative classroom materials. Furthermore, administrators must be open to suggestions for block scheduling and for integrating curricula, perhaps even arranging for interested teachers to be placed together in team-teaching situations that are premised on the constructivist approach.

To strengthen the school's position on accountability, assessment specialists who understand constructivism can be brought in to connect local standards with instruction and with evidence that learning is taking place. Teachers will undoubtedly appreciate assistance in investigating and evaluating a variety of assessment strategies.

The list of challenges I have described here is not exhaustive. There are certainly others, and the challenges outnumber the solutions at the moment. But articulating these challenges is a significant step in helping educators create and sustain a classroom culture that values diversity in learning and offers a new vision of the roles of teachers and learners—the culture of constructivism.

Notes

1. Pam Bolotin-Joseph, "Understanding Curriculum as Culture," in Pam Bolotin-Joseph, Stevie Bravman, Mark Windschitl, Edward Mikel, and Nancy Green, eds., *Cultures of Curriculum* (Mahwah, N.J.: Erlbaum, forthcoming).

2. Thomas Russell, "Learning to Teach Science: Constructivism, Reflection, and Learning from Experience," in Kenneth Tobin, ed., *The Practice of Constructivism in Science Education* (Hillsdale, N.J.: Erlbaum, 1993), pp. 247–58.

3. Corby Kennison, "Enhancing Teachers' Professional Learning: Relationships Between School Culture and Elementary School Teachers' Beliefs, Images, and Ways of Knowing" (Specialist's thesis, Florida State University, 1990).

4. Kenneth Tobin, "Constructivist Perspectives on Teacher Learning," in idem, pp. 215–26; and Kenneth Tobin and Sarah Ulerick, "An Interpretation of High School Science Teaching Based on Metaphors and Beliefs for Specific Roles," paper presented at the annual meeting of the American Educational Research Association, San Francisco, 1989.

5. Kenneth Zeichner and Robert Tabachnick, "Are the Effects of University Teacher Education Washed Out by School Experience?," *Journal of Teacher Education*, vol. 32, 1981, pp. 7–11.

6. Adriana Groisman, Bonnie Shapiro, and John Willinsky, "The Potential of Semiotics to Inform Understanding of Events in Science Education," *International Journal of Science Education*, vol. 13, 1991, pp. 217–26.

7. James H. Mosenthal and Deborah Ball, "Constructing New Forms of Teaching: Subject Matter Knowledge in Inservice Teacher Education," *Journal of Teacher Education*, vol. 43, 1992, pp. 347–56.

8. David Lebow, "Constructivist Values for Instructional Systems Design: Five Principles Toward a New Mindset," *Educational Technology, Research, and Development*, vol. 41, no. 3, 1993, pp. 4–16.

9. Jeong-Im Choi and Michael Hannafin, "Situated Cognition and Learning Environments: Roles, Structures, and Implications for Design," *Educational Technology, Research, and Development*, vol. 43, no. 2, 1995, pp. 53–69.

10. David W. Johnson, Roger T. Johnson, and Karl A. Smith, *Active Learning: Cooperation in the College Classroom* (Edina, Minn.: Interaction Book Company, 1991).

11. Robert E. Slavin, *Cooperative Learning* (Boston: Allyn and Bacon, 1995).

12. Phyllis Blumenfeld et al., "Motivating Project-Based Learning: Sustaining the Doing, Supporting the Learning," *Educational Psychologist*, vol. 26, 1991, pp. 369–98.

13. Ibid.9

Keeping in Character
A Time-Tested Solution

By Jacques S. Benninga
and Edward A. Wynne

The positive outcomes of for-character education, the authors contend, counter such misleading pictures as the one sketched by Alfie Kohn in his February Kappan *article.*

I N THE February 1997 *Kappan*, Alfie Kohn attacked modern character education for a myriad of alleged deficiencies. This essay constitutes our response to his criticisms. The basic structure of true "for-character" education relies on an approach that

- is relevant for students of all ages;
- has been time-tested and refined over 2,500 years;
- is as responsive to today's children as it was to yesterday's;
- has broad support among American citizens, including teachers and students; and
- has a research base to justify its continuation.

Illustration by Mario Noche

Increasing Disorder

Before we turn to particulars, it is important for readers to understand exactly why we and so many other American adults are worried about the character of the nation's youth. It is not, as Kohn implies, be-

---

JACQUES S. BENNINGA is a professor of education and director of the Bonner Center for Character Education and Citizenship at California State University, Fresno. EDWARD A. WYNNE is a professor of education at the University of Illinois, Chicago, and editor of the For-Character Education Web Page (www.uic.edu/~edaw/main.html).

cause we dislike young people. Instead, it is because we love them and want them to stop killing and abusing themselves and one another at record rates.

Statistics document the record-breaking rates of distress afflicting young Americans and form an essential backdrop for any discussion of for-character practices. The annual rates of death of young (15- to 19-year-old) white males by homicide and suicide are at their highest points since national record-keeping began in 1914.[1] The rates of out-of-wedlock births to young (15- to 19-year-old) white females are also at or near their highest points since national record-keeping began in

From *Phi Delta Kappan*, February 1998, pp. 439-445, 448. © 1998 by Phi Delta Kappa International, Inc. Reprinted by permission.

ANY FOR-CHARACTER SCHOOL OR CLASSROOM WILL INCLUDE A NUMBER OF FOR-CHARACTER ACTIVITIES.

1936. What's more, these high rates have occurred during an era of generally more accessible contraception, abortion, and sex education. All these indicators focus on whites—members of our most advantaged group. This suggests that the "causes" for the bulk of the disorder only incidentally involve poverty and race.

As if we needed any more bad news, the Centers for Disease Control released an important report in February 1997. That report found that "nearly three-quarters of all the murders of children in the industrialized world occur in the United States" and that the U.S. has the "highest rates of childhood homicide, suicide, and firearms-related deaths of any of the world's 26 richest nations."[2]

All these relatively precise measures of disorder indirectly measure many other uncountable forms of profound despair, injury, and wrongdoing that affect the young.

- Most murders of young persons are committed by young murderers.
- Every identified young death by homicide undoubtedly subsumes many other less violent crimes, such as battery, woundings, and beatings.
- Out-of-wedlock births are also indices of victimization of vulnerable females by males or of risky acts of promiscuity.
- The suicides are also indicators of previously attempted suicides and other symptoms of deep depression.

High school students themselves are very well situated to see what is happening among their peers. They clearly recognize that many deeply flawed contemporary education policies have enmeshed our young in a disorderly, low-demand world—a world in which too many adults confuse being caring with being permissive. Recent evidence from a national sample of high school students shows that 50% of the respondents said that "schools fail to challenge pupils to do their best," 71% said that there were "too many disruptive students," 79% said that learning would improve if "schools ensured students got their work done on time and completed their assignments," 86% said that schools should teach students the value of "hard work," 71% would require after-school classes for students who get D's and F's in major subjects, 73% said requiring exit tests before graduation would cause students to learn more, and 50% said that "too

many students get away with being late to class or not doing their work."[3] As we will show, these student opinions are quite congruent with the for-character approach.

Some Qualifications

We have both done considerable research and writing on issues involving student character. For instance, each of us, acting separately and with the help of local educators, has organized school recognition programs, one in the Chicago area and the other in the Fresno area. These programs identify elementary and secondary schools that maintain exemplary character formation policies and curricula. Over 13 yearly cycles, approximately 400 elementary, middle, and secondary schools have participated in these programs. Thus we have examined a variety of good, bad, and indifferent for-character activities. From that base, after some important background information, we will assess Kohn's key contentions.

One other qualification should be expressed. Many of Kohn's criticisms are essentially aimed at the ambitious claims made for packaged character education curricula. We and many leading figures in the character education movement are not sanguine about expecting notable results from any such quick-fix approach.[4] However, well-conceived packages may be useful if they are part of a holistic school- or classroom-wide for-character approach. Indeed, it is to express our distance from quick-fix activities that we use the phrase "for-character education" rather than the more common "character education." Such use stresses the need to integrate for-character elements into many typical school activities. Thus there can be for-character policies, for-character cocurricular activities, and even for-character lunchroom policies. To further stress the issue of systematically planning for-character activities, one of the authors even published a list of 100 for-character activities that can be used in and around schools.[5] Though 100 is not a sacred number, the point is that any for-character school or classroom will include a number of for-character activities, most of which will be integrated into its day-to-day operations.

Character and For-Character Education

The word *character* derives from the Greek word "to mark" or "to engrave" and is associated with the writings of philosophers such as Plato and Aristotle. People with good character habitually display good behavior, and these people are known by their behavior. Thus a generous person may be seen giving notable gifts, or a brave person may perform heroic acts. A courteous person behaves properly and with civility toward others.

There may be no specific consensus on a list of desirable character traits or habits. But considerable agreement exists on the desirable virtues—moral qualities regarded as good or meritorious—that underlie these traits. Throughout history thoughtful philosophers and educators have been concerned about the cultivation of such virtues as honesty, kindness, courage, perseverance, and loyalty and about the cultivation of their concomitant traits. The renewed interest in such virtues is evident in the huge success of *The Book of Virtues*, by William Bennett. The book is a collection of inspiring classic literature for children and adults. It addresses 10 particular virtues. In recent years, we have also witnessed the publication of a spate of nonsectarian character-oriented books by psychologists, educators, and distinguished scholars.[6]

The consensus is that traits—and, to some degree, virtues—are not innate. They must be acquired through learning and practice in homes, schools, neighborhoods, churches, and other agencies. They must be transmitted to be internalized. However, a child's state of mind *is* relevant to this process. That is, for-character educators do not advocate having children behave solely according to a set of principles or rules without understanding them. Rather, for-character educators agree with William Frankena, who proposed that "we regard the morality of principles and the morality of traits of character, or being and doing, not as rival kinds of morality between which we must choose, but as two complimentary aspects of the same morality."[7]

The character tradition stresses the importance of whole environments operating systematically to foster good character formation. But environments mean not only the physical elements surrounding students, but also the people surrounding them, the good or bad examples they provide, and the expectations they establish. Profound character education involves managing classrooms or whole schools so that they will advance student character.

Here is where Alfie Kohn missed the mark. His criticisms extend far beyond the defects of relying solely on packages. He takes offense because for-character educators have developed a perspective, a "particular style of moral training." And it is true that there are good and bad ways to teach character. Kohn then proposes his alternative to character education. Let us, in his words, get straight to the educational point. His alternative is a set of various approaches that we have met before, collected under the umbrella of developmental education. The umbrella currently includes such panaceas as the whole-language approach, constructivism, and, most recently, democratic education. These approaches have already been tried in our own era, without generating either "good people" or notable academic learning.[8]

True, the policies have attractive labels. But such labels are deceptive. Who, for example, could be against democratic education? Yet such ambiguous labels are riddled with inconsistencies that foreclose careful analysis. For example, many educators now favor emotive terminology, such as "educating for democracy," without being able to define or evaluate the policies advocated to advance such ends. Various notions, such as self-esteem education and inclusion, are now contained in the "democratic education" package. Few of these programs have undergone rigorous evaluation to determine their effects, and, when they have been evaluated, the results often fail to support their ambitious claims.

But that doesn't seem to matter to some. In the words of educational theorist Amy Guttman, democratic education "commits us to accepting nondiscriminatory and nonrepressive policies as legitimate even when they are wrong."[9] Even when such practices lead to lower academic achievement, she states, they are necessary to advance the "virtues of citizenship," and even when student participation threatens to produce disorder within schools, it may be defended on "democratic grounds."[10]

These conceptions of democracy are probably not what America's founders had in mind two centuries ago, but they seem to be exactly what Alfie Kohn believes. That is, he wants us to engage elementary school children in "deep, critical reflection about certain ways of being"; to teach reflection over diligence, respect, patriotism, and responsibility; to teach self-determination and skepticism over self-control and obedience. He does not suggest where skepticism should begin or end. Still, he is at least skeptical about patriotism: he compares the Pledge of Allegiance to the Flag to a form of "loyalty oath to the Fatherland" (with its obvious Nazi overtones). It would seem consistent with such cynicism to approve as well of 10-year-olds' skepticism toward their parents, although wiser students may choose to reserve their skepticism for persons who recommend such questionable doctrines.

The Five Questions

Kohn poses five basic questions that might be asked of character education programs. In answer to the first question—"At what level are problems addressed?"—Kohn reiterates the liberal argument that crime and urban decay are political outcomes of unemployment and the consolidation of great wealth in the hands of the few. These "bad things" are the cause of any character problems our young people might have. In other words, "It's all someone else's fault!" Our reply is brief, since we are neither criminologists nor economists—but neither, we believe, is Kohn.

- The data we have already cited on steadily rising youth disorder dealt just with whites. Presumably, such a group, even though afflicted with disorder, is not composed of poor inner-city residents.

- The long-term economic trends affecting most young white Americans involve economic improvements over their parents. Our college students, when we ask them for a show of hands on such matters, usually agree that they will be better off than their parents regarding such things as length of education, quality of housing, length of life span, and quality of health. It appears that the long-term increase in disorder is not caused by the spread of grinding poverty.

- The causal connection, if any, between crime and personal income is actually hotly debated. As James Wilson and Richard Herrnstein have emphasized, the overall statistical relationship between crime and the unemployment rate is not very strong.[11] Though many criminals may be poorly educated and are often unemployed, the factors underlying the development of the criminal personality are more complicated.

View of Human Nature

Next, Kohn addresses for-character's view of human nature. And surprise, the for-character educators do not see everything as sweetness and roses. "Fix-the-kids," say prominent for-character educators, who take a "dim view of human nature" (William Kilpatrick), who hold a "pessimistic view of human nature" (Edward Wynne), who say that "children are self-centered" (Kevin Ryan), and who seek to "control [children's] impulses and defer [their] gratification" (Amitai Etzioni).

Kohn is absolutely right! We are horrified and distressed at the harm so many young people are doing to themselves and to one another. We also desperately want to change the destructive conduct of many young people—to protect them and their possible victims. As for being anti-youth, our opinions and prescriptions are generally similar to those approved by young people themselves, as reported in the national high school student poll quoted near the beginning of this article. Are the students also anti-youth?

If modern for-character educators are not utopian in their attitudes toward children, they certainly are

not alone. In a recent national survey of American adults, 72% of the respondents said there was an excess of "drugs and violence in their local schools." When the responses were broken down by race, the comparable figures were 58% (whites) and 80% (blacks).[12] Are the blacks who think there's too much violence in their children's schools also anti-youth?

There are important historic precedents for our current concerns. Many of history's best minds have realized that most children and adults don't naturally set about "doing good for intrinsic reasons," as Kohn would suggest. A revealing dialogue from Plato's *Republic* (Book II) is instructive. Glaucon, a character in *The Republic*, maintains in a discussion with Socrates that it is natural for people to pursue their own interests despite the needs of others or the need for an orderly society. As evidence, Glaucon tells the story of Gyges, an otherwise rather decent shepherd. Gyges found a magic ring that enabled him to become invisible. The result? Gyges "seduced the queen and with her help attacked and murdered the king and seized the throne."[13] Of course, the tale of Gyges is a story—all made up. However, does anyone doubt the psychological truth of the ring story? When people receive uncontrolled power, there is a real possibility that they will abuse it. Or, as James Madison put it, "If men were angels, no government would be necessary."

Similarly, Horace Mann, the founder of public education in the U.S., believed that "moral education is a primal necessity of social existence. The unrestrained passions of men are not only homicidal, but suicidal."[14] But contrary to what Kohn would surmise, Mann hoped to form a literate, diligent, productive, and responsible citizenry committed to the conception that the best society was one in which people governed themselves through elected officials and representative institutions. Both Aristotle and Plato advocated a curriculum of music, literature, mathematics, and gymnastics that would result in a "well-balanced and harmonious character."

It would certainly be wrong to characterize these men or the contemporary for-character educators mentioned by Kohn as promoting a totalitarian educational agenda based on their conceptions of an unschooled human nature. To the contrary, it seems more reasonable to conclude that the current for-character perspective represents the collective and rather consistent perspective of the best minds of the past 2,500 years. Such a conclusion seems more promising than the utopian, New Age perspective proposed by Kohn.

Furthermore, the Founders of our nation, from their extensive reading of history, concluded that the greatest threat to democracy was the danger of tyranny that might evolve from the failure of powerful men to meet their civic responsibilities. To prevent such destructive patterns, citizens had to possess such virtues as self-discipline, responsibility, and prudence. Lacking such virtuous citizens, any democracy would gradually decay into a morass of selfishness and jealousy.

John Adams and his wife Abigail exemplified this "republican virtue" in their role as parents. Adams, absent for long periods from his family, wrote to his wife, "Train [our children] to virtue. Habituate them to industry, activity, and spirit."[15] Similarly, George Washington compiled and learned early a set of 110 "Rules of Civility and Decent Behavior in Company and Conversation," which thereafter governed his private behavior and tempered his impulsiveness.[16] The models left us by these men are still worth emulating.

Rather than holding a dark, bleak vision of human nature, these leaders had purpose and courage in the face of danger and suffering. They were indifferent to material circumstances and believed that their legacies would consist of the good and virtuous lives they lived. It is understandable that some citizens in our hedonistic and pedestrian era (What is the going price for a night in Lincoln's bed?) have trouble interpreting their heroic stoicism. Still, we owe it to our young people to try and hold high models up before them. Kohn has missed the point here.

The Ultimate Goal

Kohn next attacks for-character educators for their "profoundly conservative, if not reactionary, agenda." Rather than teach the virtuous life, he wants educators to train children as "advocates for social justice." Rather than set standards for behavior, he wants educators to promote skepticism in children. Rather than, as Aristotle suggested, "learning that there are things which one is expected to do even when all concerned are aware that one does not feel like doing them . . . [and] that there are things worth doing and aiming for which are not immediately pleasant,"[17] Kohn wants us to emphasize "the cultivation of autonomy so that children come to experience themselves as 'origins' rather than 'pawns.'" Thus children should be allowed to participate "in making decisions about their learning and about how they want their classroom to be." We should, Kohn states, stress compassion over loyalty, cooperation over competition, autonomy over punctuality, self-determination over self-control. In truth, those of us concerned with the formation of character engage in no such dichotomous thinking. We want to develop all the virtues.

But children cannot be treated like miniature adults. Nowhere is this issue better exemplified than in recent public service television spots for the United Negro College Fund. In these brief ads, small children are pictured piloting advanced aircraft, sitting behind corporate desks, and teaching in a university classroom, while the announcer suggests: "A mind is a ter-

rible thing to waste." The point behind these gripping presentations is clear: children are only *potentially* capable of doing the jobs suggested by the images. They are certainly not ready in the early stages of life for the responsibilities that are inherent in adult positions. They need encouragement and training to realize their potential. Their minds are not those of adults. As both Piaget and Kohlberg have shown us, they are not miniature versions of what they will become. Rather, they are, as we now know, thinkers of a qualitatively different kind from the thinkers we hope they will become. This point seems to have been overlooked by Kohn, who seems to believe that by defining the best outcomes for adults we can infer direct implications for classrooms of children. This is just not so.

Allowing students too much freedom to "cultivate autonomy" and too much freedom to "make decisions about their learning" can be detrimental. Three quick examples may suffice to make this obvious point.

- A *New York Times* article (independently verified by one of the authors) told of one "democracy first" public high school in which a discussion took place among the students and teachers—the whole school community—about whether the students should be allowed to bring knives and to have sex on a school picnic. (They eventually voted the proposal down.)[18]
- Robert Howard described an elementary school classroom in which the students, with their classroom teacher's approval, decided that a student who was guilty of spitting on a classmate was to be punished by standing in the middle of his classmates who would each, in turn, spit on the offender. (A more experienced teacher intervened and stopped the punishment.)[19]
- Timothy Lensmire invited the students in his third-grade writing project to insert the names of fellow pupils in the stories they composed. He wrote a book on the project and its outcomes. The young authors discovered that using the names of classmates gave them the power to embarrass and shame their peers. Some students so named became very upset. Eventually, Lensmire was distressed about the pain and selfishness his innovation was generating, but—like Hamlet—he could not decide what to do. Fortunately, the principal stepped in and ended the project. Lensmire's book was sympathetically reviewed in an academic journal.[20] The reviewer disapproved of the principal's intrusion, calling it "institutionalized violence," and commented that, if the project had continued, Lensmire could have transformed his classroom into a court and could have had his writers and injured students hold an in-class lawsuit over the conflict—that is, if someone did not beat up someone else first.

A CERTAIN WELL-ROUNDEDNESS IS DESIRABLE, AND AN
EXCESS IN ANY ONE VIRTUE CAN LEAD TO IMBALANCES.

These activities bear some vague, though distorted and uninformed, resemblance to our republican form of government. We say "distorted" because they involve so little accountability for the misuse of student power. Nothing happens to authors who recklessly hurt other students' feelings. As for the picnic, if the "no knives and no sex" resolution had failed, would the students have been collectively liable for any harmful—or deadly—results? These are just the sort of in-school activities that cultivate poor character in students. Though we feel such activities are comparatively rare in our schools, we believe many readers will be able to identify less dramatic examples of similar tendencies.

What For-Character Educators Want

So what do for-character educators want? What is our ultimate goal? Simply stated, we want children and adolescents to learn to feel a sense of belonging to and responsibility for others. This goal and its rationale come from the work of Emile Durkheim almost 100 years ago. In Durkheim's view, morality and religion, the *collective conscience* as he called them, are the cohesive bonds that hold the social order together. A breakdown of these values, he believed, would lead to social instability and individual feelings of anxiety and dissatisfaction, sometimes resulting in depression, suicide, and other forms of disorder.

Durkheim exhaustively studied the topic of suicide.[21] He concluded that it—and by extension other types of youth disorder—was largely caused by the affliction of not being immediately needed. Suicide was not particularly related to poverty or to evident social injustice. Instead, people with simple, proximate obligations to others (e.g., mothers, manual laborers, teachers) tended to choose to live through the inevitable "slings and arrows of outrageous fortune." They rejected suicide because it was a betrayal of those immediate obligations. (Who will feed the chickens? Who will change the baby's diapers?) These notions are certainly generalizable. Conversely, people with abstract and unclear obligations to others are much more prone to suicide. Young people, especially in our country and in our era, are one class with very remote and vague obligations to others.

Recent sociological studies have reached conclusions generally congruent with Durkheim's broad propositions.[22] One of the authors once examined re-cords of adolescents who had committed suicide. One pitiful file told of a boy whose last act before committing suicide was to kill his beloved dog. Once the ties of responsibility were destroyed, the boy no longer had any obligation to endure the typical buffets of life. In effect, we are often saved by our obligations to others.

Durkheim's theory implies that the young are ignored, unwanted, and lacking in serious responsibilities. The solution involves creating more structured and intense responsibilities. Thus he implies that being extremely permissive toward the young makes things worse. When people are really important to us, we surround their conduct with many forms of constraint and their misconduct with notable and fast consequences. We demand that the surgeon who will cut us open first wash his or her hands. When we go to an expensive restaurant for a fine meal, we want the waiter to display a little style. When we're playing a sport to win, we want our teammates to go all out. We put people who are really important to us under pressure, and so they feel important.

But too many of today's young people are rarely expected to help support their families, nor are they called on to carry out demanding household chores. Instead, their most typical characteristic is that they are often not very much needed by anyone else. They are ignored. Their roles are largely ornamental. If many of them died, the day-to-day work of the world would continue for the immediate future. People given such freedom can find themselves bored and tempted toward irresponsible and dangerous behavior. The traditional character prescription still applies: "For Satan finds some mischief still for idle hands to do."

We believe that children need age-appropriate but significant responsibilities, in order to feel socially integrated and respected. Adults with authority (i.e., parents, teachers, coaches) should feel comfortable disciplining youngsters who fail to carry out those significant duties. It is, furthermore, the responsibility of adults to critically examine children's and adolescents' social environments and to design and manage them so those environments help our young people grow into mature and moral adults.

These intuitions, based on our collective research, are corroborated by findings about what works with regard to for-character education. Activities in which students assume responsibility (including the acceptance of authority and consequences) for their own learning and behavior and the learning and behavior of others "will result in positive changes in selected prosocial character traits." Moreover, "classroom and school climates that embody such factors as clear standards, mutual respect between students and teachers, and shared governance have been found to be associated with some limited, but nonetheless important, positive changes in student character."[23]

Which Values?

In his fourth question, Kohn wonders, "Which values" should we teach? We agree with him that "whether or not we deliberately adopt a character or moral education program, we are always teaching values." We would say, more precisely, we are always teaching virtues. But which virtues? Though Kohn agrees with the teaching of noncontroversial virtues, such as fairness or honesty, he objects to such "conservative" and "potentially controversial" guidelines as "work hard and complete your tasks." Here again, Kohn rebukes for-character educators for sneaking in their propagandistic biases—e.g., the Protestant work ethic or obedience. He would prefer that we teach empathy and skepticism.

The for-character tradition recognizes that no single virtue should always dominate, although the virtues are systematically related to form a unity of perspective. Virtuous people we know or read about and admire—e.g., George Washington, Martin Luther King, Mother Teresa—all possessed a measure of the Socratic virtues: wisdom, temperance, justice, and courage. A certain well-roundedness is desirable, and an excess in any one virtue can lead to imbalances. For example, the fictional Hamlet was reflective and loyal, but indecisive. Richard Nixon was diligent and farsighted, but also vindictive.

We do not feel qualified to strongly recommend any particular mix of values to educators or parents. We are far more concerned with the openness of the decision-making process, realizing that conflicts do occur over moral priorities. Since their inception American public schools have successfully and regularly resolved conflicts over what should be taught. Such disputes are the day-to-day routines of our democratic processes. Differences are scrutinized, pros and cons are subjected to public debate, compromises are negotiated, and votes are cast.

There are, of course, many sources that offer specific answers to the question of which virtues we should teach. One such set is embodied in the principles laid out in the U.S. Constitution, the Bill of Rights, and other founding documents (e.g., justice, the rights and responsibilities of citizenship, freedom of the press, freedom of religion, and so on). Another set of answers is the common core of virtues alluded

to throughout this article: honesty, love, compassion, duty, respect, responsibility, diligence, and so on. A third set of answers can be found in the growing number of communities that have adopted common core virtues for their own children. Yet another set of answers can be found in the six pillars growing out of the Aspen Declaration of 1992: caring, civic virtue and citizenship, justice and fairness, respect, responsibility, and trustworthiness. Since America is the world's most religious industrialized country, it would be incongruous if some of that tradition did not influence the setting of priorities with regard to virtue. This might touch on such matters as chastity, the sanctity of marriage, honoring one's parents or others in authority, or displaying charity. The list goes on.

What Is Our Theory of Learning?

The pedagogical principles we advocate are simple and direct.

- Identify and list the virtues and relevant behavior traits one hopes children will learn. (There are a variety of virtues to choose from and a variety of sources for those virtues.)
- Establish those identified virtues or traits as goals for students and the faculty.
- Provide occasions for students, either individually or as part of well-designed groups, to practice the behaviors associated with such traits or virtues.
- Praise students, either individually or as a group—publicly or privately—when desirable behavior, consistent with expectations, is displayed.
- Identify undesirable traits and prohibit them. Publicize and justify such prohibitions, and establish and enforce clear, unpleasant, and appropriate consequences for such misbehavior by individuals or groups.
- Use the school's formal curriculum and ceremonies to support such activities.
- Hire, train, and retain staff members who actively support such policies.[24]

Kohn characterizes this approach as nothing more than "exhortation and directed recitation . . . teaching as a matter of telling and compelling." Teachers in for-character classrooms, he states, are encouraged to engage in a variety of measures to get students to conform: praising children who respond correctly, prohibiting wrongdoing, and inculcating habits such as perseverance, delay of gratification, and self-control. He's correct. But this approach is far more than simplistic "exhortation." We believe that straightforward tactics will improve academic and for-character learning and help save students' lives.

As to for-character vocabulary, we intend such words as *instill in, transmit to,* and *habit formation* to describe the process of character development and mature moral decision making. These are, however, not our words. They are the words of Plato and Aristotle, of Kant and Piaget. They are the collective knowledge of our best minds over time.

So how do schools best help shape the character of the young? Our answer is clear. Effective schools share the same systemic characteristics researchers have observed in highly effective parents.[25] Similarly, less-effective schools share characteristics of less-effective, laissez-faire parents. That is, well-grounded teachers and schools set high expectations and nourish children's earned sense of competence and self-reliance. They rely on extrinsic control, clarity, consistency, nurture, and honesty of communication to shape their students' character. They are primarily concerned for the well-being of the children. We believe that schools with these characteristics are more likely to graduate students who are accomplished academically and who demonstrate the habits and character traits that lead to productive citizenship. We believe that this is what good schools have always been about.

The Bog of Intrinsic Motivation

Kohn strongly opposes all measures that involve incentives, since they rely on external motivation. His position is, in effect, that, as long as such constraints are applied, students will not be free. That is, they will not practice learning for intrinsic reasons. The matter can be put in a more critical way: Kohn is less interested in stimulating students toward excellence in academics or character formation than many other educators. His case requires him to find strong evidence that recognition, praise, and other earned rewards do not habituate people to be kind, honest, or diligent. In other words, well-deserved praise does not encourage people to make a habit of their praised conduct. This is a rather fantastic position, countered by recent research and everyday experience.[26]

Allow us to provide just one instance of such everyday experience of the deep power of extrinsic motivation over learning. As part of a study of a typical suburban high school, one of the authors identified various systems to motivate learning that were used in that school. Each system was accompanied by its own unique intrinsic and extrinsic rewards. The most powerful and effective learning systems were associated with interscholastic competitive team athletics.

This "discovery" simply represents the researcher's having stumbled into a widely recognized pattern. In many schools, a great deal of attention is given to athletics. Much of this attention consists of public praise, publicity, and other forms of conspicuous display. The point so often forgotten, though, is that such extrinsic motivation systems work very well! Student athletes work long and hard to learn how to improve their skills, and often they succeed. The members of the swimming team, for example, practiced arduously for four hours a day over the 20-day Christmas vacation. And when the members of the girls' varsity volleyball team returned to school in the fall, their coach publicly tested each player to see if she had managed to improve her jumping and speed since their last practices. All the other school teams applied equivalent begin-the-season tests. It was understood by the athletes that training started well before each season began. Obviously, extrinsic motivation to learn has not turned off student athletes; it has just made them work harder at learning their skills.

Finally, Kohn offers his example of a good school program that promotes children's moral and social development. He presents the Child Development Project (CDP), whose premise is that, "by meeting children's needs, we increase the likelihood that they will care about others." However, one of the authors helped conduct a four-year direct comparison of students in CDP schools with students attending a public school with a strong for-character program.

In contrast to the CDP schools, the for-character school established specific, measurable goals, standards, and performance indicators; conducted frequent, systematic assessments of performance; measured and rated school performance relative to the goals and published the results; publicly recognized schools, classes, and individuals for achieving goals; and supported school personnel in their efforts to achieve school goals. In other words, it was not the type of school in which Kohn would enroll his children.

Although there were major differences between the CDP program and the for-character program, both seem to have had positive effects in students, and, of the hundreds of variables studied, there were numerous areas in which neither program was significantly or consistently differentiated from the other.[27] But the teachers in the for-character school, as opposed to teachers in the CDP schools, rated their school as more businesslike, creative, and innovative, with more involved and supportive parents, a more supportive and accessible principal, a more traditional academic focus, a pleasanter atmosphere, and better relations between teachers and students. And students in the for-character school scored higher on measures of self-esteem in the third and fourth grades than did students in the CDP schools. These positive results in a school with clear for-character policies should not extinguish other experiments designed to improve student character. However, the results do counter such misleading pictures as the one sketched by Alfie Kohn.

1. The U.S. Department of Health and Human Services, Public Health Service, Bureau of Vital Statistics, and predecessor agencies have compiled annual vital statistics reports on specific topics for appropriate years (homicide and suicide, 1914–94; out-of-wedlock births, 1940–93).
2. Judith Haveman, "A Nation of Violent Children: A New Survey Finds the Epidemic Is Confined Almost Exclusively to the U.S.," *Washington Post National Weekly Edition*, 17 February 1997, p. 34.
3. Jean Johnson and Steve Farkas, *Getting By: What American Teenagers Really Think About Their Schools* (New York: Public Agenda, 1997).
4. Over the past few years many books have documented exemplary programs in character education. None of these school programs relied primarily on packaged character education programs, though some did use them. See Jacques S. Benninga, ed., *Moral, Character, and Civic Education in the Elementary School* (New York: Teachers College Press, 1991); Philip F. Vincent, *Promising Practices in Character Education: Nine Success Stories from Around the Country* (Chapel Hill, N.C.: Character Development Group, 1996); and Edward A. Wynne, *A Year in the Life of an Excellent Elementary School* (Lancaster, Pa.: Technomics, 1993).
5. "List of 100 For-Character Activities and Policies," in Edward A. Wynne and Kevin Ryan, *Reclaiming Our Schools: A Handbook on Teaching Character, Academics, and Discipline* (New York: Merrill, 1997), pp. 197–202.
6. See, for example, Stephen L. Carter, *Integrity* (New York: HarperCollins, 1996); William Damon, *Greater Expectations: Overcoming the Culture of Indulgence in America's Homes and Schools* (New York: Free Press, 1996); Jack Frymier et al., *Values on Which We Agree* (Bloomington, Ind.: Phi Delta Kappa Educational Foundation, 1995); Gertrude Himmelfarb, *The Demoralization of Society: From Victorian Virtues to Modern Values* (New York: Alfred A. Knopf., 1995); William Kilpatrick, Gregory Wolfe, and Suzanne M. Wolfe, *Books That Build Character: A Guide to Teaching Your Child Moral Values Through Stories* (New York: Simon & Schuster, 1994); Alex Molnar, ed., *The Construction of Children's Character: 96th NSSE Yearbook, Part II* (Chicago: National Society for the Study of Education, University of Chicago Press, 1997); and Wynne and Ryan, op. cit.
7. William K. Frankena, *Ethics* (Englewood Cliffs, N.J.: Prentice-Hall, 1963), p. 53.
8. See, for example, Robert E. Slavin, "Reforming State and Federal Policies to Support Adoption of Proven Practices," *Educational Researcher*, December 1996, p. 4, in which Slavin comments that "year after year, the achievement of American children remains unchanged. . . . Yet, in what other area of American life would we be satisfied to say that things have simply become no worse over the past quarter century?" Slavin was writing about the academic achievement of youths; we have shown that the moral indicators have declined over this same time period.
9. Amy Gutmann, *Democratic Education* (Princeton, N.J.: Princeton University Press, 1987), p. 288.
10. Ibid.
11. James Q. Wilson and Richard J. Herrnstein, *Crime and Human Nature.* (New York: Simon & Schuster, 1985).
12. Jean Johnson and John Immerwahr, *First Things First: What Americans Expect from the Public Schools* (New York: Public Agenda, 1994).
13. Plato, *The Republic*, trans. H.D. P. Lee (Baltimore: Penguin Books, 1955), pp. 90–91.
14. Horace Mann, as quoted in Lori Sanford Wiley, *Comprehensive Character-Building Classroom* (Manchester, N.H.: Character Development Foundation, 1997), p. 28.
15. Lawrence Cremin, *American Education: The Colonial Years.* (New York: Harper Torchbook, 1970), p. 479.
16. Richard Brookhiser, "A Man on Horseback," *Atlantic,*. January 1996, p. 61.
17. Sarah Broadie, *Ethics with Aristotle* (New York: Oxford University Press, 1991), p. 109.
18. Edward A. Wynne, "Character and Academics in the Elementary School," in Benninga, ed., p. 142.
19. Robert W. Howard, "Lawrence Kohlberg's Influence on Moral Education in Elementary Schools," in Benninga, ed., pp. 61–62.
20. John Willinsky, "The Underside of Empowerment," *Educational Researcher*, March 1995, pp. 31–32.
21. Emile Durkheim, *Suicide: A Study in Sociology*, trans. John A. Spaulding and George Simpson (Glencoe, ILL.: Free Press, 1951).
22. R. W. Marris, "Sociology of Suicide," in Seymour Perlin, ed., *A Handbook for the Study of Suicide* (New York: Oxford University Press, 1975), pp. 93–112.
23. James S. Leming, *Character Education: Lessons from the Past, Models for the Future* (Camden, ME.: Institute for Global Ethics, 1993), p. 16.
24. Edward A. Wynne, "Transmitting Character in Schools—Some Common Questions and Answers," *The Clearing House,"* January/February 1995, *pp. 151–53.*
25. See Eleanor Maccoby, *Social Development: Psychological Growth and the Parent/Child Relationship* (New York: Harcourt Brace Jovanovich, 1980), pp. 382–383; and Diane Baumrind, "The Development of Instrumental Competence Through Socialization," in Anne D. Pick, ed., *Minnesota Symposium on Child Psychology,*. vol. 7 (Minneapolis: University of Minnesota Press, 1973).
26. Judy Cameron and W. David Pierce, "The Debate About Rewards and Intrinsic Motivation: Protests and Accusations Do Not Alter the Results," *Review of Educational Research,*. vol. 66, 1996, pp. 39–51.
27. Jacques S. Benninga et al., "Effects of Two Contrasting School Task and Incentive Structures on Children's Social Development," *Elementary School Journal,*. vol. 92, 1991, pp. 149–67.

Improving Student Thinking

BARRY BEYER

Believe it or not, our students—regardless of age or grade level—not only *can* think but they *do*. They make decisions, attack problems, pose hypotheses, evaluate information, and even make inferences. Unfortunately, of course, many don't carry out these operations very skillfully or consistently, or at all the appropriate times or places, at least in our classes. Consequently, they often fail to develop the kinds of subject matter understandings, insights, and knowledge that we try so hard to help them develop. Isn't there something we can do in our classrooms to help our students improve the quality of their thinking, so they can think better and learn the subjects they study as well as they really could and as well as we would like them to?

The answer, happily, is a resounding *yes!*

Research, exemplary classroom practice, and accumulated teaching experience indicate that there are at least four things you and I can do right now in our classrooms that will improve the abilities and inclinations of our students to think better than they do when left on their own. And, we can do these *at the same time* that we engage our students in achieving the various subject matter learning objectives called for by our curricula. Specifically, we can

- provide a classroom learning environment that makes thinking possible and students willing to engage in it;
- make the invisible substance of thinking visible and explicit;
- guide and support student execution of newly encountered, difficult, or complex thinking operations during their initial efforts to apply them; and
- integrate instruction in thinking with instruction in subject matter.

Barry Beyer is professor emeritus in the Graduate School of Education at George Mason University in Fairfax, Virginia. He is the author of Improving Student Thinking: A Comprehensive Approach *(Boston: Allyn and Bacon, 1998).*

Before we consider some of the many ways to incorporate these approaches into our daily teaching, however, it is important to note that *improving* thinking differs considerably from *facilitating* thinking. The latter consists of making thinking easier. It is commonly a one-time intervention to help students overcome a temporary obstacle or to ease them through a difficult thinking task. Improving thinking, on the other hand, means making thinking work better—more rapidly, accurately, "expertly"—in the long run than it does now. This requires a continuing, systematic, long-term effort to move students toward achieving and maintaining the highest levels possible of skilled, self-directed, self-correcting thinking. The four approaches described here are especially useful for achieving that goal.

Providing Thoughtful Learning Environments

Unless the learning environments of our classrooms nurture and support student thinking, especially higher-order thinking, our students are unlikely to be very receptive to serious efforts on our part to help them improve their thinking. Among the features of such learning environments two stand out as especially crucial: (1) repeated opportunities to engage in meaningful thinking beyond the level of recall and (2) encouragement to engage and remain engaged in such thinking. By ensuring that our classrooms consistently exhibit these features, we make them "thinker-friendly" as well as "thinking-friendly." Specialists call such classrooms thoughtful classrooms (Wiggins 1987).

Providing Thinking Opportunities

The secret to providing repeated classroom opportunities to engage in thinking is to engage students in productive learning tasks. These are tasks that require students to produce knowledge new to them, rather than simply to reproduce information or knowledge claims already presented to them in texts, lectures, or media. One powerful way to do this is to frame learning assignments or lessons around thoughtful questions.

A thoughtful question is a question that—to produce an acceptable response—requires students to go substan-

 From *The Clearing House*, May/June 1998, pp. 262–267. © 1998 by Barry Beyer.

tially beyond where they are and, like the crew of the Enterprise, "to boldly go where no man has gone before." To answer these questions, students must locate and use information they may not yet possess as well as restructure familiar information to produce something they do not already know. "What did Columbus discover?" is not a very thoughtful question. "Who discovered Columbus—and why?" is much more thoughtful.

Thoughtful questions stimulate thinking and trigger additional related questions. They engage students in defining terms; posing hypotheses; identifying, finding, assessing, and manipulating data; making and testing inferences; generating and evaluating conclusions and arguments; and applying concepts, principles, and other kinds of knowledge. They are not yes/no questions. They cannot be answered simply by recall. They do not have a single preferred "right" answer (Newmann 1990; Wiggins 1987). Organizing lessons, units, or topics around such questions provides students continued opportunities to engage in all kinds of thinking to generate worthwhile and meaningful subject matter learning.

Productive learning activities also provide considerable opportunities for sustained thinking. Activities like judging the accuracy of a given claim or body of information or generating a strong argument in support of a conclusion may require as few as only one or two classroom periods (Beyer 1997). Longer tasks such as the following provide even more opportunities for continued student thinking:

> Create and justify the "good citizenship merit badge" requirements for a specific kind of person in a given culture or place at a particular time in history, such as for a Nez Perce youth in the 1870s, an enslaved or free African American in the 1850s, or a king's vassal in the Middle Ages.

Organizing our lessons around thoughtful questions and productive learning tasks helps make thinking a central part of student learning in our classrooms.

Encouraging Student Thinking

Providing opportunities to think, however, is fruitless unless students take advantage of them. And, as we all know, too many students frequently do not! It is thus also essential that we encourage students to seize and sustain engagement in thinking opportunities if we are to create and maintain a thoughtful learning environment.

The kind of encouragement required here is not the redouble-your-effort kind derived from simple cheerleading or from exhortations like, "Think! Think again! Now think harder!" On the contrary, it is the kind of encouragement that *emboldens* students to engage in thinking. This means providing them some tangible aid, prompt, or other support that gives them reason to feel that they will or can succeed at the task at hand.

We can provide such encouragement by arranging students so they face each other as well as by surrounding them with bulletin board displays of quotations, cartoons, puzzles, and copies of their own work that illustrate the importance and value of good thinking. Providing wait time for them to think before we accept their responses to our questions or claims and before we respond to their assertions or answers also serves that purpose (Rowe 1974). So, too, does our modeling the behaviors and dispositions of skillful thinking and helping our students exhibit these behaviors and dispositions. Rather than cutting thinking off with remarks such as, "Good answer!," we can build on their responses to sustain continued thinking by, for instance, asking for evidence to support the accuracy of a response or for examples or more details or assumptions underlying it.

We can also encourage student thinking by minimizing or eliminating the negative risks of thinking (Lipman 1991; Nickerson 1988–89). We can consistently emphasize the positive value of rejected hypotheses and "wrong answers" in leading us to valid hypotheses and "answers." We can constantly employ the language of thinking by using precise thinking terms to denote the specific cognitive actions, skills, conditions, or products in which we wish to engage students. For instance, instead of asking, "What do you think will happen next?" we should ask, "What do you *predict* will happen next?" (Olson and Astington 1990; Perkins 1992). And we can keep classroom discourse focused on truth and proof rather than on who says what, welcome and explore divergent or unusual views, and reward the validated products of high-risk thinking (Newmann 1990).

When engaging in new or difficult thinking tasks is a normal and expected part of our classrooms and "emboldening boosts" are consistently given, students have reason to believe that they can engage successfully in such thinking. It is this kind of support—combined with the topics we ask them to think about—that encourages them to take advantage of the thinking opportunities we provide.

Making Thinking Visible

Before we can repair or strengthen something that is broken or is not working as well as it should be, we need to be aware of exactly how it presently functions. We also need to be aware of how it works or might work when functioning as it could or should function. This is as true of student thinking as it is of any other procedure or process. The first step in improving student thinking thus consists of making students conscious of how they presently think and how others more skilled than they carry out the same thinking operations. This means we need to make the seemingly invisible thinking processes visible and explicit, especially when our students are focusing on new or complex thinking operations.

The Invisible Substance of Thinking

What is there we can make visible and explicit about any act of thinking? Cognitive scientists assert that every thinking skill (operation, strategy, or act) consists of three elements: one or more *procedures* (series of steps and/or rules) by which it is or can be executed skillfully and efficiently; the *conditions* under which it is appropriately employed; and any *declarative knowledge* associated with it, such as the criteria employed in making judgments or evaluations or the heuristics (rules of thumb) that guide expert application of a procedure (Anderson 1983; Nickerson 1988–89). Students benefit immensely from becoming conscious of and articulating exactly how they presently execute a given thinking operation or skill as well as how experts do it, of where and when it is appropriate to employ the operation, and of anything they know—or should know—that would make its application more efficient, effective, and "expert" (Papert 1980; Vygotsky 1962).

Making the Invisible Visible

We help students make visible and explicit these normally unarticulated elements of any thinking skill in several ways. One is by engaging students in reflecting on what they did to carry out a thinking operation they have just completed. This is known as *metacognitive reflection.* Once students have completed a thinking task, we have them think back on exactly what they did mentally, step by step, to complete it, and why they took those steps. In doing this, students articulate what they recall doing, listen to how some of their peers believe they did the same thing, and then analyze these accounts to identify apparently useful, and even additional unarticulated, steps and rules. By continuously articulating and then comparing these procedural descriptions with each other and with explicit procedures employed by individuals more skilled than they in carrying out the same operation, students can spot weaknesses or omissions in the way they do it, identify steps or rules that appear to be especially useful in carrying out the thinking operation, and adapt or incorporate these into how they execute it in the future (Beyer 1997; Nickerson, Perkins, and Smith 1985; Sternberg 1984).

Another way to make the invisible of thinking visible and explicit is to model a thinking operation to be developed (Pressley and Harris 1990; Rosenshine and Meister 1992). *Modeling* consists of demonstrating step-by-step how a skill is executed, with accompanying explanation noting the key steps in the procedure and why these steps are important. If we are proficient at executing the thinking skill in question and can verbalize clearly how we do it, we ourselves can model it for our students. We may also use written protocols or videos or essays that model this procedure, if any are available. Occasionally, a student who has demonstrated skill in carrying out the thinking operation can model the procedure. Then, if we provide an immediate opportunity to apply the modeled procedure while it is still visible to them, students can attempt to replicate it. With continued practice and reflection they can adopt or adapt it to develop a skilled routine of their own for executing the skill.

The key here is making students conscious of exactly how they presently carry out a thinking act or skill (imperfect as their awareness or execution may be), of how their peers do it, and of how more skilled thinkers do it. Metacognitive reflection and modeling serve these ends well. Improving the quality of student thinking requires repeated use of both of these techniques with each thinking skill we teach.

Guiding and Supporting Student Thinking

Providing continuing guidance and support to students who are trying to apply newly encountered thinking skills proves indispensable to moving them toward skillful, autonomous use of these skills (Rosenshine and Meister 1992). Two kinds of such guidance and support prove especially effective to this end: scaffolding and cueing. Once students have become conscious of a procedure or routine for executing a new thinking operation, scaffolding and cueing can be used to guide their continuing follow-up practice and application of the procedure in a variety of contexts.

Scaffolding Thinking

A scaffold is a skeletal framework of a thinking procedure—such as a checklist—that makes the steps in that thinking procedure explicit. Students use the scaffold to steer themselves through these steps as they try to carry them out. Such devices allow students to concentrate on applying the rules and steps of an unfamiliar or complex thinking procedure to a given body of information without having also to try to recall what steps to employ. Use of thinking scaffolds minimizes procedural errors in trying to apply a newly encountered thinking skill and enables students to internalize a more effective skill-using routine sooner than they otherwise might if they had to carry out the skill, from memory, exclusively on their own (McTighe and Lyman 1988).

There are three kinds of devices that prove especially effective as scaffolds for thinking. *Procedural checklists,* such as that for decision making shown in figure 1, are the most explicit. They provide a list, in order, of the mental steps by which a specific thinking procedure can be effectively carried out. *Process-structured questions* are less explicit. Like the example in figure 1, these devices walk students through the steps in a thinking procedure not by telling them the steps directly but by asking a series of questions that require students to execute in sequence each of the steps that constitutes the given thinking procedure. *Graphic organizers,* like that in figure 1, are charts or diagrams that present visually—and occasionally with

FIGURE 1
Scaffolds for Student Thinking

A Procedural Checklist
for Decision Making

- Identify a choosing opportunity.
- State the problem/goal.
- State the criteria of the "best" choice/decision.
- List the possible alternative choices.
- List the possible consequences of selecting each alternative.
- Evaluate each consequence in terms of the criteria identified above.
- Select the alternative that best meets the identified criteria.

Process-Structured Questions
for Decision Making

1. What do you want to make a decision about?
2. What do you want to accomplish by making this decision?
3. How will you know when you have made the "best" choice?
4. What are all the alternatives you have to choose from?
5. What are the possible consequences of each alternative—long range as well as short range?
6. What are the pluses and minuses of each consequence?
7. Which alternative is "best"? Why?

A Graphic Organizer
for Decision Making

Situation/opportunity:				
Problem:		Goal/criteria:		
Alternatives:	Consequences/costs/etc.:			Evaluation:
Decision:		Reasons:		

written prompts—the steps in a thinking procedure (McTighe and Lyman 1988). As students fill in the various sections of the thinking skill organizer, they move through these steps. Graphic organizers provide less explicit support and guidance than either checklists or process-structured questions but can still effectively scaffold or structure student thinking.

Not all checklists, lists of questions, or graphic organizers scaffold thinking, however. Many checklists and questions trigger thinking but do not, by the way they are arranged or worded, effectively move students through the steps in a cognitive procedure. Furthermore, as commonly used, many webs, matrices, charts, and diagrams tend to represent the products of thinking—products such as concepts, generalizations, and so on—rather than a procedure by which a thinking product is generated. To be effective in scaffolding thinking, checklists, question sets, and

graphic organizers must activate and present a cognitive procedure in a clear, step-by-step fashion.

Cueing Thinking

A *cue* is a prompt that reminds us of what to do or say next without telling us all that we are to do or say. Cueing thinking consists of prompting students to employ a specific thinking operation. Cues are usually much less explicit than scaffolds. They also depend much more for their effectiveness on the degree to which students have already internalized—stored in memory—under that cue label or signal the procedures and the rules that constitute the action or skill they seek to call forth. Cueing thinking proves helpful to improving student thinking only after students have become consciously aware (through metacognitive reflection and/or modeling) of an effective skill-using procedure and have had enough scaffolded practice in applying it to have stored that specific knowledge in memory.

Thinking cues take many forms (Rosenshine and Meister 1992). They range from the more explicit, such as previewing and rehearsing a skill about to be applied, to simply naming that operation, to even less explicit devices such as mnemonics and symbols. We can *preview* a thinking operation that students are about to employ by having volunteers provide its various names, report any special rules or heuristics that they know might guide its use (including the criteria it applies, if it is a critical thinking operation), tell why it is appropriate to use at this point, and define it. Asking for the definition last allows students to use the preceding volunteered information as cues for searching their memories for this definition or as information from which to construct an appropriate working definition.

We can help students *rehearse* a thinking skill they are about to practice by having volunteers report one or more routines or procedures by which it can be effectively employed and/or any rules, criteria, and heuristics that direct or inform its use. When students have been applying a skill for some time, however, merely *stating the technical label* of the skill—or words associated with it—customarily serves as a sufficient cue. *Mnemonics,* if devised or learned earlier by the students when they were first articulating or devising skilled procedures for executing a skill, also can serve as useful thinking cues. For example, consider the acronym **DECIDE** as a cue for the process of decision making:

Define goal
Enumerate alternatives
Consider consequences
Investigate effects
Determine best alternative
Execute

Acronyms like this one not only aid students in recalling the skill to employ but can actually cue the steps in a procedure for executing it (Beyer 1997).

Integrating Instruction in Thinking with Subject Matter

Thinking is affected and shaped as much by the subject matter to which it is applied as that subject matter is shaped by the kind of thinking that is employed to process it and the skill with which that thinking is applied. Efforts to improve student thinking, therefore, need to be carefully integrated into instruction in subject matter (Resnick and Klopfer 1989). *We can and should teach thinking and subject matter at the same time.*

To accomplish this, we must do at least two things. First, we must ensure that our students have repeated opportunities throughout our courses to apply the thinking skills in which they need to improve. This can be done, in part, by focusing on topics and themes within our subjects that are relevant to our students and to life today and in the future. It can also be accomplished by building student study around productive thinking activities and questions, as described above.

In addition, we must provide explicit instruction and then guided practice—as appropriate—in each thinking operation to be improved the first dozen or so times students are called upon to apply it. One way to plan for this instruction is to identify prior to beginning a course the specific thinking skills we believe our students will need to improve. Next, we can plan specific opportunities for the students, once they have first encountered the need to use these skills, to apply each at first frequently and then intermittently thereafter. Then we can design in advance the appropriate skill instruction for each point in this skill-using sequence using the subject matter our students are to be studying along the way.

Another way to provide such instruction is to be always alert while teaching to any thinking skills with which our students seem to be having difficulty. The first time we notice such difficulty we then can switch our instructional focus from subject matter to how to carry out the skill by introducing that skill. John Bransford (1993) calls this "just-in-time teaching." Appropriate guided practice can follow, over a sequence of subsequent lessons, as described above.

Both of these teaching approaches capitalize on what research tells us about student motivation to learn. And that is that students are more willing to attempt and to attend to learning a new skill when they are introduced to it and provided guidance in applying in at a time they have a perceived need to use it but realize they cannot do it effectively (Sigel 1984). Such skill lessons do not ignore the topic or subject being studied at the time. Indeed, they should use this subject matter as a vehicle for articulating the skill so students learn about this content while they also improve their proficiency in executing the skill.

Once a thinking skill has been introduced—made visible and explicit—we need to provide guided practice in it each time the students must apply it to develop further subject matter learning. Such practice not only helps students move toward skilled, autonomous use of the skill but also helps them develop the kinds of complex subject matter learning we usually wish them to develop. In guided practice of a skill, students first attend to how they executed the skill and then to the subject matter knowledge developed by its application. In time, little attention at all need be given to the skill. Upon our cue, students will soon be able to execute it effectively and eventually can do so on their own initiative. By combining instruction in thinking and subject matter in this way we capitalize on the symbiotic relationship between content and thinking: content serves as a vehicle for applying thinking and thinking serves as a tool for understanding content and producing knowledge.

Combining These Approaches to Improve Student Thinking

Many of us have long been aware of these four teaching approaches. However, we have too often elected to employ only one of them, the one that we or someone deems is "best" for us or our students. This is most unfortunate because, in order to improve the quality of student thinking and subject matter learning, we need to use all—rather than just one—of these approaches in our classrooms.

Each of the four approaches described here addresses a different element of what is required to improve thinking. Thoughtful classrooms provide the kind of nurturing thinking environment so essential for all the other approaches to "take." Making the invisible substance of thinking visible and explicit requires such an environment and establishes the baseline from which improvement can proved. Scaffolding and cueing student thinking provide the guidance and support students need to apply with increasing efficiency, ease, and what math instructors call "elegance" the thinking procedures that they are developing. And employing all of these approaches in the subject matter being studied gives purpose to and motivates continued student skill development.

Is This Worth Doing?

Is the effort to do this worth it? Of course it is. All our students think. But most of them can think better—more often—and with greater success than they now do. And many, if not most, of them certainly can learn more or better in our courses than they do now. Interestingly, research demonstrates that in classes where teachers attend continuously and explicitly to the cognitive skills needed to understand subject matter, students not only improve their proficiency in these thinking skills but they also attain higher achievement in subject matter (Estes 19723). Use of the teaching approaches described here will help us accomplish precisely these goals.

REFERENCES

Anderson, J. R. 1983. *The architecture of cognition.* Cambridge, Mass.: Harvard University Press.

Beyer, B. K. 1997. *Improving student thinking: A comprehensive approach.* Boston: Allyn and Bacon.

Bransford, J. 1993. Teaching thinking. Presentation at the ASCD National Conference on Thinking and Learning, San Antonio, Tex. (26 Feb.).

Estes, T. H., 1972. Reading in the social studies: A review of research since 1950. In *Reading in the content areas,* edited by J. Laffery. Newark, Del." International Reading Association.

Lipman, M. 1991. *Thinking in education.* Cambridge: Cambridge University Press.

McTighe, J., and F. T. Lyman, Jr. 1988. Cueing thinking in the classroom: The promise of theory embedded tools. *Educational Leadership* 45 (April): 18–24.

Newmann, F. M. 1990. Higher order thinking in teaching social studies. *Journal of Curriculum Studies* 22 (Jan.–Feb.): 41–56.

Nickerson, R. 1988–1989. On improving thinking through instruction. In *Review of research in education* (vol. 15), edited by E. Z. Rothkopf. Washington, D.C.: American Educational Research Association.

Nickerson, R. S., D. N. Perkins, and E. E. Smith. 1985. *The teaching of thinking.* Hillsdale, N.J.: Lawrence Erlbaum Associates.

Olson, D. R., and J. W. Astington. 1990. Talking about text: How literacy contributes to thought. *Journal of Pragmatics* 14: 705–21.

Papert, S. 1980. *Mindstorms: Children, computers and powerful ideas.* New York: Basic Books.

Perkins, D. 1992. *Smart schools.* New York: The Free Press.

Pressley, M., and K. R. Harris. 1990. What we really know about strategy instruction. *Educational Leadership* 48 (Sept.): 31–34.

Resnick, L., and L. E. Klopfer, eds. 1989. *Toward the thinking curriculum.* Alexandria, Va.: Association for Supervision and Curriculum Development.

Rosenshine, B. V., and C. Meister. 1992. The use of scaffolds for teaching higher level cognitive strategies. *Educational Leadership* 49 (April): 26–33.

Rowe, M. B. 1974. Wait time and rewards as instructional variables. *Journal of Research in Science Teaching* 11: 8–94.

Sigel, I. E. 1984. How can we teach intelligence? *Educational Leadership* 42 (Sept.): 38–50.

Sternberg, R. J. 1984. How can we teach intelligence? *Educational Leadership* 42 (Sept.): 38–50.

Vygotsky, L. S. 1962. *Thought and language.* Cambridge, Mass.: MIT Press.

Wiggins, C. 1987. Creating a thought-provoking curriculum. *American Educator* 11 (winter): 12–13.

The Intelligence-Friendly Classroom

It Just Makes Sense

By Robin Fogarty

Ms. Fogarty provides guidelines that serve as a bridge between theory and practice in the intelligence-friendly classroom.

Illustration by Mario Noche

ROBIN FOGARTY has taught at all levels, from kindergarten through college. She lives in Chicago and trains teachers around the world in cognitive strategies and cooperative interaction. Her most recent book is Brain-Compatible Classrooms (SkyLight Training and Publishing, Inc., 1998).

I F WE KNOW that intelligence is emotional, then it just makes sense to use visceral hooks. If we know that intelligence is nurturable, then it just makes sense to create rich environments. If we know that intelligence is constructed, then it just makes sense to provide tools for the mind. If we know that intelligence is experiential, then it just makes sense to challenge through doing. If we know that intelligence is multiple, then it just makes sense to target many dimensions. If we know that intelligence is modifiable, then it just makes sense to mediate learning. If we know that intelligence is elusive, then it just makes sense to vary the ways we measure it.

If we know all these things and believe what we know to be true, then the "intelligence-friendly classroom" should be a given. It is as simple and logical as an "if . . . then" syllogism.

Defining Intelligence-Friendly Classrooms

Let's look more closely at the term "intelligence-friendly classroom" and see just what it means. An intelligence-friendly classroom is a classroom in which the teaching/learning process is governed by what is known about developing the intellectual potential of human beings. Literally, intelligence-friendly means "friendly to intelligence," which can be translated into friendly to the growth patterns of human intellect and friendly to the

"The Intelligence-Friendly Classroom" by Robin Fogarty, © 1998 by SkyLight Training and Publishing Inc., was originally published in the May 1998 issue of *Phi Delta Kappan,* Volume 79, Number 9, and is reprinted here by permission of SkyLight Training and Publishing Inc., Arlington Heights, Illinois.

learner in fostering intelligent behavior for problem solving, decision making, and creative thinking. Figuratively, the intelligence-friendly classroom serves as a caring companion and mindful guide to the intellect of each and every child in it. Just as a friend in the real world furnishes certain kinds of support that are reliable, time-tested, and tried and true, so intelligence-friendly classrooms provide similar systems of support that foster the ongoing development of human intelligence potential.

In brief, intelligence-friendly classrooms are classrooms that celebrate the joy of the learner's emotional and intellectual world, not through rhetoric and repetition, but through richness and relationships. In this article, I'll take a closer look at these intelligence-friendly classrooms and investigate their theoretical underpinnings briefly and their practical implications in more depth.

Theoretical Underpinnings

Guidelines for the intelligence-friendly classroom are grounded in the works of the leading voices in the field. First, I offer a cursory examination of the various theories of intelligence and then suggest what each of them implies for the intelligence-friendly classroom.

- *Traditional theory of general intelligence.* Intelligence is inherited and unchanging.
- *Piaget's theory of developmental psychology.* Intelligence is developmentally constructed in the mind by the learner and moves from concrete to abstract stages of understanding.
- *Vygotsky's theory of social mediation.* Intelligence is a function of activity mediated through material tools, psychological tools, and other human beings.
- *Feuerstein's theory of structural cognitive modifiability.* Intelligence is a function of experience and can be changed through guided mediation.
- *Gardner's theory of multiple intelligences.* Intelligence is made up of eight realms of knowing (verbal, visual, mathematical, musical, bodily, interpersonal, intrapersonal, naturalistic) for solving problems and creating products valued in a culture.
- *Sternberg's successful intelligence.* Intelligence is triarchic, with analytic, creative, and practical components that need to be balanced.

- *Perkins' theory of learnable intelligence.* Intelligence is made up of neural, experiential, and reflective components that help us know our way around the good use of our minds.
- *Costa's theory of intelligence behaviors.* Intelligence is composed of acquired habits or states of mind that are evident in such behaviors as persistence, flexibility, decreased impulsiveness, enjoyment of thinking, and reflectiveness.
- *Goleman's theory of emotional intelligence.* Intelligence is both cognitive and emotional, with the emotional (self-awareness, self-regulation, motivation, empathy, and social skill) ruling over the cognitive.
- *Coles' theory of moral intelligence.* Intelligence is composed of cognitive, psychological or emotional, and moral realms.

Implications for Application

The intelligence-friendly classroom is an intricate and complex microcosm of nuance and activity that propels the teaching/learning process. The following eight guidelines, derived from the various theories of intelligence, have compelling implications for today's classroom. I explain each guideline briefly and offer a sampling of useful strategies. While some readers may find the suggestions familiar and already part of their current teaching repertoire, others may discover new ideas or, perhaps, novel ways to revisit an old idea with a fresh approach. Whatever the case, the guidelines serve as a bridge between theory and practice in the intelligence-friendly classroom.

1. *Set a safe emotional climate.* The intelligence-friendly classroom is a safe and caring place for all learners, regardless of race, color, creed, age, aptitude, or ability to go about the business of learning. In setting a climate for thinking, risk-taking becomes the norm, and learners understand that to learn is to make mistakes as well as to experience successes.

Specific strategies to use include the following: establishing classroom rules, being aware of verbal and nonverbal teaching behaviors (e.g., wait time), organizing diverse small-group work that feels "safe," tapping into the emotional and moral intelligences, setting up the room to facilitate student-to-student interactions as well as

student-to-teacher interactions, and incorporating learner-centered structures (e.g., multi-age groupings) that foster the creation of intelligence-friendly learning communities.

2. *Create a rich learning environment.* An enriched environment requires attention to the physical aspects of the intelligence-friendly classroom. The ideal classroom resembles a children's museum, in which students are repeatedly and implicitly invited to interact with the learning environment. In such a stimulus-rich setting, explorations, investigations, and inquiries are irresistible.

This enriched environment presents science equipment, art supplies, tools and workbenches, toys and building blocks, optical illusion posters, and an electronic circus of computers, telephones, and fax machines. The intelligence-friendly classroom has different mini-environments for quiet reflection, noisy projects, learning centers, and one-on-one tutorials. The sensory input—ranging from print-rich materials, music, and recordings to visually appealing bulletin boards and to signs, games, puzzles, and lab setups—provides an intriguing and engaging place for teaching for intelligence.

3. *Teach the mind-tools and skills of life.* Teaching the skills of life involves both mind and body "tools" that range from communication and social skills to the microskills of thinking and reflecting, to the technological skills needed for the Information Age, to the skills needed for solving algebraic equations or programming computers, and even to the skills needed to learn a craft or participate in athletics.

More specifically, these skills might include critical thinking skills (e.g., prioritizing, comparing, and judging), creative thinking skills (e.g., inferring, predicting, and generalizing), social skills (e.g., communicating, team building, leading, and resolving conflicts), technological skills (e.g., keyboarding, surfing the Net, and taking virtual field trips), visual skills (e.g., painting, sculpting, and drawing), skills in the performing arts (e.g., dancing, acting, and playing a musical instrument), and skills of the elite athlete (e.g., diving, skiing, and swimming).

4. *Develop the skillfulness of the learner.* The developmental path of skill training moves through fairly predictable stages: novice, advanced beginner, competent user, proficient user, expert. Inherent in this developmental arc is the understanding that skillfulness is achieved through mediation, practice, coaching, and rehearsal.

Skill development often occurs through formal teaching/learning structures, such as direct instruction models, that demonstrate the skill for students. Skills are also developed through independent readings and research and through the dialogue, discussion, and articulation of peer coaching, mentoring, or internships. Skill development can even happen with experiences in which the skill is embedded in application and in poised moments for achieving peak performances.

5. *Challenge through the experience of doing.* Learning is a function of experience and is shaped by internal processes that actually construct ideas in the mind, as well as by the external processes of social interaction. In the intelligence-friendly classroom, a construc- tivist philosophy of education reigns. Active, experiential learning is the norm, as the learner is invited to become an integral part of the teaching/learning process.

Specific strategies that abound in the constructivist classroom include hands-on learning with lots of manipulatives and lab-like situations; small-group, cooperative tasks; the frequent use and unique application of graphic organizers (e.g., concept maps, attribute webs, flow charts, and Venn diagrams); and authentic experiential curriculum models (e.g., problem-based learning, case studies, project and service learning, performance tasks, and the use of relevant overarching themes).

6. *Target multiple dimensions of intelligence.* The multiple intelligences (MI) approach taps into the unique profile of intelligences of each learner. The education community embraces MI theory because it provides a natural framework for inspired practice. MI approaches to curriculum, instruction, and assessment target a full spectrum of teaching/learning strategies that encompass the many ways of knowing and of expressing what we know. The MI classroom is abuzz with activity as all eight of the intelligences are given

fair time in the curriculum for authentic, relevant opportunities for development.

This does not mean that every lesson shows evidence of all eight intelligences, but rather that the learning is structured in naturally integrated ways that call upon various intelligences. For example, while creating a school newspaper, students interview (interpersonal), write (verbal), design and lay out (visual), and critique (logical) as natural parts of the process.

7. *Transfer learning through reflection.* The reflective use of learning is the cornerstone of the intelligence-friendly classroom. It drives personal application and transfer of learning. It makes learning personal, purposeful, meaningful, and relevant and gives the brain reason to pay attention, understand, and remember. Reflection is sometimes the missing piece in today's classroom puzzle, as the pacing of the school day often precludes time for reflection. Yet reflection, introspection, and mindfulness must accompany collaborations and discussions because the time for reflection is the time for internalizing the learning.

Specific strategies that enhance reflection include the use of reading-response journals in which the reader writes a personal, immediate response to what has been read; learning logs that record the learner's thoughts, comments, and questions prior to or following a learning experience; lab reports; personal diaries; sketch books; writer's notebooks; portfolios; partner dialogues and conversations with a mentor; mediation interventions; and metacognitive strategies of planning, monitoring, and evaluating through self-regulation.

8. *Balance assessment measures.* Human nature demands feedback. Whether that feedback is internally motivated or externally given, all of us who are intent on learning anxiously await the critique, the judgment. In the intelligence-friendly classroom, this critical phase of the learning process

is integral to all other interactions. The feedback, analysis, and evaluation are ongoing as well as summative.

Assessment occurs by the traditional means of grades and rankings for required classwork, homework assignments, quizzes, criterion-referenced tests, and standardized tests. In addition, to provide the proper balance to the assessment process, both portfolio assessments (e.g., project portfolios, best-work portfolios, electronic portfolios, and videotape analysis) and performance assessments (speeches, presentations, plays, concerts, athletic performances, and lab experiments) occur.

A Final Note

In closing, let's circle back for a moment and revisit the title of this article: "The Intelligence-Friendly Classroom: It Just Makes Sense." Think about how I've described the intelligence-friendly classroom and about how it matches or fails to match any preconceived notions you might have had as you began to read. Intelligence-friendly? What does that mean? What does that look like? Sound like? Did you learn in an intelligence-friendly classroom? Do you teach in one? Would you know one if you saw one?

Of course you would. The intelligence-friendly classroom is no enigma. It makes perfect sense. It draws on the many powers of intelligence of both the teacher and the learner. It is the teaching/learning process in all its glorious colors. It is the science of good, sound pedagogy coupled with the art of uniquely creative minds.

The intelligence-friendly classroom is part of the noble vision of schooling that led many of us into the field. It is the reason that we do what we do. It's about children, and it's about helping those children be as smart as they can be in every way they can be. The intelligence-friendly classroom just makes sense.

Mapping a Route Toward Differentiated Instruction

Even though students may learn in many ways, the essential skills and content they learn can remain steady. That is, students can take different roads to the same destination.

Carol Ann Tomlinson

Developing academically responsive classrooms is important for a country built on the twin values of equity and excellence. Our schools can achieve both of these competing values only to the degree that they can establish heterogeneous communities of learning (attending to issues of equity) built solidly on high-quality curriculum and instruction that strive to maximize the capacity of each learner (attending to issues of excellence).

A serious pursuit of differentiation, or personalized instruction, causes us to grapple with many of our traditional—if questionable—ways of "doing school." Is it reasonable to expect all 2nd graders to learn the same thing, in the same ways, over the same time span? Do single-textbook adoptions send inaccurate messages about the sameness of all learners? Can students learn to take more responsibility for their own learning? Do report cards drive our instruction? Should the classroom teacher be a solitary specialist on all learner needs, or could we support genuinely effective generalist-specialist teams? Can we reconcile learning standards with learner variance?

The questions resist comfortable answers—and are powerfully important. En route to answering them, we try various roads to differentiation. The concreteness of having something ready to do Monday morning is satisfying and inescapable. After all, the students will arrive and the day must be planned. So we talk about using reading buddies in varied ways to support a range of readers or perhaps developing a learning contract with several options for practicing math skills. Maybe we could try a tiered lesson or interest centers. Three students who clearly understand the chapter need an independent study project. Perhaps we should begin with a differentiated project assignment, allowing students to choose a project about the Middle Ages. That's often how our journey toward differentiation begins.

The nature of teaching requires doing. There's not much time to sit and ponder the imponderables. To a point, that's fine—and, in any case, inevitable. A reflective teacher can test many principles from everyday interac-

From *Educational Leadership,* September 1999, pp. 12-16. © 1999 by the Association for Supervision and Curriculum Development. All rights reserved. Reprinted by permission.

tions in the classroom. In other words, philosophy can derive from action.

We can't skip one step, however. The first step in making differentiation work is the hardest. In fact, the same first step is required to make all teaching and learning effective: We have to know where we want to end up before we start out and plan to get there. That is, we must have solid curriculum and instruction in place before we differentiate them. That's harder than it seems.

Looking Inside Two Classrooms

Mr. Appleton is teaching about ancient Rome. His students are reading the textbook in class today. He suggests that they take notes of important details as they read. When they finish, they answer the questions at the end of the chapter. Students who don't finish must do so at home. Tomorrow, they will answer the questions together in class. Mr. Appleton likes to lecture and works hard to prepare his lectures. He expects students to take notes. Later, he will give a quiz on both the notes and the text. He will give students a study sheet before the test, clearly spelling out what will be on the test.

Mrs. Baker is also teaching about ancient Rome. She gives her students graphic organizers to use as they read the textbook chapter and goes over the organizers with the class so that anyone who missed details can fill them in. She brings in pictures of the art and the architecture of the period and tells how important the Romans were in shaping our architecture, language, and laws. When she invites some students to dress in togas for a future class, someone suggests bringing in food so that they can have a Roman banquet—and they do. One day, students do a word-search puzzle of vocabulary words about Rome. On another day, they watch a movie clip that shows gladiators and the Colosseum and talk about the favored "entertainment" of the period. Later,

Mrs. Baker reads aloud several myths, and students talk about the myths that they remember from 6th grade. When it's time to study for the test, the teacher lets students go over the chapter together, which they like much better than working at home alone, she says.

She also wants students to like studying about Rome, so she offers a choice of 10 projects. Among the options are creating a poster listing important Roman gods and goddesses, their roles, and their symbols; developing a travel brochure for ancient Rome that a Roman of the day might have used; writing a poem about life

in Rome; dressing dolls like citizens of Rome or drawing the fashions of the time; building a model of an important ancient Roman building or a Roman villa; and making a map of the Holy Roman Empire. Students can also propose their own topic.

Thinking About the Two Classrooms

Mr. Appleton's class is not differentiated. He does not appear to notice or respond to student differences. Mrs. Baker's is differentiated—at least by some definitions. Each class has serious flaws in its foundations, however, and for that reason, Mrs. Baker's class may not be any more successful than Mr. Appletons's—and perhaps less so.

Successful teaching requires two elements: student understanding and student engagement. In other words, students must really understand, or make sense of, what they have studied. They should also feel engaged in or "hooked by" the ways that they have learned. The latter can greatly enhance the former and can help young

people realize that learning is satisfying.

Mr. Appleton's class appears to lack engagement. There's nothing much to make learning appealing. He may be satisfied by his lecture, but it's doubtful that many of the students are impressed. It is also doubtful that much real student understanding will come from the teaching-learning scenario. Rather, the goal seems to be memorizing data for a test.

Memorizing and understanding are very different. The first has a short life span and little potential to transfer into a broader world. However, at least Mr. Appleton appears clear

> We have to know where we want to end up before we start out—and plan to get there.

about what the students should memorize for the test. Mrs. Baker's class lacks even that clarity.

Students in Mrs. Baker's classroom are likely engaged. It is a lively, learner–friendly place with opportunity for student movement, student choice, and peer work. Further, Mrs. Baker's list of project options draws on different student interests or talents—and she is even open to their suggestions.

Although Mrs. Baker succeeds to some degree with engagement, a clear sense of what students should understand as a result of their study is almost totally missing. Thus her careful work to provide choice and to build a comfortable environment for her learners may not net meaningful, long-term learning. Her students are studying "something about ancient Rome." Nothing focuses or ties together the ideas and information that they encounter. Activities are more about being happy than about making meaning. No set of common information, ideas, or skills will stem from completing the various projects. In essence, she has accomplished little for the long haul. Her "differentiation" provides varied avenues to "mush"—multiple versions of fog. Her students work with different tasks, not differentiated ones.

Mr. Appleton's class provides little engagement, little understanding, and scant opportunity for attending to student differences. Mrs. Baker's class provides some engagement, little understanding, and no meaningful differentiation.

An Alternative Approach

To make differentiation work—in fact, to make teaching and learning work—teachers must develop an alternative approach to instructional planning beyond "covering the text" or "creating activities that students will like."

Ms. Cassell has planned her year around a few key concepts that will help students relate to, organize, and retain what they study in history. She has also developed principles or generalizations that govern or uncover how the concepts work. Further, for each unit, she has established a defined set of facts and terms that are essential for students to know to be literate and informed about the topic. She has listed skills for which she and the students are responsible as the year progresses. Finally, she has developed essential questions to intrigue her students and to cause them to engage with her in a quest for understanding.

Ms. Cassell's master list of facts, terms, concepts, principles, and skills stems from her understanding of the discipline of history as well as from the district's learning standards. As the year evolves, Ms. Cassell continually assesses the readiness, interests, and learning profiles of her students and involves them in goal setting and decision making about their learning. As she comes to understand her students and their needs more fully, she modifies her instructional framework and her instruction.

Ms. Cassell is also teaching about ancient Rome. Among the key concepts in this unit, as in many others throughout the year, are culture, change, and interdependence. Students will be responsible for important

terms, such as *republic, patrician, plebeian, veto, villa,* and *Romance language;* names of key individuals, for example, Julius Caesar, Cicero, and Virgil; and names of important places, for instance, the Pantheon and the Colosseum.

For this unit, students explore key generalizations or principles: Varied cultures share common elements. Cultures are shaped by beliefs and values, customs, geography, and resources. People are shaped by and shape their cultures. Societies and cultures change for both internal and external reasons. Elements of a society and its cultures are interdependent.

Among important skills that students apply are using resources on history effectively, interpreting information from resources, blending data from several resources, and organizing effective paragraphs. The essential question that Ms. Cassell often poses to her students is, How would your life and culture be different if you lived in a different time and place?

Looking Inside the Third Classroom

Early in the unit, Ms. Cassell's students begin work, both at home and in class, on two sequential tasks that will extend throughout the unit as part of their larger study of ancient Rome. Both tasks are differentiated.

For the first task, students assume the role of someone from ancient Rome, such as a soldier, a teacher, a healer, a farmer, a slave, or a farmer's wife. Students base their choice solely on their own interests. They work both alone and with others who select the same topic and use a wide variety of print, video, computer, and human resources to understand what their life in ancient Rome would have been like. Ultimately, students create a first-person data sheet that their classmates

can use as a resource for their second task. The data sheet calls for the person in the role to provide accurate, interesting, and detailed information about what his or her daily schedule

> Successful differentiation is squarely rooted in student engagement plus student understanding.

would be like, what he or she would eat and wear, where he or she would live, how he or she would be treated by the law, what sorts of problems or challenges he or she would face, the current events of the time, and so on.

Ms. Cassell works with both the whole class and small groups on evaluating the availability and appropriate use of data sources, writing effective paragraphs, and blending information from several sources into a coherent whole. Students use these skills as they develop the first-person data sheets. The teacher's goal is for each student to increase his or her skill level in each area.

The second task calls on students to compare and contrast their own lives with the lives of children of similar age in ancient Rome. Unlike the first task, which was based on student interest, this one is differentiated primarily on the basis of student readiness. The teacher assigns each student a scenario establishing his or her family context for the task: "You are the eldest son of a lawmaker living during the later years of the period known as Pax Romana," for example. Ms. Cassell bases the complexity of the scenario on the student's skill with researching and thinking about history. Most students work with families unlike those in their first task. Students who need continuity between the tasks, however, can continue in a role familiar from their first investigation.

All students use the previously developed first-person data sheets as well as a range of other resources to gather background information. They must address a common set of specified questions: How is what you eat shaped by the economics of your family and by your location? What is your level of education and how is that affected by your status in society? How is your life interdependent with the lives of others in ancient Rome? How will Rome change during your lifetime? How will those changes affect your life? All students must also meet certain research and writing criteria.

Despite the common elements, the task is differentiated in several ways. It is differentiated by interest because each student adds questions that are directed by personal interests: What games did children play? What was the practice of science like then? What was the purpose and style of art?

Readiness differentiation occurs because each student adds personal research and writing goals, often with the teacher's help, to his or her criteria for success. A wide range of research resources is available, including books with varied readability levels, video and audio tapes, models, and access to informed people. The teacher also addresses readiness through small-group sessions in which she provides different sorts of teacher and peer support, different kinds of modeling, and different kinds of coaching for success, depending on the readiness levels of students.

Finally, the teacher adds to each student's investigation one specific question whose degree of difficulty is based on her most recent assessments of student knowledge, facility with research, and thinking about history. An example of a more complex question is, How will your life differ from that of the previous generation in your family, and how will your grandchildren's lives compare with yours? A less complex, but still challenging question is, How will language change from the generation before you to two generations after you, and why will those changes take place?

Learning-profile differentiation is reflected in the different media that students use to express their findings: journal entries, an oral monologue, or a videotape presentation. Guidelines

for each type of product ensure quality and focus on essential understandings and skills established for the unit. Students may work alone or with a "parallel partner" who is working with the same role, although each

student must ultimately produce his or her own product.

At other points in the study of ancient Rome, Ms. Cassell differentiates instruction. Sometimes she varies the sorts of graphic organizers that students use when they read, do research, or take notes in class. She may use review groups of mixed readiness and then conduct review games with students of like readiness working together. She works hard to ask a range of questions that move from concrete and familiar to abstract and unfamiliar in all class discussions. She sometimes provides homework options in which students select the tasks that they believe will help them understand important ideas or use important skills best. Of course, the class also plans, works, reviews, and debates as a whole group.

Students find Ms. Cassell's class engaging—and not just because it's fun. It's engaging because it shows the connection between their own lives and life long ago. It helps them see the interconnectedness among times in history and make links with other subjects. It tickles their curiosity. And it provides a challenge that pushes each learner a bit further than is comfortable—and then supports success. Sometimes those things are fun. Often they are knotty and hard. Always they dignify the learner and the subject.

Ms. Cassell's class is highly likely to be effective for her varied learners, in part because she continually attempts to reach her students where they are and move them on—she dif-

ferentiates instruction. The success of the differentiation, however, is not a stand-alone matter. It is successful because it is squarely rooted in student engagement plus student understanding.

> Differentiation is not so much the "stuff" as the "how." If the "stuff" is ill conceived, the "how" is doomed.

This teacher knows where she wants her students to arrive at the end of their shared learning journey and where her students are along that journey at a given time. Because she is clear about the destination and the path of the travelers, she can effectively guide them, and she varies or differentiates her instruction to accomplish this goal. Further, her destination is not merely the amassing of data but rather the constructing of understanding. Her class provides a good example of the close and necessary relationship between effective curriculum and instruction and effective differentiation.

The First Step Is the Compass

Mr. Appleton may have a sense of what he wants his students to know at the end of the road, but not about what his students should understand and be able to do. He teaches facts, but no key concepts, guiding principles, or essential questions. With a fact-based curriculum, differentiating instruction is difficult. Perhaps some students could learn more facts and some, fewer. Perhaps some students could have more time to drill the facts, and some, less. It's difficult to envision a defensible way to differentiate a fact-driven curriculum, probably because the curriculum itself is difficult to defend.

Mrs. Baker also appears to lack a clear vision of the meaning of her subject, of the nature of her discipline and what it adds to human understanding, and of why it should matter to a young learner to study old times. There is little clarity about facts—let alone concepts, guiding principles, or essential questions. Further, she confuses folly with engagement. She thinks that she is differentiating instruction, but without instructional clarity, her activities and projects are merely different—not differentiated. Because there is no instructional clarity, there is no basis for defensible differentiation.

Ms. Cassell plans for what students should know, understand, and be able to do at the end of a sequence of learning. She dignifies each learner by planning tasks that are interesting, relevant, and powerful. She invites each student to wonder. She determines where each student is in knowledge, skill, and

understanding and where he or she needs to move. She differentiates instruction to facilitate that goal. For her, differentiation is one piece of the mosaic of professional expertise. It is not a strategy to be plugged in occasionally or often, but is a way of thinking about the classroom. In her class, there is a platform for differentiation.

Ms. Cassell helps us see that differentiated instruction must dignify each learner with learning that is "whole," important, and meaning making. The core of *what* the students learn remains relatively steady. *How* the student learns—including degree of difficulty, working arrangements, modes of expression, and sorts of scaffolding—may vary considerably. Differentiation is not so much the "stuff" as the "how." If the "stuff" is ill conceived, the "how" is doomed.

The old saw is correct: Every journey *does* begin with a single step. The journey to successfully differentiated or personalized classrooms will succeed only if we carefully take the first step—ensuring a foundation of best-practice curriculum and instruction.

Carol Ann Tomlinson is Associate Professor of Educational Leadership, Foundations and Policy at the Curry School of Education, University of Virginia, Charlottesville, VA 22903 (e-mail: cat3y@virginia.edu). She is the author of *The Differentiated Classroom: Responding to the Needs of All Learners* (ASCD, 1999).

Educating the Net Generation

As technology becomes an integral part of our classrooms and schools, educators can look to the students—the Net Generation—to help make the shift to more student-centered learning.

Don Tapscott

Every time I enter a discussion about efforts to get computers into schools, someone insists that computers aren't the answer. "It won't help to just throw computers at the wall, hoping something will stick. I've seen lots of computers sitting unused in classrooms."

> **Digital kids are learning precisely the social skills required for effective interaction in the digital economy.**

Agreed. Computers alone won't do the trick. They are a necessary but insufficient condition for moving our schools to new heights of effectiveness. We've still got to learn how best to use this technology. And I have become convinced that the most potent force for change is the students themselves.

Why look to the kids? Because they are different from any generation before them. They are the first to grow up surrounded by digital media. Computers are everywhere—in the home, school, factory, and office—as are digital technologies—cameras, video games, and CD-ROMs. Today's kids are so bathed in bits that they think technology is part of the natural landscape. To them, digital technology is no more intimidating than a VCR or a toaster. And these new media are increasingly connected by the Internet, that expanding web of networks that is attracting one million new users a month.

The Net Generation

The Net affects us all—the way we create wealth, the nature of commerce and marketing, the delivery system for entertainment, the role and dynamics of learning, and the nature of government. It should not surprise us that those first to grow up with this new medium are defined by their relationship to it. I call them the Net Generation—the N-Geners.

According to Teenage Research Unlimited (1997), teens feel that being online is as "in" as dating and partying! And this exploding popularity is occurring while the Net is still in its infancy and, as such, is painfully slow; primitive; limited in capabilities; lacking complete security, reliability, and ubiquity; and subject to both hyperbole and ridicule. Nevertheless, children love it and keep coming back after each frustrating experience. They know its potential.

What do students do on the Net? They manage their personal finances; organize protest movements; check facts; discuss zits; check the scores of their favorite team and chat online with its superstars; organize groups to save the rain forest; cast votes; learn more about the illness of their little sister; go to a virtual birthday party; or get video clips from a soon-to-be-released movie.

From *Educational Leadership,* February 1999, pp. 6-10. © 1999 by the Association for Supervision and Curriculum Development. All rights reserved. Reprinted by permission.

Chat groups and computer conferences are populated by young people hungry for expression and self-discovery. Younger kids love to meet people and talk about anything. As they mature, their communications center on topics and themes. For all ages, "E-mail me" has become the parting expression of a generation.

Digital Anxiety

For many adults, all this digital activity is a source of high anxiety. Are kids really benefitting from the digital media? Can technology truly improve the process of learning, or is it dumbing down and misguiding educational efforts? What about Net addiction? Is it useful for children to spend time in online chat rooms, and what are they doing there? Are some becoming glued to the screen? What about cyberdating and cybersex? Aren't video games leading to a violent generation? Is technology stressing kids out—as it seems to be doing to adults? Has the Net become a virtual world—drawing children away from parental authority and responsible adult influence—where untold new problems and dangers lie? What is the real risk of online predators, and can children be effectively protected? How can we shield kids from sleaze and porn? As these children come of age, will they lack the social skills for effective participation in the work force?

These questions are just a sampling of the widespread concern raised not just by cynics, moralists, and technophobes, but also by reasonable and well-meaning educators, parents, and members of the community.

Everybody, relax. The kids are all right. They are learning, developing, and thriving in the digital world. They need better tools, better access, better services—*more* freedom to explore, not less. Rather than convey hostility and mistrust, we need to change *our* way of thinking and behaving. This means all of us—parents, educators, lawmakers, and business leaders alike.

Digital kids are learning precisely the social skills required for effective interaction in the digital economy. They are learning about peer relationships, teamwork, critical thinking, fun, friendships across geographies, self-expression, and self-confidence.

Conventional wisdom says that because children are multitasking—jumping from one computer-based activity to another—their attention span is reduced. Research does not support this view. Ironically, the same people who charge that today's kids are becoming "glued to the screen" also say that kids' attention spans are declining.

The ultimate interactive learning environment is the Internet itself.

At root is the fear that children will not be able to focus and therefore will not learn. This concern is consistent with the view that the primary challenge of learning is to absorb specific information. However, many argue—and I agree—that the content of a particular lesson is less important than learning how to learn. As John Dewey wrote,

> Perhaps the greatest of all pedagogical fallacies is the notion that a person learns only the particular thing he is studying at the time. Collateral learning . . . may be and often is more important than the spelling lesson or lesson in geography or history that is learned. (1963, p. 48)

The Challenge of Schooling

The new technologies have helped create a culture for learning (Papert, 1996) in which the learner enjoys enhanced interactivity and connections with others. Rather than listen to a professor regurgitate facts and theories, students discuss ideas and learn from one another, with the teacher

acting as a participant in the learning. Students construct narratives that make sense out of their own experiences.

Initial research strongly supports the benefits of this kind of learning. For example, in 1996, 33 students in a social studies course at California State University in Northridge were randomly divided into two groups, one taught in a traditional classroom and the other taught virtually on the Web. The teaching model wasn't fundamentally changed—both groups received the same texts, lectures, and exams. Despite this, the Web-based class scored, on average, 20 percent higher than the traditional class. The Web class had more contact with one another and were more interested in the class work. The students also felt that they understood the material better and had greater flexibility to determine how they learned (Schutte, n.d.).

The ultimate interactive learning environment is the Internet itself. Increasingly, this technology includes the vast repository of human knowledge, the tools to manage this knowledge, access to people, and a growing galaxy of services ranging from sandbox environments for preschoolers to virtual laboratories for medical students studying neural psychiatry. Today's baby will tomorrow learn about Michelangelo by walking through the Sistine Chapel, watching Michelangelo paint, and perhaps stopping for a conversation. Students will stroll on the moon. Petroleum engineers will penetrate the earth with the drill bit. Doctors will navigate the cardiovascular system. Researchers will browse through a library. Auto designers will sit in the back seat of the car they are designing to see how it feels and to examine the external view.

Eight Shifts of Interactive Learning

The digital media is causing educators and students alike to shift to new ways of thinking about teaching and learning.

1. From linear to hypermedia learning. Traditional approaches to learning are linear and date back to using books as a learning tool. Stories, novels, and other narratives are generally linear. Most textbooks are written to be tackled from the beginning to the end. TV shows and instructional videos are also designed to be watched from beginning to end.

Students need better tools, better access, better services—more freedom to explore, not less.

But N-Gen access to information is more interactive and nonsequential. Notice how a child channel surfs when watching television. I've found that my kids go back and forth among various TV shows and video games when they're in the family room. No doubt that as TV becomes a Net appliance, children will increasingly depend on this nonlinear way of processing information.

2. From instruction to construction and discovery. Seymour Papert says,

> The scandal of education is that every time you teach something, you deprive a child of the pleasure and benefit of discovery. (de Pommereau, 1996, p. 68)

With new technologies, we will experience a shift away from traditional types of pedagogy to the creation of learning partnerships and learning cultures. This is not to say that teachers should not plan activities or design curriculums. They might, however, design the curriculum in partnership with learners or even help learners design the curriculum themselves.

This constructivist approach to teaching and learning means that rather than assimilate knowledge that is broadcast by an instructor, the learner constructs knowledge anew. Constructivists argue that people learn best by *doing* rather than simply

by *listening.* The evidence supporting constructivism is persuasive, but that shouldn't be too surprising. When youngsters are enthusiastic about a fact or a concept that they themselves discovered, they will better retain the information and use it in creative, meaningful ways.

3. From teacher-centered to learner-centered education. The new media focus the learning experience on the individual rather than on the transmitter. Clearly, learner-centered education improves the child's motivation to learn.

The shift from teacher-centered to learner-centered education does not suggest that the teacher is suddenly playing a less important role. A teacher is equally crucial and valuable in the learner-centered context, for he or she creates and structures what happens in the classroom.

Learner-centered education begins with an evaluation of abilities, learning styles, social contexts, and other important factors that affect the student. Evaluation software programs can tailor the learning experience for each individual child. Learner-centered education is also more active, with students discussing, debating, researching, and collaborating on projects with one another and with the teacher.

4. From absorbing material to learning how to navigate and how to learn. This means learning how to synthesize, not just analyze. N-Geners can assess and analyze facts—a formidable challenge in a data galaxy of easily accessible information sources. But more important, they can synthesize. They are engaged in information sources and people on the Net, and then they construct higher-level structures and mental images.

5. From school to lifelong learning. For young baby boomers looking forward to the world of work, life often felt divided—between the period when you *learned* and the period when you *did.* You went to school and maybe to university and learned a trade or profession. For the rest of your life, your challenge was simply to keep up with developments in your field. But things have changed. Today, many

I have become convinced that the most potent force for change is the students themselves.

boomers reinvent their knowledge base constantly. Learning has become a continuous, lifelong process. The N-Gen is entering a world of lifelong learning from day one, and unlike the schools of the boomers, today's educational system can anticipate how to prepare students for lifelong learning.

6. From one-size-fits-all to customized learning. The digital media enables students to be treated as individuals—to have highly customized learning experiences based on their backgrounds, individual talents, age levels, cognitive styles, and interpersonal preferences.

As Papert puts it,

> What I see as the real contribution of digital media to education is a flexibility that could allow every individual to find personal paths to learning. This will make it possible for the dream of every progressive educator to come true: In the learning environment of the future, every learner will be "special." (1996, p. 16)

In fact, Papert believes in a "community of learning" shared by students and teachers:

> Socialization is not best done by segregating children into classrooms with kids of the same age. The computer is a medium in which what you make lends itself to be modified and shared. When kids get together on a project, there is abundant discussion; they show it to other kids, other kids want to see it, kids learn to share knowledge with other people—much more than in the classroom. (1997, p. 11)

7. From learning as torture to learning as fun. Maybe torture is an exaggeration, but for many kids, class is not exactly the highlight of their day. Some educators have decried the fact that a generation schooled on *Sesame Street* expects to be entertained at school—and to enjoy the learning experience. They argue that learning and entertainment should be clearly separated.

Why shouldn't learning be entertaining? In *Merriam-Webster's Collegiate Dictionary,* the third definition of the verb *to entertain* is "to keep, hold, or maintain in the mind" and "to receive and take into consideration." In other words, entertainment has always been a profound part of the learning process, and teachers throughout history have been asked to convince their students to entertain ideas. From this perspective, the best teachers were the entertainers. Using the new media, the learner also becomes the entertainer and, in doing so, enjoys, is motivated toward, and feels responsible for learning.

8. From the teacher as transmitter to the teacher as facilitator. Learning is becoming a social activity, facilitated by a new generation of educators.

The topic is saltwater fish. The 6th grade teacher divides the class into teams, asking each team to prepare a presentation on a fish of its choice. Students have access to the Web and are allowed to use any resources. They must cover the topics of history, breathing, propulsion, reproduction, diet, predators, and "cool facts." They must also address questions to others in their team or to others in the class, not to the teacher.

Two weeks later, Melissa's group is first. The students have created a shark project home page with hot links for each topic. As the students talk, they project their presentation onto a screen at the front of the class. They have video clips of different types of sharks and also a clip from Jacques Cousteau discussing the shark as an endangered species. They then use the Web to go live to Aquarius, an underwater site located off the Florida Keys. The class can ask questions of the Aquarius staff, although most inquiries are directed to the project team. One such discussion focuses on which is greater: the dangers posed by sharks to humans or the dangers posed by humans to sharks.

The class decides to hold an online forum on this topic and invites kids from classes in other countries to participate. The team asks students to browse through its project at any time, from any location, because the forum will be up for the rest of the school year. In fact, the team decides to maintain the site by adding new links and fresh information throughout the year. The assignment becomes a living project. Learners from around the world find the shark home page helpful and build links to it.

In this example, the teacher acts as consultant to the teams, facilitates the learning process, and participates as a technical consultant on the new media. The teacher doesn't have to compete with Jacques Cousteau's expertise on underwater life; her teaching is supported by his expertise.

Turning to the Net Generation

Needless to say, a whole generation of teachers needs to learn new tools, new approaches, and new skills. This will be a challenge, not just because of resistance to change by some teachers, but also because of the current atmosphere of financial cutbacks, low teacher morale, increased workloads, and reduced retraining budgets.

But as we make this inevitable transition, we may best turn to the generation raised on and immersed in new technologies. Give students the tools, and they will be the single most important source of guidance on how to make their schools relevant and effective places to learn.

References

de Pommereau, I. (1997, April 21). Computers give children the key to learning. *Christian Science Monitor,* p. 68.

Dewey, J. (1963). *Experience and education.* London: Collier Books.

Papert, S. (1996). *The connected family: Bridging the digital generation gap.* Marietta, GA: Longstreet Press.

Schutte, J. G. (n.d.). *Virtual teaching in higher education* [On-line]. Available: http://www.csun.edu/sociology/virtexp.htm.

Teenage Research Unlimited, Inc. (1996, January). Press release. Northbrook, IL: Author.

Teenage Research Unlimited, Inc. (1997, Spring). Teenage marketing and lifestyle update. Northbrook, IL: Author.

Copyright © 1999 Don Tapscott.

Don Tapscott is President of New Paradigm Learning Corporation and Chairman of Alliance for Converging Technologies, 133 King St. E., Ste. 300, Toronto, ON M5C 1G6, Canada (Website:http://nplc.com; e-mail: nplc@nplc.com).

Unit 5

Unit Selections

Key Points to Consider

❖ Discuss several ways to motivate both at-risk and typical students. What difference is there?

❖ Why should motivational style be consistent with instructional techniques?

❖ How are motivation and classroom management related?

❖ Discuss several ways to discipline both typical students and those with exceptionalities.

❖ How are classroom management and discipline different? Discuss whether discipline can be developed within students, or whether it must be imposed by teachers, supporting your argument with data derived from your reading.

DUSHKIN ONLINE Links   www.dushkin.com/online/

These sites are annotated on pages 4 and 5.

The term *motivation* is used by educators to describe the processes of initiating, directing, and sustaining goal-oriented behavior. Motivation is a complex phenomenon, involving many factors that affect an individual's choice of action and perseverance in completing tasks. Furthermore, the reasons why people engage in particular behaviors can only be inferred; motivation cannot be directly measured.

Several theories of motivation, each highlighting different reasons for sustained goal-oriented behavior, have been proposed. We will discuss three of them: behavioral, humanistic, and cognitive. The behavioral theory of motivation suggests that an important reason for engaging in behavior is that reinforcement follows the action. If the reinforcement is controlled by someone else and is arbitrarily related to the behavior (such as money, a token, or a smile), then the motivation is extrinsic. In contrast, behavior may also be initiated and sustained for intrinsic reasons such as curiosity or mastery.

Humanistic approaches to motivation are concerned with the social and psychological needs of individuals. Humans are motivated to engage in behavior to meet these needs. Abraham Maslow, a founder of humanistic psychology, proposes that there is a hierarchy of needs that directs behavior, beginning with physiological and safety needs and progressing to self-actualization. Some other important needs that influence motivation are affiliation and belonging with others, love, self-esteem, influence with others, recognition, status, competence, achievement, and autonomy.

The dominant view of motivation in the educational psychology literature is the cognitive approach. This set of theories proposes that our beliefs about our successes and failures affect our expectations and goals concerning future performance. Students who believe that their success is due to their abilities and efforts are motivated toward mastery of skills. Students who blame their failures on inadequate abilities have low self-efficacy and tend to set ability and performance goals that protect their self-image.

William Glasser, in the unit's first selection, argues that when teachers use coercive management techniques, students feel that teachers do not care about them and they become unmotivated. When choice theory is implemented, however, the student-teacher relationship is nurtured, and students want to learn. The next two selections address achievement motivation. Penny Hauser-Cram introduces the concept of mastery motivation. She describes how parents and caregivers can negatively affect mastery motivation by being too directive, and offers suggestions for encouraging mastery motivation. The goal is for all children to learn to persist in the face of difficulty and to seek challenge. Then, Martin Covington explores students' intrinsic appreciation for the subject matter under study.

No matter how effectively students are motivated, teachers always need to exercise management of behavior in the classroom. Classroom management

is more than controlling the behavior of students or disciplining them following misbehavior. Instead, teachers need to initiate and maintain a classroom environment that supports successful teaching and learning. The skills that effective teachers use include preplanning, deliberate introduction of rules and procedures, immediate assertiveness, continual monitoring, consistent feedback to students, and specific consequences.

The first two articles in this subsection describe the most current thinking about classroom management techniques that best meet the needs of learner-centered classrooms. Mary McCaslin and Thomas Good believe that teachers who value teaching for understanding need to help students internalize a commitment to certain standards of behavior, rather than settle for compliance. They suggest that this can be accomplished by teaching students to coordinate their multiple academic and social goals. Next, Nancy Martin argues that student-teacher relationships need to be nurtured in student-centered classrooms. Teacher-centered classroom management techniques conflict with the philosophy of student-centered instruction and can undermine its effectiveness.

The next three articles address specific disciplinary issues facing teachers today: disciplining students in inclusive classrooms, confrontational students, and violence in the schools. The first, "Teaching Students to Regulate Their Own Behavior," gives advice to teachers with inclusive classrooms about how to help students with special needs learn to regulate their own behavior, and at the same time, take some of the time demands away from the teacher. Next, Geoff Colvin, David Ainge, and Ron Nelson observe that even effective classroom managers are sometimes faced with confrontational students. The authors discuss defusing tactics that can minimize the likelihood of escalating conflict. Finally, Ian Elliot describes a model program for reducing violence in schools. He describes the PeaceBuilders program and the techniques adopted by schools and teachers to help students care about each other and solve problems appropriately.

A New Look at School Failure and School Success

BY WILLIAM GLASSER, M.D.

*The cause of both school failure and marriage failure is that almost all people believe in and practice stimulus/response psychology, Dr. Glasser contends. He suggests a better alternative—CHOICE THEORY*SM*—to nurture the warm, supportive human relationships that students need to succeed in school and that couples need to succeed in marriage.*

JOHN IS 14 years old. He is capable of doing good work in school. Yet he reads and writes poorly, has not learned to do more than simple calculations, hates any work having to do with school, and shows up more to be with his friends than anything else. He failed the seventh grade last year and is well on his way to failing it again. Essentially, John chooses to do nothing in school that anyone would call educational. If any standards must be met, his chances of graduation are nonexistent.

We know from our experience at the Schwab Middle School, which I will describe shortly, that John also knows that giving up on school is a serious mistake. The problem is he doesn't believe that the school he attends will give him a chance to correct this mistake. And he is far from alone. There may be five million students between the ages of 6 and 16 who come regularly to school but are much the same as John. If they won't make the effort to become competent readers, writers, and problem solvers, their chances of leading even minimally satisfying lives are over before they reach age 17.

Janet is 43 years old. She has been teaching math for 20 years and is one of the teachers who is struggling unsuccessfully with John. She considers herself a good teacher but admits that she does not know how to reach John. She blames him, his home, his past teachers, and herself for this failure.

---

*William Glasser, M.D., is the founder and president of the William Glasser Institute in Chatsworth, Calif. In 1996 he changed the name of the theory he has been teaching since 1979 from "control theory" to CHOICE THEORY*SM*. He is currently writing a new book on the subject. All his books are published by HarperCollins.*

All who know her consider her a warm, competent person. But for all her warmth, five years ago, after 15 years of marriage, Janet divorced. She is doing an excellent job of caring for her three children, but, with only sporadic help from their father, her life is no picnic. If she and her husband had been able to stay together happily, it is almost certain that they and their children would be much better off than they are now.

To persuade a teacher like Janet to give up what she implicitly believes to be correct is a monumental task.

Like many who divorce, Janet was aware that the marriage was in trouble long before the separation. But in the context of marriage as she knew it, she didn't know what to do. "I tried, but nothing I did seemed to help," she says. She is lonely and would like another marriage but, so far, hasn't been able to find anyone she would consider marrying. There may be more than a million men and women teaching school who, like Janet, seem capable of relationships but are either divorced or unhappily married. No one doubts that marriage failure is

 From *Phi Delta Kappan*, April 1997, pp. 596–602. © 1997 by Phi Delta Kappa, Inc. Reprinted by permission.

a huge problem. It leads to even more human misery than school failure.

I bring up divorce in an article on reducing school failure because there is a much closer connection between these two problems than almost anyone realizes. So close, in fact, that I believe the cause of both these problems may be the same. As soon as I wrote those words, I began to fear that my readers would jump to the conclusion that I am blaming Janet for the failure of her marriage or for her inability to reach John. Nothing could be further from the truth. The fact that she doesn't know something that is almost universally unknown cannot be her fault.

If you doubt that the problems of John and Janet are similar, listen to what each of them has to say. John says, "I do so little in school because no one cares for me, no one listens to me, it's no fun, they try to make me do things I don't want to do, and they never try to find out what I want to do." Janet says, "My marriage failed because he didn't care enough for me, he never listened to me, each year it was less fun, he never wanted to do what I wanted, and he was always trying to make me do what he wanted." These almost identical complaints have led John to "divorce" school, and Janet, her husband.

Are these Greek tragedies? Are all these students and all these marriages doomed to failure no matter what we do? I contend they are not. *The cause of both school failure and marriage failure is that almost no one, including Janet, knows how he or she functions psychologically.* Almost all people believe in and practice an ancient, commonsense psychology called stimulus/response (SR) psychology. I am one of the leaders of a small group of people who believe that SR is completely wrongheaded and, when put into practice, is totally destructive to the warm, supportive human relationships that students need to succeed in school and that couples need to succeed in marriage. The solution is to give up SR theory and replace it with a new psychology: *choice theory.*

To persuade a teacher like Janet to give up what she implicitly believes to be correct is a monumental task. For this reason I have hit upon the idea of approaching her through her marriage failure as much as through her failure to reach students like John. I think she will be more open to learning something that is so difficult to learn if she can use it in both her personal and her professional lives. From 20 years of experience teaching choice theory, I can also assure her that learning this theory can do absolutely no harm.

If John could go to a school where choice theory was practiced, he would start to work. That was conclusively proved at the Schwab Middle School. To explain such a change in behavior, John would say, "The teachers care about me, listen to what I have to say, don't try to make me do things I don't want to do, and ask me what I'd like to do once in a while. Besides, they make learning fun." If Janet and her husband had practiced choice theory while they still cared for each other, it is likely that they would still be married. They would have said, "We get along well because every day we make it a point to show each other we care. We listen to each other, and when we have differences we talk them out without blam-

ing the other. We never let a week go by without having fun together, and we never try to make the other do what he or she doesn't want to do."

Where school improvement is concerned, I can cite hard data to back up this contention. I also have written two books that explain in detail all that my staff and I try to do to implement choice theory in schools. The books are *The Quality School* and *The Quality School Teacher.*[1] Where marriage failure is concerned, I have no hard data yet. But I have many positive responses from readers of my most recent book, *Staying Together,*[2] in which I apply choice theory to marriage.

The most difficult problems are human relationship problems. Technical problems, such as landing a man on the moon, are child's play compared to persuading all students like John to start working hard in school or helping all unhappily married couples to improve their marriages. Difficult as they may be to solve, however, relationship problems are surprisingly easy to understand. They are all some variation of "I don't like the way you treat me, and even though it may destroy my life, your life, or both our lives, this is what I am going to do about it."

READERS familiar with my work will have figured out by now that choice theory used to be called control theory because it teaches that the only person whose behavior we can control is our own. I find choice theory to be a better and more positive-sounding name. Accepting that you can control only your own behavior is the most difficult lesson that choice theory has to teach. It is so difficult that almost all people, even when they are given the opportunity, refuse to learn it. This is because the whole thrust of SR theory is that we do not control our own behavior, rather, our behavior is a response to a stimulus from outside ourselves. Thus we answer a phone in response to a ring.

Choice theory states that we never answer a phone because it rings, and we never will. We answer a phone—and do anything else—because it is the most satisfying choice for us at the time. If we have something better to do, we let it ring. Choice theory states that the ring of the phone is not a stimulus to do anything; it is merely *information.* In fact, all we can ever get from the outside world, which means all we can give one another, is information. But information, by itself, does not make us do anything. Janet can't make her husband do anything. Nor can she make John do anything. All she can give them is information, but she, like all SR believers, doesn't know this.

What she "knows" is that, if she is dissatisfied with someone, she should try to "stimulate" that person to change. And she wastes a great deal of time and energy trying to do this. When she discovers, as she almost always does, how hard it is to change another person, she begins to blame the person, herself, or someone else for the failure. And from blaming, it is a very short step to punishing. No one takes this short step more frequently and more thoroughly than husbands, wives, and teachers. As they attempt to change their mates, couples develop a whole repertoire of coercive behaviors aimed at punishing the other for being so obstinate. When teachers attempt to deal with students such as John, punishment—masquerading as "logical consequences"—rules the day in school.

Coercion in either of its two forms, reward or punishment, is the core of SR theory. Punishments are by far the more common, but both are destructive to relationships. The difference is that rewards are more subtly destructive and generally less offensive. Coercion ranges from the passive behaviors of sulking and withdrawing to the active behaviors of abuse and violence. The most common and, because it is so common, the most destructive of coercive behaviors is criticizing—and nagging and complaining are not far behind.

Choice theory teaches that we are all driven by four psychological needs that are embedded in our genes: the need to belong, the need for power, the need for freedom, and the need for fun. We can no more ignore these psychological needs than we can ignore the food and shelter we must have if we are to satisfy the most obvious genetic need, the need for survival.

Whenever we are able to satisfy one or more of these needs,

> # When Janet punishes John, she gives him more reasons to keep her and math out of his quality world.

it feels very good. In fact, the biological purpose of pleasure is to tell us that a need is being satisfied. Pain, on the other hand, tells us that what we are doing is not satisfying a need that we very much want to satisfy. John suffers in school, and Janet suffers in marriage because neither is able to figure out how to satisfy these needs. If the pain of this failure continues, it is almost certain that in two years John will leave school, and of course Janet has already left her marriage.

If we are to help Janet help John, she needs to learn and to use the most important of all the concepts from choice theory, the idea of the *quality world*. This small, very specific, personal world is the core of our lives because in it are the people, things, and beliefs that we have discovered are most satisfying to our needs. Beginning at birth, as we find out what best satisfies our needs, we build this knowledge into the part of our memory that is our quality world and continue to build and adjust it throughout our lives. This world is best thought of as a group of pictures, stored in our brain, depicting with extreme precision the way we would like things to be—especially the way we want to be treated. The most important pictures are of people, including ourselves, because it is almost

impossible to satisfy our needs without getting involved with other people.

Good examples of people who are almost always in our quality worlds are our parents and our children—and, if our marriages are happy, our husbands or wives. These pictures are very specific. Wives and husbands want to hear certain words, to be touched in certain ways, to go to certain places, and to do specific activities together. We also have special things in our quality world. For example, the new computer I am typing this article on is very much the computer I wanted. I also have a strong picture of myself teaching choice theory, something I believe in so strongly that I spend most of my life doing it.

When we put people into our quality worlds, it is because we care for them, and they care for us. We see them as people with whom we can satisfy our needs. John has long since taken pictures of Janet and of most other teachers—as well as a picture of himself doing competent schoolwork—out of his quality world. As soon as he did this, neither Janet nor any other SR teacher could reach him. As much as they coerce, they cannot make him learn. This way of teaching is called "bossing." Bosses use coercion freely to try to make the people they boss do what they want.

To be effective with John, Janet must give up bossing and turn to "leading." Leaders never coerce. We follow them because we believe that they have our best interests at heart. In school, if he senses that Janet is now caring, listening, encouraging, and laughing, John will begin to consider putting her into his quality world. Of course, John knows nothing about choice theory or about the notion of a quality world. But he can be taught and, in a Quality School, this is what we do. We have evidence to show that the more students know about why they are behaving as they do, the more effectively they will behave.

Sometime before her divorce, Janet, her ex, or both of them took the other out of their quality worlds. When this happened, the marriage was over. If they had known choice theory and known how important it is to try to preserve the picture of a spouse in one's quality world, they could have made a greater effort than they did to care, listen, encourage, and laugh with each other. They certainly would have been aware of how destructive bossing is and would have tried their best to avoid this destructive behavior.

As I stated at the outset, I am not assigning blame for the failure of Janet's marriage. I am saying that, as soon as one or the other or both partners became dissatisfied, the only hope was to care, listen, encourage, and laugh and to completely stop criticizing, nagging, and complaining. Obviously, Janet and her ex-husband would have been much more likely to have done this if they had known that the only behavior you can control is your own.

When Janet, as an SR teacher, teaches successfully, she succeeds with students because her students have put her or the math she teaches (or both) into their quality worlds. If both she and the math are in their quality worlds, the students will be a joy to teach. She may also succeed with a student who does not particularly want to learn math, but who, like many students, is open to learning math if she gives him a little attention.

John, however, is hard core. He is more than uninterested; he is disdainful, even disruptive at times. To get him interested will require a real show of interest on her part. But Janet resents any suggestion that she should give John what he needs. Why should she? He's 14 years old. It's his job to show interest. She has a whole classroom full of students, and she hasn't got the time to give him special attention. Because of this resentment, all she can think of is punishment.

When Janet punishes John, she gives him more reasons to keep her and math out of his quality world. Now he can blame her; from his standpoint, his failure is no longer his fault. Thus the low grades and threats of failure have exactly the opposite effect from the one she intends. That is why she has been so puzzled by students like John for so many years. She did the "right thing," and, even though she can see John getting more and more turned off, she doesn't know what else to do. She no more knows why she can't reach John than she knows why she and her husband found it harder and harder to reach each other when their marriage started to fail.

FROM THE beginning to the end of the 1994–95 school year, my wife Carleen and I worked to introduce Quality School concepts into the Schwab Middle School, a seventh- and eighth-grade school that is part of the Cincinnati Public School System. (Carleen actually began training many staff members in choice theory during the second semester of the 1993–94 school year.) This school of 600 regularly attending students (750 enrolled) has at least 300 students like John, who come to school almost every day. With the help of the principal, who was named best principal in Ohio in 1996, and a very good staff, we turned this school around.

By the end of the year, most of the regularly attending students who were capable of doing passable schoolwork were doing it.[3] Indeed, some of the work was much better than passable. None of the students like John were doing it when we arrived. Discipline problems that had led to 1,500 suspensions in the previous year slowly came under control and ceased to be a significant concern by the end of the school year.

By mid-February, after four months of preparation, we were able to start a special program in which we enrolled all the students (170) who had failed at least one grade and who also regularly attended school. Most had failed more than one grade, and some, now close to 17 years of age, had failed four times. Teachers from the regular school staff volunteered for this program. Our special program continued through summer school, by the end of which 147 of these 170 students were promoted to high school. The predicted number of students who would go to high school from this group had been near zero. Getting these students out of the "on-age" classes where they had been disruptive freed the regular teachers to teach more effectively, and almost all the "on-age" students began to learn. The "on-age" seventh-graders at Schwab had a 20%

increase in their math test scores, another positive outcome of the program.

We were able to achieve these results because we taught almost all the teachers in the school enough choice theory to understand how students need to be treated if they are to put us into their quality worlds. Using these concepts, the teachers stopped almost all coercion—an approach that was radically different from the way most of these students had been treated since kindergarten. When we asked the students why they were no longer disruptive and why they were beginning to work in school, over and over they said, "You care about us." And sometimes they added, "And now you give us choices and work that we like to do."

What did we do that they liked so much? With the district's permission, we threw out the regular curriculum and allowed the students to work at their own pace. We assigned lessons that, when successfully completed, proved that the students were ready for high school. The seven teachers in the special program (called the Cambridge Program)—spurred on by the challenge that this was their school and that they could do anything they believed necessary—worked day and night for almost two months to devise these lessons, in which the students had to demonstrate that they could read, write, solve problems, and learn the basics of social studies and science.

We told the students that they could not fail but that it was up to them to do the work. We said that we would help them learn as much as we could, and teachers from the "on-age" classes volunteered their free periods to help. Some of the students began to help one another. The fear began to dissipate as the staff saw the students begin to work. What we did was not so difficult that any school staff, with the leadership of its principal, could not do it as well. Because we had so little time, Carleen and I were co-leaders with the principal. A little extra money (about $20,000) from a state grant was also spent to equip the room for the Cambridge Program with furniture, carpeting, and computers, but it was not more than any school could raise if it could promise the results we achieved.

THESE Quality School ideas have also been put to work for several years in Huntington Woods Elementary School in Wyoming, Michigan. This nearly 300-student K–5 school is located in a small middle-class town and is the first school to be designated a Quality School. There were very few Johns in this school to begin with, so the task was much easier than at Schwab. Nonetheless, the outcomes at Huntington Woods have been impressive.

- All students are doing competent schoolwork, as measured by the Michigan Education Assessment Program (MEAP). The percentages of Huntington Woods students who score satisfactorily as measured against a state standard are 88% in reading and 85% in math (Compared to state averages of 49% in reading and 60% in math).
- As measured by both themselves and their teachers, all students are doing some quality work, and many are doing a great deal of quality work.

- While there are occasional discipline incidents, there are no longer any discipline problems.
- The regular staff works very successfully with all students without labeling them learning disabled or emotionally impaired.
- Even more important than these measurable outcomes, the school is a source of joy for students, teachers, and parents.

I emphasize that no extra money was spent by the district to achieve these results. The school, however, did some fund raising to pay for staff training.

I CITE Schwab and Huntington Woods because I have worked in one of these schools myself and have had a great deal of contact with the other. They are both using the ideas in my books. Huntington Woods has changed from an SR-driven system, and Schwab has made a strong start toward doing so. Moreover, Schwab's start has produced the results described above. And more than 200 other schools are now working with me in an effort to become Quality Schools.

So far only Huntington Woods has evaluated itself and declared itself a Quality School. Even Schwab, as improved as it is, is far from being a Quality School. But, in terms of actual progress made from where we found it, what Schwab has achieved is proportionally greater than what Huntington Woods has achieved.

While many schools have shown interest in what has been achieved at Huntington Woods and at Schwab, very few of them have accepted the core idea: change the system from SR theory to choice theory. Indeed, there are many successful SR schools around the country that are not trying to change the fundamental system in which they operate, and I believe their success is based on two things.

First, for a school to be successful, the principal is the key. When an SR school succeeds, as many do, it is led by a principal whose charisma has inspired the staff and students to work harder than they would ordinarily work. This kind of success will last only as long as the principal remains. I am not saying that some charismatic principals do not embrace many of the ideas of the Quality School, or that the principal doesn't have to lead the systemic change that choice theory makes possible. However, once the system has been changed, it can sustain itself (with the principal's support, of course, but without a charismatic leader).

Second, the SR schools that are working well have strong parental support for good education and few Johns among their students. Where such support is already present or can be created by hard- working teachers and principals, schools have a very good chance of being successful without changing their core system. After all, it is these schools that have traditionally made the SR system seem to work. In such schools, Janet would be a very successful teacher.

While Huntington Woods had the kind of support that would have made it a good school without changing the system, the staff wanted it to become a Quality School and set about changing the system from the outset. With the backing of the superintendent, the staff members were given an empty building and the opportunity to recruit new staff members, all of whom were anxious to learn the choice theory needed to change the system. The fact that Huntington Woods has a charismatic leader is certainly a plus, but it is her dedication to the ideas of choice theory that has led to the schools' great success. With very high test scores, no discipline problems, and no need for special programs, Huntington Woods has gone far beyond what I believe the typical SR school could achieve. Many educators who have visited the school have said that it is "a very different kind of school."[4]

Schwab today is also very different from the school it was. And what has been accomplished at Schwab has been done with almost no active parental support. The largest number of parents we could get to attend any meeting—even when we served food and told them to bring the whole family—was 20, and some of them were parents of the few students who live in the middle-class neighborhood where the school is located. Almost all the Schwab students who are like John are bused in from low-income communities far from the school, a fact that makes parents' participation more difficult.

At Schwab an effort was made to teach all the teachers choice theory. Then Carleen and I reminded them continually to use the theory as they worked to improve the school. At Huntington Woods, not only were the teachers and principal taught choice theory in much more depth than at Schwab and over much more time that we had at Schwab, but all the students and many parents were also involved in learning this theory and beginning to use it in their lives.

Unfortunately, Janet has never taught in a school that uses choice theory. When she brings up her problems with John in the teachers' lounge, she is the beneficiary of a lot of SR advice: "Get tough!" "Show him right away who's boss." "Don't let him get away with anything." "Call his mother, and demand she do something about his behavior." "Send him to the principal." Similarly, like almost everyone whose marriage is in trouble, Janet has been the beneficiary of a lot of well-intended SR advice from family and friends—some of which, unfortunately, she took.

Her other serious problem is that she works in an SR system that is perfectly willing to settle for educating only those students who want to learn. The system's credo says, "It's a tough world out there. If they don't make an effort, they have to suffer the consequences." Since Janet is herself a successful product of such a system, she supports it. In doing so, she believes it is right to give students low grades for failing to do what she asks them to do. She further believes it is right to refuse to let them make up a low grade if they don't have a very good attitude—and sometimes even if they do.

In her personal life, she and her husband had seen so much marriage failure that, when they started to have trouble, it was easy for them to think of divorce as almost inevitable. This is bad information. It discourages both partners from doing the hard work necessary to learn what is needed to put their marriage back together. Life is hard enough without the continuing harangues of the doomsayers. In a world that uses choice theory, people would be more optimistic.

There has been no punishment in the Huntington Woods School for years. There is no such thing as a low grade that cannot be improved. Every student has access to a teacher or another student if he or she needs personal attention. Some students will always do better than others, but, as the MEAP scores show, all can do well. This is a Quality system, with an emphasis on continual improvement, and there is no settling for good enough.

Unfortunately for them, many Schwab students who experience success in school for the first time will fail in high school. The SR system in use there will kill them off educationally, just as certainly as if we shot them with a gun. They didn't have enough time with us and were too fragile when we sent them on. However, if by some miracle the high school pays attention to what we did at Schwab, many will succeed. There was some central office support for our efforts, and there is some indication that this support will continue.

The Huntington Woods students are less fragile. They will have had a good enough start with choice theory so that, given the much stronger psychological and financial support of their parents, they will probably do well in middle school. Indeed, data from the first semester of 1995–96 confirm that they are doing very well.

It is my hope that educators, none of whom are immune to marriage failure, will see the value of choice theory in their personal lives. If this happens, there is no doubt in my mind that they will begin to use it with their students.

---

1. William Glasser, *The Quality School* (New York: HarperCollins, 1990); and idem, *The Quality School Teacher* (New York: HarperCollins, 1994).
2. William Glasser, *Staying Together* (New York: HarperCollins, 1995).
3. The school also had about four classes of special education students who were in a special program led by capable teachers and were learning as much as they were capable of learning.
4. See Dave Winans, "This School Has Everything," *NEA Today,* December 1995, pp. 4–5.

I Think I Can, I Think I Can: Understanding and Encouraging Mastery Motivation in Young Children

Penny Hauser-Cram

"She works very hard when she's trying to build a block construction." "He is so curious about how gadgets work." These are comments often made by parents and teachers in their conversations about young children. Children's motivation to solve and complete tasks they set out to do is a central part of the way teachers and parents view children. Is such motivation intrinsic? Are children with developmental disabilities as motivated as other children? How is motivation influenced by caregivers? Does motivation vary in different contexts, such as the classroom and the home? What do we know about motivation, and how can preschool teachers encourage it?

Perspectives on motivation

Based largely on Piaget's (1952) writings, developmental theorists (White 1959; Hunt 1965) have proposed

Penny Hauser-Cram, Ed.D., is an associate professor of developmental and educational psychology at the School of Education at Boston College. Penny's research focuses on the development of children with disabilities.

This is one of a regular series of Research in Review columns. The column in this issue was invited by Research in Review Editor Martha B. Bronson, Ph.D., professor at Boston College, Chestnut Hill, Massachusetts.

that children's motivation to explore the world around them is the foundation upon which learning occurs. Such motivation is considered to be intrinsic, universal, and an integral part of development. All children are born with curiosity and a desire to learn about the world.

White (1959) contended that children have a need to produce an effect on their environment and that they achieve this through exploration and play. He proposed that children have "an urge toward competence," and he defined this urge as effectance or competence motivation. Harter (1975) further defined effective motivation as a "desire to solve cognitively challenging problems for gratification inherent in discovering the solution" (p. 370). She highlighted several key components: curiosity, preference for challenge, internal criteria of success, and working for one's own satisfaction.

In studying motivation in school-age children, Dweck (1986) described some children as "mastery-oriented" (i.e., challenge seeking and persistent in attempting to solve difficult problems) and others as "helpless" (i.e., challenge avoidant and low in persistence). She maintained that some children exhibit "learned helplessness" because they believe, based on past experiences, that they have little control over the events that affect them. Children who exhibit patterns of learned helplessness attribute their successes to external factors, such as luck, and their failures to internal factors, such as ability (Dweck & Elliott 1983). Researchers suggest that teachers

From *Young Children*, July 1998, pp. 67–71. © 1998 by the National Association for the Education of Young Children. Reprinted by permission.

can promote mastery-oriented, rather than helpless, behavior by providing tasks in which the goal is learning (i.e., developing different strategies) rather than performance (i.e., focusing on correct or incorrect responses) (Stipek 1996).

Studies on toddlers and preschool-age children have focused on mastery motivation, which is assumed to be a precursor to later development of motivation to achieve academically. *Mastery motivation* is defined as a "psychological force that stimulates an individual to attempt independently, in a focused and persistent manner, to solve a problem or master a skill or task which is at least moderately challenging for him or her" (Morgan, Harmon, & Maslin-Cole 1990, 319). Key components of this definition include (1) attempts to master a task independent of adult direction; (2) persistence in mastering a task even when difficulties arise; and (3) selection of a task that is neither extremely easy nor extremely difficult. Researchers have stressed the importance of individually determined moderate challenge as children persist less with tasks that they find too easy or too difficult (Redding, Morgan & Harmon 1988). Thus, by identifying the kinds of tasks individual children engage in and persist with, teachers can provide opportunities that will offer optimal challenges.

Regardless of their theoretical background, intelligent, sensitive adults who closely observe children discover the same things—because that's the way children are—there are a number of "universals."

How does mastery motivation change during early childhood?

Most developmental psychologists contend that children begin life as motivated beings. Children strive to understand the world and to affect it. Developmentally, children progress through several shifts in motivation, so the motivated child behaves differently at different phases of life. The motivated infant, younger than six months of age, explores objects through reaching, mouthing, and visual exploration. Around nine months infants begin to understand simple notions of cause-and-effect, and the motivated infant of this age begins to engage in goal-directed activity with unfamiliar tasks (Jennings 1993). Another transition occurs around 18 months of age

when children begin to be able to compare their behavior with that of a standard (Jennings 1993). The motivated toddler attempts to approximate the standard. During the preschool years motivated children begin to self-select challenging tasks and prefer tasks that "make them think" to those that are easy for them to accomplish (Stipek 1996).

How does motivation relate to cognition?

Motivation and cognition are conceptually different, but researchers have found that the two constructs are intertwined during infancy (Yarrow et al. 1982; Yarrow et al. 1983). Infant mastery motivation measures have been found to be better predictors of preschool measures of cognition than are standardized infant developmental quotients (Messer et al. 1986). Measures of mastery motivation may be good indicators of the way in which children approach learning about objects. Infants and toddlers who appear more motivated may take full advantage of a range of spontaneous learning opportunities and ultimately demonstrate more advanced cognitive performance.

During the preschool period, correlations between measures of motivation and those of intelligence are only modestly related (Morgan, MacTurk, & Hrncir 1995). While the motivated preschooler is one who persists at difficult tasks, and thus creates and engages in cognition enriching activities, cognitively advanced preschoolers are not necessarily highly motivated. The low correlation between intelligence and motivation indicates that aspects of children's lives other than cognition, such as the actions of important adults, may explain differences in mastery motivation.

How do caregivers affect mastery motivation?

Motivation is often assumed to be intrinsic, but it also appears to be affected by the transactions between children and their parents and other caregivers. The role played by caregivers, however, varies with the age of the child (Busch-Rossnagal, Knauf-Jensen, & DesRosiers 1995). For example, Yarrow and his colleagues (Yarrow et al. 1984) reported that parents who provided more sensory stimulation for their young infants had infants who were more persistent in their exploration of objects. After children begin engaging in cause-and-effect actions with objects, during the latter part of the first year of life, caregivers' role in providing stimulation becomes more complex. Parents who interfere in children's attempts to engage in autonomous activity diminish children's motivated behavior (Frodi, Bridges, & Grolnick 1985; Wachs 1987; Hauser-Cram 1993). Researchers (e.g., Morgan et al. 1991) contend that parents who are highly directive may encourage children to be efficient respond-

© Elisabeth Nichols

Eriksonians emphasize the industriousness of children in this age range. They have a strong, innate urge to become competent. During the preschool years, motivated children begin to self-select challenging tasks and prefer tasks that "make them think" to those that are easy for them to accomplish. Motivation is intrinsic, but it also is affected by transactions between children and the important adults in their lives.

too, often highly direct children with disabilities (Hauser-Cram, Bronson, & Upshur 1993; Bronson, Hauser-Cram, & Warfield 1997). In both settings children with disabilities may have little opportunity for executing autonomy and independence in attempts to master tasks.

Can parents and teachers accurately assess mastery motivation?

Although the preponderance of studies on mastery motivation have been based on behavioral assessments, an increasing number are incorporating parents' or teachers' ratings of children's motivated behavior. Ratings are quicker and easier to gather, and they have been found to correlate significantly with behavioral assessments (Morgan et al. 1993). Furthermore, ratings can take advantage of parents' and teachers' knowledge of children in multiple settings and with a wide range of tasks.

The Dimensions of Mastery Questionnaire (DMQ) has been found to be a reliable and valid source of ratings of children's persistence on object-oriented tasks, social-symbolic activities, and gross-motor play (Morgan et al. 1993). In studies in which parents and teachers have been asked to use the DMQ to rate the same child's mastery motivation, parents usually provide more positive ratings.

This trend was reported in a recent study of three-year-old children with developmental disabilities (Hauser-Cram et al. 1997). Results of this study also in-

ers but not effective initiators. In contrast, parents who provide a range of challenges and support children's autonomy have children who display high levels of mastery motivation.

What do we know about motivation in children with developmental or physical disabilities?

Although less research has been conducted on motivation in children with disabilities, a picture of motivated behavior has begun to emerge. Researchers studying children with physical disabilities and mental retardation (MacTurk et al. 1985; Hauser-Cram 1996) have reported that levels of persistence on challenging tasks are similar for children with and without disabilities during the infant and toddler years. Discrepancies in mastery motivation of children with and without disabilities begin to emerge during the preschool and early school-age years (Harter & Zigler 1974; Jennings, Connors, & Stegman 1988).

Although the cause of the decline in motivated behavior of children with disabilities has not been determined, home and classroom factors may provide a clue. Studies of parent-child interaction in the home indicate that many parents of children with developmental disabilities and delays are highly directive in their play (Mahoney, Fors, & Wood 1990). Preschool classroom observation studies indicate that teachers,

© Elisabeth Nichols

dicated that parents' ratings of mastery motivation were more predictive of children's later performance than were teachers' ratings. Therefore, parents' perceptions of children's motivated behavior offer unique and valuable information to teachers.

What can teachers do to encourage mastery motivation?

Research on mastery motivation does not have a long history, but much of the research has been undertaken with a view toward application and intervention. Several important suggestions emerge from the studies conducted so far.

1. Provide a moderate choice of activities. Choosing activities promotes autonomy and offers children some control over their own learning. Research indicates that a modest number of choices, rather than no choice or a large number of choices, is optimal in enhancing intrinsic motivation (Stipek 1996).

2. Provide children with activities that offer opportunities to learn rather than opportunities only to be correct or incorrect. For example, provide problem-posing tasks, games, or other activities in which there are several possible ways to solve the problems posed.

3. Support children's activities in ways that do not interfere with autonomy. Sometimes this requires adults to wait rather than anticipate a child's needs when she encounters difficulty with a task. If the child is getting very frustrated, a well-timed suggestion (e.g., "Maybe if you turn that piece around . . .") rather than a direct command (e.g., "That piece fits here") may support her attempts to persist.

4. Ask parents about their perspectives on their child's motivation. Parents know what children enjoy doing and what challenges provide them with pride in accomplishment.

What future research is needed on children's mastery motivation?

Current work on mastery motivation is somewhat limited by a focus on the individual child's independent activities, yet preschool classrooms are social organizations where children play and learn together. Future work on mastery motivation will benefit by considering the influence of the social context in which children learn. To what extent do peers challenge each other as they persist together on a joint enterprise? To what extent do the social dynamics of a classroom offer a range of challenges appropriate for each child? To what extent do children develop a sense of shared agency in making a difference in their preschool classroom? Many questions will undoubtedly emerge as we extend the construct of mastery motivation to include the collective intricacies of the social settings in which children engage in learn-

ing. Adults, siblings, and peers are all potential partners in children's motivation, and future research can help us understand these partnerships and the ways in which all can contribute to optimizing mastery-oriented behavior in young children.

References

Bronson, M. B., P. Hauser-Cram, & M. E. Warfield. 1997. Classrooms matter: Relations between the classroom environment and the social and mastery behavior of five-year-old children with disabilities. *Applied Developmental Psychology* 18: 331–48.

Busch-Rossnagel, N. A., D. E. Knauf-Jensen, & F. S. DesRosiers. 1995. Mothers and others: The role of the socializing environment in the development of mastery motivation. In *Mastery motivation: Origins, conceptualizations, and applications*, eds. R. H. MacTurk & G. A. Morgan, 117–45. Norwood, NJ: Ablex.

Dweck, C., & E. S. Elliot. 1993. Achievement motivation. In *Handbook of child psychology, Vol. 4: Socialization, personality, and social development*. 4th ed., series ed. P. H. Mussen, vol. ed. E. M. Hetherington, 643–91. New York: Wiley.

Dweck, C. S. 1986. Motivational processes affecting learning. *American Psychologist* 41: 1040–48.

Frodi, A., L. Bridges, & W. Grolnick. 1985. Correlates of mastery-related behavior: A short-term longitudinal study of infants in their second year. *Child Development* 56: 1291–98.

Harter, S. 1975. Developmental differences in the manifestations of mastery motivation on problem-solving tasks. *Child Development* 46: 370–78.

Harter, S., & E. Zigler. 1974. The assessment of effectance motivation in normal and retarded children. *Developmental Psychology* 45:661–69.

Hauser-Cram, P. 1993. Mastery motivation in three-year-old children with Down syndrome. In *Mastery motivation in early childhood: Development, measurement, and social processes*, ed. D. J. Messer, 230–50. London: Routledge.

Hauser-Cram, P. 1996. Mastery motivation in toddler with developmental disabilities. *Child Development* 67: 236–48.

Hauser-Cram, P., M. B. Bronson, & C. C. Upshur. 1993. The effects of the classroom environment on classroom behaviors of young children with disabilities. *Early Childhood Research Quarterly* 8: 479–97.

Hauser-Cram, P., M. W. Krauss, M. E. Warfield, & A. Steele. 1997. Congruence and predictive power of mothers' and teachers' ratings of mastery motivation in children with mental retardation. *Mental Retardation* 35: 355–63.

Hunt, J. McV. 1965. Intrinsic motivation and its role in psychological development. In *Nebraska symposium on motivation*, ed. D. Levine, 189–282. Lincoln: University of Nebraska Press.

Jennings, K. D. 1993. Mastery motivation and the formation of self-concept from infancy through early childhood. In *Mastery motivation in early childhood: Development, measurement, and social processes*, ed. D. J. Messer, 36–54. London: Routledge.

Jennings, K. D., R. E. Connors, & C. E. Stegman. 1988. Does a physical handicap alter the development of mastery motivation during the preschool years? *Journal of the American Academy of Child and Adolescent Psychiatry* 27: 312–17.

MacTurk, R., P. M. Vietze, M. E. McCarthy, S. McQuiston, & L. J. Yarrow. 1985. The organization of exploratory behavior in Down syndrome and nondelayed infants. *Child Development* 56: 573–81.

Mahoney, G., S. Fors, & S. Wood. 1990. Maternal directive behavior revisited. *American Journal on Mental Retardation* 94: 398–406.

Messer, D. J., M. E. McCarthy, S. McQuiston, R. H. MacTurk, L. J. Yarrow, & P. M. Vietze. 1986. Relations between mastery motivation in infancy and competence in early childhood. *Developmental Psychology* 22: 336–72.

Morgan, G. A., R. J. Harmon, & C. A. Maslin-Cole. 1990. Mastery motivation: Definition and measurement. *Early Education and Development* 1: 318–39.

Morgan, G. A., R. H. MacTurk, & E. J. Hrncir. 1995. Mastery motivation: Overview, definitions, and conceptual issues. In *Mastery motivation:*

Origins, conceptualizations, and applications, eds. R. H. MacTurk & G. A. Morgan. Norwood, NJ: Ablex.

Morgan, G. A., C. A. Maslin-Cole, Z. Biringer, & R. J. Harmon. 1991. Play assessment of mastery motivation in infants and young children. In *Play diagnosis and assessment,* eds. C. E. Schaefer, K. Gitlin, & A. Sandgrund, 65–86. New York: Wiley.

Morgan, G. A., C. Maslin-Cole, R. J. Harmon, N. A. Busch-Rossnagel, K. Jennings, P. Hauser-Cram, & L. Brockman. 1993. Parent and teacher perceptions of young children's mastery motivation: Assessment and review of research. In *Mastery motivation in early childhood: Development, measurement, and social processes,* ed. D. Messer, 109–31. London: Routledge.

Piaget, J. 1952. *The origins of intelligence in children.* New York: International Universities Press.

Redding, R. E., G. A. Morgan, & R. J. Harmon. 1988. Mastery motivation in infants and toddlers: Is it greatest when tasks are moderately challenging? *Infant Behavior and Development* 11: 419–30.

Stipek, D. J. 1996. Motivation and instruction. In *Handbook of educational psychology,* eds. D. Berliner & R. Calfee, 85–113. New York: Macmillan.

Wachs, T. D. 1987. Specificity of environmental action as manifest in environmental correlates of infant's mastery motivation. *Developmental Psychology* 23: 782–90.

White, R. W. 1959. Motivation reconsidered: The concept of competence. *Psychological Review* 66: 297–333.

Yarrow, L., R. H. MacTurk, P. M. Vietze, M. E. McCarthy, R. P. Klein, & S. McQuiston. 1984. Developmental course of parental stimulation and its relationship to mastery motivation during infancy. *Developmental Psychology* 20: 492–503.

Yarrow, L., S. McQuiston, R. MacTurk, M. McCarthy, R. Klein, & P. Vietze. 1983. Assessment of mastery motivation during the first year of life: Contemporaneous and cross-age relationships. *Developmental Psychology* 19: 159–71.

Yarrow, L., G. Morgan, K. Jennings, & R. Harmon. 1982. Infants' persistence at tasks: Relationships to cognitive functioning and early experience. *Infant Behavior and Development* 5: 131–41.

Editor's note: As Penny Hauser-Cram tells us, developmental psychologists have focused mainly on mastery motivation in individual children and are now beginning to consider the influence of the social context in which children learn.

The latter is one of the areas of expertise of excellent early childhood educators. They have learned much through their work, which is with groups, about the group dynamics, interpersonal relations, cooperative behaviors, and peer example that power or impede children as they strive to create a project, conquer a difficulty, or solve a problem they've encountered.

We will all benefit when specialists in these two related areas—developmental psychology and early childhood education—pool their knowledge and move on to learn more.

Caring About Learning: The Nature and Nurturing of Subject-Matter Appreciation

Martin V. Covington
University of California at Berkeley

Many observers despair of the prospects of encouraging intrinsic values among students in a world controlled by extrinsic rewards. The purpose of this article is to explore the question of whether intrinsic objectives such as subject-matter appreciation can coexist to any degree, let alone flourish, in the face of competing, if not higher, loyalties that involve a performance ethic based on scrambling for extrinsically oriented rewards, such as high grades, and avoiding punishments in the form of failing grades. Based on research conducted in ongoing classroom contexts at the college level, it is concluded that the pursuit of high grades and valuing what one is learning are not necessarily incompatible goals as long as certain conditions prevail. More specifically, students are more likely to value what they are learning and to enjoy the achievement process more: (a) when they are attaining their grade goals, (b) when what they are studying is of personal interest, and (c) when the dominant reasons for learning are task oriented, not self-aggrandizing or failure avoidant.

Teacher: What did you get out of the class?
Student: I got an A.

Perhaps nothing frustrates teachers more than when students forsake learning for the pursuit of grades and in the process fail to appreciate the power of learning for the sake of self-expression, personal growth, and meaningful discovery. Certainly, many students are grade driven, not to say, "grade grubbing," and this preoccupation begins surprisingly early in life. Such a reaction seems inevitable in a society like ours in which a primary determinant of one's status and worth is the ability to perform successfully. And grades are widely regarded as an index of ability. As a result, nothing contributes more to the young student's sense of worth than does a good report card, nor destroys it so completely as do poor grades (Glasser, 1976; Oakes, 1985).

This dependency of one's worth on good grades intensifies as students grow older, so that by the college years, one's grade point average is often of paramount, sometimes of overweening, importance. For example, virtually without exception, we have found that college students rate achieving the highest grade possible as the main reason for undertaking school assignments, with such reasons as overcoming a personal challenge or developing an appreciation for what one is learning rated as less important (Covington & Wiedenhaupt, 1997).

These same students as well as many educational observers are quite clear about whom they consider responsible for this scramble for grades. For instance, George Leonard (1968) pointed to society's use of grades as the primary means by which individuals are distributed proportionally across the available jobs, some of which are more attractive than others. In truth, competitive grading has long been a central mechanism for assigning talent according to job demands and availability, a reality that has also troubled David Campbell (1974), who points out that the whole frantic scrambling to win over others is essential for the kind of institutions that our schools have become—"bargain-basement personnel screening agencies for business and government" (pp. 145–146). Campbell's remark, perhaps more than any other, lays bare the fundamental incompatibility of the mission confronting all of education: Schools are not only places of learning but also places for sorting out students and giving further encouragement to those capable of learning the most and the quickest. Given this selective-sorting function of schools, it is little wonder that many students become preoccupied with grades, especially because grades not only largely determine future occupational placement but also are judged indicative of the individual's personal worth. Rightly or wrongly, students often see teachers as the main gatekeepers in this process of selective sorting and, ironically, accuse teachers of not recognizing and rarely encouraging the same intrinsic aspects of learning that teachers, in their turn, lament that students have come to disregard—that is, feeling that one has learned something of personal value apart from any grade, of seeking to learn more on one's own, or of feeling poised, ready to learn more. These dispositions remind us of other higher order objectives in whose service the acquisition and valuing of knowledge is widely justified. Basically, these objectives involve the processes of change that we hope to initite in our students—encouraging changes that move individuals from novice to expert and the shedding of an emotional dependency on authority so that students will eventually become independent learners (Carnegie Foundation for the Advancement of Teaching, 1989). These changes embody perhaps the most elevated purpose of all schooling: to encourage a love of learning now and for a lifetime, not only because of the presumed personal benefits of learning for the sake of perspective or for enhanced well-being (e.g., Dewey, 1938/1963), but also because task-engaged students are better, more receptive learners. For example, task-engaged students are more likely to employ deep-level, meta-cognitive strategies in their studies (e.g., Ames & Archer, 1987). Likewise, when students become personally involved in an assignment, they exhibit greater comprehension of the subject matter, attend to the task for longer periods, and remember more of what they learned (e.g., Alexander, Kulikowich, & Schulze, 1994; Hidi & Anderson, 1992).

Given the significance accorded these intrinsic objectives by educators, it is sobering to note that they are more often honored in the breach than in the observance. Many observers have despaired of the prospects of ever encouraging intrinsic values such as subject-matter appreciation in a world controlled by extrinsic rewards (e.g., Kohn, 1993). If high marks in school become increasingly important as students grow older, not only for the tangible future benefits they are expected to bestow—being the gateway to prestigious occupations—but also as an indication of one's personal worth, then what becomes of the value of learning? Is caring about learning marginalized?

The purpose of this article is to explore the question of whether intrinsic objectives such as subject-matter appreciation can coexist to any degree, let alone flourish, in the face of competing, if not higher, loyalties that involve a performance ethic based on external constraints and incentives such as school grades.

In addressing this question, I rely heavily on research conducted under the auspices of the Teaching/Learning Project at the University of California at Berkeley (Covington, 1992, 1998). The overall purpose of this large-scale investigation was to explore the nature of intrinsic motivation and its relation to the various extrinsic rewards that dominate classroom life. The database consists of five separate yearly cohorts of some 500 Berkeley undergraduates each year, all of whom were enrolled in different offerings of the introductory psychology course. Overall, this database represents a series of interlocking studies conducted under actual classroom conditions, with each inquiry designed to address some specific aspect of the relation between intrinsic and extrinsic motivation, the facilitation of subject-matter appreciation, and the role of personal interest in learning. As a group, these studies represent a variety of methodological approaches, including the use of hypothetical, role-playing scenarios; true experimental designs; diaries; free-response essays; life-history interview data; and correlational time sample studies.

By far, the most important feature of this research is that it was fully integrated into the ongoing life of the classroom. For instance, in one study we tracked changes in student reasons for continuing work on class assignments as they progressed from week to week as well as sampling the kinds of self-inducements they used to sustain their work (e.g., "I considered denying myself little treats like taking a break, if I did not stay on schedule"). Thus, data collection became a continual and sustaining part of the curriculum. In the process, students became valued informants and involved observers—not merely passive or disinterested research subjects—involved because these investigations were situated in an authentic, high-stakes, grade-driven context of great personal significance for students. Although laboratory research has contributed immeasurably to our understanding of the issues to be discussed here, I believe we cannot truly understand how students come to appreciate and deeply hold the values of exploration and discovery unless the processes involved are also studied in the context of real-life schooling where success and failure carry enormous public promise and penalties, respectively.

A final note regarding this research: The population we have chosen to study is clearly unrepresentative of the vast majority of students who pass through the American educational system. In one sense, however, it is an ideal group to lay bare the essence of the phenomena under study. Where else does caring about what one learns hang more in the balance than among those students whose very sense of self is so completely defined by a past history of competitive accomplishments? Yet, this benefit limits the generalizability of this research. Clearly, any temptation to ascribe college dynamics wholesale to other groups differing by age, experience, and ability must be avoided. In this cautionary spirit, I offer our findings largely as a means to raise and illustrate motivational issues that may have broader application across the grade levels and for a variety of student groups.

OBSTACLES TO THE VALUING OF LEARNING

The most important initial question to ask in situating our inquiries was: "What are the various factors thought to undercut intrinsic valuing and personal engagement in schools?"

We identified three interlocking obstacles, each of which follow from one fundamental reality of school life: All motivational dynamics, whether they be construed as intrinsic or extrinsic, owe their very existence to the different kinds of incentives and rewards prevailing in classrooms. Every classroom reflects some type of reward structure within which all academic work is embedded (Doyle, 1983). It is this structure that conveys information to students, explicitly or implicitly, about how they are to be evaluated and what they must do if they hope to be successful. The resulting achievement dynamics have been likened to a game, albeit a serious one (Alschuler, 1973). The purpose of this game for students is to amass as many points (rewards) as possible and to avoid losing points, which occurs when students fail to do well academically or fail to comply with the rules of the game, which include submission to teacher authority and a willingness to try hard. A wide variety of rewards for doing well is potentially available in this game. They range from edibles, such as candy and ice cream for younger students, to social reinforcers, such as teacher praise and recognition for students of all ages. Punishments also abound for noncompliance with a work ethic as well as for doing poorly in one's studies, ranging from teacher reprimands, to warnings, and even the enforced isolation of miscreants.

School grades are the ultimate embodiment of all such rewards and punishments. The overarching importance of grades comes from their formal, summative power as a single index for judging overall success and failure in school. Moreover, grades enjoy great credibility among both parents and college admissions officers. And, as already noted, grades hold extraordinary power, not only to determine who goes to college and even which college but, more importantly, the power to shape one's sense of worth as a person.

The Nature of Rewards

The first potential obstacle to the valuing of what one learns in school concerns the nature of the rewards that dominate in the learning game, namely, the fact that gold stars, praise, and grades are by their very nature extrinsic—extrinsic because they are essentially unrelated to the act of learning itself (Condry & Chambers, 1978). For this reason, learning is in danger of becoming the means to an end, that is, for the acquisition of rewards per se, not an end in itself, so that when rewards are no longer offered or available learning is likely to wane, to say nothing of subject-matter appreciation.

Moreover, as typically administered, these rewards focus student attention on performance outcomes, such as high test scores, not on the process of learning itself, which may be attended by curiosity, personal creativity, and an appreciation for what one is learning. However, according to some observers, if teachers attempt to correct this situation and reward these intrinsic values directly—say, by praising students for pursuing their interests—then, paradoxically, these values may actually be discouraged. This phenomenon is the so-called overjustification effect. Such discouragement is thought to occur because, according to one interpretation, the value of an already justifiable activity becomes suspect by the promise of additional rewards—hence the term *overjustification*—so that the individual believes, in effect, "If someone has to pay me to do this, then it must not be worth doing for its own sake" (Leeper, Greene & Nisbett, 1973; for a recent debate on this topic, see the Spring 1996 issue of the *Review of Educational Research*).

Scarcity of Rewards

A second impediment to subject-matter appreciation involves not merely the presence of extrinsic rewards but the fact that the typical method for distributing them appears highly abrasive. Many classroom reward structures encourage what has been referred to as an "ability game" (Covington & Teel,

1996). The rules of this competitive game dictate that an inadequate supply of rewards (e.g., good grades) be distributed unequally with the greatest number going to the best performers or to the fastest learners. This arrangement amounts to a zero-sum scoring system. When one student (player) wins (or makes points), then other students must lose (points). Here success depends heavily on one's academic ability because rewards are more available to the most able.

According to the self-worth theory of achievement motivation (Covington, 1992; Covington & Beery, 1976), this competitive arrangement undermines task engagement by threatening one's sense of worth. Students come to perceive themselves to be only as worthy as their ability to achieve competitively, and because only a few can win at this game, the majority of students must content themselves with the dubious satisfaction of either avoiding failure or, in the event of actually failing, of at least avoiding the implication of failure—that they are incompetent, hence unworthy.

Reasons for Achieving

The negative impact of the ability game is exacerbated by the presence of a third obstacle, one that lies within the individual, namely, the presence of trait-like personality characteristics that dispose some students to depend on extrinsic rewards for self-definition. These so-called failure avoiders (Atkinson, 1957, 1964) equate their worth with the ability to achieve high grades and in the process become preoccupied with avoiding failure, because typically in school there are insufficient rewards for all students to succeed. The self-protective strategies chosen by these students to deflect the implication that they are incompetent, ironically enough, are likely to cause the very failures they are trying to avoid. For instance, when individuals jeopardize their academic standing in school by procrastinating or by taking too heavy a course load, they virtually insure failure, but at least it is failure with honor, that is, failure that reflects little on their ability because no one else could be expected to do very well when the academic burdens are so great, time so short, or the opportunities for study so few. For these failure-avoidant students, the reasons for achieving are concerned less with the value of what they might learn than with issues of psychological survival (Covington, 1998).

By contrast, *success-oriented* students (Atkinson, 1957, 1964) are typically drawn to the challenges posed by achieving noteworthy accomplishments, but challenges crafted within realistic limits. These students establish learning objectives slightly beyond their current capacity to achieve yet still within reach if they only work a little harder or in more effective ways. This means that failure is robbed of much of its potential threat. Because success is within the grasp of these students, failure to reach their goals does not necessarily imply incompetency, as it does for failure-avoiding students, but rather is seen as a temporary shortfall that can be redressed by renewed effort. It is for these reasons that success-oriented students tend to define their worth in terms of self-improvement, discovering new perspectives, and pushing the envelope of skills and understanding through diligence and the application of hard work.

This self-worth perspective on motivation and schooling presents a troubling picture. Basically, it portrays classrooms as battlefields where the rules favor sabotage, lackluster effort, and self-deception. In such a climate students are placed at risk for ever valuing what they have learned. Not only has it been argued here that students are discouraged from satisfying their curiosities when they are rewarded tangibly for these positive impulses but also, because of the scarcity of these rewards, the majority of students must struggle to avoid failure rather than to approach success. Nonetheless, despite these realities and an almost universal disliking for them, the college students in our samples chose to enter the fray. And in doing so they widely embrace, as their first priority, achieving the highest grades possible—an objective they often hold in contempt because they generally consider grades grossly inadequate reflections of what they have actually learned or have come to value about learning.

Caring About Learning

Taken in their entirety, these dynamics would seem to leave little room for intrinsic task engagement. Yet, despite these formidable obstacles, our inquiries provide unmistakable signs that much of what students learn is acquired out of personal interest and not just for the sake of high grades. In fact, many of our informants sought to reassure us on this point, often protesting at what they sensed was a skepticism on our part regarding the genuineness of their positive feelings toward learning. Perhaps, after all, there is life after grades! But if true, what are the characteristics of such intrinsic knowledge from the student perspective? Why is it valued by students, and how deeply are these convictions held?

As a first step in addressing these questions, we solicited the thoughts of students by means of several open-ended essays. First, our students' collective responses reassured us that, as a minimum at least, they could readily describe and generally agree on what one informant called "surplus knowledge," that is, knowledge acquired above and beyond grade-driven considerations. Moreover, the sophistication of their analyses convinced us that what they had in mind was vivid, inescapable, and real. For instance, for some informants, surplus knowledge was distinguishable not by any specific content but rather by the reasons that lead to its acquisition—for the sake of curiosity or out of the pursuit of personal interests. Other students differentiated surplus knowledge by the means of its acquisition—through active discovery contrasted to the kind of passive acquisition involved in memorizing material for an examination. Still other students identified surplus knowledge by the emotions it creates. They spoke of these emotions as intense and uplifting, as in the distinction between *wonder* and *worry,* the latter feeling being associated with narrow performance goals.

Second, it also became clear that such knowledge was held in high regard. Students valued what they were learning for the information that it provided in making life choices and for the philosophical perspectives it promoted. Others mentioned the potential of surplus knowledge to transform an individual

for the better, with frequently cited moral lessons involving increased compassion for others, patience, and personal fortitude.

Third, and finally, we wondered just how frequently students had what might be called, with apologies to Abraham Maslow (1970), "educational peak experiences," and to what degree these events were perceived to impact them positively. If such experiences were valued by students largely for their rarity, then they would likely exert little influence despite the esteem, even reverence, in which these experiences were sometimes held. We asked one cohort of several hundred introductory psychology students to note such events as they occurred on a daily basis throughout all their classes for an entire semester. Students were provided with descriptive categories based on various themes that emerged from earlier essays, including, for instance, references to "feeling that personal priorities (who you are or where you are headed) seemed clearer." Most students recorded numerous instances of such positive experiences and often rated them as having a substantial, positive impact on their thinking about themselves.

Overall, these data along with the essay material convinced us of the durability and depth of student appreciation for much of what they were learning, apart from any immediate grade benefits. But assuming that this appreciation for learning was genuine, how could such intrinsic values coexist, even thrive, in the presence of selective sorting, extrinsically conditioned rewards, and an overarching grade focus? Was it somehow a matter of balancing grade goals and sources of appreciation? And, if so, how was it managed and at what costs? Finally, we wondered just how adversarial are grade goals and the love of learning anyway? These questions came to occupy center stage in our evolving inquiries.

We again appealed directly to our students for guidance through another series of open-ended essays. Several important points emerged from these data.

First, our informants provided us with the key to understanding why a dominant grade focus does not necessarily preclude the valuing of learning. It all depends, they suggested, on one's reasons for achieving. All students strive for the highest grade possible, but for different reasons, and it is these reasons in turn that determine the degree to which knowledge is valued. For instance, when students strive for high grades as a mark of personal worth, to impress others, or to avoid failure, learning will be valued only to the extent it serves to aggrandize one's ability status, not for any inherent merit of the material itself. If, on the other hand, the reasons for grade striving serve a task-oriented purpose, for instance, using grades as feedback for how one can improve, then one's accomplishments will be appreciated more for their positive instrumental properties.

In effect, it is not necessarily the presence of grades per se, or even a dominant grade focus among students, that influences the degree to which learning is appreciated, but rather the valuing of what one learns depends on the initial reasons for learning and the meaning students attach to their grades. This implies that striving for good grades and caring for learning are not necessarily incompatible goals.

Second, if this goal compatibility depends on one's reasons for learning, then perhaps it also depends on whether one's grade goals are achieved. Our students offered plenty of anecdotal support for this assertion. Restating their comments most simply: Being successful in one's studies promotes an appreciation for what one is learning; whereas falling short of one's grade goals either intensifies one's concentration on studying, to the exclusion of appreciation, or causes a sense of hopelessness about ever succeeding, feelings that bode ill for both the goals of achievement and appreciation.

Third, our informants also indicated that they often deliberately manipulated academic circumstances in an effort to create a tolerable balance between grade goals and caring. The most frequently mentioned of these strategies, especially among success-oriented students, was to arrange one's course of study around personal interests. As one student remarked,

I do realize . . . that students are competing against fellow students, but I do not perceive it that way. The classes I am enrolled in are ones that I choose to take because I have an interest in them. Thus I am already learning for personal satisfaction.

Another student admonished his peers thus: "Students must learn how to incorporate classes they need to take with classes they want to take . . . the best of both worlds. This, in turn, causes feelings of enjoyment, and happiness in the school system." And, when success-oriented students are limited by necessity in their choice of classes, they report seeking out what might interest them even in an otherwise uninviting class. Or, failing this prospect, they find personal satisfaction in the expenditure of energy for a job well done. To cite another student, "I try to believe that as long as I put forth my best effort to learn, I definitely receive personal satisfaction." Recall that it is success-oriented students who perceive effort expenditure as the primary means to success, whereas for failure-avoiding students, the prospect of trying hard and failing anyway raises doubts about their ability, and hence effort can become a threat (Covington & Omelich, 1979) rather than a source of personal satisfaction. Perhaps this is one reason that among some failure-avoiding students we detected a sense of resignation regarding the prospects of ever appreciating what was being learned, or at least of having to postpone such enjoyment until after the joyless gauntlet of the college years had ended.

A PROPOSAL

In summary of these essay responses, we proposed that students are more likely to value what they are learning, and to enjoy the process when: (a) they are achieving their grade goals; (b) what they are studying is of personal interest; and (c) the dominant reasons for learning are task oriented, not self-aggrandizing or failure avoidant.

Although, in retrospect, it seemed self-evident that success and failure experiences will influence one's appreciation for learning, its obviousness became clearly manifest (at least to us) largely because of the real-life context in which we con-

ducted our investigations. To my knowledge, little prior research on valuing has considered the degree to which students were succeeding (or not) in learning the material they were expected to value. Because of this, and the clear saliency of this factor in the minds of students, we decided to conduct a more formal inquiry into these dynamics. Additionally, we were intrigued to determine the extent to which the potentially debilitating effects of a disappointing grade on valuing might be offset for students by their having at least studied a topic that interested them.

This formal study took the form of a series of role-playing scenarios that were subsequently administered to a new sample of some 500 students. They were directed to imagine themselves beginning work on a final assignment in a course. The general situation was portrayed in ways that closely approximated the actual achievement experiences of students to increase the realism of this hypothetical mode. The conditions under which this final, fictitious assignment occurred were varied along two dimensions: first, whether students had succeeded gradewise on several highly similar prior assignments or, by contrast, had consistently received disappointing grades on these earlier assignments; and second, whether the subject matter of the course was personally meaningful to the students. These two conditions were crossed so that all students responded to each of the four possible combinations in a within-subject, repeated measure design. One between-subject factor was also introduced consisting of type of student, either success oriented or failure avoiding.

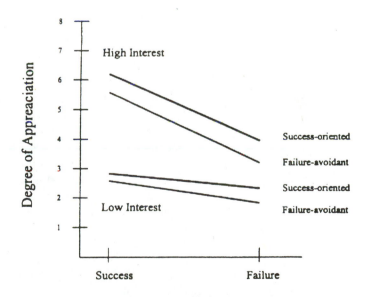

FIGURE 1 Degree of subject-matter appreciation expressed under conditions of high and low interest and success or failure for success-oriented and failure-avoidant students.

For all four scenarios our informants indicated (on a 7-point scale) the degree to which they would likely appreciate and value what they had learned from working on this final assignment. The mean values of these ratings for each scenario separated for success-oriented and failure-oriented students are presented in Figure 1.

Grade Goal

The effect for achieving one's grade goal or not was significant for all levels of student type and interest. In effect, doing well in one's studies was associated with an increased valuing of what one has learned, whereas doing poorly diminished valuing. The negative impact of failure experiences on valuing is scarcely surprising. Much previous research has consistently demonstrated that feeling unsuccessful generates fear of being judged incompetent by others (e.g., Hagtvet, 1984, Thompson, 1993, 1996) and, in turn, ability-linked anxiety is well known to narrow one's attention to matters of self-preservation, especially the creation of self-serving excuses to deflect the causes of poor performance away from insufficient ability (Urdan, Midgley, & Anderman, 1998). These fears and the defensive positioning that follows are exacerbated for failure-avoiding students (Covington & Omelich, 1981, 1988), the very students who in this study expected the least intrinsic benefits in the event of failure.

By contrast, the expectation of achieving high grades enhanced the valuing of knowledge gained. This finding might be considered somewhat unexpected, given the previously mentioned concern that providing tangible rewards might dampen intrinsic task engagement. In light of the results, however, these concerns appear at least overstated if not doubtful. At present our understanding of why extrinsic rewards might enhance, and not necessarily discourage, subject-matter appreciation is not well advanced. There is little to fall back on by way of explanation except, perhaps, the well-known generalization that human beings like and appreciate those things they do well (e.g., Renninger, Hidi, & Krapp, 1992). Although undoubtedly true, we are left wondering what the mechanisms responsible for this relation are.

To deepen our understanding in this matter, we asked one group of students to hypothesize why this generalization might be true in their experience and a second group to assess how credible these student-generated hypotheses were. The explanation judged most likely and for which the most convincing personal anecdotes were offered assumed that doing well caused positive feelings like pride, which in turn increased students' enthusiasm for what they were learning. Other possibilities with varying degrees of anecdotal support involved the observation that doing well reduces worry about failing so that students are freer to explore what is potentially most interesting to them. Another highly regarded candidate assumed that being successful stimulated students to study more, and, according to our informants, the more one learns, the more interesting the material is likely to become.

At present, we are planning further inquiries into the possible linkages between feeling successful, gradewise, and increased interest. Meanwhile, it seems clear that the relation between tangible rewards like good grades and intrinsic processes is far from simple. As a minimum at least, it appears that offering extrinsic rewards does not necessarily undermine interest in learning.

Subject-Matter Interest

The effect for subject-matter interest was also significant at all levels of success and failure and student type. In short, people enjoy and appreciate learning more about what already interests them than about topics that hold little interest. What is intriguing about this bit of otherwise common-sense wisdom is that these results applied to failure as well as to success experiences. Indeed, what most merits our attention here is the degree to which pursuing one's interests offsets failure experiences when it comes to valuing learning. The power of this dynamic is illustrated in our data by the fact that an appreciation for what one is learning was far greater in a failing but task-interested cause than it was when the same student succeeded, gradewise, but for subject-matter content that held little or no interest.

We asked our students, what is it about the nature of interest that seems to buffer the negative effects of a disappointing grade? Although it was generally agreed that subject-matter interest is typically sustained and sometimes even created by doing well, gradewise, our informants also made it clear that interest was not simply the product of social approval or of academic success. They argued that at its core a deeply held, abiding interest possesses a private, protected side in which the rewards that sustain it are largely undiminished by a mediocre record of objective school performance. These alternative rewards involve surpassing one's own idiosyncratic standards of excellence, the playful discovery of hidden talents, and the personal freedom to pick and choose different ways of pursuing whatever invites one's attention.

Another possible explanation for why interest does not necessarily wane, despite the failure to do well, is provided by the work of Richard Newman (1990). Newman found that when individuals pursue their own interests, observers interpret requests for help as the result of being novices—that is, of being ignorant, but not stupid. In effect, in self-worth terms it is not ignorance, or the temporary lack of knowledge or skills, that is threatening. Rather it is feeling stupid that triggers ability-linked anxiety with the implication that one can never become knowledgeable. As long as students follow their interests and struggle for self-improvement and personal enlightenment, then temporary failures along the way do not necessarily count against their reputations for competency.

Another possible explanation concerns the potential impact of interests on one's perceptions of the meaning and purpose of grades. We have found that when task-interested students acknowledge that they would be graded—nothing obscures this fact of school life for long—they tend to believe that the presence of grades actually inspires them to do their best work (Covington & Wiedenhaupt, 1997). This sentiment included the conviction that disappointing grades act as potential feedback for future improvement. Thus, even poor school marks may offer positive benefits for those who are pursuing their interests. This uplifting possibility stands in stark contrast to the reactions of these same students when they express little interest in an assignment. Now students tend to perceive grades as a strategy employed by teachers to ensure a minimum amount of effort! This latter meaning of grades carries with it the feeling of being controlled by others, with a resulting diminution of task engagement (Deci, 1975; Deci & Ryan, 1985, 1994).

Finally, this study underscores the positive motivational impact of successfully pursuing one's interests. It is this success-interest combination that elicits the greatest degree of subject-matter appreciation. It is not success or interest by themselves alone but a synergistic combination of the two that is reflected in a significant interaction in these data. This combination is likely powerful for several interlocking reasons. As previously observed, a successful performance may minimize the distractions caused by the fear of failure as well as increase self-confidence in one's ability to continue succeeding, thereby elevating more positive, task-focused reasons for achieving, all in the context of already deeply held interests that also carry their own positive motivational weight.

The many questions stimulated by this modest study indicate how little we understand about the prospects of encouraging intrinsic goals in a world controlled by extrinsic rewards. However, I believe that when taken together the three factors explored here will provide important insights into these concerns and may even hold the key to a reconsideration of the long-standing assumption that intrinsic and extrinsic motives are necessarily antagonistic. In essence, based on these findings, I suggest that it is not the presence of a dominant grade focus that influences the extent to which learning is appreciated; rather, caring for what is learned depends on the reasons for the grade focus—either task oriented or failure avoidant, on whether one succeeds in achieving one's grade goals, and on one's initial interest level in the subject-matter topic being studied.

FAILURE WITH APPRECIATION

Naturally, as educators we seek other reasons besides subject-matter interest to encourage an appreciation for what students are learning. After all, learning cannot always be arranged around personal preferences, nor do students always succeed. What other characteristics of the teaching and learning act might promote personal valuing and subject-matter appreciation, even in a losing cause, gradewise?

We also put this question to our students. They were asked to recall a time, if any, when despite receiving a disappointing course grade, they still felt they learned a lot that was worthwhile and remained excited about the subject matter. They were asked further to describe the circumstances of this event, to indicate how intense their disappointment was (on a 7-point scale), to say why they believed they had received a disappointing grade, and finally to tell why they still found the course material worthwhile. Irrespective of the circumstances of the individual scenarios, the degree of disappointment expressed, and the alleged reasons for the poor grade, our informants consistently cited three reasons for the undiminished value of these otherwise disappointing learning experiences.

First, our students remarked on the pivotal role of teachers as models of enthusiasm for their subject. Not surprisingly, it appears that teacher enthusiasm encourages positive attitudes in the minds of students toward what they are learning, irrespective of the grade received. This result complements the findings of Ray Perry and his associates (Perry & Dickens, 1984; Perry & Magnusson, 1987), who report that teacher charisma encourages positive, nonability attributions among students for their disappointing performances such as inadequate effort.

Second, our students also reported maintaining enthusiasm for subject-matter material, despite a disappointing course grade, when what they learned was germane to their larger life and career goals outside the classroom. In addition, appreciation comes from working on tasks over which students have some choice and control and through which they can produce things of value to others, including, for instance, the creation of educational material such as new bibliographies or instructional manuals. In effect, information that serves an instrumental purpose of high relevance to the individual is valued, irrespective of grades received.

Third, our students remarked that the negative effects of a disappointing grade were further offset, and a sense of subject-matter appreciation maintained, when instructors directly reinforced positive reasons for learning. Specifically, our evidence suggests that although virtually all students focus primarily on the prospects of getting a good grade, they are also more likely to invest greater time and energy (beyond what is necessary for a good grade) in those assignments for which there are additional tangible, yet intrinsically oriented payoffs. These payoffs include the opportunity for students to share the results of their work with other students or the chance to explain to someone more deeply and personally about why what they learned was important to them. In effect, these are the means by which individuals gain the respect of their peers and co-workers and the admiration of their mentors. I suggest these are the kinds of inducements that enhance subject-matter appreciation and sustain task preservation, even after an assignment has been completed and grade credits are no longer at issue.

These observations imply that, far from being incompatible, intrinsic and extrinsic reasons for learning are both encouraged by tangible rewards, but—and this is the important point—by different kinds of tangible rewards. This proposition sheds an entirely new light on the current debate about the allegedly harmful influence of tangible rewards on the will to learn—the so-called overjustification effect. It is not the offering of tangible rewards that undercuts personal task engagement and appreciation for what is learned as much as it is the absence of those kinds of payoffs that encourage and recognize the importance of being involved in and caring about what one is learning.

CONCLUSION

We are left with the question of how schools can encourage the goals of subject-matter acquisition and appreciation. The issue is not fundamentally one of an incompatibility between learning and caring. The act of learning is not inherently abrasive. Quite to the contrary, learning is a natural, wholesome process. Nor is learning inconsistent with appreciation. In fact, they are mutually reinforcing. Our informants made this clear: The more students learn about a topic, they told us, the more students are likely not only to appreciate the knowledge gained, but also to appreciate the processes by which the knowledge was attained.

Learning is abrasive and undercuts caring only when it becomes a measure of one's worth. From this self-worth perspective, a balance between learning and caring will most likely be struck when educators approach the task in a twofold, coordinated fashion: First, we must discourage negative reasons for learning, including the avoidance of failure and the aggrandizement of one's status at the expense of others; and second, at the same time, encourage those positive reasons for learning linked to self-improvement, discovery, and creativity. To the extent these two objectives are met, subject-matter appreciation will likely flourish.

As to discouraging negative reasons for learning, we have already noted that successful achievement likely offsets ability-linked fear and dampens defensive posturing, which otherwise erodes an appreciation for what and how one is learning. Yet success alone is unlikely to ensure caring for everyone, because for some students successful performances are driven by negative reasons. For example, those students whom we have identified as *overstrivers* (Covington & Omelich, 1991) are highly successful, gradewise. However, because they succeed largely as a way to avoid failure, knowledge gained is never fully appreciated for its own sake. For such students success is seen only as a temporary respite from the continual need to prove themselves worthy in the face of additional and likely more difficult challenges in the future.

More is needed than academic success to offset the forces that distract the value of learning. Negative reasons for learning need to be addressed directly. One approach is to initiate grading policies based on absolute, or merit-based, criteria, that is, holding students to specific, clearly defined requirements so that any number of pupils can achieve a given grade as long as they live up to the quality of workmanship demanded by the teacher. This procedure has been shown to discourage negative reasons for learning associated with competitive pressure among such diverse groups as Berkeley undergraduates (Covington & Omelich, 1985) and at-risk minority students at the middle-school level (Covington & Teel, 1996; Teel, De-Bruin-Parecki, & Covington, 1998). In the latter instance, investigators controlled the quality and quantity of student work by applying a simple rule: the better the grade students want, the more credit they must earn, irrespective of how well others are doing. Substantial amounts of grade credit were given based on how much students improved and for redoing assignments after having received corrective feedback. A variety of ways to express ideas was also encouraged, including drawings and role playing. As a result, these at-risk youngsters could now enter fully into the intellectual life of the classroom.

Another approach, one emphasizing positive reasons for learning, features exploratory learning and the cultivation of personal interests. We have already noted the motivational benefits of an interest-based approach and recall the idiosyn-

cratic yet powerful rewards that our informants identified as accompanying the pursuit of one's own goals.

Finally, a word of guidance from our college informants respecting the nature of the relation between the goals of learning and caring. Our students repeatedly confirmed having feelings of great conflict regarding these goals, but not necessarily feelings of incompatibility. The conflict arises, they suggest, largely because the demands of academic life leave little room to pursue either goal fully, let alone both goals simultaneously. Given the pressure of schoolwork in the face of sometimes overwhelming personal and financial burdens, students must often choose between, say, narrowing the focus of their study, for efficiency sake, to what they believe will be tested versus attending to the personal meaning of what they are studying. Students made it clear which choice they often felt forced to make. But they also lamented what they lost in the bargain. In effect, students typically prioritize their goals, in this case, acquisition over appreciation. But that does not necessarily mean these goals are incompatible. They have merely been prioritized. From this perspective our task as educators is to help students to redress these priorities in favor of caring.

REFERENCES

Alexander, P. A., Kulikowich, J. M., & Schulze, S. K. (1994). How subject-matter knowledge affects recall and interest. *American Educational Research Journal, 31,* 313–337.

Alschuler, A. S. (1973). *Developing achievement motivation in adolescents.* Englewood Cliffs, NJ: Educational Technology Publications.

Ames, C., & Archer, J. (1987, April). *Achievement goals in the classroom: Student learning strategies and motivation processes.* Paper presented at the annual meeting of the American Educational Research Association, Washington, DC.

Atkinson, J. W. (1957). Motivational determinants of risk-taking behavior. *Psychological Review, 64,* 359–372.

Atkinson, J. W. (1964). *An introduction to motivation.* Princeton, NJ: Van Nostrand.

Campbell, D. N. (1974, October). On being number one: Competition in education. *Phi Delta Kappan,* 143–146.

Carnegie Foundation for the Advancement of Teaching. (1989). *Missions of the college curriculum: A contemporary review with suggestions.* San Francisco: Jossey-Bass.

Condry, J. D., & Chambers, J. (1978). Intrinsic motivation and the process of learning. In M. R. Lepper & D. Greene (Eds.), *The hidden costs of reward: New perspectives on the psychology of human motivation.* Hillsdale, NJ: Lawrence Erlbaum Associates, Inc.

Covington, M. V. (1992). *Making the grade: A self-worth perspective on motivation and school reform.* New York: Cambridge University Press.

Covington, M. V. (1998). *The will to learn: A guide for motivating young people.* New York: Cambridge University Press.

Covington, M. V., & Beery, R.G. (1976). *Self-worth and school learning.* New York: Holt, Rinehart & Winston.

Covington, M. V., & Omelich, C. L. (1979). Effort: The double-edged sword in school achievement. *Journal of Educational Psychology, 71,* 169–182.

Covington, M. V., & Omelich, C. L. (1981). As failures mount: Affective and cognitive consequences of ability demotion on the classroom. *Journal of Educational Psychology, 73,* 799–808.

Covington, M. V., & Omelich, C. L. (1985). Ability and effort valuation among failure-avoiding and failure-accepting students. *Journal of Educational Psychology, 73,* 799–808.

Covington, M. V., & Omelich, C. L. (1988). Achievement dynamics: The interaction of motives, cognitions and emotions over time. *Anxiety Journal, 1,* 165–183.

Covington, M. V., & Omelich, C. L. (1991). Need achievement revisited: Verification of Atkinson's original 2 × 2 model. In C. D. Spielberger, I. G. Sarason, Z. Kulcsár, & G. L. Van Heck (eds.), *Stress and emotion: Anxiety, anger, and curiosity* (Vol. 14, pp. 85–105). Washington, DC: Hemisphere.

Covington, M. V., & Teel, K. M. (1996). *Overcoming student failure: Changing motives and incentives for learning.* Washington, DC: American Psychological Association.

Covington, M. V., & Wiedenhaupt, S. (1997). Turning work into play: The nature and nurturing of intrinsic task engagement. In R. Perry & J. C. Smart (Eds.), *Effective teaching in higher education: Research and practice, special edition* (pp. 101–114). New York: Agathon Press.

Deci, E. L. (1975). *Intrinsic motivation.* New York: Plenum.

Deci, E. L., & Ryan, R. M. (1985). *Intrinsic motivation and self-determination in human behavior.* New York: Plenum.

Deci, E. L., & Ryan, R. M. (1994). Promoting self-determined education. *Scandinavian Journal of Educational Research, 38,* 3–14.

Dewey, J. (1963). *Experience and education.* New York: Collier. (Original work published 1938)

Doyle, W. (1983). Academic work. *Review of Educational Research, 53,* 159–199.

Glasser, W. (1976). *Schools without failure.* New York: Harper & Row.

Hagtvet, J. A. (1984). Fear of failure, worry and emotionality: Their suggestive causal relationships to mathematical performance and state anxiety. In H. M. van der Ploeg, R. Schwarzer, & C. D. Spielberger (Eds.), *Advances in test anxiety research* (pp. 211–224). Hillsdale, NJ: Lawrence Erlbaum Associates, Inc.

Hidi, S., & Anderson, V. (1992). Situational interest and its impact on reading and expository writing. In K. A. Renninger, S. Hidi, & A. Krapp (Eds.), *The role of interest in learning and development* (pp. 215–238). Hillsdale, NJ: Lawrence Erlbaum Associates, Inc.

Kohn, A. (1993). *Punished by rewards.* New York: Houghton Mifflin.

Leonard, G. B. (1968). *Education and ecstasy.* New York: Delacorte.

Lepper, M. R., Greene, D., & Nisbett, R. E. (1973). Undermining children's intrinsic interest with extrinsic rewards: A test of the "overjustification" hypothesis. *Journal of Personality and Social Psychology, 28,* 129–137.

Maslow, A. H. (1970). *Religions, values, and peak experiences.* New York: Viking.

Newman, R. S. (1990). Children's help-seeking in the classroom: The role of motivational factors and attitudes. *Journal of Educational Psychology, 82,* 92–100.

Oakes, J. (1985). *Keeping track: How schools structure inequality.* New Haven, CT: Yale University Press.

Perry, R. P., & Dickens, W. J. (1984). Perceived control in the college classroom: Response-outcome contingency training and instructor expressiveness effects on student achievement and causal attributions. *Journal of Educational Psychology, 76,* 966–981.

Perry, R. P., & Magnusson, J. -L. (1987). Effective instruction and students' perceptions of control in the college classroom: Multiple-lectures effect. *Journal of Educational Psychology, 79,* 453–460.

Renninger, K. A., Hidi, S., & Krapp, A. (1992). *The role of interest in learning and development.* Hillsdale, NJ: Lawrence Erlbaum Associates, Inc.

Teel, K. M., DeBruin-Parecki, A., & Covington, M. V. (1998). Teaching strategies that honor and motivate inner-city African American students: A school university collaboration. *Teaching and Teacher Education, 14,* 479–495.

Thompson, T. (1993). Characteristics of self-worth protection in achievement behavior. *British Journal of Educational Psychology, 63,* 469–488.

Thompson, T. (1996). Self-worth protection in achievement behavior: A review and implications for counselling. *Australian Psychologist, 31,* 41–51.

Urdan, T., Midgley, C., & Anderman, E. M. (1998). The role of classroom goal structure in students' use of self-handicapping strategies. *American Educational Research Journal, 35,* 101–122.

Moving beyond Management as Sheer Compliance: *Helping Students to Develop Goal Coordination Strategies*

Specific classroom situations require individualized management techniques, not a "rubber-stamp" approach. A cohesive relationship between teaching style and behavior management style is essential.

by Mary McCaslin and Thomas L. Good

Historically classroom management has been seen largely as controlling students—getting them to respond quickly to teacher demands, needs, and goals. Although for some educators this conception is beginning to change, much emphasis remains on behavioral control.[1] This is especially the case in "packaged" prescriptive management programs.[2] When control strategies fail, students' noncompliance is met with an arsenal of punishment and removal strategies.[3]

We begin by noting that there are distinctly different ways to conceptualize management goals and, within a particular management goal, there are many competing views of how to think about management. We will argue that teachers can and should promote the goal for students to develop their capacity for self-regulation. Although there are no foolproof prescriptions for successful management, teachers can help students to achieve more capacity for self-direction by encouraging them to conceptualize problem-solving behaviors vis-à-vis their

Mary McCaslin and Thomas L. Good are associate professor and professor, respectively, of educational psychology in the College of Education at the University of Arizona, Tucson.

Reprinted with permission from *Educational Horizons,* Summer 1998, pp. 169–176. © 1998 by Phi Lambda Theta, Inc., international honor society and professional association in education, Bloomington, IN 47404-6626.

When control strategies fail, students' noncompliance is met with an arsenal of punishment and removal strategies.

own academic and social goals (much as one teaches curriculum content in a problem-solving fashion). Helping students to develop strategies for coordinating their goals is one important aspect of facilitating student capacity for adaptive self-regulation of their learning, motivation, and behavior.

Discipline Goals

It is possible to distinguish among three discipline goals: compliance, identification, and internalization.[4] Compliance is achieved when an individual behaves simply to get a reward or to avoid a punishment. Identification occurs when an individual acts "appropriately" when a valued model is salient (especially when they are present in a situation). Internalization is inferred when an individual's behavior is stable across a variety of settings in the absence of external inducements. In our opinion, these three discipline goals differ in terms of students' commitment to a standard of action (compliance = I'll stop or start when you tell (consequate) me to do it; identification = I'll start because I know you would want me to; internalization = I act this way because I have accepted your value as my own). Sheer compliance is a sufficient goal for many classroom tasks (e.g., raise your hand for recognition in school whether or not you value hand raising or sanctioned recognition). For other tasks, however, compliance is at best a starting point.

We write this paper for educators who want to achieve more than sheer compliance. However, make no bones about it, compliance is a major goal of classroom management (students must be safe, bullies cannot harass, students must be on time, individuals cannot continuously monopolize classroom discussion). Whether or not a student prefers or values aggression, it cannot be tolerated. Similarly, a student who complies by accepting peer conflict resolution rather than fighting after school represents a favorable

discipline outcome (whether or not the student values conflict resolution).

We prefer goals that include internalization rather than only sheer compliance for three basic reasons. First, the success of a compliance model depends upon constant monitoring (if the teacher turns her or his back, students misbehave; if the electricity in the fence goes off, the cattle flee). Second, if compliance obtained through the judicious use of rewards (and to a lesser extent punishment) is the only controlling mechanism, appropriate behavior and dispositions will not transfer from one setting to another (students may not steal in school, but may do so in the mall; students may try to do their best when the popcorn party is this week, but not take their work seriously the week after the party). In short, compliance with rules and acceptable standards of behavior is, of course, always one goal, but sheer compliance is less durable and transferable than compliance that occurs because of identification (with sports stars who don't smoke or fight—i.e., the "squash it" campaign) or internalization (fighting and smoking are detrimental and things I will not do). A third reason to promote more than compliance is that some complex forms of instruction simply cannot occur if students operate at only a sheer compliance level. For example, if small-group instruction is to work effectively, it is necessary that students value and support cooperative and divergent exchanges. Additionally, students' behavior in small groups often is unsupervised; thus, group management will vary widely as a function of students' commitment to a standard of action and valuing of diversity.

Representations of Management

There are multiple ways to conceptualize management issues in school settings. Indeed, how a teacher or administrator frames a management problem is a critical determinant of how he or she responds to a specific classroom issue. For example, different beliefs about why a student misbehaves influences specific strategies that teachers use in attending to particular classroom events. As can be seen in Table 1, students may misbehave for different reasons and, of course, some of these reasons occur simultaneously.

Table 1: Reasons Why Students Misbehave

1. Lonely or scared
2. Out of control or hostile
3. Face-saving or don't know what to do
4. Have failed to learn, bored or frustrated
5. Physiological need (pain, sleep deprivation, withdrawal) or satiation
6. Distracted by peers, events, or memories

A student who is bored because the work is inappropriately difficult is different from the student who is bored because he or she is satiated and needs a change of activity. Similarly, students who misbehave because they do not know what to do require a different response than students who misbehave because they are distracted by peers. The possible reasons for misbehavior are countless but Table 1 helps to make the point—students misbehave because of cognitive, emotional, and physiological reasons. This analysis also helps to explain why prescriptive programs with regimented responses for student misbehavior often miss the mark. If teachers have management goals other than sheer compliance, then it is important to determine *why* students misbehave. And, even if sheer compliance is the goal, knowing why students misbehave prevents inefficient and potentially counterproductive use of discipline strategies (offering help to a student bored with unchallenging work).

It also is possible to discuss management in terms of *when* students misbehave as somewhat independent from *why* they misbehave (see Table 2).

Table 2: When Misbehavior Occurs

1. Before the lesson starts
2. In the initial stages of a lesson
3. Transition from one lesson activity to another
4. Transition from teacher-directed to student-directed control of the lesson
5. Conclusion of a lesson

Data illustrate that the times listed in Table 2 are when misbehavior most often occurs—especially when whole-class instructional models are being used. The literature on classroom management provides strategies for how to proactively circumvent these "time-based" problems.[5] Further, it's important to understand that these timing problems typically occur because of teachers' instructional or managerial errors. Informed teachers recognize that sometimes students misbehave for reasons that are primarily due to teacher behavior.

Another conceptualization of management is problem ownership. Table 3 defines five types of problem ownership: teacher-owned, student-owned, shared between teacher and student, class-owned, and school-owned problems.[6] If a teacher is angry (as in teacher-owned problem situations) the teacher must recognize the anger to deal capably with student misbehavior (i.e., do more than punish).

Educators who conceptualize management from the perspective of problem ownership have provided rich strategies for dealing with different types of problem students (e.g., shy, hostile, hyperactive) as a

Table 3: Problem Ownership Definitions	
Ownership	**Problem**
Teacher-owned	Student behavior prevents teacher need satisfaction (makes teacher angry)
Student-owned	Student need satisfaction is stymied by someone other than teacher
Shared	Teacher and student partially prevent one another's need satisfaction
Class-owned	Classroom structure prevents students' and teachers' need satisfaction
School-owned	School policies keep students and teachers from achieving needs

function of problem ownership.[7] Most classification systems for dealing with problem ownership have dealt only with the first three types of problems that are caused by other persons. However, it is also possible to conceptualize problems that are classroom-based or school-based due to official *policies,* not only the individuals who enforce them. Some schools, for example, have allowed businesses (McDonald's, Pizza Hut) to advertise in schools and sponsor school programs. Channel One monitors the news that students watch and advertises products along with news broadcasts.[8] One critic of such practices illustrates how a school-level function (allowing tennis shoes to be advertised) may create classroom-level problems (fighting over tennis shoes). Alex Molnar puts it this way, "At a time when poor children have been killed for their shoes, they are forced to watch advertising messages for high-priced sneakers. At a time when American children are increasingly overweight and at risk of coronary disease, they have been taught how the heart functions from a poster advertising junk food and then served high-fat meals by the fast food concessionaires that run their school cafeterias. At a time when too many children abuse alcohol, they are taught history by a brewery."[9]

Yet another way to conceptualize management is the possible interaction between the roles that teachers and students may adopt. Here, the number of comparisons is almost infinite; however, for discussion purposes, some examples are provided in Table 4. As is the case in most representations, this conception interacts with others. For example, an authoritarian teacher typically has a lower threshold for "seeing" a management problem in the first place (especially defiance) than does a laissez-faire teacher.

Table 4 has been organized to show how a particular teacher role may exacerbate certain types of problems students have and how certain student roles may highlight vulnerabilities in certain types of teachers. For example, teachers differ in the amount of control they exert in the classroom. Laissez-faire teachers tend to be relatively tolerant of a range of student behavior (e.g., noise, movement), choosing not to intervene unless required to do so. These teachers' management "plan" is more about reaction and remediation than proactive prevention. In these classrooms students who do not provoke teacher attention do not receive teacher attention. Thus, in such classrooms, the shy or passive student is likely to receive too little structure, demands, or guidance to become more actively engaged and self-regulating. In contrast, the authoritarian teacher who runs a "tight ship" is apt to be over-controlling and thereby triggers the defiant student who likes to test boundaries. Similarly, teachers differ in their relative emphasis of academic or social goal orientation in their classroom. Teachers who value academic goals relatively more than social ones may well find themselves "locking horns" with the underachiever who has grown comfortable with the "gentleman's C." Teachers who attend to social development as a primary goal will likely confront the "I'm the best, I'm the king/queen of the

---

Table 4: Management as a Function of Teacher Role and Student Role	
Teacher Role	**Student Role**
1. Laissez-faire Control	Passive student
2. Authoritarian Control	Defiant student
3. Academic Focus	Underachieving student
4. Social Focus	Self-aggrandizing student

Table 5: Five Personality Factors

1. Agreeableness, Altruism, Affection vs. Hostility
2. Extroversion, Energy, Enthusiasm vs. Introversion
3. Conscientiousness, Control, Constraint vs. Impulsiveness
4. Neuroticism, Negativism, Nervousness vs. Emotional Stability
5. Intellectual Openness, Originality, Flexibility vs. Narrowness, Simplicity, Shallowness

This table has been condensed from Richard Snow, Lyn Corno, and Doug Jackson, III, "Individual Differences in Affective and Conative Functions," in D. Berliner and R. Calfee, eds., Handbook of Educational Psychology (New York: Macmillan, 1996), 243-310.

---

world" student as a major challenge to their instructional goals. Table 4 presents two anchors of teacher behavior on each of two dimensions. Consider the likely management issues that arise when, for example, a laissez-faire teacher with an academic focus implements project-based science. What types of behavior would you predict from each of the student roles listed? What if they were members of the same group?

Researchers who have examined the extensive literature on individual differences have noted that five major personality factors describing dispositions teachers and students bring to the classroom can be derived from the research (see Table 5).[10] As suggested by Table 5, a teacher with one personality orientation necessarily must deal with many students whose personalities may differ in major ways from one another and from the teacher. An introverted teacher who prefers to be low-key in the classroom, for example, can (and sometimes must) project enthusiasm, firmness, or assertiveness as the educational context affords or demands.

Table 5 indicates the complexity of potential interactions. For example, each factor (e.g., agreeable vs. hostile) is associated with multiple characteristics (affectionate, unselfish, trusting, etc.); however, even the most agreeable person will be cold and unfriendly in some situations. Basic personality dispositions (e.g., honesty) are more likely to be exhibited in some situations but not others (e.g., Joan would never cheat on an exam but would copy off another student's homework). Given such complexity it simply is not possible to understand student disposition, behavior, and needs without *listening* to them.[11]

As seen through the representations we have introduced, classroom management is complex: what constitutes a good management strategy depends (at least) upon the teacher's role, personality, goals, and strategies; characteristics of the management "problem"; and the role, personality, developmental level, and goals of the students. Again, we emphasize a key premise of this article—if teachers want to influence students and want them to respond for reasons other than sheer compliance, teachers cannot let packaged, prescriptive programs do their thinking for them.

Teach for Understanding; Manage for Compliance: Any Questions?

Ironically, and unfortunately, many who write about classroom management answer "no" to the above question. We contend that to teach for understanding while managing for compliance is self-defeating. Too many classroom-management writers ignore the important link

It seems highly unlikely that students will profit from the incongruous messages we send when we manage for obedience and teach for exploration and risk taking.

between the need for more advanced management approaches (i.e., moving beyond sheer compliance) if certain types of instructional processes and goals are to be achieved. It is not uncommon to find educational writers who strongly advocate a thinking or problem-solving curriculum while directly, or indirectly, arguing for behavioral control of students. For example, Carolyn Evertson and her colleagues note that Walter Doyle incorrectly " . . . suggests that classrooms with complex organization will require more direct management and control than simpler settings."[12] In marked contrast to Doyle's position, Evertson and colleagues note that classroom researchers contend that "instead of more teacher control, these settings will need a different *kind* of teacher control."[13] They argue that when complex instructional goals are required, it is more efficacious for the teacher to delegate authority to students or groups of students, rather than attempting to supervise directly the multitude of overlapping activities, claiming that "direct supervision is more appropriate to [and, we would add, theoretically consistent with] simpler routine tasks."[14] Simply put, if the teacher is trying to create a trusting, cooperative learning environment for students, then the management system must also promote these same dispositions, behaviors, and skills—in part through opportunities for thinking and problem solving in the academic *and* social spheres.

Goal Coordination: Moving beyond Compliance

We have presented several representations of management and each one provides a legitimate lens for thinking about how to conceptualize and implement classroom management goals and strategies. Now we want to introduce another representation;

one that we feel is especially relevant for contemporary classrooms. Elsewhere, we have suggested that in many classrooms there is a fundamental mismatch in the promotion of a problem-solving curriculum while using a behavioral control approach to management.[15] It seems highly unlikely that students will profit from the incongruous messages we send when we manage for obedience and teach for exploration and risk taking. We put our argument this way:

> Educators have created an oxymoron: a curriculum that urges problem solving and critical thinking and a management system that requires compliance and narrow obedience. The management system at least dilutes, if not obstructs, the potential power of the curriculum for many of our students. Students are asked to think and understand, but in too many classrooms they are asked to think noiselessly, without peer communication or social exchange. And the problems they are asked to think about must be solved, neatly, within (at most) forty-five-minute intervals. In the problem-solving curriculum, in too many cases, the teacher sets the performance goals, identifies relevant resources, establishes criteria for evaluation, and eventually announces winners and losers. Students generally gain recognition and approval by paying close attention to recommended procedures and by taking few academic risks (e.g., reading and extensively footnoting fifteen secondary sources rather than venturing their own informed opinions).[16]

If we want students to develop thoughtful work habits it seems necessary to help them think about how they acquire, elaborate, and integrate academic knowledge; consider the relations among their knowledge, beliefs, and identity; and locate those processes and persons who support them in complicated learning. Simply put, if we want students to understand (i.e., not memorize) academic content, value the process of academic learning, and internalize their education, then we need to help students understand their own behavior in school settings and develop a capacity for managing and regulating themselves and others in a way that supports their learning goals.

Multiple Goals

Teachers can help students become more adept at self-management, or "self-regulation," by helping them learn to coordinate their social and academic lives. This involves identifying goals and their interrelationships and strategically coordinating among them. Students (like teachers) pursue multiple

goals simultaneously (with more and less success). Often students must choose between competing goals (asking the teacher a question about the trig assignment at the end of class or catching up with a friend who won't be seen the rest of the school day to ask about substituting that afternoon at McDonald's). Further, as we note in *Listening in Classrooms,* students often pursue a goal for multiple reasons (e.g., strategic use of study time as a way both to learn and ensure weekend privileges), and strategies and goals can be *multi-functional* (e.g., "obvious" effort may promote achievement and it is also an effective impression-management strategy).[17] Also, relations among goals are multidimensional. When multiple goals are pursued at the same time and do not overlap, time pressure can make it difficult to establish priorities and then pursue goals sequentially. In addition, goal coordination becomes more complex when multiple goals are difficult (i.e., they take time, attention, and energy to achieve). Third, personal goals often clash with others' needs and interests. Conflict with others makes goal pursuit and coordination more difficult and costly. Teachers sometimes inadvertently create goal conflict and thwart learning goal coordination. For example, teachers typically give deadline extensions when performance events occur midweek. Students who receive extensions do not learn how to prioritize and follow through; instead, they learn that the teacher devalues school work. Peers without extensions may learn to prioritize; however, they also may learn that their multiple goals and time constraints are not noteworthy. Both groups of students have had another piece added to their friendship task.

Dealing with multiple goals is a part of life and people who can do so successfully are apt to be more productive and satisfied than those who cannot. Single-mindedness—all the eggs in one basket—is not a healthy

Teachers can help students become more adept at self-management, or "self-regulation," by helping them learn to coordinate their social and academic lives.

Table 6: Goal-coordination Strategies

1. *A single, integrative strategy:* Although this is the most efficient and inclusive strategy, the goals obviously need to be compatible. One example is the high-ability, highly focused student who is involved in the school yearbook and student government, has a part-time job at the local Quick Print, and hopes to attend college to study journalism. This student's achievement, belongingness, power, independence, and present and future career needs are met with a single broad, integrative strategy.

2. *Multiple, simultaneous strategies:* Simultaneous strategies require goals to be compatible with or independent of each other and for some to be less difficult so that the student can do more than one thing at a time. Academically more-capable students are often able to meet the demands of the task, follow procedures, and catch up on the "chit-chat" with their group members. Thus, they follow the routines like "good" students, successfully complete the task like "smart" students, and maintain friendly banter like "popular" students.

3. *Deferment strategies:* Deferment strategies result when the student realizes that she or he can't "have it all" and prioritizes. Nonpriority goals are put on the back burner, not abandoned. As compared with the integrative and simultaneous strategies, deferment means less gets done because less can get done. We suspect this is the initial reasoning as students begin to restrict their hobbies: piano is deferred for now to allow more time for flute and the school band; soccer takes priority over track, etc.

4. *Modification strategies:* Goals or the criteria for their successful attainment are modified to make goals more compatible. Students may decide that each and every paper in English does not have to be their best; it is important that some of their time be spent on science class, too. Learning to modify goals is a particularly important skill that teachers can help students to develop. Adolescents as well as first-graders can easily lose a sense of proportion in the goals they set and their abilities to meet them.

5. *Goal substitution:* One goal replaces the original goal. Although goal substitution need not have a negative connotation, it is often offered as an explanation for student gang membership and general theories of "negative identity." That is, students who are unable to achieve belongingness in family or sense of place and recognition in school substitute membership and status in gangs to fulfill unmet needs. All of us have had "goal-substitution" experiences, however, and they typically are positive, involving more realistic aspirations. Consider the student who wants to be part of the school play; although stage fright and basic lack of talent may prohibit being cast in an acting role, scenery always needs painting.

6. *Goal abandonment.* By goal abandonment we mean to simply give up on a goal without deferring, modifying, or substituting another. In the specific instance, goal abandonment may be appropriate. For example, simply giving up and going home to regroup may help a student cope with temporary embarrassment. Giving up the goal to always be the best at whatever one does is probably a good idea—as long as it does not translate into giving up trying or giving up altogether.

This table has been adopted (slightly condensed) from McCaslin and Good, Listening in Classrooms.

ask one student to explain to another (who has been unable to answer) how a process works or why an answer is incorrect. Students may solve the goal-conflict by feigning ignorance—friendship matters more than being right and a "good" student. Incompatible goals also might negate one another. A student who strives to improve her game, meet the no-pass-play academic criterion, and "party hearty" risks failure of academic and athletic goals. And, if "caught," she neither plays, nor remains in school, nor is allowed to go out with friends. Prioritizing and choosing among independent and incompatible goals is essential if students are to meet any of them. Think of how much energy, time, and emotion is spent futilely because an individual does not realize that he cannot have his cake and eat it too, and as a result, achieves neither experience.

Goal-Coordination Strategies

In addition to helping students recognize the degree of compatibility (or lack thereof) among goals, teachers can also help students develop strategies to coordinate among them. In Table 6 we describe four strategies that Dodge and colleagues argue promote goal coordination.[19] We add two strategies (points 5, 6) to their list and place the strategies on a continuum of inclusiveness from greater inclusiveness to less.

School-Wide Co-regulation

If teachers are to be notably effective in helping students to develop goal-coordination strategies and, more broadly, to increase their capacity for self-regulation, teachers will need to work with colleagues at earlier and later grade levels. Elsewhere it has been argued that often first- and second-grade

life strategy. Students must learn to identify individual goals, assess their relative importance, and their relationship. Teachers also need to understand the goal coordination task that they impose on students when they assign multiple, simultaneous, and difficult requirements. Teachers who are mindful of students' goal coordination tasks can co-regulate students' learning how to strategically organize and achieve them. Teachers can help students accomplish personal goals by teaching (a) goal-compatibility features and (b) goal-coordination strategies.

Goal Compatibility

Educational researchers have argued that goals can be *compatible* in three ways.[18]

First, they may be compensatory as effort (to some extent) can compensate for ability. Second, compatible goals can be complementary as, for example, cooperative behavior complements cooperative learning. Third, compatible goals can be instrumental—studying now makes it easier to be admitted to college later. Goals (like many classroom goals) can be largely *independent* of each other. For example, wanting to be on time to sit with friends at lunch is usually independent of wanting to do well on a chemistry test. Finally, goals can be *incompatible* by interfering or negating one another. Goal interference can occur when teachers inadvertently place students, especially preadolescents, in a conflict between the goal of being a good student and the goal of being a good friend. For example, often teachers

Students should be allowed, taught, and expected to assume more responsibility for their goals and behavior as they progress through school.

students have more opportunity for self-direction, self-evaluation, and choice than do sixth-grade or twelfth-grade students.[20] Unfortunately, the progress that one teacher makes in helping students to develop their capacity for self-regulation in a given year can be dissipated the following year when the next teacher imposes a more controlling (and therefore regressive) system.[21] As we have noted previously, it is time to examine the connectedness of classroom management systems. Educators need to become more sensitive to building better bridges between grades.[22] Students should be allowed, taught, and expected to assume more responsibility for their own goals and behavior as they progress through school.

In this article, we have argued that there are many ways to conceptualize classroom management and we have recommended that teachers can benefit from using multiple perspectives. We argue that successful management has to be conceptualized as fluid and transitional: that is, teachers must continue to adjust their management systems to changes in context, including students' expanding needs and abilities.

1. See Mary McCaslin and Thomas L. Good, *Listening in Classrooms* (New York: Harper Collins, 1996); Mary McCaslin and Tom Good, "Compliant Cognition: the Misalliance of Management and Instructional Goals in Current School Reform," *Educational Researcher* 21 (1992): 4–17; Carolyn Evertson and Catherine Randolph, "Perspectives on Classroom Management for Learner-centered Classrooms," in H. Waxman and H. Walberg, eds., *New Directions for Research on Teaching* (Berkeley, Calif.: McCutchan, in press); and Alfie Kohn, *Beyond Discipline: From Compliance to Community* (Alexandria, Va.: Association for Supervision and Curriculum Development, 1996).

2. For an example of one type of the packaged management programs that we find self-defeating, see Lee Canter and Marlene Canter, *Assertive Discipline: Positive Behavior Management for Today's Classroom* (Santa Monica, Calif.: Lee Canter and Associations, 1992).

3. Some of the school-level control strategies in popular use are blatantly contradictory. For example, some schools that have zero-tolerance programs for drugs (i.e., students are kicked out of school for any violation and placed on the street where they can acquire drugs among other things) have tough policies on student truancy that are imposed by state law (e.g., prosecute parents of heavy-truancy students). Apparently it is okay for the school to allow students not to go to school, but the same option does not exist for parents!

4. Herbert C. Kelman, "Compliance, Identification, and Internalization: Three Processes of Attitude Change," *Journal of Conflict Resolution*, vol. 2 (1958): 51–60; and Herbert C. Kelman, "Processes of Opinion Change," *Public Opinion Quarterly* 25 (1961): 57–78.

5. See Thomas L. Good and Jere Brophy, *Looking in Classrooms*, 7th ed. (New York: Harper Collins, 1997).

6. Thomas Gordon, *Teacher Effectiveness Training* (New York: Wyden, 1974); and Jere Brophy and Mary McCaslin, "Teachers' Reports of How They Perceive and Cope with Problem Students," *Elementary School Journal* 93, no. 1 (1992): 3–68.

7. Ibid, Brophy and McCaslin, "Teachers' Reports."

8. Bradley Greenberg and Jeffrey Brand, "Channel 1: But What about the Advertising?" *Educational Leadership* 51 (1994): 56–58.

9. See Alex Molnar, *Giving Kids the Business: The Commercialization of American Schools* (New York: Westview Press, 1996), 49.

10. See Richard Snow, Lyn Corno, and Doug Jackson III, "Individual Differences in Affective and Conative Functions," in D. Berliner and R. Calfee, eds., *Handbook of Educational Psychology* (New York; Macmillan, 1996), 243–310.

11. Mary McCaslin and Thomas L. Good, *Listening in Classrooms* (New York: Harper Collins, 1996).

12. See Carolyn Evertson, K. Weeks, and C. Randolph, *Creating Learning-centered Classrooms: Implications for Classroom Management* (Nashville, Tenn.: Vanderbilt University, March 1997, mimeo); Walter Doyle, "Classroom Organization and Management," in M. Wittrock, Ed., *Handbook of Research on Teaching*, 3rd ed. (New York: MacMillan, 1986), 392–431.

13. See Hermine Marshall, "Beyond the Workplace Metaphor: Toward Conceptualizing the Classroom as a Learning Setting," *Theory into Practice* 29 (1990): 94–101; and Alfie Kohn and Lotan, "Teachers as Supervisors of Core Technology," *Theory into Practice* 29 (1990): 78–84.

14. Ibid, Marshall, "Beyond the Workplace."

15. See Mary McCaslin and Thomas L. Good, "Compliant Cognition: the misalliance of Management and Instructional Goals in Current School Reform," *Educational Researcher* 21 (1992): 4–17.

16. Ibid.

17. See McCaslin and Good, *Listening in Classrooms*, 65, 66.

18. See Kenneth Dodge, Steven Asher, and Jennifer Parkhust,"Social Life as a Goal-Coordination Task," in C. Ames and R. Ames, eds., *Research on Motivation and Education: Volume 3: Goals and Cognition* (New York; Academic Press, 1989), 107–135.

19. Ibid.

20. Thomas L. Good, "What Is Learned in Elementary Schools," in Tommy Tomlinson and Herbert Walberg, eds., *Academic Work and Educational Excellence* (Berkeley, Calif.: McCutchan, 1986), 87–114.

21. Nedra Fetterman, *The Meaning of Success and Failure: A Look at Social Instructional Environments of Four Elementary School Classrooms*, unpublished doctoral dissertations. Bryn Mawr College, Bryn Mawr, Pa.

22. Mary McCaslin and Thomas L. Good, "Classroom Management and Motivated Student Learning," in Tommy Tomlinson, ed., *Motivating Students to Learn; Overcoming Barriers to High Achievement* (Berkeley, Calif.: McCutchan, 1993), 245–261.

Connecting Instruction and Management in a Student-Centered Classroom

Nancy K. Martin

Ms. Thompson's seventh grade students have been studying the solar system and are busily working in cooperative learning groups. Each group has been assigned one planet and their objective is to create a description of a being that could live on "their" planet. Because Ms. Thompson has done a good job of orchestrating positive interdependence, students are relying on their groups to achieve their objective while the teacher serves as a facilitator (Johnson, Johnson, Holubec, & Roy, 1988). The noise level here is slightly higher than in the typical classroom as students interact with each other and fulfill their assigned roles. The teacher explained the rules for behavior to the students prior to beginning the project: "Keep hands, feet, and objects to yourself," "Let others have a chance to speak," and "Contribute to your group. "She has predetermined consequences for both appropriate and inappropriate behavior and shared those with the class.

Ray and Bill have been having trouble getting along together and today does not seem to be an exception as they continue to "pick on" each other. Even though a warning has been issued to both students, there is yet another altercation between them. Ms. Thompson explains, "Boys, this means detention for both of you." Ray turns pale and looks upset. Bill continues poking Ray with his pencil and says, "Detention's no big deal. I don't care." Ms. Thompson explains to Bill that a call to his parents will be made.

The classroom environment promoted by this teacher is typical of many middle school teachers. The instruction was creative and student centered, but the classroom management techniques were expedient and teacher centered. There can be little doubt that an interesting, well-organized lesson is the single best means to prevent off-task behavior. Still, when coupled with teacher-centered behavior management methods, the subtle but unmistakably clear message students receive is: "It's 'us' against 'them.' "

Classroom atmosphere is an important consideration for educators at all levels. However, it is especially important for teachers at the middle level because of the many developmental changes their students experience simultaneously. In addition to physical, social, and cognitive changes, young adolescents also encounter new academic demands and are required to make the adjustment from a small self-contained classroom with one teacher to a larger, possibly less personal school structure (Santrock, 1987). The purpose of this article is to consider the elements of a student-centered learning environment and the connection between the teacher's instructional methods and his or her approach to classroom management.

Historically classroom have been teacher-centered. Instructors were accepted as experts conveying the subject matter. The focus in this type of classroom was on the teacher's needs (e.g., the content to be covered and student obedience). Student activity was limited and students were, at best, passive learners. They spoke when recognized by the teacher and were typically not allowed to interact with each other during lessons. Although rote learning may have flourished in the teacher-centered classroom, active learning (problem-solving and critical thinking) was unlikely to emerge. As we prepare to enter the 21st cen-

Nancy K. Martin teaches at the University of Texas at San Antonio.

From *Middle School Journal*, March 1997, pp. 3–9. © 1997 by the National Middle School Association (NMSA). Reprinted by permission.

tury, this type of learning environment is no longer favorable. If the classroom is to be the center of "intellectual inquiry, students and teachers must feel free to pursue ideas and make mistakes" (Prawat, 1992, p. 10). Recently, student-centered instruction has gained new advocacy (Aaronsohn, 1993).

Unlike classrooms of the past, student-centered classrooms focus on students "interaction with meaningful content, with each other, and with the teacher as facilitator of that independence" (Aaronsohn, 1993, p. 3). Today quality instruction is characterized by developmentally appropriate methods that consider the intrinsic needs of students. Students' decision-making skills are fostered and opinions are validated by focusing on creativity

"Can't I be student centered in my instruction and teacher centered in my classroom management?" The answer is no; you are trying to mix oil with water.

and critical thinking rather than role learning.

Although often considered separately, classroom management and instruction cannot be isolated from each other because they work together to create a classroom atmosphere (Martin & Baldwin, 1994). Yet many schools across the country encourage and use student-focused instructional methods while simultaneously adopting packaged approaches to classroom management, even though these approaches may not be designed to support student-centered instruction. Without student-centered instruction and classroom management, a truly learner-focused environment cannot exist.

Still, when I try to convey this connection to teachers, I am frequently met with skepticism: "Can't I be student centered in my instruction and teacher centered in my classroom management?" The answer is no; you are trying to mix oil with water.

The student-centered classroom is an outgrowth of a philosophy sensitive to the whole child. Therefore, by definition it must focus on the psychological and emotional aspects of the child as well as on the cognitive and intellectual domains. As Wilson (1994) explains, "teachers who view their students simply as academic learners fail to consider the impact of each student's affective state on achievement in the middle school. . . . Teachers who appear too busy to respond to significant social/affective related needs of young adolescents assure an incomplete learning ethos in their classrooms, counter-productive to excellence in scholarship" (p. 53).

The Goal of Classroom Management

This brings to light important questions. First, what is the overall goal of classroom management? In the teacher-centered classroom, control is key to being able to "cover" the material. Keeping pupils still and quiet in the most expedient fashion possible is the primary objective. Traditional, teacher-centered classroom management techniques usually require appropriate behavior in response to some type of reward. Therefore, the teacher must be present to view the behavior and dispense the reinforcer. By utilizing systems such as these, we run the risk of creating a situation in which students behave only for what they "get" and the teacher's absence implies permission to misbehave.

One of the most widely used teacher-centered paradigms is Canter's (1992) *Assertive Discipline*. More than 750,000 teachers have been trained in the use of this model which advocates the use of incentive systems and punishment and focuses on teacher control and student obedience (Hill, 1990). Canter (1992) defines the assertive teacher as, "One who clearly and firmly communicates her expectations to her students, and is prepared to reinforce her words with appropriate actions. She responds in a manner which maximizes her potential to get her needs to teach met, but in no way violates the best interest of the students" (p. 14). This model consists of a set of rules and a hierarchy of predetermined rewards and consequences. When the child misbehaves, he or she is allowed one warning before the predetermined consequence is automatically doled out without consideration of the individual child or the motivation of the misbehavior.

Consider the following scenario typical of the assertive discipline classroom. As Mr. Martinez is presenting his lesson, he sees Emily turn and whisper to Jason. "Emily, that's a warning."

"But, Mr. Martinez, I . . ."

"No 'buts', Emily. You know the rules. Next time, you go to detention. "The classroom belongs only to Mr. Martinez; there is no sense of community here. Emily is likely to become resentful and other students may be upset or angry by observing similar interactions.

In the student-centered classroom, however, Mr. Martinez's response would be very different. Here, the teacher might simply ask, "Emily, is there something I can help you with?"

"What page are we on, Mr. Martinez? I didn't hear you say."

"Page 53, Emily, but remember that the assignment is always written on the board so you can look there in the future." In this simple exchange, the teacher has first tried to be

(Mendler, 1993, p. 5). In the student-centered classroom, misbehavior is considered a golden opportunity to foster self-discipline and responsibility. To that end, consequences are tailored to individual students and their needs. The consequences for appropriate and inappropriate behavior should not be predetermined but, instead, considered on an individual basis. Unlike the physician who gives all patients aspirin or the teacher who doles out the same consequences to all students, one should consider the specific situation and tailor the response to fit the needs and motives of the "patient."

Student-centered classrooms are characterized by the teacher's consideration of the student's developmental tasks, needs, motives, and feelings. As middle school students struggle with the development of a personal identity and greater social independence, the student-centered environment fosters the development of an internalized moral code (Alexander, 1965/1995). Student input, discussion, and compromise are important parts of this teacher's classroom management plan so self-discipline and responsibility are encouraged. Therefore, classroom rules and policies could be the objective for a cooperative learning assignment at the beginning of the year. To foster a student-centered environment, students could brainstorm ideas, discuss, and possibly vote on how the classroom community should function within the broader school context.

> **When a physician has a waiting room full of patients with different illnesses, he or she does not come out and say: "Today is aspirin day; all patients will be treated equally and given aspirin to solve their ailments."**

pro-active by putting information on the board. But when Emily did not remember or notice, she was still given the benefit of the doubt. She was listened to and respected. In this scenario, we see reciprocal interaction; not a one-way or topdown exchange.

Assertive Discipline, on the other hand, treats all students the same. But being fair means not treating all children the same. When a physician has a waiting room full of patients with different illnesses, he or she does not come out and say: "Today is aspirin day; all patients will be treated equally and given aspirin to solve their ailments"

Student-Centered Classroom Management Sounds Good, But . . .

Another important question is this: Why are teachers reluctant to implement student-centered theories of classroom management that encourage self-discipline and responsibility? In my work with teachers, I have found six frequently expressed reasons.

1. What will others think if . . . ? Teachers often feel pressured to create a quiet and orderly classroom environment so material can be "covered" and/or because of concern about the opinions of others (e.g., administrators, colleagues, or parents). Aaronsohn (1993) quotes a student teacher who said, "[My cooperating teacher] evaluated me on how I controlled the class—on who was off task. . . . How am I going to make the school people happy?" (p. 26). Indeed, the piece of advice probably most often given to new teachers is, "Go in there, take control and don't smile until Christmas."

On the other hand, student-centered, intrinsic classroom management strategies focus on the whole child, his or her needs and motives. A consequence for inappropriate behavior is only successful if it results in students realizing the repercussions of their actions, envisioning other behavioral choices, and making a sincere plan to use those choices in the future. The student-centered classroom may be lively with active learners but intrinsic classroom management techniques are also needed for students to become self-disciplined, independent learners.

The importance of administrative and collegial encouragement is paramount in overcoming the "what will people think" obstacle. Without such support, it is unlikely that a student-focused atmosphere will materialize. School administrators and fellow teachers must provide the moral support and professional development opportunities necessary if student-centered classroom management practices are to predominate.

2. Forget classroom management theory. If it works, use it. This is the "fly-by-the-seat-of-the-pants" approach to classroom management. Teachers have been using it for decades. Aaronsohn (1993) explains, "'the way it is' is a powerful model . . . since 'it's always been that way'" (p. 7). Traditionally educators have learned how to manage classrooms from each other where the focus is on practice rather than theory. When classroom management is taught and learned in this manner we run the risk of making the same mistakes year after year without realizing why.

Theory is important because it provides us with an explanation of observations. We may all see and experience the same things but our explanation for the underlying causes of these events can be very different. A consistent theoretical perspective lends the teacher a coherent base from which to draw. Without it, we are left with a mere "bag of tricks" and are often at a loss for alternatives when a particular discipline method inevitably fails. Dismissing theory as unimportant is analogous to walking a tightrope without a net.

The teacher's transition to a student-centered classroom environment is a gradual process that involves a great deal of introspection and cannot be accomplished overnight. It is not unusual to see practicing teachers who want to hang on to the old, comfortable classroom management techniques because they "work," even though they may not be appropriate. Many things work; this does not mean they are necessarily appropriate. Extra work given as punishment, writing "lines," and teacher sarcasm are all examples of interventions that may "work" in that they temporarily stop the behavior but are never appropriate.

No one wants to develop a pool of techniques that does not work; that would be silly. At the same time, educators have a responsibility to critically evaluate classroom management techniques. Are these techniques accomplishing what we think they are and, if so, how well? When a student misbehaves, we typically use a discipline technique, see its immediate impact, and think it is effective. Claiming it "works," we prepeatedly use it. If it really worked, we would not need it again. Even worse, at times educators embarrass and humiliate students into compliance. Strategies such as these can leave deep emotional scars and have long-term negative effects. Both teacher-centered and student-centered models of classroom management can be used effectively for short-term control of children's classroom behavior. However, it is dangerous to value discipline for its own sake "without regard for the effects of these programs on the overall learning and development of children" (Benshoff, Poidevant, & Cashwell, 1994, p. 166). It is imperative that we consider what happens later. What happens to the student's self-esteem, motivation for learning, or dig-

As an individual, I can influence others, but I cannot actually control anyone except myself— and sometimes even this is difficult.

nity (Mendler, 1993)? Any interaction that diminishes these is inappropriate, even though it may stop the misbehavior.

3. My philosophy is "eclectic." I use a combination of models and classroom management techniques. Without student-centered classroom management techniques, there can be no student-centered classroom. Altering curriculum and instruction is of little use if the overall classroom atmosphere is still teacher-centered. This is difficult change to make as it usually requires letting go of some of the teacher implemented rules and requirements.

As a result, teachers have a tendency to combine conflicting models that sound good with ones that "feel" right to them as traditional teachers (e.g., Canter's (1992) *Assertive Discipline* with Glasser's (1986) *Control Theory* or Ginott's (1972) ideas with behavior modification). In theory as well as in practice, this is impossible. It cannot be done. When the teacher "combines" a teacher-centered model of classroom management with a student-centered model, at least one of them is bastardized—usually the student-centered one.

The teacher-student relationship is at the heart of student-centered classroom management. Mutual respect and trust are prerequisite to success. When teachers try to combine conflicting models, students learn that they are only listened to when they agree with the teacher. One experienced teacher explained his professional transition as follows:

> In the past, I have combined many different ideas. Many of those ideas send conflicting signals to students. I want trust in a classroom but I also want students to do what I say when I say. I want to meet the needs of students but I also want students to sit down and shut up. I want to talk to students when I want to talk to students. When I look at all that is happening in my classroom, I realize that what I do is a major part of behavior problems. I have to let go. I have to free myself from past experiences and provide an environment that meets the needs of my students instead of meeting only my needs.

Traditionally, classroom management techniques were likely drawn from no particular theoretical base at all or from theories such as behaviorism where the focus is on extrinsic control via reinforcements. Classic behavior modification does not recognize students as active participants in the learning process but instead views them as passive learners who simply respond to the environment. Behaviorally based models of classroom management such as Canter's (1992) *Assertive Discipline* or Jones's (1987) model cannot co-exist with a student-centered curriculum.

Others present very different theories and models for classroom management that focus on the individual and advocate free will rather than determinism (e.g., Dreikurs, Grunwald, & Pepper, 1982; Glasser, 1986; Ginott, 1972, Gordon, 1974). Glasser (1986) described all behavior as a choice and believes that, "None of what we do is caused by any situation outside of ourselves" (p. 17). A good teacher is one who considers his or her role as one of a modern manager who shares power, rather than the traditional, teacher-centered manager who does not (Glasser, 1986).

Similarly, Dreikurs, Grunwald, and Pepper (1982) maintained that humans are social beings and all behavior is enacted with some purpose in mind. Specifically, humans attempt to find their place in the group in which they function such as the family or class. Again, the focus is on the individual and the origin of behaviors. In other words, both Glasser and Dreikurs addressed the underlying cause for the behaviors of both the teacher and the student. Control—and therefore, responsibility—lies within each individual. Likewise, Ginott (1972) and Gordon (1974) encouraged teachers to invite students' cooperation and encouraged the use of "I-messages," realizing that students make their own decisions and choices regarding behavior.

4. How can we teach students respect for authority if we give them too much control? I answer this question with another question. How can we teach students respect for anyone if we do not show them the respect all people deserve? Teaching respect begins by giving respect. Teacher-centered models of classroom management are focused on the teacher and, therefore, by definition disregard students' needs.

In addition, the idea that control is ours to give is an illusion. Any "control" one has over another exists only because the recipient allows it. As an individual, I can influence others, but I cannot actually control anyone except myself—and sometimes even this is difficult. Because students may be used to teacher-centered classrooms, they may not be aware that they are the ones who control their behavior. As a result, they may be giving others more power over their lives than they should. Student-centered classroom management models teach students that they—not others—are responsible for their behavior.

If students are out of control today, it is partly because their sense of personal control has been taken away from them. They have felt disregarded and disempowered by traditional, teacher-centered—sometimes authoritarian—school systems. A sense of validation can go a long way to facilitate some of the developmental struggles associated with young adolescence.

Unfortunately, not all authority figures have children's best interests in mind. Because we have seen an increase in drug use, gang activity, reported cases of child abuse and molestation, students today should be encouraged to differentiate between those who do and do not deserve their trust and respect. It is a dangerous proposition to teach our children otherwise.

5. Some classroom management theories are not appropriate for the type of student I teach. Younger (older, "typical," exceptional) students need more teacher control. Simultaneously, other teachers say, "I should use a less controlling (student-centered) classroom management model because my students are younger (older, typical, exceptional)." Neither age nor exceptionality is the issue. If the classroom management theory is appropriate for one group, it is appropriate for another. Although this may seem to conflict with the previous "aspirin" analogy, it does not. A theory is an umbrella that encompasses a collection of techniques. In the student-focused classroom, interventions are designed with the particular students and specific situations in mind. Although the manner in which the theory is implemented in specific instances may differ, the theoretical base does not.

6. I like the sound of this theory but I do not see how to actually use it. It looks good on paper but may be too idealistic. Teachers often see the merit of a student-centered classroom management theory or model and want to put it into practice but do not see how to bridge the all-important gap between theory and application. Attending workshops or university classes pertaining to classroom management and instruction is an important first step. Exposure to ideas must occur before change can happen. However, an equally important issue surrounds what happens after teachers return to their classrooms. After educators have been exposed to new theories and techniques, do they actually translate them into practice? There is a temptation to try the new techniques learned and, if they do not work the way the teacher thinks they should or do not show "results" in a short time period, discard them as not practical for the real classroom.

Old habits are hard to break. Fortunately, there are several student-centered "packages" of classroom management that provide clear guidelines for implementation and can serve as "training wheels" for the teacher until student-centered classroom management comes naturally. Based on student-focused, intrinsic theories, Albert (1989), Gathercoal (1990), and Dinkmeyer, McKay, and Dinkmeyer (1980) present student-focused models of classroom management.

To illustrate how a student-centered model might look in practice, return to the classroom scenario with Ms. Thompson, Ray, and Bill. Using a teacher-centered classroom management model, Ms. Thompson assigned the predetermined consequence to both boys. However, a more student-centered Ms. Thompson would take a holistic perspective and consider all she knows about both students before she acts. As Ray and Bill "pick on" each other, Ms. Thompson notes, "You two seem to have a problem. In a little while, I would like to discuss what I can do to help you solve it but in the meantime, I want you two to move away from each other." Bill says, "I ain't going anywhere 'cause I wasn't doing anything!" Ray moves a few seats away from Bill, seems to calm down, and is on task the rest of the class period.

Bill, on the other hand, is a much tougher customer to deal with because of the emotion his defiance is likely to evoke. Automatic detention may only serve to make him more angry—not a lasting solution to the problem. He is lashing out at the teacher and, although tempted to respond in a similar manner, Ms. Thompson explains, "Bill, solving this problem is more important than punishing you for your misbehavior. I'd like to help you do that. Fill out this card and we will visit in a few minutes." Bill is given a card with the following four questions on it (Charles, 1992, p. 121):

1. What were you doing when the problem started?
2. Was it against the rules?
3. Can we work things out so it won't happen again?
4. What could you and I do to keep it from happening?

When Ms. Thompson finds a few spare minutes, the answers are used to structure a conversation between her and Bill.

Based on Glasser's intrinsic theory of motivation, the objectives of the conference are three-fold: to print out the connection between Bill's behavior and its results, to obtain a sincere commitment from Bill to do better, and to plan a strategy more likely to be successful for Bill in the future (Charles, 1992). Ms. Thompson also explains to Bill that he is the only one who can truly control his behavior. His behavior is his choice and under his control. In pointing this out to Bill, she is not losing control; she is only acknowledging something he already has. Such acknowledgment will only lead to validation of his self-worth and decrease the likelihood that the misbehavior will re-occur.

Since Roy and Bill control their own behavior but can be influenced by others, their parents may be involved to work as partners with the teacher and their child—but this would be a last resort. This is a very different perspective than the teacher-centered approach of calling the parent and charging them with "fixing" their child. No one can be "fixed" without their cooperation and input.

Summary & Conclusion

If learning is fostered by a student-centered environment, then quality instruction requires the creation of a "learning community" within the classroom. In such a community, students feel psychologically and intellectually safe to explore, to try, to make mistakes, and explore again. Their needs are acknowledged and validated. In order for such an environment to exist, all components of it must be addressed and in place.

As knowledge is dynamic and changing, so is society. If our schools are to be effective in the next century, we must respond to this evolution. "Simple" changes in curriculum and instruction techniques are not enough to create a student-centered environment; classroom management theory and models must also follow suit in order for a truly student-focused learning environment to exist. This is especially important when dealing with young adolescents who are in the midst of myriad developmental changes. As they seek to develop a clear sense of self, they may try on a number of personas. Student-focused classroom environments facilitate the development of a healthy identity and an internalized moral structure.

Both student- and teacher-centered approaches to classroom management can create orderly environments, provide structure, and set limits. Still, no matter how expedient, teacher-centered models do not address students' emotional needs or long-term concerns regarding self-discipline, responsibility, or critical reasoning. They do not touch the students' humanness. Teacher-centered, obedience models of classroom management many appear to allow us the opportunity to cover more material and teach more facts, but at what cost? The irony is that the more control we take the more control we loose. When the focus is on controlling others, there is little freedom left for us. Comprehensive student-focused classroom communities are necessary to develop independent, self-disciplined, life-long learners. Communities such as these only come about when both the instruction and the classroom management center on the students.

References

Aaronsohn, E. (1993, April). *Supporting student-centered teaching: Reconceptualizing the roles or teacher and teacher educator.* Paper presented at the annual meeting on the American Educational Research Association, Atlanta, GA.

Albert, L. (1989). *A teacher's guide to cooperative discipline: How to manage your classroom and promote self-esteem.* Circle Pines, MN:AGS.

Alexander, W. M. (1995). The junior high school: A changing view. *Middle School Journal, 26*(3), 21–24. (Reprinted from *Readings in Curriculum,* pp. 418–425, by G. Hass & K. Wiles, Eds., 1965, Boston: Allyn and Bacon.)

Benshoff, J. M., Poidevant, J. M., & Cashwell, C. S. (1994). School discipline programs: Issues and implications for school counselors. *Elementary School Guidance and Counseling, 17,* 163–169.

Canter, L. (1992). *Assertive discipline: Positive behavior management for today's classroom.* Santa Monica, CA: Lee Canter & Associates.

Charles, C. M. (1992). *Building classroom discipline* (4th ed.). White Plains, NY: Longman.

Dinkmeyer, D., McKay, G. D., & Dinkmeyer, D. (1980). *STET: Systematic training for effective teaching.* Circle Pines, MN: AGS.

Dreikurs, R., Grunwald, B. B., & Pepper, F. C. (1982). *Maintaining sanity in the classroom* (2nd ed.). New York: Harper & Row.

Gathercoal, F. (1990). *Judicious discipline.* Davis, CA: Caddo Gap Press.

Ginott, H. (1972). *Teacher and child.* New York: Avon Books.

Glasser, W. (1986). *Control theory in the classroom.* New York: Harper & Row.

Gordon, T. (1974). *Teacher effectiveness training.* New York: Wyden.

Hill, D. (1990). Order in the classroom. *Teacher, 1*(7), 70–77.

Johnson, D. W., Johnson, R. T., Holuber, E. J., Roy, P. (1988). *Circles of learning: Cooperation in the classroom.* Reston, VA: Association for Supervision and Curriculum Development.

Jones, F. (1987). *Positive classroom discipline.* New York: McGraw-Hill.

Martin, N. K., & Baldwin, B. (1994, January). *Beliefs regarding classroom management style: Differences between novice and experienced teachers.* Paper presented at the annual meeting of the Southwest Educational Research Association, San Antonio, TX.

Mendler, A. N. (1993). Discipline with dignity in the classroom: Seven principles. In F. Schultz (Ed.), *Education 94/95.* (pp. 110–112). Guilford, CT: The Dushkin Publishing Group.

Prawat, R. S. (1992). From individual differences to learning communities: Our changing focus. *Educational Leadership, 49*(7), 9–13.

Santrock, J. W. (1987). *Adolescence* (4th ed.). Dubuque, IA: Wm. C. Brown Publishers.

Wilson, J. H. (1994). An open letter to middle level educators: A parent's concern. *Middle School Journal, 26*(1), 53.

Teaching Students to Regulate Their Own Behavior

> During the 1994–95 school year, 43% of all students with disabilities were served in general education classrooms (18th Annual Report, 1997).

> Children and Adults with Attention Deficit Disorders (CHADD) estimates that there are 3.5 million children with ADHD (CHADD, 1993).

> Of the 5.4 million children nationwide with disabilities, 8.7% are identified as emotionally disturbed/behavior disordered, and 80% of these children are co-diagnosed with ADHD (Mathes & Bender, 1997).

Lewis R. Johnson • Christine F. Johnson

Before general education teachers refer a child to special education services, the teachers must implement program modifications and strategies and document that the modifications were insufficient to remedy the student's problem. For these reasons, general educators and special education teachers/consultants need methods to successfully include students with disabilities in general education programs.

A Question of Generalization

Sometimes, consultants and classroom teachers collaboratively develop prereferral interventions or behavior management plans that require the teacher to monitor, record, and issue contingent reinforcers. This type of behavior management program is time-consuming; and if more than one student in the class is "on a plan," it can be overwhelming.

In 1973 Glynn, Thomas, and Shee described an effective procedure for general education teachers to employ so students can self-monitor and improve their on-task behavior. Although recent research has focused on the use of self-regulation techniques for students with disabilities in special education settings, it is peculiar that the technique is not used more in general education classrooms as prereferral interventions and to facilitate inclusion of students with disabilities.

Self-regulation techniques can be used with students from preschool age through post-secondary age when educators adapt the level of sophistication to the age group. One limitation of self-regulation training conducted by special education teachers in the special education setting is the lack of generalization of the behavior change in the general education setting.

One way to facilitate generalization of skills is to provide the training in the setting in which you want the generalization to occur (Guevremont, Osnes, & Stokes, 1988). In this article we present a description of self-regulation and the specific procedures for teaching students to employ self-regulation of classroom work-study behavior.

Components of Self-Regulation

Self-regulation requires students to stop, think about what they are doing, compare their behavior to a criterion, record the results of their comparison, and receive reinforcement for their behavior if it meets the criterion (Webber, Scheuermann, McCall, & Coleman, 1993). Self-monitoring involves all the steps in self-regulation, except the issuing of reinforcement.

When you begin the program, first teach students to ask the monitoring question aloud. Then, as the program becomes more

> **Self-regulation requires students to stop, think about what they are doing, compare their behavior to a criterion, record the results of their comparison, and receive reinforcement for their behavior if it meets the criterion.**

routine, students ask the monitoring question in a whisper. In the initial stages of self-regulation, use a tone sounded in the classroom at random intervals to cue the students to ask the question. Cued monitoring is much more effective than uncued monitoring. When you must conduct a training session outside the general classroom, the use

From *Teaching Exceptional Children*, March/April 1999, pp. 6-10. © 1999 by The Council for Exceptional Children. Reprinted by permission.

of the same tone aids in maintaining the skills across settings.

The Steps of Self-Regulation

Students use the following sequence of steps to use self-regulation:

1. Self-observation—looking at one's own behavior given a predetermined criterion.
2. Self-assessment—deciding if the behavior has occurred, through some self-questioning activity.
3. Self-recording—recording the decision made during self-assessment on a private recording form.
4. Self-determination of reinforcement—setting a criterion for success, and selecting a reinforcer from a menu of reinforcers.
5. Self-administration of reinforcement—administering a reinforcer to oneself (Glynn et al., 1973).

According to Barkley (1990), 3%–5% of all school-age children may have attention deficit hyperactivity disorder (ADHD).

Target Behavior

Self-regulation is most widely used during independent seatwork; however, you may apply the technique to a variety of classroom activities. Here are kinds of behavior commonly targeted by self-regulation:

- Staying on task.
- Assignment completion (productivity).
- Appropriate classroom behavior (such as staying in one's seat).
- Accuracy of completed work (percent correct).

The student should focus on positive behavior. The choice of a target behavior for self-regulation is important and may be individually selected, depending on student needs.

Initially, you may want to select a single target behavior for the entire class group. Then, after the students learn the technique, you may want to select different kinds of behavior to target to meet the needs of individual students. Although teachers most frequently select on-task behavior, improvement in on-task behavior may not promote improved academic outcomes. Researchers have found that a *combination* of types of target behavior, including both work-study and accuracy of assignment completion, seems to work best (Rooney, Polloway, &

Hallahan, 1985). Young students respond to task completion as a criterion, whereas older students respond best to completion of tasks with an accuracy criteria (Maag, Reid, & DiGanni, 1993).

Procedure

Before you begin a self-regulatory program, collect program data to determine the students' current level of performance regarding the behavior problem. The special education teacher/consultant or a classroom assistant can collect preintervention "on-task" data using an interval observation method on several students over several visits.

For interval observation, the observer records "+" or "–" every 10 seconds to indicate if the student was on/off task during that interval. The observer then divides the number of intervals marked "+" by the total number of intervals in the observation to get a percentage of time on task (see Figure 1). Then the teacher begins the procedure for teaching the students to self-regulate their behavior, as follows:

1. Model the procedure, using a suitable behavior. Model being cued to engage in self-observation/recording by a tone provided by an audiotape (available from ADD Warehouse; see box, "Internet Sites").
2. Students observe you modeling the procedure.
3. The students practice self-observation/recording on a single behavior.

Internet Sites for ADHD

Children and Adults with Attention Deficit Disorders

http://www.chadd.org

Teaching Children with ADHD

http://www.kidsource.com/kidsource/content2/add.html

A.D.D. Warehouse (catalog)

http://www.addwarehouse.com

ADD Treatment Information

http://www.mediconsult.com/add/shareware/decad_brain/cope.html

---

The Five Steps of Self-Regulation

1. Self-observation.
2. Self-assessment.
3. Self-recording.
4. Self-determination of reinforcement.
5. Self-administration of reinforcement.

---

4. Students employ the procedure daily.
5. The students graph their own observation data, in a manner appropriate to the age and ability of students.
6. Introduce self-reinforcement, such as "I did a good job staying on task," to the students. Better grades and teacher praise are effective reinforcers of accurate and honest self-recording.
7. Collect posttraining data over several observation sessions.
8. Suggest that some students self-observe and record a different behavior, based on individual student need.
9. With each student, review the weekly self-recording data. Introduce the concept of self-determination of a goal and self-reinforcement.

To teach students to use the self-regulation procedure, use the following direct instruction approaches—modeling and guided practice.

Format for Training Grade 2 Students: Modeling

1. "Class, I am concerned that when a student correctly responds to a question, I have not been providing praise as regularly as I should have. I need to find a way to improve how I respond to students who answer my questions."
2. *Thinking aloud,* say: "I will use this tape, which makes a sound every so often to remind me to ask myself, 'Did I offer praise for correct student answers?' If I did offer praise since the last tone, I will put a mark in the *yes*

Figure 1. Classroom Observation of "On-Task" Student Behavior

Student	1	2	3	4	5	6	7	8	9	10	11	12	13	14	15	16	17	18	19	20	%

column on my record sheet if I said something like 'thank you' or 'that's correct.' " (See Figure 2 for the recording sheet.)

3. "Class, what am I going to ask myself?" Group response—

4. "Class, if I said something like 'thank you' or 'that's correct' to a student, what will I mark?" Group response—

You should then begin the tape, which has several tones at intervals of 2–4 minutes, and then begin a short group lesson that lends itself to individual student responding. At the sound of each tone, the teacher will ask in a volume so all students can hear, "Did I offer praise?" Each time, record on the chalkboard or on an overhead a mark in the "Yes" or "No" column.

Self-regulation techniques can be used with students from preschool age through postsecondary age. Self-regulation is most widely used during independent seatwork.

After the short lesson is done, "think aloud," making comments about the number of marks in each column and how the students responded to the lesson. This think-aloud action is necessary to demonstrate to the students the relationship between the data collection and an evaluation of the outcome—the lesson.

After you have fully modeled the self-regulation procedure with the "think alouds," begin training the class using the single target behavior, such as on-task behavior.

Format for Training Group 2 Students: Guided Practice

1. Distribute a "Check Yourself" recording form to each student, and make a "Yes/No" box on the chalkboard. Say, "Class, when you hear the tone, ask yourself, 'Am I working?' " Provide examples of what is considered working and not working. This aspect of training is important so students will be able to make a quick decision and record it without asking you about a common task-related behavior. (Figures 3 and 4 show variations on the "Check Yourself" student form.)

2. Begin the tape of the tones and continue talking: "When you hear the tone, ask yourself in your quiet voice, 'Am I working?' Put a check mark in the 'Yes' box or the 'No' box. Are you always going to be working or listening to the lessons? No, sometimes you won't. That's OK. This strategy will help you become a better student. It is not possible to always be working on an assignment."

3. Continue teaching the group lesson started during the modeling phase and the tape of the recorded tones. When the class hears the first tone, the students (with your assistance) ask out loud, "Am I working?" You answer "Yes" and record a check in the "Yes" box on the chalkboard. Each student will record the response on his or her record sheet. The procedure continues with tones at random intervals, which are frequent enough to allow four or five recordings within a 10–15-minute time period.

4. At the conclusion of the lesson, say, "You did a good job asking the 'Am I working?' question and recording your answer. We will practice this again later."

Graphing and Record Keeping

Graphing the self-recording data can be an excellent activity for upper elementary age students to help them keep a long-term record of their performance and begin to set behavior goals. Older students can compute and record the percentage of "Yes" responses. Younger students may need to count total number of checks, "Yes" and "No," and record that total on a graph. Then they will count just the "Yes" checks and record that total on the graph. The goal is to make the distance be-

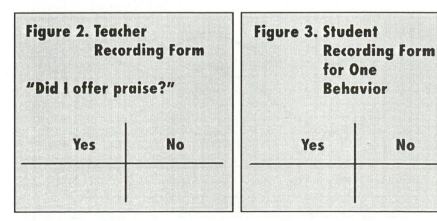

Figure 2. Teacher Recording Form

"Did I offer praise?"

Yes	No

Figure 3. Student Recording Form for One Behavior

Yes	No

Figure 4. Student Recording Form for Several Types of Behavior

	Yes	No
"Am I working?"		
"Did I stay in my seat?"		
"Did I do my work?"		

tween the total number of checks and number of "Yes" checks as small as possible. (See Figure 5 for an example of student data and a sample graph.)

Benefits and Potential

The strengths of the self-regulatory program include the following:

• Reduced teacher time for monitoring and responding to student behavior.
• The ability to vary the target behavior from simple on-task behavior to the complex self-monitoring of strategy usage.

• The ability to individualize target behavior to accommodate a variety of student ability levels.

The teaching of self-regulation has the potential of providing students with a skill that will have an ongoing benefit as students become self-directed, lifelong learners.

References

18th Annual Report affirms CEC's policy on inclusive settings. (1997). *CEC Today, 3*(7), 1.

Barkley, R. A. (1990). *Attention-deficit hyperactivity disorder: A handbook for the diagnosis and treatment.* New York: Guilford.*

> Researchers have found that a *combination* of types of target behavior, including both work-study and accuracy of assignment completion, seems to work best.

Children and Adults with Attention Deficit Disorders. (1993). *CHADD facts 8: The national organization working for children and adults with attention deficit disorders.* Washington, DC: Author.*

Glynn, E. L., Thomas, J. D., & Shee, S. M. (1973). Behavioral self-control of on-task behavior in an elementary classroom. *Journal of Applied Behavior Analysis, 6*(1), 105–113.

Guevremont, D. C., Osnes, P. G., & Stokes, T. P. (1988). The functional role of preschoolers' verbalizations in the generalization of self-instructional training. *Journal of Applied Behavior Analysis, 21*(1), 45–55.

Maag, J. W., Reid, R., & DiGanni, S. A., (1993). Differential effects of self-monitoring attention, accuracy, and productivity. *Journal of Applied Behavior Analysis, 26*(3), 329–344.

Mathes, M. Y., & Bender, W. N. (1997). The effects of self-monitoring on children with attention-deficit/hyperactivity disorder who are receiving pharmacological interventions. *Remedial and Special Education, 18*(2), 121–128.

Rooney, K. J., Polloway, E. A., & Hallahan, D. P. (1985). The use of self-monitoring procedures with low IQ learning disabled students. *Journal of Learning Disabilities, 18,* 384–389.

Webber, J., Scheuermann, B., McCall, C., & Coleman, M. (1993). Research on self-monitoring as a behavior management technique in special education classrooms: A descriptive review. *Remedial and Special Education, 14*(2), 38–56.

BooksNow

To order books marked by an asterisk (*), please call 24 hrs/365 days: 1–800–BOOKS–NOW (266–5766) or (801) 261–1187, or visit them on the Web at http://www.BooksNow.com/TeachingExceptional.htm. Use VISA, M/C, or AMEX or send check or money order + $4.95 S&H ($2.50 each add'l item) to: Books Now, Suite 125, 448 East 6400 South, Salt Lake City, UT 84107.

Lewis R. Johnson *(CEC Chapter #345), Assistant Professor, Department of Special Education;* **Christine E. Johnson,** *Graduate Student, Department of Speech Pathology, Arkansas State University, State University.*

Address correspondence to Lewis R. Johnson, P.O. Box 1450, Arkansas State University, State University, AR 72467 (e-mail: Ljohnson@kiowa.astate.edu).

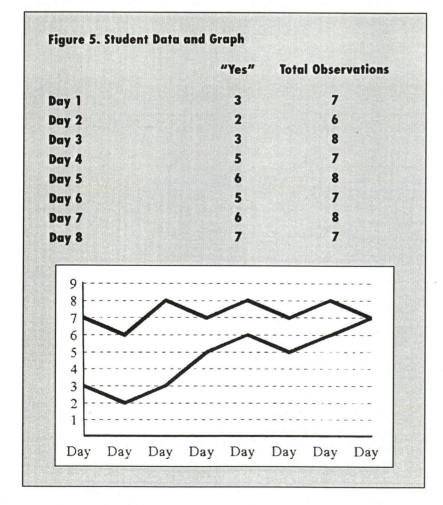

Figure 5. Student Data and Graph

	"Yes"	Total Observations
Day 1	3	7
Day 2	2	6
Day 3	3	8
Day 4	5	7
Day 5	6	8
Day 6	5	7
Day 7	6	8
Day 8	7	7

HOW TO DEFUSE
CONFRONTATIONS

DEFIANCE THREATS CHALLENGES

The T-Shirt attention getter...
Prohibited cookies on the bus...
Profanity in class...
Outright refusal to do classwork...
Chair-throwing...

A comprehensive system of behavior management has three critical components: prevention, defusion, and follow-up.

Geoff Colvin
David Ainge
Ron Nelson

■

Do some of your students engage in confrontational behavior like this? Here's a litany of such behavior: attention-getting, defiance, challenges, disrespect, limit testing, verbal abuse, blatant rule violations, threats, and intimidation. Some students test the patience of teachers who have what they thought was an effective behavior-management system. This article presents teacher-tested ways to *defuse* such behavior and allow the students to learn and participate in positive ways.

Special education teachers have always had the task of managing students who display seriously disturbing behavior. More recently, these teachers are expected to provide support and consultation to general education teachers who need assistance on managing the behavior of all students in inclusive classrooms. Special education teachers can assist other educators in a comprehensive system of behavior management composed of three critical components: prevention, defusion, and follow-up (see box, "Three Approaches to Behavior Management").

We focus here particularly on *defusion,* an approach that is helpful with students who are continually confrontational. Such behavior not only leads to class disruption, but also can readily escalate to more serious behavior—and threats to the safety of both staff and students. Let's look at some examples of confrontational behavior and then explore how we can deal with it.

Three Confrontational Students

• Joe steps onto the school bus holding a monster cookie in his hand. Above his head is a large sign that reads, "No food

on the bus." Joe looks at the driver, takes a huge bite of the cookie, and takes another step on the bus. The bus driver points to the sign and says quite emphatically, "Look, no food on the bus. You'll have to give me that cookie." Joe says equally emphatically, "No," and takes another bite. The driver looks him right in the eye and says, "If you don't give me the cookie, you will not ride the bus." Joe says, "So," takes another bite of the cookie, and begins to move toward his seat. The driver calls transportation to have the student removed from the bus.

• Sarah walks into the classroom wearing a T-shirt displaying a toilet bowl with an arrow coming up out of the bowl and a written statement underneath, "Up your AZ." Some students giggle, and another asks, "Where did you get that?" The teacher comes over and says, "Sarah, that shirt is not acceptable in a public school. You had better go to the restroom and turn it inside out." Sarah looks at the teacher and says, "I'm not gonna do that. My dad gave it to me and you can't make me turn it inside out." The teacher says that if she does not cooperate, she will be sent to the office. Sarah throws her book down and heads to the back of the room.

• Jamie is sitting at his desk, arms folded, shoulders rounded, feet firmly planted on the floor, and staring at the floor with a scowl on his face, while the rest of the class is working on an independent math assignment. The teacher eventually approaches Jamie and prompts him to start on his math. He scowls and says in a harsh tone that he can't do it. So the teacher offers to help him. He says he still can't do it. The teacher provides more detail with the explanation and directs him to make a start. He says he hates math. The teacher tells him that he needs to start or he will have to do his math during the break. He utters a profanity and storms out of the room.

From *Teaching Exceptional Children,* July/August 1997, pp. 47–51. © 1997 by The Council for Exceptional Children. Reprinted by permission.

What Happened?

In each case, the supervising staff person reacts to a problem behavior in a direct manner. There is a high likelihood that the student *expects* a response. In fact, the student not only expects a response, but he or she expects a *particular* response.

For all practical purposes, the staff person is *already set up for confrontation.* In other words, the student displays engaging behavior that is highly likely to elicit a predictable response from staff that includes a clear direction. The student refuses to follow the direction, which engages staff further, leading to ultimatums and additional problem behavior.

Moreover, if the staff person becomes confrontational at this point, there is a strong likelihood that the student will react with more serious behavior. In effect, we can see a pattern—a cycle—of successive interactions beginning with problem behavior leading to more serious behavior, such as throwing a book (Sarah), continuing to disregard requests (Joe), or profanity (Jamie). These vignettes have five common features:

1. The student displays defiant, challenging, or inappropriate behavior.
2. The supervising staff person reacts to the problem behavior and provides a direction in opposition to the student's behavior.
3. The student challenges the direction by not complying and by displaying other inappropriate behavior.
4. The staff person reacts to the non-compliance and presents an ultimatum.
5. The student takes up the challenge of the ultimatum with further defiance and exhibits hostile and explosive behavior.

What Strategies Can Help?

When students exhibit confrontational behavior, you need approaches that are likely to defuse the problem behavior, rather than lead to more serious behavior. Defusing strategies minimize the likelihood that interactions between you and the student will escalate the confrontation. We have found five defusing strategies that work—in order of least intrusive student behavior to more serious confrontational behavior. These strategies range from ignoring the behavior to delaying a response and allowing the student to calm down.

Focus on the Task to Defuse Minor Attention-Getting Behavior

Students often display minor problem behavior to secure attention: talking out in class, moving out of their seats, starting work slowly, and pencil tapping. Once you re-

spond to such behavior, the student may exhibit more attention-getting behavior. The basic approach for managing this level of problem behavior is to use a *continuum* of steps based on the level of attention you provide:

- Attend to the students exhibiting expected behavior, and ignore the students displaying the problem behavior.
- Redirect the student to the task at hand. Do not respond to or draw attention to the problem behavior.
- Present a choice between the expected behavior and a small negative consequence (such as a loss of privilege).

For example, Michael is out of his seat wandering around the room while other students are seated and engaged in a class activity. The teacher moves among the students who are on task, acknowledges their good work and ignores Michael. Michael continues to move around the class. The teacher approaches him and says privately, "Michael, listen, it's math time. Let's go," and points to his seat. Michael still does not return to his seat. The teacher secures his attention and says calmly and firmly, "Michael, you have been asked to sit down and start work or you will have to do the work in recess. You decide." The teacher follows through on whatever Michael chooses to do.

Present Options Privately in the Context of a Rule Violation

Sometimes students will break a rule to challenge you. They know you will react and give a direction. The student will then refuse to follow the direction. In this way, a confrontation scene is established. For example, in the cases of Joe and Sarah, the staff member gave the students a direction that the students refused to follow—the cookie was not turned in to the driver, the T-shirt was not turned inside out. Here are steps to follow in such cases:

- State the rule or expectation.
- Request explicitly for the student to "take care of the problem."
- Present options for the student on how to take care of the problem.

In this way, you lessen the chance of confrontation when you present options and focus [on] how the student might decide to take care of the problem, rather than whether the student follows a specific direction.

For example, the bus driver might have quietly said something like this to Joe: "Look, there is no food on the bus, thank you. You had better take care of that. You can eat it before you get on or leave it here and collect it later." Note the options the bus driver might have provided.

Or, to deal with Sarah's offensive T-shirt, the teacher might take Sarah aside and say, "Sarah, that shirt is not OK in a public school. It has a rude message. You can turn it inside out, get a shirt from the gym, or wear a jacket."

Reduce Agitation in a Demand Situation

Sometimes students are already agitated when they enter a situation. When you or other people place demands on them, their behavior will likely escalate.

---

*F*irst, communicate concern to the student. Then allow the student time and space. Give the student some choices or options.

For example, Jamie's body posture and tone of voice suggest he is upset. When the teacher tries to prompt him to work, even in a very reasonable manner, his behavior escalates to storming out of the room. Here, the teacher might have used agitation-reduction techniques.

Signs of Agitation. Students show agitation by either increasing distracting behavior or decreasing active, engaged behavior (Colvin, 1992). Here are common signs of increases in *distracting behavior:*

- Darting eyes
- Nonconversational language
- Busy hands
- Moving in and out of groups
- Frequent off-task and on-task behavior
- Starting and stopping activities
- Moving around the room

Paradoxically, sometimes agitation doesn't seem to live up to its name. Some students can be agitated and not show it. Watch for the following *decreases in behavior* and a lack of engagement in class activities:

- Staring into space
- Subdued language
- Contained hands
- Lack of interaction and involvement in activities
- Withdrawal from groups and activities
- Lack of responding in general
- Avoidance of eye contact

Techniques for Reducing Agitation. Once you recognize that the student's behavior is agitated, your primary goal is to use strategies to calm the student down and assist him or her to become engaged in the

*T*he most important thing to remember is that your responses can change things.

present classroom activity. Because these strategies are supportive in nature, you need to use them *before* the behavior becomes serious; otherwise, you risk reinforcing the seemingly endless chain of inappropriate behavior. The critical issue is *timing*. Use the following techniques at the *earliest* indications of agitation:

Teacher support: Communicate concern to the student.

Space: Provide the student with an opportunity to have some isolation from the rest of the class.

Choices: Give the student some choices or options.

Preferred activities: Allow the student to engage in a preferred activity for a short period of time to help regain focus.

Teacher proximity: Move near or stand near the student.

Independent activities: Engage the student in independent activities to provide isolation.

Movement activities: Use activities and tasks that require movement, such as errands, cleaning the chalkboard, and distributing papers.

Involvement of the student: Where possible, involve the student in the plan. In this way, there is more chance of ownership and generalization to other settings.

Relaxation activities: Use audiotapes, drawing activities, breathing and relaxation techniques.

Now let's replay Jamie's situation. This time, the teacher determines that Jamie seems to be agitated—he shows a *decrease* in behavior. The teacher says, as privately as possible, "Jamie, it's time for math. Are you doing OK? Do you need some time before you start?" In this way, the teacher is recognizing the agitation, communicating concern to Jamie, and giving him time to regain his focus.

Preteach and Present Choices to Establish Limits and Defuse Noncompliance

Use this strategy to establish limits and to defuse sustained noncompliance. Essentially, the student is refusing to follow the teacher's directions.

For example, suppose that Scott has been off task and distracting other students for several minutes. The teacher has tried to provide assistance, redirect him, and give a formal direction to begin work. Scott refuses to cooperate. At this point, the teacher wants to communicate to him that "enough is enough," and to establish some classroom

limits. When the teacher tries to establish limits, however, Scott may become more hostile and aggressive.

The following steps in the preteaching strategy can establish limits without escalating the behavior. Role-playing these steps can help students learn how to use self-control.

Preteach the procedures: Carefully rehearse the procedures with the student, give explanations, model the steps, and describe the consequences. Do preteaching at a neutral time when the student is relatively calm and cooperative.

Deliver the information to the students without being confrontational:

1. Present the expected behavior and the negative consequence as a decision; place responsibility on the student.
2. Allow a few seconds for the student to decide. This small amount of time helps the student calm down, enables face saving in front of peers, enables you to pull away from the conflict, and leaves the student with the decision.
3. Withdraw from the student and attend to other students. You thus help the student focus on the decision, not attend to you.

Follow through: If the student chooses the expected behavior, briefly acknowledge the choice and continue with the lesson or activity. If the student has not chosen the expected behavior, deliver the negative consequence. Debrief with the student and problem solve.

For example, if Sarah refused to take care of the T-shirt problem, the teacher could say, "Sarah, you have been asked to take care of the shirt (expected behavior), or I will have to make an office referral (negative consequence). You have a few seconds to decide." The teacher moves away from Sarah and addresses some other students or tasks. The teacher follows through on the choice made by the student.

Disengage and Delay Responding in the Presence of Serious Threatening Behavior

Students may escalate to a point of serious confrontational behavior involving threats or intimidation. For example, the teacher may

*D*efusing strategies minimizes the likelihood that interactions between you and the student will escalate the confrontation.

Three Approaches to Behavior Management

Prevention. The teacher places a strong focus on teaching desirable behavior and orchestrating effective learning activities. These proactive strategies are designed to establish a positive classroom structure and climate for students to engage in productive, prosocial behavior.

Defusion. Teachers use strategies designed to address problem behavior after the behavior has commenced. The goal here is to arrest the behavior before it escalates to more serious behavior and to assist the student to resume class activities in an appropriate manner.

Follow-up. A teacher or an administrator may provide consequences for the problem behavior and endeavors to assist the student to terminate the problem behavior and to engage in appropriate behavior in the future.

The goal of these approaches is to provide information to the student on the limits of behavior and to use problem-solving strategies to enable the student to exhibit alternative appropriate behavior in subsequent events (Biggs & Moore, 1993; Colvin & Lazar, 1997; Kameenui & Darch, 1995; Myers & Myers, 1993; Sprick, Sprick & Garrison, 1993; Sugai & Tindal, 1993; Walker, Colvin, & Ramsey, 1995).

have presented options, given the student time, and provided a consequence: "Eric, you are asked to start work or you will have to stay after school. You have a few seconds to decide." Eric walks over to the teacher and says, "I know where you live."

Suppose a more serious situation occurs, such as this real incident: An administrator told a student to go to the in-school suspension area or he would call his probation officer. The student picked up a cup of coffee from the secretary's desk, moved to the administrator, held the coffee in his face, and said, "You call my P.O. and I will throw this in your f_____ face."

In each of these cases, there is a direct threat to a staff member and the danger that the student's behavior may escalate. Whether the student's behavior becomes more serious *depends on the staff member's initial response to the threat*. The primary intent of this strategy is to avoid responding directly to the student's behavior and to disengage momentarily and then to redirect the student.

We are *not* suggesting that this strategy is all you need to do. Rather, the primary purpose of this strategy is to defuse a crisis situation. Once the crisis has been avoided, you should follow up and address the previous threatening behavior so that such behavior does not arise again. Here are steps to use in disengaging and delaying:

Break the cycle of successive interactions by delaying responding: This pattern consists of successive hostile or inflammatory interactions between you and the student—the student challenges you to respond. The first step is to *delay responding,* because the student is expecting an immediate response. To delay responding, very briefly look at the student, look at the floor, look detached, and pause.

Prevent explosive behavior by making a disengaging response: Do not leave the student waiting too long; otherwise, an "extinction burst" may occur. That is, if events do not go the way the student expects them to, he or she may exhibit explosive behavior, such as throwing a chair at the wall (or staff, or another student), or throwing the coffee cup. To prevent this burst, disengage swiftly and engage in something neutral or unrelated (Lerman & Iwata, 1995). For example, say to the student, "Just a minute," and move and pick up something on your desk.

Return to the student, redirect, and withdraw: If the student has not exhibited further problem behavior and is waiting, simply return to the student and present the original choice.

For example, approach the student and say, "You still have a moment or two to decide what you wish to do," and withdraw. If the student engages in more serious behavior, implement emergency procedures and policies established by the school or district.

Follow through: If the student chooses the expected behavior, acknowledge the choice briefly and debrief later. If the student does not choose the expected behavior, deliver consequences and debrief later.

> *Sometimes students will break a rule to challenge you; others are already agitated when you try to correct them.*

Debrief: The debriefing activity is designed to help the student problem solve by reviewing the incident and events leading up to the incident, identifying the triggers, and examining alternatives. The debriefing finishes with a focus or agreement on what the student will try to do next time that would be an appropriate response to the situation (Sugai & Colvin, in press).

Now Let's Debrief

How many Sarahs and Jamies and Erics do you know? Are you tired of throwing up your hands and sending these students to the office, or facing hostility and muttered challenges—or even threats to your own safety? Are you equally concerned that these students (and other students in your class) may be missing out on learning opportunities?

The most important thing to remember is that *your responses can change things.* Go back to the section on "Disengage and Delay Responding" and memorize it. Then follow the steps in "Preteaching," and you are on your way to helping students control their own behavior and create a better environment for learning.

References

Biggs, J. B., & Moore, P. J. (1993). *The process of learning.* New York: Prentice Hall.

Colvin, G. (1992). *Video program: Managing acting-out behavior.* Eugene, OR: Behavior Associates.

Colvin, G., & Lazar, M. (1997). *The effective elementary classroom: Managing for success.* Longmont, CO: Sopris West.

Kameenui, E. J., & Darch, C. B. (1995). *Instructional classroom management: A proactive approach to behavior management.* White Plains, NY: Longman.

Lerman, D., & Iwata, B. (1995). Prevalence of the extinction burst and its attenuation during treatment. *Journal of Applied Behavior Analysis, 28,* 93–94.

Myers, C. B., & Myers, L. K. (1993). *An introduction to teaching and schools.* Fort Worth, TX: Rinehart and Winston.

Sprick, R., Sprick, M., & Garrison, M. (1993). *Interventions: Collaborative planning for students at risk.* Longmont, CO: Sopris West.

Sugai, G., & Colvin, G. (in press). Debriefing: A proactive addition to negative consequences for problem behavior. *Education and Treatment of Children.*

Sugai, G., & Tindal, G. (1993). *Effective school consultation: An interactive approach.* Pacific Grove, CA: Brooks/Cole.

Walker, H., Colvin, G., & Ramsey, E. (1995). *Antisocial behavior in school: Strategies and best practices.* Pacific Grove, CA: Brooks/Cole.

Geoff Colvin *(Oregon Federation), Research Associate, Special Education and Community Resources, University of Oregon, Eugene.* **David Ainge,** *Senior Lecturer, Special Education Department, James Cook University, Queensland, Australia.* **Ron Nelson** *(CEC Chapter #374), Associate Professor, Applied Psychology Department, Eastern Washington University, Spokane.*

Address correspondence to Geoff Colvin, Special Education and Community Resources, University of Oregon, Eugene, OR 97405 (e-mail: geoff_colvin@ccmail.uoregon.edu).

Salinas, California:
Peace Breaks Out

Teaching K–8 pays a visit to a K–6 school, where every day is a good day to discourage violence

IAN ELLIOT

We were still a block away from the Jesse G. Sanchez School in Salinas, California, when we got our first taste of the PeaceBuilders™ program in action. A sharp-eyed member of the *Teaching K–8* team, drawing on her many years of experience as a classroom teacher, spotted it right away.

"See those boys over there?" she said, indicating several groups of students on their way to school. "They're not grabbing bookbags or running into each other. They're just walking peacefully."

Nothing earthshaking about that, of course; nevertheless, it's typical of what's been going on in Salinas for the past two years. No, Salinas is not one big, ever-so-peaceful community, but it's getting there, thanks to PeaceBuilders.

Background. *Teaching K–8* was in Salinas recently to find out more about PeaceBuilders and how it works in a K–6 school. Our first stop was the central office of the Alisal Union School District, where we spoke with Roberta Emmerson, the district's curriculum director. Since Roberta plays a leading role in implementing the program in the district's seven elementary schools (with a total of over 6,000 students), she was able to provide us with some much-needed background.

Sanchez School, she told us, is located in a low socio-economic area. The student body is about 96 percent Spanish-speaking with about 80 percent of the students classified as "limited English-speaking."

This means they speak almost no English when they enter school.

To make matters even more challenging for Sanchez educators, many of the students are chil-

CLAY PETERSON

*A **large** billboard (above) in front of the school has a message in English and Spanish. Left above: These buttons are worn by many faculty members.*

dren of migrant workers. The youngsters leave town (and school) with their families when crops need to be harvested elsewhere, and are gone for many weeks at a time.

It's a serious problem if ever there was one, but it's not the school district's *only* serious problem. There's also the problem of violence around the schools.

From the February 1998 issue of *Teaching K-8* magazine, pp. 36-40. © 1998 by Early Years, Inc., Norwalk, CT 06854. Reprinted by permission.

Want to Learn More?

For more information about the Peace-Builders program, contact Heartsprings, Inc., P.O. Box 12158, Tucson, AZ 85732; 520–322–9977; fax, 520–322–9983; e-mail, mik@heart-springs.org

"In this area of Salinas," Roberta said, "we've had a lot of problems with rival gangs—the North gangs and the South gangs—who wear clothing and certain colors that identify them. We've had a lot of shootings and a lot of school violence.

"The community knew it had to do something about the problem and so it worked hard to clean up a dangerous part of town, and to get neighbors to know each other and combat violence.

"PeaceBuilders got the schools involved. We recognized that we had to intervene early. It's too late to wait until middle school and junior high, and so PeaceBuilders was put into effect in all seven elementary schools during the 1995–96 school year."

Successful? No doubt about it. On the community level, negative behavior (including violence) is down significantly all across the board. Other communities plagued by the same problem now regard Salinas and Peace-Builders as helpful models. And in 1996, President Clinton visited Salinas to praise the community's efforts of "fighting crime and rescuing children."

PeaceBuilders has been no less successful in the district's elementary schools. A survey taken at the end of the program's first year showed the following reductions in negative behavior: disciplinary actions by 49%; serious violence episodes by 59%; tardiness by 20%; absences by 31%; vandalism incidents by 61%; and vandalism costs by 61%.

Getting started. The PeaceBuilders program was created by Dr. Dennis Embry of Tucson, Arizona, who played a major role in getting the Salinas program off the ground by conducting inservice sessions for all teachers and non-teaching staff in the district.

Four basic principles are at the heart of the program: 1) Praise people; 2) Give up putdowns; 3) Notice hurts and right wrongs; and 4) Seek wise people.

"They're very simple principles," Roberta pointed out. "The program is not so much a curriculum as a way of life. If it's going to be successful in the schools—or anywhere, for that matter—it has to be modeled by adults. It's not going to work in the classroom if the teacher doesn't buy into it. Actually, most of our teachers have been really comfortable with it."

Judging from the decor in all of the classrooms at Sanchez school, "comfortable" may be the understatement of the year. PeaceBuilders posters in English and in Spanish, were on every classroom

Nora Bustos, who teaches grades 3 and 4, English only, goes over a PeaceBuilders book with Principal Ruben Pulido.

wall—and that's just the start of it. Here are a few more reminders that PeaceBuilders is alive and well at Sanchez:

- Teaching a peace pledge in sign language.
- PeaceBuilders boards, where children can write peace notes to one another.
- PeaceBuilders buttons and T-shirts.
- Monday morning assemblies, where the school acknowledges PeaceBuilders of the Week in front of the student body. Example: A student on his way to school noticed that a driver was pushing his car at a busy intersection. The boy put his books down on the corner and helped push the car out of the intersection. (Salinas

Pauline Torres' third and fourth grade classroom is bilingual – and shows it in the books and posters on display.

No matter how you look at it – front or back – this is definitely a PeaceBuilders tee-shirt.

BARBARA MAZZUCA MAHAFFEY, *6th grade:* "I integrate PeaceBuilders all day long, from the time I come in until the time I leave. I use it in writer's workshop. I tell students to go home and write a two-page essay on 'How Were You a PeaceBuilders today?' I use it in physical education, too. There may be a conflict when we go outside and the kids have to right some wrongs.

"We're always praising. I try to be a role model with other teachers in front of my students. I've noticed a big plus. I have minor discipline problems, like talking in class, but I don't have major ones. I've never sent a child to the office. If we have a problem, we settle it right there, not at the end of the day."

Community program. What with all the emphasis on PeaceBuilders in the classroom, it's easy to forget that this is a community program, not just a school program. In addition to the Alisal Union School District, Salinas' business community, youth agencies, churches, law enforcement agencies, doctors, health care providers, libraries, service clubs and parents are all active, enthusiastic supporters of the program.

Principal Ruben Pulido gave *Teaching K–8* an indication of just how enthusiastic the community can be when it comes to supporting PeaceBuilders.

"Our kickoff for PeaceBuilders the last two years has been a march that promoted non-violence," he said. "We had a host of community people coming out to join us. They were so enthusiastic, because we were marching to promote safety and security.

"As we were walking around the community, parents and others were coming out of their homes to join us—not just the families of migrant workers, but second and third generation families, too. We started out with a student body of about 960 and came back to school with at least 1,300 participants."

Feeling safer. Assistant Principal Donna Kiernan was equally enthusiastic about the community's activism. "I'm amazed at the community's support

Successful Model

According to Assistant Principal Donna Kiernan, the J. M. Smuckers Company in Salinas has been a successful model for the entire community.

"They've joined the school as PeaceBuilders to enhance the education of children and the self-esteem of their workers," she said.

"They've held reading and writing contests (for which they gave students gift certificates and book bags), supported our choir and soccer teams, sent readers once a month to classrooms, donated turkeys to our families at Christmas and provided awards for the Students of the Month."

police officers also recognize the program by issuing citations when they see students doing something helpful; the citations can be exchanged for a free video at the video store.)

Two views. How do classroom teachers view the PeaceBuilders program? Here's what two of them have to say.

MOREY FUGATE, *1st and 2nd grades:* "I think PeaceBuilders is a way of life, something that we instill in children when they're young. We give them skills they'll carry with them for the rest of their lives. This carries over to the work they're doing. There's definitely an increase in academic skills."

Sanchez Principal *Ruben Pulido and Assistant Principal Donna Kiernan.*

Reciting the PeaceBuilders pledge *is a daily ritual for these primary graders.*

The PeaceBuilders *pledge adorns a classroom wall.*

A patch *for a quilt links "forever" Jesse G. Sanchez School and the PeaceBuilders program.*

Colorful skirts aswirl, *Sanchez girls rehearse a dance for cinco de mayo, a Mexican holiday. The girls are taught by Dana Mills-Helman,*

About Jesse G. Sanchez School

No. of students: Approx. 855 students without children of migrant workers; approx. 940 with these children.

No. of teachers: 31, plus resource teachers.

No. of classrooms: 31 (4 or 5 per grade level); 1 multi-age classroom and. many combination classrooms.

Class size: Aprox. 30 students per classroom, except for 1st grade, which has approx. 20 students per classroom.

Types of classroom (based on English proficiency): Spanish, pre-transitional, transitional, post-transitional, English only.

School organization: Divided into 3 mini-schools, primarily to make school more approachable for parents.

After-school programs: Title V Extended Day, coordinated by Devorah Duncan. The Title V collaborative, the largest after-school program, has been named an exemplary program by the State of California.

Pauline Torres *leads her first graders in reciting the PeaceBuilders pledge.*

Children study *plant growth and native plants in this greenhouse.*

Students came up *with a wide variety of colors and designs for patches for a PeaceBuilders quilt.*

Jesse G. Sanchez School *is located in a spacious park-like setting. with plenty of room for sports or just running around.*

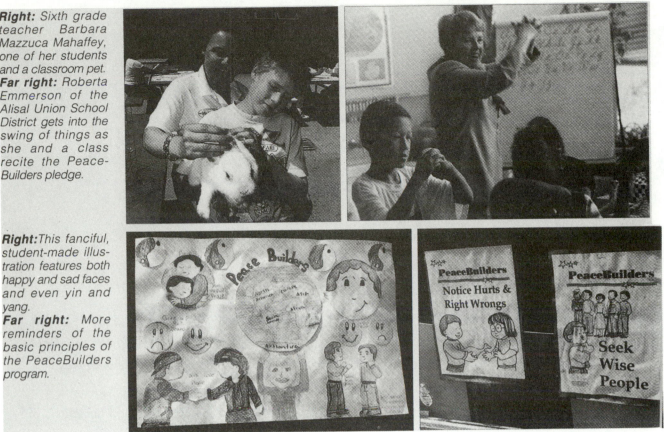

Right: Sixth grade teacher Barbara Mazzuca Mahaffey, one of her students and a classroom pet.
Far right: Roberta Emmerson of the Alisal Union School District gets into the swing of things as she and a class recite the Peace-Builders pledge.

Right: This fanciful, student-made illustration features both happy and sad faces and even yin and yang.
Far right: More reminders of the basic principles of the PeaceBuilders program.

and at how people want to get together to help out.

"It doesn't matter what position a person holds. We've had the Mayor, a Councilman and a Congressman here. Salinas knows there's a problem and is doing something about it, but there's still a lot of work to be done.

"I think that basically, the children feel safer. They feel that when they come to school, they're secure. We're certainly not having the problems at school we used to have. It's been a great success because of teamwork and collaboration."

In the future. What next in the Alisal Union School District? Well, as you read this, there's an ongoing effort to provide more in-depth training of faculty and staff, along with an effort to involve more people in the home environments by bringing them into the schools. The City of Salinas is in high gear, too, and is implementing the Peace-Builders program in the city's middle schools.

There will certainly be more ahead. A lot more. Sanchez and the other district schools have helped cut violence in half in a little over two years—but that's just the beginning. Recently, the school held another march and had a turnout of about 1,200. With those kind of numbers, it's obvious that someone must be doing something right.

Unit Selections

Key Points to Consider

❖ What are some important principles for assessing young children? How is the purpose of the assessment related to these principles?

❖ How can assessment be integrated with instruction? Does this change the traditional way teachers assess students?

❖ What are some examples of alternative assessment? What are the strengths and limitations of these assessments?

❖ Many educators believe that schools should identify the brightest, most capable students. What are the assessment implications of this philosophy? How would low-achieving students be affected?

❖ What principles of assessment should teachers adopt for their own classroom testing? Is it necessary or feasible to develop a table of specifications for each test? How do we know if the tests that teachers make are reliable and if valid inferences are drawn from the results?

❖ How can teachers grade thinking skills such as analysis, application, and reasoning? How should objectives for student learning and grading be integrated? What are some grading practices to avoid? Why?

 **Links** **www.dushkin.com/online/**

These sites are annotated on pages 4 and 5.

In which reading group does Jon belong? How do I construct tests? How do I know when my students have mastered the course objectives? How can I explain test results to Mary's parents? Teachers answer these questions, and many more, by applying principles of assessment. Assessment refers to procedures for measuring and recording student performance and constructing grades that communicate to other levels of proficiency or relative standing. Assessment principles constitute a set of concepts that are integral to the teaching-learning process. Indeed, a significant amount of teacher time is spent in assessment activities, and with more accountability has come a greater emphasis on assessment.

Assessment provides a foundation for making sound evaluative judgments about students' learning and achievement. Teachers need to use fair and unbiased criteria in order to assess student learning objectively and accurately and to make appropriate decisions about student placement. For example, in assigning Jon to a reading group, the teacher will use his test scores as an indication of his skill level. Are the inferences from the test results valid for the school's reading program? Are his test scores consistent over several months or years? Are they

consistent with his performance in class? The teacher should ask and then answer these questions so that he or she can make intelligent decisions about Jon. On the other hand, will knowledge of the test scores affect the teacher's perception of classroom performance and create a self-fulfilling prophecy? Teachers also evaluate students in order to assign grades, and the challenge is to balance "objective" test scores with more subjective, informally gathered information. Both kinds of evaluative information are necessary, but both can be inaccurate and are frequently misused.

The first article in this unit discusses standardized aptitude and achievement tests. Then, Grant Wiggins discusses performance-based, "authentic" assessment. This form of assessment has great potential to integrate measurement procedures with instructional methods more effectively and to focus student learning on the application of thinking and problem-solving skills in real-life contexts. A related form of assessment, using portfolios, is described in "Lessons Learned about Student Portfolios."

In the last article, Gregory Cizek examines grading practices and makes suggestions for how to assign grades so that the results provide accurate and helpful information as well as motivate students.

Why Standardized Tests Don't Measure Educational Quality

Educators are experiencing almost relentless pressure to show their effectiveness. Unfortunately, the chief indicator by which most communities judge a school staff's success is student performance on standardized achievement tests.

W. James Popham

These days, if a school's standardized test scores are high, people think the school's staff is effective. If a school's standardized test scores are low, they see the school's staff as ineffective. In either case, because educational quality is being measured by the wrong yardstick, those evaluations are apt to be in error.

One of the chief reasons that students' standardized test scores continue to be the most important factor in evaluating a school is deceptively simple. Most educators do not really understand why a standardized test provides a misleading estimate of a school staff's effectiveness. They should.

What's in a Name?

A standardized test is any examination that's administered and scored in a predetermined, standard manner. There are two major kinds of standardized tests: aptitude tests and achievement tests.

Standardized *aptitude* tests predict how well students are likely to perform in some subsequent educational setting. The most common examples are the SAT-I and the ACT both of which attempt to forecast how well high school students will perform in college.

But standardized *achievement*-test scores are what citizens and school board members rely on when they evaluate a school's effectiveness. Nationally, five such tests are in use: California Achievement Tests, Comprehensive Tests of Basic Skills, Iowa Tests of Basic Skills, Metropolitan Achievement Tests, and Stanford Achievement Tests.

A Standardized Test's Assessment Mission

The folks who create standardized achievement tests are terrifically talented. What they are trying to do is to create assessment tools that permit someone to make a valid inference about the knowledge and/or skills that a given student possesses in a particular content area. More precisely, that inference is to be norm-referenced so that a student's relative knowledge and/or skills can be compared with those possessed by a national sample of students of the same age or grade level.

Such relative inferences about a student's status with respect to the mastery of knowledge and/or skills in a particular subject area can be quite informative to parents and educators. For example, think about the parents who discover that their 4th grade child is performing really well in language arts (94th percentile) and mathematics (89th percentile), but rather poorly in science (39th percentile) and social studies (26th percentile). Such information, because it illuminates a child's strengths and weak-

From *Educational Leadership*, March 1999, pp. 8-15. © 1999 by the Association for Supervision and Curriculum Development. All rights reserved. Reprinted by permission.

nesses, can be helpful not only in dealing with their child's teacher, but also in determining at-home assistance. Similarly, if teachers know how their students compare with other students nationwide, they can use this information to devise appropriate classroom instruction.

But there's an enormous amount of knowledge and/or skills that children at any grade level are likely to know. The substantial size of the content domain that a standardized achievement test is supposed to represent poses genuine difficulties for the developers of such tests. If a test actually covered all the knowledge and skills in the domain, it would be far too long.

So standardized achievement tests often need to accomplish their measurement mission with a much smaller collection of test items than might otherwise be employed if testing time were not an issue. The way out of this assessment bind is for standardized achievement tests to sample the knowledge and/or skills in the content domain. Frequently, such tests try to do their assessment job with only 40 to 50 items in a subject field—sometimes fewer.

Accurate Differentiation As a Deity

The task for those developing standardized achievement tests is to create an assessment instrument that, with a handful of items, yields valid norm-referenced interpretations of a student's status regarding a substantial chunk of content. Items that do the best job of discriminating among students are those answered correctly by roughly half the students. Developers avoid items that are answered correctly by too many or by too few students.

As a consequence of carefully sampling content and concentrating on items that discriminate optimally among students, these test creators have produced assessment tools that do a great job of providing relative comparisons of a student's content mastery with that of students nation-wide. Assuming that the national norm group is genuinely representative of the nation at large, then educators and parents can make useful inferences about students.

One of the most useful of those inferences typically deals with students' relative strengths and weaknesses across subject areas, such as when parents find that their daughter sparkles in mathematics but sinks in science. It's also possible to identify students' relative strengths and weaknesses within a given subject area if there are enough test items to do so. For instance, if a 45-item standardized test in mathematics allocates 15 items to basic computation, 15 items to geometry, and 15 items to algebra, it might be possible to get a rough idea of a student's relative strengths and weaknesses in those three realms of mathematics. More often than not, however, these tests contain too few items to allow meaningful within-subject comparisons of students' strengths and weaknesses.

A second kind of useful inference that can be based on standardized achievement tests involves a student's growth over time in different subject areas. For example, let's say that a child is given a standardized achievement test every third year. We see that the child's percentile performances in most subjects are relatively similar at each testing, but that the child's percentiles in mathematics appear to drop dramatically at each subsequent testing. That's useful information.

Unfortunately, both parents and educators often ascribe far too much precision and accuracy to students' scores on standardized achievement tests. Several factors might cause scores to flop about. Merely because these test scores are reported in numbers (sometimes even with decimals!) should not incline anyone to attribute unwarranted precision to them. Standardized achievement test scores should be regarded as rough approximations of a student's status with respect to the content domain represented by the test.

> Parents and educators often ascribe far too much precision and accuracy to students' scores on standardized achievement tests.

To sum up, standardized achievement tests do a wonderful job of supplying the evidence needed to make norm-referenced interpretations of students' knowledge and/or skills in relationship to those of students nationally. The educational usefulness of those interpretations is considerable. Given the size of the content domains to be represented and the limited number of items that the test developers have at their disposal, standardized achievement tests are really quite remarkable. They do what they are supposed to do.

But standardized achievement tests should not be used to evaluate the quality of education. That's not what they are supposed to do.

Measuring Temperature with a Tablespoon

For several important reasons, standardized achievement tests should not be used to judge the quality of education. The overarching reason that students' scores on these tests do not provide an accurate index of educational effectiveness is that any inference about educational quality made on the basis of students' standardized achievement test performances is apt to be invalid.

Employing standardized achievement tests to ascertain educational quality is like measuring temperature with a tablespoon. Tablespoons have a different measurement mission than indicating how hot or cold something is. Standardized achievement tests have a different measurement mission than indicating how good or bad a school is. Standardized achievement tests should be used to make the comparative interpretations that they were intended to provide. They should not be used to judge educational quality. Let's look at three significant reasons that it is thoroughly invalid to base inferences about the caliber of education on standardized achievement test scores.

Testing-Teaching Mismatches

The companies that create and sell standardized achievement tests are all owned by large corporations. Like all for-profit businesses, these corporations attempt to produce revenue for their shareholders.

Recognizing the substantial pressure to sell standardized achievement tests, those who market such tests encounter a difficult dilemma that arises from the considerable curricular diversity in the United States. Because different states often choose somewhat different educational objectives (or, to be fashionable, different content standards), the need exists to build standardized achievement tests that are properly aligned with educators' meaningfully different curricular preferences. The problem becomes even more exacerbated in states where different counties or school districts can exercise more localized curricular decision making.

At a very general level, the goals that educators pursue in different settings are reasonably similar. For instance, you can be sure that all schools will give attention to language arts, mathematics, and so on. But that's at a general level. At the level where it really makes a difference to instruction—in the classroom—there are significant differences in the educational objectives being sought. And that presents a problem to those who must sell standardized achievement tests.

In view of the nation's substantial curricular diversity, test developers are obliged to create a series of one-size-fits-all assessments. But, as most of us know from attempting to wear one-size-fits-all garments, sometimes one size really can't fit all.

The designers of these tests do the best job they can in selecting test items that are likely to measure all of a content area's knowledge and skills that the nation's educators regard as important. But the test developers can't really pull it off. Thus, standardized achievement tests will always contain many items that are not

aligned with what's emphasized instructionally in a particular setting.

To illustrate the seriousness of the mismatch that can occur between what's taught locally and what's tested through standardized achievement tests, educators ought to know about an important study at Michigan State University reported in 1983 by Freeman and his colleagues. These researchers selected five nationally standardized achievement tests in mathematics and studied their content for grades 4–6. Then, operating on the very reasonable assumption that what goes on instructionally in classrooms is often influenced by what's contained in the textbooks that children use, they also studied four widely used textbooks for grades 4-6.

Employing rigorous review procedures, the researchers identified the items in the standardized achievement test that had not received meaningful instructional attention in the textbooks. They concluded that between 50 and 80 percent of what was measured on the tests was not suitably addressed in the textbooks. As the Michigan State researchers put it, "The proportion of topics presented on a standardized test that received more than cursory treatment in each textbook was never higher than 50 percent" (p. 509).

Well, if the content of standardized tests is not satisfactorily addressed in widely used textbooks, isn't it likely that in a particular educational setting, topics will be covered on the test that aren't addressed instructionally in that setting? Unfortunately, because most educators are not genuinely familiar with the ingredients of standardized achievement tests, they often assume that if a standardized achievement test asserts that it is assessing "children's reading comprehension capabilities," then it's likely that the test meshes with the way reading is being taught locally. More often than not, the assumed match between what's tested and what's taught is not warranted.

If you spend much time with the descriptive materials presented in the manuals accompanying standardized achievement tests, you'll find that the descriptors for what's tested are often fairly general. Those descriptors need to be general to make the tests acceptable to a nation of educators whose curricular preferences vary. But such general descriptions of what's tested often permit assumptions of teaching-testing alignments that are way off the mark. And such mismatches, recognized or not, will often lead to spurious conclusions about the effectiveness of education in a given setting if students' scores on standardized achievement tests are used as the indicator of educational effectiveness. And that's the first reason that standardized achievement tests should not be used to determine the effectiveness of a state, a district, a school, or a teacher. There's almost certain to be a significant mismatch between what's taught and what's tested.

A Psychometric Tendency to Eliminate Important Test Items

A second reason that standardized achievement tests should not be used to evaluate educational quality arises directly from the requirement that these tests permit meaningful comparisons among students from only a small collection of items.

A test item that does the best job in spreading out students' total-test scores is a test item that's answered correctly by about half the students. Items that are answered correctly by 40 to 60 percent of the students do a solid job in spreading out the total scores of test-takers.

Items that are answered correctly by very large numbers of students, in contrast, do not make a suitable contribution to spreading out students' test scores. A test item answered correctly by 90 percent of the test-takers is, from the perspective of a test's efficiency in providing comparative interpretations, being answered correctly by too many students.

Test items answered correctly by 80 percent or more of the test takers, therefore, usually don't make it past the final cut when a standardized

FIGURE 1

A 3rd grade standardized achievement test item in mathematics

Sally had 14 pears. Then she gave away 6. Which of the number sentences below can you use to find out how many pears Sally has left?

A. $14 + 6 = \_$

B. $6 + 14 = \_$

C. $\_ - 6 = 14$

D. $14 - 6 = \_$

achievement test is first developed, and such items will most likely be jettisoned when the test is revised. As a result, the vast majority of the items on standardized achievement tests are "middle difficulty" items.

As a consequence of the quest for score variance in a standardized achievement test, items on which students perform well are often excluded. However, items on which students perform well often cover the content that, because of its importance, teachers stress. Thus, the better the job that teachers do in teaching important knowledge and/or skills, the less likely it is that there will be items on a standardized achievement test measuring such knowledge and/or skills. To evaluate teachers' instructional effectiveness by using assessment tools that deliberately avoid important content is fundamentally foolish.

Confounded Causation

The third reason that students' performances on these tests should not be used to evaluate educational quality is the most compelling. Because student performances on standardized achievement tests are heavily influenced by three causative factors, only one of which is linked to instructional quality, asserting that low or high test scores are caused by the quality of instruction is illogical.

> The better the job that teachers do in teaching important knowledge and/or skills, the less likely it is that there will be items on a standardized achievement test measuring such knowledge and/or skills.

FIGURE 2

A 6th grade standardized achievement test item in social studies

If someone really wants to conserve resources, one good way to do so is to:

A. leave lights on even if they are not needed.

B. wash small loads instead of large loads in a clothes-washing machine.

C. write on both sides of a piece of paper.

D. place used newspapers in the garbage.

To understand this confounded-causation problem clearly, let's look at the kinds of test items that appear on standardized achievement tests. Remember, students' test scores are based on how well students do on the test's items. To get a really solid idea of what's in standardized tests, you need to grub around with the items themselves.

The three illustrative items presented here are mildly massaged versions of actual test items in current standardized achievement tests. I've modified the items' content slightly, without altering the essence of what the items are trying to measure.

The problem of confounded causation involves three factors that contribute to students' scores on standardized achievement tests: (1) what's taught in school, (2) a student's native intellectual ability, and (3) a student's out-of-school learning.

What's taught in school. Some of the items in standardized achievement tests measure the knowledge or skills that students learn in school. In certain subject areas, such as mathematics, children learn in school most of what they know about a subject. Few parents spend much time teaching their children about the intricacies of algebra or how to prove a theorem.

So, if you look over the items in any standardized achievement test, you'll find a fair number similar to the mathematics item presented in Figure 1, which is a mildly modified version of an item appearing in a standardized achievement test intended for 3rd grade children.

This mathematics item would help teachers arrive at a valid inference about 3rd graders' abilities to choose number sentences that coincide with verbal representations of subtraction problems. Or, along with other similar items dealing with addition, multiplication, and division, this item would contribute to a valid inference about a student's ability to choose appropriate number sentences for a variety of basic computation problems presented in verbal form.

If the items in standardized achievement tests measured only what actually had been taught in school, I wouldn't be so negative about using these tests to determine educational quality. As you'll soon see, however, other kinds of items are hiding in standardized achievement tests.

A student's native intellectual ability. I wish I believed that all children were born with identical intellectual abilities, but I don't. Some kids were luckier at gene-pool time. Some children, from birth, will find it easier to mess around with mathematics than will others. Some kids, from birth, will have an easier time with verbal matters than will others. If children came into the world having inherited identical intellectual abilities, teachers' pedagogical problems would be far more simple.

Recent thinking among many leading educators suggests that there are various forms of intelligence, not just one (Gardner, 1994). A child who is born with less aptitude for dealing with quantitative or verbal tasks, therefore, might possess greater "interpersonal" or "intrapersonal" intelligence, but these latter abilities are not tested by these tests. For the kinds of items that are most commonly found on standardized achievement tests, children differ in their innate abilities to respond correctly. And some items on standardized achievement tests are aimed directly at measuring such intellectual ability.

Consider, for example, the item in Figure 2. This item attempts to measure a child's ability "to figure out" what the right answer is. I don't think that the item measures what's taught in school. The item measures what students come to school with, not what they learn there.

In Figure 2's social studies item for 6th graders, look carefully at the four answer options. Read each option and see if it might be correct. A "smart" student, I contend, can figure out that choices A, B, and D really would not "conserve resources" all that well; hence choice C is the winning option. Brighter kids will have a better time with this item than their less bright classmates.

But why, you might be thinking, do developers of standardized tests include such items on their tests? The answer is all too simple. These sorts of items, because they tap innate intellectual skills that are not readily modifiable in school, do a wonderful job in spreading out test-takers' scores. The quest for score variance, coupled with the limitation of having few items to use in assessing students, makes such items appealing to those who construct standardized achievement tests.

But items that primarily measure differences in students' in-born intellectual abilities obviously do not contribute to valid inferences about "how well children have been taught." Would we like all children to do well on such "native-smarts" items? Of course we would. But to use such items to arrive at a judgment about educational effectiveness is simply unsound.

Out-of-school learning. The most troubling items on standardized achievement tests assess what students have learned outside of school. Unfortunately, you'll find more of these items on standardized achievement tests than you'd suspect. If children come from advantaged families and stimulus-rich environments, then they are more apt to succeed on items in standardized achievement test items than will other children whose environments don't mesh as well with

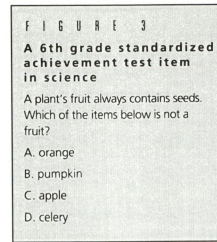

FIGURE 3

A 6th grade standardized achievement test item in science

A plant's fruit always contains seeds. Which of the items below is not a fruit?

A. orange

B. pumpkin

C. apple

D. celery

what the tests measure. The item in Figure 3 makes clear what's actually being assessed by a number of items on standardized achievement tests.

This 6th grade science item first tells students what an attribute of a fruit is (namely, that it contains seeds). Then the student must identify what "is not a fruit" by selecting the option without seeds. As any child who has encountered celery knows, celery is a seed-free plant. The right answer, then, for those who have coped with celery's strings but never its seeds, is clearly choice D.

But what if when you were a youngster, your folks didn't have the money to buy celery at the store? What if your circumstances simply did not give you the chance to have meaningful interactions with celery stalks by the time you hit the 6th grade? How well do you think you'd do in correctly answering the item in Figure 3? And how well would you do if you didn't know that pumpkins were seed-carrying spheres? Clearly, if children know about pumpkins and celery, they'll do better on this item than will those children who know only about apples and oranges. That's how children's socioeconomic status gets mixed up with children's performances on standardized achievement tests. The higher your family's socioeconomic status is, the more likely you are to do well on a number of the test items you'll encounter in such a test.

Suppose you're a principal of a school in which most students come from genuinely low socioeconomic situations. How are your students likely to perform on standardized achievement tests if a substantial number of the test's items really measure the stimulus-richness of your students' backgrounds? That's right, your students are not likely to earn very high scores. Does that mean your school's teachers are doing a poor instructional job? Of course not.

Conversely, let's imagine you're a principal in an affluent school whose students tend to have upper-class, well-educated parents. Each spring, your students' scores on standardized achievement tests are dazzlingly high. Does this mean your school's teachers are doing a super instructional job? Of course not.

One of the chief reasons that children's socioeconomic status is so highly correlated with standardized test scores is that many items on standardized achievement tests really focus on assessing knowledge and/or skills learned outside of school—knowledge and/or skills more likely to be learned in some socioeconomic settings than in others. Again, you might ask why on earth would standardized achievement test developers place such items on their tests? As usual, the answer is consistent with the dominant measurement mission of those tests, namely, to spread out students' test scores so that accurate and fine-grained norm-referenced interpretations can be made. Because there is substantial variation in children's socioeconomic situations, items that reflect such variations are efficient in producing among-student variations in test scores.

You've just considered three important factors that can influence students' scores on standardized achievement tests. One of these factors was directly linked to educational quality. But two factors weren't.

What's an Educator to Do?

I've described a situation that, from the perspective of an educator, looks

pretty bleak. What, if anything, can be done? I suggest a three-pronged attack on the problem. First, I think that you need to learn more about the viscera of standardized achievement tests. Second, I think that you need to carry out an effective educational campaign so that your educational colleagues, parents of children in school, and educational policymakers understand what the evaluative shortcomings of standardized achievement tests really are. Finally, I think that you need to arrange a more appropriate form of assessment-based evidence.

Learning about standardized achievement tests. Far too many educators haven't really studied the items on standardized achievement tests since the time that they were, as students, obliged to respond to those items. But the inferences made on the basis of students' test performances rest on nothing more than an aggregated sum of students' item-by-item responses. What educators need to do is to spend some quality time with standardized achievement tests—scrutinizing the test's items one at a time to see what they are really measuring.

Spreading the word. Most educators, and almost all parents and school board members, think that schools should be rated on the basis of their students' scores on standardized achievement tests. Those people need to be educated. It is the responsibility of all educators to do that educating.

If you do try to explain to the public, to parents, or to policymakers why standardized test scores will probably provide a misleading picture of educational quality, be sure to indicate that you're not running away from the need to be held accountable. No, you must be willing to identify other, more credible evidence of student achievement.

Coming up with other evidence. If you're going to argue against standardized achievement tests as a source of educational evidence for determining school quality, and you still are willing to be held educationally accountable, then you'll need to ante up some other form of evidence to show the world that you really are doing a good educational job.

I recommend that you attempt to assess students' mastery of genuinely significant cognitive skills, such as their ability to write effective compositions, their ability to use lessons from history to make cogent analyses of current problems, and their ability to solve high-level mathematical problems.

If the skills selected measure really important cognitive outcomes, are seen by parents and policymakers to be genuinely significant, and can be addressed instructionally by competent teachers, then the assembly of a set of pre-test-to-post-test evidence showing substantial student growth in such skills can be truly persuasive.

What teachers need are assessment instruments that measure worthwhile skills or significant bodies of knowledge. Then teachers need to show the world that they can instruct children so that those children make striking pre-instruction to post-instruction progress.

The fundamental point is this: If educators accept the position that standardized achievement test scores should not be used to measure the quality of schooling, then they must provide other, credible evidence that can be used to ascertain the quality of schooling. Carefully collected, nonpartisan evidence regarding teachers' pretest-to-post-test promotion of undeniably important skills or knowledge just might do the trick.

Right Task, Wrong Tools

Educators should definitely be held accountable. The teaching of a nation's children is too important to be left unmonitored. But to evaluate educational quality by using the wrong assessment instruments is a subversion of good sense. Although educators need to produce valid evidence regarding their effectiveness, standardized achievement tests are the wrong tools for the task.

References

Freeman, D. J., Kuhs, T. M., Porter, A. C., Floden, R. E., Schmidt, W. H., & Schwille, J. R. (1983). Do textbooks and tests define a natural curriculum in elementary school mathematics? *Elementary School Journal*, 83(5), 501–513.

Gardner, H. (1994). Multiple intelligences: The theory in practice. *Teacher's College Record*, 95(4), 576–583.

Author's note: A longer version of this article will appear in the final chapter of W. James Popham's book *Modern Educational Measurement: Practical Guidelines for Educational Leaders,* 3rd ed., (forthcoming); Needham Heights, MA: Allyn & Bacon.

W. James Popham is a UCLA Emeritus Professor. He may be reached at IOX Assessment Associates, 5301 Beethoven St., Ste. 190, Los Angeles, CA 90066 (e-mail: wpopham@ucla.edu).

Practicing What We Preach in

Designing Authentic Assessments

Designing credible performance tasks and assessments is not easy—but we can improve our efforts by using standards and peer review.

Grant Wiggins

What if a student asked for a good grade merely for handing the paper in? What if student divers and gymnasts were able to judge and score their own performances in meets, and did so based on effort and intent? Native ideas, of course—yet this is just what happens in schools every day when *faculty* submit new curricular frameworks or design new assessments.

Most faculty products are assessed, if at all, merely on whether we worked hard: Did we hand in a lengthy report, based on lots of discussion? Did we provide students with a test that we happen to like? Only rarely do we demand formal self- or peer-assessment of our design work, against standards and criteria. This not only leads to less rigorous reports and designs but also seems a bit hypocritical: We ask students to do this all the time. We need to better practice what we preach.

But how do we ensure that ongoing design and reform work is more rigorous and credible? At the Center on Learning, Assessment, and School Structure (CLASS) in Princeton, New Jersey, we use design standards and a workable peer review process for cri-

tiquing and improving all proposed new curricular frameworks, tests, and performance assessments. At the heart of the work is making adult work standards-based, not process-based or merely guided by good intentions. Using such standards can go a long way in helping parents, students, and the community have faith in locally designed systems.

Standard-Based vs. Process-Based Reform Work

Many new curriculum frameworks and assessment systems produce a significant (and often understandable) backlash. A major reason is that the work is typically produced without reference to specific standards for the proposals and final product.

Think of a typical districtwide curriculum reform project. Twelve teachers and supervisors hold meetings all school year to develop a new mathematics curriculum. Their work culminates in a report produced over a three-

week period in the summer, at district behest and with district financial support, resulting in a new local mathematics curriculum framework. They follow a time-tested *process* of scanning national reports, searching for consensus about themes and topics

© Susie Fitzhugh

From *Educational Leadership,* December 1996–January 1997, pp. 18–25. © 1997 by the Association for Supervision and Curriculum Development. All rights reserved. Reprinted by permission.

and logical progressions, and summarizing their findings and recommendations. But against what standards is their *product* (as opposed to their *process*) to be judged? The usual answer is: no legitimate standards at all, other than the implicit one that when the authors deem their work finished, the report is complete.

By contrast, what if all report-writers had to answer these questions: Is the report useful to readers? Does it engage and inform the readers? Does it anticipate the reactions of its critics? Does it meet the professional standards of curriculum design or measurement? Does it meet the purposes laid out in a charge to the committee? Most important: *Did the writers regularly self-assess and re-*

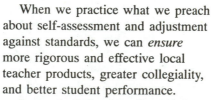

The purpose of assessment is to find out what each student is able to do, with knowledge, in context.

vise their work in progress against such criteria and standards? Did they regularly seek feedback from faculty affected en route?—the same writing process questions we properly put to students. Their report would have far greater impact if they addressed such questions. By contrast, with no self-assessment and self-adjustment along the way, the work is predictability ineffective in getting other faculty to change practice or in helping skeptical parents understand the need to do so.

Similarly with new assessments. Almost every teacher designs tests under the most naive premise: "If I designed it and gave it, it must be valid and reliable." Yet we know from research, our own observations, and the process of peer review that few teacher-designed tests and assessments meet the most basic standards for technical credibility, intellectual defensibility, coherence with system goals, and fairness to students.

© Susie Fitzhugh

When we practice what we preach about self-assessment and adjustment against standards, we can *ensure* more rigorous and effective local teacher products, greater collegiality, and better student performance.

In standards-based reform projects, in short, we must seek a disinterested review of products against standards all along the way—not just follow a process in the hope that our work turns out well. The challenge for

school reformers is to ensure that their work has *impact,* like any other performance. Desired effects must be *designed in;* they must inform all our work from the beginning.[1] As with student performances, then, we will meet standards only by "backwards design"—making self-assessment and peer review against performance standards central to the process of writing and revision—*before* it is too late.

Complex performance tasks focus on understanding as an educational goal, as opposed to mere textbook knowledge.

Rather than teaching a lock-step process of design, we at CLASS teach faculties to see that design is always *iterative*. We constantly rethink our designs, using feedback based on clear design standards. We will likely never revisit our original designs if we lack powerful criteria and a review process with the implicit obligation to critique all work against the criteria. We are often satisfied with (and misled by) our effort and good intentions.

Assessment Design Standards

Standards-based reform work begins with clear standards for eventual products. At CLASS, we instruct faculties involved in performance-based assessment reform in the use of a design template, a design process, and a self-assessment and peer review process based on ultimate-product standards. In addition, we work with leaders to make such standards-based design work more routine in and central to local faculty life (linked to job descriptions, department meetings, and performance appraisal systems, as well as individual and team design work). The template is also the database structure for assessment tasks and rubrics on our World Wide Web site, http://www.classnj.org.

The standards guide all design decisions. The three main criteria for judging emerging tasks are *credibility, user-friendliness,* and *feasibility.* The standards are fixed by specific models that serve to anchor the self-assessment and peer review process (just as in the assessment of student writing). Each criterion is broken down further into subcriteria: Under credibility, for example, the designer (in self-assess-

ing) and the peers (in peer reviewing) ask such questions as:

■ Does it measure what it says it measures? Is this a valid assessment of the intended achievement?

■ Are the scoring criteria and rubrics clear, descriptive, and explicitly related to district goals and standards?

■ Is the scoring system based on genuine standards and criteria, derived from analysis of credible models?

■ Does the task require a sophisticated understanding of required content?

■ Does the task require a high degree of intellectual skill and performance quality?

■ Does the task simulate or replicate authentic, messy, real-word challenges, contexts, and constraints faced by adult professionals, consumers, or citizens?

■ Does the scoring system enable a reliable yet adequately fine discrimination of degrees of work quality?

■ Is the task worthy of the time and energy required to complete it?

■ Is the task challenging—an appropriate stretch for students?

Naturally, in parallel to what we ask of students, there are rubrics for self- and peer-assessment of these questions.

Anticipating Key Design Difficulties

We ask designers to pay particular attention to three crucial, ever-present problems in local assessment design: whether a sophisticated understanding of core content is required by the task, whether the criteria and rubrics used are authentic and appropriate for such a task and target, and whether the tasks really measure the targeted achievement. This last problem can be stated as a single injunction that must be constantly invoked: Beware the temptation of confusing a neat instructional activity with an appropriate performance task.

1. Validity in design. Validity is essential. The purpose of assessment is to find out what each student is able to do, with knowledge, in context. But we must sample from a large domain. In asking students to do a *few* tasks well, we believe we are on solid ground because we view the tasks as apt—at the heart of the subject, and able to yield more general inferences about achievement in a subject.

When we worry about validity in design, we are thinking backwards from the evidence we need. The task must yield the right kind of information and must enable us to elicit and observe the most salient performance, given the (more general) achievements we seek to measure.

In instruction, our worries are different. We typically try to develop activities that give rise to an educational experience and ask questions that differ from those that apply to assessment design: Will the students be engaged? Will we accommodate different styles, levels, and interests? Will the activity give rise to thinking and learning at the heart of my goal for the unit? Such questions are essential to teaching, but unlikely to ensure that we will have adequate assessment evidence for *each* student when the activity is over.

Easy to say, but what to do? That's where the peer review process comes in. We are now forced to *justify* our design in a nonconfrontational way. In peer review, we often discover that the design does not yet work as a sound assessment. (Eventually, our self-assessment becomes so skilled that we can foresee these kinds of problems without much peer review.)

These are the questions we use in peer review for validity:

■ Does the task evoke the right kind of evidence, given the target? Does the task evoke sufficient evidence?

■ Can a student master the task for the "right" reasons only? Or does the task unwittingly assess for a different outcome than intended by the designer?

Yes, it measures what it's supposed to if the task can only be done well if students are in control of the key achievements.

No, it doesn't measure what it should if students (1) can perform the task well without achieving the intended result or (2) fail to perform the task well for inappropriate reasons, that is, abilities or knowledge unrelated to the target.

■ Are the criteria apt? That is, given the achievements to be assessed and the nature of the task, are these the right traits of performance to assess and the right descriptions of differences in work quality?

■ Is the weighting of the different criteria appropriate, given the nature and purpose of such performance?

■ Do the scoring rubrics discriminate levels of quality appropriately and not arbitrarily?

■ Does the task imply a rich and appropriate understanding of the intended target? Or is the task implicitly based on a questionable or inappropriate definition of the achievement?

■ Do the rubrics honor the criteria and achievement? Or are they implicitly based on questionable or inappropriate definitions of exemplary performance?

2. Assessment for understanding. Because any complex performance tends to focus on fairly general aca-

> **Peer review can yield a profound result: the beginning of a truly professional relationship with colleagues.**

demic skills, performance tasks often unwittingly lack sufficient intellectual rigor and credibility.[2] Many tasks simply reveal whether students can "communicate" or "problem solve"—and often allow great leeway in subject-matter content. Consider the specific knowledge required to perform these complex tasks developed by teachers in North Carolina:

Birds and Soldiers. Wildlife officials and politicians are at odds because of the rare red-cockade

---

FIGURE 1

What Does Understanding Mean?

Complete the following sentence to help construct an authentic, credible performance assessment in any subject matter:

The students *really* understand (the idea, issue, theory, event being assessed) only when they can . . .

■ provide credible theories, models, or interpretations to explain . . .
■ avoid such common misunderstandings as . . .
■ make such fine, subtle distinctions as . . .
■ effectively interpret such ambiguous situations or language as . . .
■ explain the value or importance of . . .
■ critique . . .
■ see the plausibility of the "odd" view that . . .
■ empathize with . . .
■ critically question the commonly held view that . . .
■ invent . . .
■ recognize the prejudice within that . . .
■ question such strong personal but unexamined beliefs as . . .
■ accurately self-assess . . .

---

woodpecker on the Fort Bragg military base. Fort Bragg officials have to limit military training exercises because of the protection required for the birds under the Endangered Species Act. The Act states that an endangered bird's environment cannot be tampered with. Almost half the known red-cockade woodpecker population is located on the base. Your task is to propose a workable solution to the problem, based on a careful review of the military's needs and the relevant law. You will write a report and make a speech to a simulated EPA review board.

Federal/Confederation. This task involves three parts: a) the student is asked to assume the role of a resident of North Carolina on the eve of secession and deliver a speech from that person's perspective on whether or not North Carolina should secede from the union, b) the student then synthesizes the points from all speeches given and writes a letter to the editor of the local newspaper reflecting this person's re-examined point of view, and c) writes a reflective piece in the person's journal, 15 years later, re-examining the wisdom of the earlier stands.

It's Your Choice: Health Insurance. Co-payment? Pretreatment estimate? Deductible? Is health care language a foreign language for you? Students take on the role of a financial analyst and must communicate to each of three different families, in a convincing manner, the best choice of coverage for their needs and budget.

These tasks focus on *understanding* as an educational goal, as opposed to mere textbook knowledge. We at CLASS have developed a complex schema for teaching and assessing understanding, drawing not only on our own research of the past decade but also the fine work of Howard Gardner (1992), David Perkins (1992), and their Project Zero colleagues. As we see it, to assess for understanding means to assess for five related capacities: sophistication of explanations and interpretations; insight gained from perspective; empathy; contextual know-how in knowledge application; and self-knowledge based on knowing our talents, limits, and prejudices.

What is the evidence we need to gather? At CLASS, we use the exercise in Figure 1 as a reminder. As a prompt, we ask teachers to brainstorm ways to complete the sentence stem that reads, "The students understand the idea only when they can . . ." Then we integrate the brainstormed ideas by building a rubric of sophisticated understanding on a novice-to-expert continuum. For example, take key events in history: What is a novice versus a sophisticated understanding of the Civil War? What sorts of judgments and discriminations is an expert likely to make that a novice student is unlikely to make? Such questions force us to predict how students are likely to perform.

The most exciting effect of this exercise is to realize that we must be able to predict students' inevitable misunderstandings. Of all the assessment strategies we have used, this is the one that causes the most "Aha!" responses. To teach and assess *mindful of misunderstanding* requires not only rubrics for levels of understanding and misunderstanding, but a new perspective on teaching: If you can now predict student misunderstandings, what are you doing to avoid or aggressively compensate for them in your curriculum and instruction?[3]

3. Critique and revision of rubrics and criteria. The designer of assessments *always* has a blind spot about something. Peers can discover and help to remedy oversights. The following represent typical errors with most rubrics:

■ Turning a quality into a quantity. Thus, students improperly get a higher score for "more" library sources or footnotes, as opposed to "more apt" sources.

■ Using comparative or evaluative language alone, such as "6" or "excellent" and "5" or "good," and so forth, when observable traits of performance are more meaningful.

■ A lack of continuity in the "distance" between score points. Thus, in the descriptors for a 6, 5, and 4, the differences may be slight. Suddenly, a 3 is just awful and not passing, so the score points are bunched at one end and spread out at another, causing misleading results.

Other pitfalls to watch for include combining traits, such as "creative"

and "organized," in the same descriptor, and confusing a criterion with its indicators. For example, "asking questions" is an indicator of *good listening,* but silence in church doesn't mean that people aren't listening. Inappropriate questions don't indicate good listening, either. In addition, most rubrics overemphasize content and form of the work and underemphasize or ignore the *impact* of performance—criteria at the heart of what we mean by "performance."

Most of us make these mistakes when we begin writing rubrics. Peer review, based on design standards, ensures that rubrics are debugged of common mistakes.

Peer Review

Besides improving the process of developing performance assessments, peer review can yield a profound result: the beginning of a truly professional relationship with colleagues. In CLASS projects, teachers have termed peer review one of the most satisfying (if initially scary) experiences in their careers. As a 32-year veteran teacher put it, "This is the kind of conversation I entered the profession to have, yet never had. I'm rejuvenated. I'm optimistic."

Peer reviewers serve as consultants to the designer, not glib judges. The process itself is evaluated against a basic criterion in support of that goal: *The designer must feel that the design was understood and improved by the process, and the reviewers must feel that the process was insightful and team building.* As the following guidelines reveal, the reviewers give specific, focused, and useful feedback:

Stage 1: Peers review task without designer present.[4] The designer states issues he or she wishes highlighted, self-assesses (optional), and then leaves. The peers read the materials, referring to the *assessment design criteria.* Working individually, the peers summarize the works' strengths and weaknesses and then report to the group. The group fills out a sheet summarizing the key feedback and guidance, thus rehearsing the oral report to

follow. Reviewers rate the task against the task rubric, if appropriate.

Stage 2: Peers discuss review with designer. Appointing a timekeeper/facilitator is crucial. The facilitator's job is to gently but firmly ensure that the designer listens (instead of defending). First, the designer clarifies technical or logistical issues (without elaboration)—*The design must stand by itself as much as possible.* Second, the peers give oral feedback and guidance. Third, the group and the designer discuss the feedback; the designer takes notes and asks questions. Finally, the group decides what issues should be presented to the faculty as a whole—lessons learned and problems evoked.

Criteria for peer review:

1. The core of the discussion involves considering: To what extent is the "targeted achievement" well assessed? To what extent do the task and rubric meet the design criteria? What would make the assessment more valid, reliable, authentic, engaging, rigorous, fair, and feasible?

2. The reviewers should be friendly, honest consultants. The designer's intent should be treated as a given (unless the unit's goal and means are unclear or lack rigor). *The aim is to improve the designer's idea, not substitute it with the reviewers' aesthetic judgments, intellectual priorities, or pet designs.*

3. The designer asks for focused feedback in relation to specific design criteria, goals, or problems.

4. The designer's job in the second session is primarily to listen, not explain, defend, or justify design decisions.

5. The reviewers' job is first to give useful *feedback* (did the effect match the intent?), and only then, useful *guidance.*

Note that we distinguish here between feedback and guidance. The best feedback is highly specific and descriptive of how the performance met standards. Recall how often a music teacher or tennis coach provides a steady flow of feedback (Wiggins 1993). Feedback is *not* praise and blame or mere encouragement. Try becoming better at any performance if all you hear is "Nice effort!" or "You can do better" or "We didn't like it." Whatever the role or value of praise and dislike, they are not feedback: The information provided does not help you improve. In feedback and guidance, *what matters is judging the design against criteria related to sound assessment.* Peer reviewers are free to offer concrete guidance—suggestions on how the design might be improved—assuming the designer grasps and accepts the feedback.[5]

Assessment System Criteria

Beyond reviewing specific performance tasks and rubrics, we need to evaluate entire assessment systems. For such systemic assessments, a more complex set of criteria includes credibility, technical soundness, usefulness, honesty, intellectual rigor, and fairness (Wiggins 1996).

Again, a key to credibility is *disinterested* judging—using known and intellectually defensible tasks and criteria—whether we are talking about student or faculty work. A psychometrician may well find a local assessment system not up to a rigid technical standard; but such a system can still be credible and effective within the real-world constraints of school time, talent, and budgets.

Credibility is a concern of the whole school community. We need other feedback—not just from peer reviewers, teacher-designers, or psychometricians, but from parents, school boards, college admissions officers, and legislators. Alas, what one group finds credible, another often doesn't. Clients for our information have differing needs and interests in the data; if we fail to consider these clients, our local assessment systems may be inadequate and provincial. But if we improperly mimic large-scale, audit testing methods in an effort to meet psychometric standards for local assessment design, we often develop assessment systems that are

neither authentic nor effective as feedback.

Peer review should always consider the possible customers for the assessment information, to determine whether both the task and the reporting of results are apt and adequate (Wiggins 1996). The primary customer is always the student.

Principles Underlying the Standards and Criteria

When proposing standards and criteria for performance assessments, we need to remember—and clearly state—the underlying values of our proposals. Assessment is not merely a blind set of techniques, after all, but a means to some valued end. Effective and appropriate school assessment is based on five principles:

1. *Reform focuses on the purpose, not merely the techniques, of assessment.* Too many reform projects tamper with the technology of assessment without reconnecting with the purposes of assessment. Assessment must recapture essential educational aims: to help the student learn and to help the teacher instruct. All other needs, such as accountability testing and program evaluation, come second. Merely shifting from multiple-choice questions to performance testing changes nothing if we still rely on the rituals of year-end, secure, one-shot testing.

2. *Students and teachers are entitled to a more instructional and user-friendly assessment system than provided by current systems and psychometric criteria.* A deliberately instructional assessment makes sure that tests enlighten students about real-world intellectual tasks, criteria, context, and standards; and such an assessment is built to ensure user-friendly, powerful feedback. Conventional tests often prevent students from fully understanding and meeting their intellectual obligations. And teachers are entitled to an accountability system that facilitates better teaching.

3. *Assessment is central, not peripheral, to instruction.* We must design curriculums backwards from complex and exemplary challenges. A performance-based system integrates curriculum and assessment design, thereby making the sequence of work more coherent and meaningful from the learner's point of view.

4. *Authentic tasks must anchor the assessment process, so that typical test questions play a properly subordinate role.* Students must see what adults really do with their knowledge; and all students must learn what athletes already know—that performance is more than just the drill work that develops discrete knowledge and skill. Genuine tasks demand challenges that require good judgment, adaptiveness, and the habits of mind—such as craftsmanship and tolerance for ambiguity—never tested by simplistic test items.

5. *In assessment, local is better.* Site-level assessments must be of higher intellectual quality—more tightly linked to instruction—than superficial standardized tests can ever be. No externally run assessment can build the kind of local capacity for and interest in high-quality assessment at the heart of all genuine local improvement. But local assessment must be credible—and that means inviting disinterested assessment by people other than the student's teachers, and including oversight of the entire assessment design and implementation system (for case studies in assessment reform, see CLASS 1996).

By keeping these principles in mind, we can continually improve our reform work. Process-driven improvement efforts can become rigid and noncreative; we resort to following the letter of the law only. The real power of standards-based reform is that we are free to innovate and divert from process—if we see a better way to approach the standards and better honor our principles. Thus, our reform efforts, not just our designs, also demand constant self-assessment and self-adjustment, based on comparing emerging work against our principles.[6]

Professionalism depends on standards-based work and peer review. Despite the long-standing habits of schools where teachers are left alone to design assessments, we believe that such practices are counterproductive to both local credibility and professional development. Every school and district ought to require peer review of major assessments, based on sound and agreed-upon standards and criteria of design and use.

Notes

1. For student performance tasks, too, rubric and task writers should emphasize impact-related criteria so that students know the purpose of the task. Thus, instead of just scoring for organization, clarity, and accuracy in essay writing, we should include criteria related to how persuasive and engaging the piece is.

2. Bob Marzano believes that performance assessment is ill-suited for assessing understanding of subject matter. I disagree: Intellectual understanding is demonstrated by doing well at certain types of performance, but designing such tasks is indeed difficult.

3. A full development of this schema of understanding will appear in 1997 in a new ASCD book and training program, co-authored by Jay McTighe and myself, and tentatively titled *Understanding by Design.*

4. Some may wonder about the utility or ethics of discussing the work in the designer's absence. We have found that this first stage gives the peers freedom to express vague concerns and complete criticisms. When the designer is always present, we find that the session bogs down as the designer justifies and explains all decisions.

5. Video and print material on the peer review process is available from CLASS.

6. Fairtest (1995) has developed standards and indicators for assessment processes and systems. Contact Fairtest at National Center for Fair & Open Testing, 342 Broadway, Cambridge, MA 02139. Phone: (617) 864-4810; fax: (617) 497-2224; e-mail; FairTest@aol.com.

References

Center on Learning, Assessment, and School Structure (CLASS). (1996). *Measuring What Matters: The Case for Assessment Reform* (video). Princeton, N.J.: CLASS.

Fairtest: National Center for Fair and Open Testing. (1995). *Principles and Indicators for Student Assessment Systems.* Cambridge, Mass.: Fairtest.

Gardner, H. (1992) *The Unschooled Mind.* New York: Basic Books.

Perkins, D. (1992). *Smart Schools: Better Thinking and Learning in Every Child.* New York; Free Press.

Wiggins, G. (1993). *Assessing Student Performance: Exploring the Purpose and Limits of Testing.* San Francisco: Jossey-Bass.

Wiggins, G. (1996). "Honesty and Fairness: Toward Better Grading and Reporting," in *Communicating Student Learning,* edited by T. Guskey. 1996 ASCD Yearbook. Alexandria, Va.: ASCD.

Grant Wiggins is President of the Center on Learning, Assessment, and School Structure (CLASS), 648 The Great Road, Princeton, NJ 08540. He can be reached by e-mail at gpw@ classnj.org.

Lessons Learned About Student Portfolios

By Elizabeth A. Hebert

The idea of going beyond test scores to collect more substantive evidence of a school's curriculum and teaching initiatives seemed innovative to faculty members at Crow Island School a decade ago, Ms. Hebert notes. What they didn't know then was that the process of selecting samples of work and assembling them into a portfolio is profoundly important to children.

A DECADE ago we began a project with student portfolios at Crow Island School in Winnetka, Illinois. Influenced by Howard Gardner's theory of multiple intelligences, our faculty explored the many learning experiences of our students and decided to encourage the children to gather their work over time so that they themselves could see evidence of their learning. During the past 10 years we have learned so much more than we imagined. We now know quite a bit about what a portfolio is and probably more about what a portfolio is not. But what continues to energize our thinking after all this time is what a portfolio can be.

When we started this project, we didn't fully understand the possibilities that portfolios could offer. The

ELIZABETH A. HERBERT is the principal of Crow Island School, Winnetka, Ill.

Illustration by John Berry

notion that there could be some child-centered, qualitative supplement to the single-number characterizations of learning emphasized by our testing culture seemed reason enough to organize our efforts and those of our students. The idea of collecting more substantive evidence of our curriculum and teaching initiatives to counteract narrowly defined test scores seemed innovative at the time. What we didn't know then was that the process of selecting samples of one's own work and assembling them into a portfolio is profoundly important to children. We also learned that all children have a natural ability and desire to tell their story through the contents of the port-

 From *Phi Delta Kappan*, April 1998, pp. 583–585. © 1998 by Phi Delta Kappa, Inc. Reported by permission.

folio. Even now, we remain excited about capturing the individual voices of our students through portfolio collections.

Over the past 10 years we've discussed and rethought many aspects of our understanding of portfolios. Here are some of the lessons we've taken to heart:

• *Don't get too focused on delineating the contents of the portfolio.* In the early years of our work, we were far too concerned about the specific contents of the portfolios. Looking back, I believe that discussing this matter is a natural way to explore the purposes of portfolios; however, it's important not to become rigid about what goes into a portfolio. I'm always reminded of the wonderful definition offered by staff developers Pearl Paulsen and Leon Paulsen: "Portfolios tell a story. . . . Put in anything that helps to tell the story." The real contents of a portfolio are the child's thoughts and his or her reasons for selecting a particular entry. That selection process reflects the interests and metacognitive maturity of the child and the inspiration and influence offered by the teachers.

When teachers first get involved with portfolios, they tend to have different ideas and suggestions about what to put on the portfolio "must list." Fortunately, we never committed ourselves to making such a list, and I suspect that is why, in part, we are still so fascinated with this topic. After 10 years we realize that there is no best notion of what goes into a portfolio; rather, portfolios serve as a metaphor for our continued belief in the idea that children can play a major role in the assessment of their own learning. This perspective, rather than a predetermined list of curriculum samples, should be the guideline for placing particular items into a portfolio.

• *The "container" issue.* Initially, most teachers gathered children's work in a wide variety of containers. Hanging file folders became a popular organizing tool. The issue of what work was sent home and what work stayed in the classroom was important in the early years. It took time to establish the expectation that most of the children's work would stay at school. Faculty members spent many hours discussing details: the type and color of containers, the location and labeling of the intermediate gathering folders, the importance of dating all student work, and the directions we would give to the students about selections. Some tensions and anxieties surfaced in response to our open conversations, and there were some disagreements about the contents and purposes of portfolios. Thus the security of knowing we would definitely be using red, yellow, blue, and green legal-sized folders in grades 1–4 and black binders in grade 5 was a source of great comfort. Issues of giving tangible form to the often unwieldy openness of student-centered portfolios need to be addressed but must be secondary to the larger and more fundamental discussions about what a portfolio can represent about a child's learning.

• *Whose portfolio is it?* Because our initial understanding was that portfolios might counterbalance the narrowness of test scores with concrete examples of our students' interests and abilities, we assumed the role of portfolio managers. The notion that children could or should participate in the selection of the contents of the portfolios was intriguing to us, but we didn't have a clear plan to implement that idea.

How does the child know what to choose? What if a child doesn't select balanced evidence of the teacher's curriculum for his or her portfolio? Is it appropriate for a child to present a portfolio that excludes a major content area? These questions continue to be a part of our ongoing discussions as we discover the ever-growing metacognitive voices of our children—voices that we train to become competent and thoughtful tellers of the stories of their learning.

We now believe that the selection of the contents of the portfolio is an evolving process shared by child and teacher. When children are just beginning to understand what a portfolio is, they require clear scaffolding. We advise students about including certain pieces of work that we feel will be valued—if not now, at a later time. We have discovered that the conversations that take place as portfolios are being compiled give the children the security to suggest additional entries that are more personal or unique to their own school experience. One message about child ownership is very clear: we do not assign a letter grade or evaluation to the portfolio. We honor the child's world that is represented by the portfolio. We want to learn more about that world so that we can more sensitively help each child grow.

• *An archive adds a sense of history to the portfolio.* As children's work was gathered, we were uncertain what to do with it at the close of the school year. Our faculty discussions emphasized how important it was for the children to have access to their work over time so that they could develop a better understanding of their histories as students. We decided to use the term *portfolio* when referring to a single year's selection of works and *archive* for the total collection, which could span up to six years (K–5). Establishing the physical space to house an archive (in our school, the library/resource center) was an important step: It signaled to all children that each of them was an important part of the history of our school.

• *Defining an audience is crucial.* The notion of gathering work to "tell your story" is far too abstract for young students unless they know who is listening to that story. The question of the contents of a portfolio becomes much clearer once an audience is defined. For our students; the parents were the most natural audience. Other audiences could be siblings, other students from the same or different grade levels, prior teachers in the school, or senior citizens in the community.

• *Attaching meaning to the contents of the portfolio contributes to the child's metacognitive growth.* The collecting of student work was initially overwhelming. Some students saved everything, and others were reluctant to make a decision about what to select for their portfolios. We needed a mechanism to assist students—and ourselves—in managing the size of an individual portfolio and, more important, to inject more thoughtfulness into the selection process. The idea of "reflection tags" quickly worked its way around the building. The basic idea is to consider reasons for including a piece of work in the portfolio, to record these statements of value on a tag of paper, and to attach the tag to the sample of student work. This idea is usually presented in a rug-time discussion with students.

In the early grades, conversations with children focus on the purposes of maintaining a portfolio. In first grade, students are reminded of the baby books that their parents have put together. This example introduces the concepts of purposeful selection, life history, and evidence of change over time. "Now that you're in first grade, you will select some of your first-grade work, and we'll keep it in a portfolio." The first-graders love the sound of this grown-up word and remember that their kindergarten teachers introduced this idea to them last spring. Often fifth-grade student buddies assist the children in sorting through their work and selecting items for their portfolios.

In second grade, children may be asked, "Why would you put something in your portfolio?" "Because it's my best work" is usually the first response. With patience, the teacher elicits further value statements from the students. "Because I'm proud of it." "Because I didn't think I could do this." "Because I worked very hard on it." The teacher records these thoughts on tags of paper and asks the children to affix them to particular entries in their portfolios. "Do you have any blank tags?" asks another student, demonstrating that further ideas have occurred about why one keeps artifacts in a portfolio and indicating that the transfer of ownership from teacher to child has begun. The use of individual reflection tags (or some other open-ended written reflection) about the contents of a portfolio is an important element in portfolio construction. The physical act of attaching meaning to a specific piece of work contributes significantly to the child's metacognitive growth.

• *A celebratory event brings child, portfolio, and audience together.* Trying to balance the micro and macro issues surrounding our portfolio project was no small task. Discussions about contents, containers, file folders, and the location of the archive, together with the philosophical issues of portfolio ownership, the role of portfolios in assessment, and educating parents about the use of portfolios, had us going in many directions at once. What we needed was a unifying experience that would consolidate all our discussions and concerns and that would clearly communicate to both students and parents the value we assigned to portfolios.

Learning is worth celebrating, and children can be competent participants in that celebration. Gradually we have developed structures to express that belief as part of our school culture. By far, the most powerful celebration of student competence has been the Portfolio Evening, an opportunity for children to present their portfolios to their own parents. At one of our regularly scheduled conferences with parents, the children are given the responsibility to present their portfolios individually to their parents and to explain to them the process by which the materials were generated, the self-reflections involved in the selection of the materials, the conversations with the teacher that spurred particular choices, and any other aspects of their "learning stories" they want to share.

To prepare for this event, the children spend several weeks talking about their portfolios and archives with their teachers, with peers, and often with older students. Specific lessons are focused on how to organize selections of work; how to place them in chronological order; how to think about work as evidence of competence in more than one subject area; how to compare earlier work with present work, showing the acquisition of more advanced skills; and, most important, how to reflect on the portfolio as a whole. Students complete portfolio means called "Ask me about" sheets. On these organizing sheets the students highlight the contents of their portfolios and emphasize learning experiences that are important to their portfolio story.

Another aspect of the Portfolio Evening is the production of a classroom videotape of approximately 15 to 20 minutes in length. The video is intended to portray a day in the life of this particular group of students, including the learning that takes place in special subject areas of art, music, physical education, Spanish, and computers. In addition, many videotapes include recess activities and selected field trips. The project of organizing, scripting, and filming these videotapes is one that the children look forward to with great enthusiasm. Of greater value, however, is the fact that the production of this brief videotape provides an important metacognitive task for each group of children as they reflect on and develop descriptive language for each segment of the school day—as they understand it.

The dates of the Portfolio Evenings appear on the annual school calendar, and parents are also invited by letter. The event takes place over two nights, with half of the class and their parents attending each night for approximately 90 minutes. In the days just prior to the event, the children add final touches to their presentations and select an area of the classroom where they can hold a private conversation with their parents.

• *Parent education is required.* Another lesson we have learned is that we need to deliberately teach the parents about the value of student portfolios—what they mean to us, how we use them as a part of our curriculum, their immeasurable value to the children, and how they fit into an assess-

ment program for our school. It's important to emphasize that portfolios do not replace more standardized measures. Standardized tests address the question "Which child knows more?" whereas portfolios address the question. "What does this child know?" One question is not better than the other; posing both questions will provide a more comprehensive perspective of a child's work in school.

For the past three years a panel of eight faculty members representing grades K–5 have presented an informational program for our parents. At this evening meeting, the teachers speak briefly about their understanding of the value and purposes of portfolios for the particular age group they teach. From our years of conversations and direct experience, we are able to provide the scaffolding that enables parents to better understand their children's portfolio presentations and gain a more in-depth view of their children as learners.

These are some of the lessons we've learned about portfolios over the past 10 years. When the adoption of portfolios is first being considered, it's important to begin with a discussion of beliefs about children and learning and the connection between them. And then, of course, there's the question "What is our role in all of this?" More than any book we've read or speaker we've listened to, our own ongoing discussions about portfolios—what they can do and represent—provide direction for our own professional growth. It is important for us to continue to take the time we need to pursue this topic in depth, and we continue to share with one another any new activities and suggestions that might be helpful.

The involvement, the sense of connectedness, and the self-discovery that children demonstrate in compiling their portfolios have taught us that our work over these 10 years has to a large extent fulfilled many of the promises that we though portfolios held. Of course, we know that there are many more lessons to be learned as we listen intently to the children during this process and learn more about the meaning and value they assign to the development of their portfolios.

Grades: The Final Frontier in Assessment Reform

By Gregory J. Cizek

The task of reforming educational assessment has just begun. New forms of assessment cannot provide clearer or more complete information about student achievement unless the ways in which achievement is communicated are refined. The real challenge for assessment reform will be to bring assessment and grading practices into the fold.

Assessment reform has become a centerpiece of efforts to improve U.S. education (Stiggins, 1988; Wolf, LeMahieu, and Eresh, 1992). The list of innovations is familiar: Students are preparing portfolios of their work to demonstrate complex characteristics like employability skills. Teachers are gathering and synthesizing more information about students involving a greater diversity of valuable educational outcomes. Administrators are evaluating the use of new forms of assessment. Districts are rethinking promotion and retention policies and the measures used to inform those decisions. Professional associations are promulgating new standards for both content and assessment. Test publishers are incorporating a wider variety of alternative assessment formats into their products. Nationally, the importance of assessment can be seen in the Goals 2000 legislation and other federal initiatives.

Gregory J. Cizek is associate professor of educational research and measurement, University of Toledo, Ohio; readers may continue the dialogue on the Internet at **gcizek@utnet.utoledo.edu.**

Reprinted with permission from *NASSP Bulletin,* December 1996, pp. 103-110. © 1996 by the National Association of Secondary School Principals. For more information concerning NASSP services and/or programs, please call (703) 860-0200.

One might conclude that assessment reform efforts are making great strides toward a common goal: improving the range and quality of information about educational performance available to students, teachers, parents, administrators, and the public. But, maybe not.

How Performance Is Communicated

Despite all the other changes, a student's educational performance is still primarily reported using grades. Actually, the older term "marks" might be more accurate than grades, because the way achievement is reported does not always involve the use of grades. Instead, the marks *might* be in the form of letters (A, B, C, D, F); numbers (percent correct); symbols (S = Satisfactory, N = Needs Improvement, U = Unsatisfactory); descriptors (Emerging, Developing, Maturing); or other systems.

Regardless of the kinds of marks, however, at the local level, where an individual student's performance matters most to the student, parents, teachers, and others intimately involved in the student's education, grades continue to be relied upon to communicate important information about performance and progress. But they probably don't.

What's Wrong with Grades?

Grades in whatever form are primitive tools for doing the job they are asked to accomplish. As communication devices, they are more like two tin cans and a length of string

Despite all the other changes, a student's educational performance is still primarily reported using grades.

than a cellular phone. It's an interesting contrast: As bubble sheets whiz through a scanner in a district testing office, a teacher mulls a pile of papers with stickers and happy faces on them, concluding that this student's work merits an A for the marking period.

In a recent study, teachers from midwestern schools were asked about their assessment and grading practices. The findings revealed great differences in what teachers do, and great uncertainty about what they

should do. For example, teachers were asked to indicate what factors they consider when assigning marks to assignments and tests. A clear majority (83 percent) indicated they considered the percent or number correct on the assignment; from one-third to one-half the teachers, however, also said they considered the difficulty of the assignment, how the class performed overall, the individual students' ability levels, and the effort a student put into the work.

It appears that nearly *everything* is considered when assigning a mark. There are probably two reasons for this. First, educators want to consider all relevant aspects of a student's classroom experience when assigning a mark. At the same time, there is apparently no clear consensus about which factors *are* relevant to assigning a grade.

What about final grades? To this question, teachers responded that they combined the marks they had assigned to individual assignments and tests—that uncertain mix described above—with three other kinds of information:

• Formal achievement-related measures (attendance, class participation)
• Informal achievement-related measures (answers in class, one-on-one discussions)
• Other informal information (impressions of effort, conduct, teamwork, leadership, and so on).

Unfortunately, this mix of factors is difficult to disentangle. In an attempt to clear things up, teachers were asked to explain how they combine these diverse factors into a single mark. The interviews led to other revealing perspectives on classroom assessment practice.

Deciding on a Grade

Many teachers expressed a clear preference for non-cognitive outcomes. As one elementary teacher said, "Getting the child through the level with a positive attitude and good memories is more important than a raw number grade.... Shaping the kids' minds through group interaction, effort, and participation is more important than averaging tests and quiz scores."

Another teacher reported that "assignments, quizzes, and tests are not crucial in [her] grading policies." This teacher "stresses group interaction and uses several other subjective methods combined with intuition to formulate a final grade." Attendance and participation were also highly valued by the teachers in the study, and these factors were also considered in assigning a final grade.

It was particularly interesting to learn how teachers reported combining the divergent sources of information into the final grade. Although many teachers did not provide much detail regarding how the composite was formed, one teacher said she "considers attendance, participation, effort, conduct,

and teamwork, and adds to this things such as tests and quizzes."

Another teacher was more specific about details. She designs the test she uses herself, and uses "an average of 16–20 grades during the grading period in calculating the final grade. However, the lower grades are not factored into the average." To this mix, she adds her "overall impressions of effort and how the class performed."

Attendance and participation were also highly valued by the teachers in the study, and these factors were also considered in assigning a final grade.

The practice described by this teacher is apparently not uncommon. Several teachers reported similar practices, throwing out the worst quiz score for each student, considering class performance as a whole, and considering impressions of a student's effort and ability.

The practice of "throwing out" one or more poor scores on formal assessments is apparently quite widespread. Ostensibly, teachers use the practice so that a single low score does not inappropriately affect a student's grade. No teacher, however, reported throwing out a single high score that might inappropriately inflate a student's final grade.

Finally, several teachers made specific mention of taking "extra credit" into account when assigning the final grade.

What Do These Practices Tell Us?

Taken together, these practices point to what might be called a *success orientation* in assigning marks. While educators consider a variety of factors in assigning a final grade, they combine the information in idiosyncratic ways: Not only do different teachers use different factors, they also combine the elements in different proportions within classrooms. The factors considered in arriving at a final grade are weighted in ways that are most advantageous for each student.

In math class, for example, a student who has not mastered fractions may still be awarded a B+ for maintaining a positive attitude, regularly participating in class discussions, and trying hard. On the other hand, an A student who has mastered fractions would usually not be downgraded for being pessimistic, silent during discussions, and "coasting."

Teachers seem to follow the advice our parents gave us: "If you can't say something nice about someone, don't say anything at all." In most cases, they are able to find something good to say.

Although our parents may be happy that we are following their advice, the parents of the students may not be so happy. They assume grades indicate achievement or content mastery. Students themselves are unlikely to be sophisticated enough to understand that their grades are complex composites. Instead, they probably assume—as nearly everyone else does—that their A's and B's mean they have successfully mastered rigorous academic work.

Perhaps the innovations accompanying assessment reform have prompted teachers to gather a more diverse array of information about student performance. The new problems, though, are "What should be done with all this information?" or "How should grades be assigned?" Unfortunately, these are questions that educators are currently not well-prepared to answer. Today many teachers are simply not comfortable with the task of assigning grades.

At least two factors contribute to the problem:

First, little training in educational assessment is available at undergraduate and graduate levels of teacher training, and competence in assessment is not always a prerequisite to licensure.[1]

The research paints an even grimmer picture about the training and experience of administrators with respect to assessment. A recent study sponsored by the National Association of Elementary School Principals (NAESP), the American Association of School Administrators (AASA), and the National Association of Secondary School Principals (NASSP) illustrates the need for educational leaders to become more "assessment literate" (Stiggins, 1991; Impara, 1993).

Second, many educators simply lack an interest in testing and grading (Hills, 1991).

Grades and Report Cards: What Can Be Done?

The lack of knowledge and interest in grading translates into a serious information breakdown in education. A recent study of how the content of report cards facilitates or hinders parents' understanding of the information they provide was not optimistic. The authors concluded that report cards are not successfully transmitting teachers' intended meaning to parents (Waltman and Frisbie, 1994).

The reform of classroom assessment and grading practices must become a top priority if educational improvement is to be effective. New forms of assessment are welcome, but there will be no educational advantage if the meaning of these measures remains murky. Assessment reforms have introduced a wealth of information to teachers, parents, and students. Our ability to *use* this information, however, has remained essentially unchanged.

The lack of knowledge and interest in grading translates into a serious information breakdown in education.

At least eight initiatives are warranted; the effort should include all who are interested in reform.

1. All educators must make a commitment to professional development.

Professional development in assessment should become a top priority. There may be different focuses for these efforts: Teachers may be more interested in classroom assessment issues and administrators may be more in need of developing a vision for integrated, planned assessment systems.

2. Training in assessment must be relevant to classrooms.

Even when teachers and administrators receive formal training in assessment, university coursework often focuses on aspects of testing and grading that may not be applicable to those who actually *do* these things. College coursework should be redesigned to provide more relevant training.

3. Professional organizations must promote sound assessment practice.

Professional organizations have become active in this area,[2] although more work is necessary to highlight the need for assessment competence and the benefits of sound assessment practices for both teachers and students.

4. Educational leaders must develop an "assessment vision."

Considering the increasing attention to assessment and all the diverse purposes it serves, it is fair to say the big picture in educational assessment is sometimes chaotic, and is perhaps the most neglected issue in assessment reform. Educational leaders should promote a clear, coordinated conception about the varieties of assessment in classrooms and the purposes and uses they serve.[3] To be effective in promoting reforms, this vision must be

communicated to teachers, parents, community members, and students.

5. Grading policies must be developed and applied consistently.

Administrators, parents, and teachers must work together to develop, disseminate, and maintain consistent grading policies. To maximize the utility of grades, developmental efforts should work to build consensus on the policies, listening closely to the information needs of parents, students, employers, and universities. A beginning effort might include discussions about what current policies reveal about the need for assessment reform: for example, many policies simply list percentage ranges for A's, B's, C's, D's, and F's and give teachers little additional guidance about sound evaluation practices.

6. End isolation.

Poor assessment practices flourish in schools where teachers are isolated and do not benefit from interaction about difficult assessment issues. Teachers must take the initiative to collaborate and cooperate on testing and grading practices. Administrators must facilitate collaboration and encourage consistency in grading practices.

7. Students must be initiated into a new grading culture.

Students often see grades and learning as separate, or value grades more than education. A significant educational reform will help students see the link between mastery of knowledge, skills, and abilities, and the grades they receive. We should teach students to value real learning.

8. Assessment experts must lend a hand.

New methods of assessment promise more and better information about student performance, but proliferation of innovative assessment formats has outstripped the development of ways to interpret and report this information. Experts in testing should explore new ways of synthesizing and communicating the information provided by alternative assessments to take full advantage of the innovations.

As the list of challenges implies, the task of assessment reform has just begun. New forms of assessment such as portfolios or performance assessments cannot provide clearer or more complete information about

---

1. These problems have been well-documented for several years. See, for example, Ward (1980), Gullickson (1986), Schafer and Lissitz (1987), O'Sullivan and Chalnick (1991), and Wise, Lukin, and Roos (1991).
2. For one example, see the Standards for Teacher Competence in Educational Assessment of Students, developed by the American Federation of Teachers, National Council on Measurement in Education, and National Education Association, Washington, D.C., 1990.
3. See Cizek and Rachor (1994) for a more detailed description about what such a vision might entail—what the authors refer to as "planned assessment systems."

student achievement unless the ways achievement is communicated are refined. The real challenge for assessment will be to make assessment and grading practices part of the reform effort.

References

American Federation of Teachers, National Council on Measurement in Education, National Education Association. *Standards for Teacher Competence in Educational Assessment of Students.* Washington, D.C.: National Council on Measurement in Education, 1990.

Cizek, G. J., and Rachor, R. E. "The Real Testing Bias: The Role of Values in Educational Assessment." *NASSP Bulletin,* March 1994.

Gullickson, A. R. "Teacher Education and Teacher-Perceived Needs in Educational Measurement and Evaluation." *Journal of Educational Measurement* 23(1986): 347–54.

Hills, J. R. "Apathy Concerning Testing and Grading." *Phi Delta Kappan* 72(1991): 540–45.

Impara, J. C. "Joint Committee on Competency Standards in Student Assessment for Educational Administrators Update: Assessment Survey Results." Presented at the Annual Meeting of the National Council on Measurement, New Orleans, La., April 1993.

O'Sullivan, R. G., and Chalnick, M. K. "Measurement-Related Course Work Requirements for Teacher Certification and Recertification." *Educational Measurement: Issues and Practice* 10(1991): 17–19, 23.

Schafer, W. D., and Lissitz, R. W. "Measurement Training for School Personnel: Recommendations and Reality." *Journal of Teacher Education* 38(1987): 57–63.

Stiggins, R. J. "Assessment Literacy." *Phi Delta Kappan* 72(1991): 534–39.

———. "Revitalizing Classroom Assessment: The Highest Instructional Priority." *Phi Delta Kappan* 69(1988): 363–68.

Waltman, K. K., and Frisbie, D. A. "Parents' Understanding of Their Children's Report Card Grades." *Applied Measurement in Education* 7(1994): 223–40.

Ward, J. G. "Teachers and Testing: A Survey of Knowledge and Attitudes." In *Testing in Our Schools,* edited by L. M. Rudner. Washington, D.C.: National Institute of Education, 1980.

Wise, S. L.; Lukin, L. E.; and Roos, L. L. "Teacher Beliefs About Training in Testing and Measurement." *Journal of Teacher Education* 42(1991): 37–42.

Wolf, D. P.; LeMahieu, P. G.; and Eresh, J. "Good Measure: Assessment as a Tool for Educational Reform." *Educational Leadership* 49(1992): 8–13.

Acknowledgment: The author is grateful for the support of this work provided by the University of Toledo College of Education and Allied Professions.

AE Article Review Form

We encourage you to photocopy and use this page as a tool to assess how the articles in **Annual Editions** expand on the information in your textbook. By reflecting on the articles you will gain enhanced text information. You can also access this useful form on a product's book support Web site at **http://www.dushkin.com/ online/.**

NAME: _____ DATE: _____

TITLE AND NUMBER OF ARTICLE: _____

BRIEFLY STATE THE MAIN IDEA OF THIS ARTICLE: _____

LIST THREE IMPORTANT FACTS THAT THE AUTHOR USES TO SUPPORT THE MAIN IDEA:

WHAT INFORMATION OR IDEAS DISCUSSED IN THIS ARTICLE ARE ALSO DISCUSSED IN YOUR TEXTBOOK OR OTHER READINGS THAT YOU HAVE DONE? LIST THE TEXTBOOK CHAPTERS AND PAGE NUMBERS:

LIST ANY EXAMPLES OF BIAS OR FAULTY REASONING THAT YOU FOUND IN THE ARTICLE:

LIST ANY NEW TERMS/CONCEPTS THAT WERE DISCUSSED IN THE ARTICLE, AND WRITE A SHORT DEFINITION:

ANNUAL EDITIONS revisions depend on two major opinion sources: one is our Advisory Board, listed in the front of this volume, which works with us in scanning the thousands of articles published in the public press each year; the other is you—the person actually using the book. Please help us and the users of the next edition by completing the prepaid article rating form on this page and returning it to us. Thank you for your help!

ANNUAL EDITIONS: Educational Psychology 00/01

ARTICLE RATING FORM

Here is an opportunity for you to have direct input into the next revision of this volume. We would like you to rate each of the 41 articles listed below, using the following scale:

1. **Excellent: should definitely be retained**
2. **Above average: should probably be retained**
3. **Below average: should probably be deleted**
4. **Poor: should definitely be deleted**

Your ratings will play a vital part in the next revision. So please mail this prepaid form to us just as soon as you complete it. Thanks for your help!

RATING

ARTICLE

1. The Year That I Really Learned How to Teach
2. Reflection Is at the Heart of Practice
3. Schools and Curricula for the 21st Century: Predictions, Visions, and Anticipations
4. What Issues Will Confront Public Education in the Years 2000 and 2020? Predictions of Chief State School Officers
5. What Do We Know from Brain Research?
6. The Moral Child
7. Reevaluating Significance of Baby's Bond with Mother
8. Helping Children Become More Prosocial: Ideas for Classrooms, Families
9. How Well Do You Know Your Kid?
10. Out of the Mouths of Babes: Voices of At-Risk Adolescents
11. Taking Inclusion into the Future
12. Good Questions to Ask: When a Child with a Developmental Delay Joins Your Class
13. Meeting the Needs of Gifted Learners in the Early Childhood Classroom
14. How All Middle-Schoolers Can Be "Gifted"
15. The Goals and Track Record of Multicultural Education
16. Multiculturalism at a Crossroads
17. Voices and Voces: Cultural and Linguistic Dimensions of Giftedness
18. Brain Basics: Cognitive Psychology and Its Implications for Education
19. In Search of . . . Brain-Based Education
20. The First Seven . . . and the Eighth: A Conversation with Howard Gardner
21. Ability and Expertise: It's Time to Replace the Current Model of Intelligence

RATING

ARTICLE

22. Caution—Praise Can Be Dangerous
23. Constructivist Theory in the Classroom: Internalizing Concepts through Inquiry Learning
24. The Challenges of Sustaining a Constructivist Classroom Culture
25. Keeping in Character: A Time-Tested Solution
26. Improving Student Thinking
27. The Intelligence-Friendly Classroom: It Just Makes Sense
28. Mapping a Route toward Differentiated Instruction
29. Educating the Net Generation
30. A New Look at School Failure and School Success
31. I Think I Can, I Think I Can: Understanding and Encouraging Mastery Motivation in Young Children
32. Caring about Learning: The Nature and Nurturing of Subject-Matter Appreciation
33. Moving beyond Management As Sheer Compliance: Helping Students to Develop Goal Coordination Strategies
34. Connecting Instruction and Management in a Student-Centered Classroom
35. Teaching Students to Regulate Their Own Behavior
36. How to Defuse Defiance, Threats, Challenges, Confrontations . . .
37. Salinas, California: Peace Breaks Out
38. Why Standardized Tests Don't Measure Educational Quality
39. Practicing What We Preach in Designing Authentic Assessments
40. Lessons Learned about Student Portfolios
41. Grades: The Final Frontier in Assessment Reform

(Continued on next page)

We Want Your Advice

||||

NO POSTAGE
NECESSARY
IF MAILED
IN THE
UNITED STATES

BUSINESS REPLY MAIL
FIRST-CLASS MAIL PERMIT NO. 84 GUILFORD CT

POSTAGE WILL BE PAID BY ADDRESSEE

Dushkin/McGraw-Hill
Sluice Dock
Guilford, CT 06437-9989

III....IIII.I.I.I.IIII.I.I.III.I.I.I.I.I.I.I.I.I.I.I.I.I.I

ABOUT YOU

Name _____   Date _____

Are you a teacher? ☐   A student? ☐

Your school's name _____

Department _____

Address _____   City _____   State ____   Zip ____

School telephone # _____

YOUR COMMENTS ARE IMPORTANT TO US !

Please fill in the following information:

For which course did you use this book?

_____

Did you use a text with this ANNUAL EDITION? ☐ yes ☐ no

What was the title of the text?

_____

What are your general reactions to the Annual Editions concept?

_____

Have you read any particular articles recently that you think should be included in the next edition?

_____

Are there any articles you feel should be replaced in the next edition? Why?

_____

Are there any World Wide Web sites you feel should be included in the next edition? Please annotate.

_____

May we contact you for editorial input? ☐ yes ☐ no

May we quote your comments? ☐ yes ☐ no